PROFESSIONAL SELLING

third edition

PROFESSIONAL SELLING

B. ROBERT ANDERSON

Prentice-Hall, Inc., Englewood Cliffs, New Jersey 07632

Library of Congress Cataloging-in-Publication Data

ANDERSON, B. ROBERT.
   Professional selling.

   Bibliography: p.
   Includes index.
   1. Selling. I. Title.
HF5438.25.A52 1987   658.8   86-17077
ISBN 0-13-725912-3

Editorial/production supervision and
  interior design: *Nancy Savio-Marcello*
Cover design: *Ben Santora*
Manufacturing buyer: *Harry P. Baisley*

Printed in the United States of America

10 9 8 7 6 5 4

ISBN 0-13-725912-3   01

PRENTICE-HALL INTERNATIONAL (UK) LIMITED, *London*
PRENTICE-HALL OF AUSTRALIA PTY. LIMITED, *Sydney*
PRENTICE-HALL CANADA INC., *Toronto*
PRENTICE-HALL HISPANOAMERICANA, S.A., *Mexico*
PRENTICE-HALL OF INDIA PRIVATE LIMITED, *New Delhi*
PRENTICE-HALL OF JAPAN, INC., *Tokyo*
PRENTICE-HALL OF SOUTHEAST ASIA PTE. LTD., *Singapore*
EDITORA PRENTICE-HALL DO BRASIL, LTDA., *Rio de Janeiro*

to my wife
Joyce
and children
Steven, David, Faith

CONTENTS

vii

PREFACE

A preface is really a personal note to the reader. This preface to the third edition of *Professional Selling* is a sheer joy to write because it signals a degree of success. In fact, there are really three signals.

The first and most important signal is the positive reaction by students and professional salespeople who have used this book. Those readers and you, the new reader, are the ultimate customer. You are the ones who must be served, be satisfied, and attain success if this book is to really work. Thus, by definition, the third edition says that the readers are successful.

The second signal is the feeling of having made a contribution. When teachers, trainers, students, and salespeople continue to buy a text, it says they have somehow succeeded and this speaks well of the book. The author shares in your success by feeling contentment at helping others to succeed. Occasionally I meet a student who recounts the story of a successful sale by saying, "I overcame the objection of the prospect by using the boomerang method." Let me tell you, that means a great deal to the author. It means you have used a technique and it worked!

The third signal is for me to continue having a good time. Writing and talking about selling are enjoyable. After four decades of selling, the thrill of the chase and the excitement of the sale have not dimmed. Writing about these experiences and having them appear in a textbook to help others are extensions of selling. What more could a dedicated salesperson seek.

As this edition goes to press, the business news suggests that our sales role in the future will grow in importance. How fitting to be part of a profession that means so much to our society.

Read. Learn. Sell. Most of all, have fun.

B. Robert Anderson

PROFESSIONAL SELLING

1

SELLING

PERFORMANCE OBJECTIVES

After you have read this chapter and completed the Questions for Class Discussion, the Case, the Sales Problem, and the Exercise, you should be able to do the following:

1. Define and explain "selling."
2. Cite the main differences between the barter system of exchange and selling.
3. List three attributes of professional salespeople.
4. Identify and compare the life-styles of sales representatives at the four levels of industry.
5. List the five phases that constitute the Heart of the Sale.
6. Differentiate among "suspect," "prospect," and "customer."

SELLING AND SOCIETY

Every salesperson has a dream, a fantasy of how to deal with the person who says, "I wish all you salespeople would stop bothering me." With a sudden wave of a magic wand, all the salespeople disappear—except for the dreamer.

"How do you feel now that no salespeople are calling?" asks the dreamer.

"It's great," comes the response. "Now I can get some work done."

"Oh? What kind of work do you do?"

"I own a service station. Do a pretty good job, if I do say so myself."

"I notice your supply of tires is running low. How are you going to replace them?"

"No trouble," smiles the station owner. "I'll get them the next time the tire distributor comes in."

"And the chemicals you use to wash cars?"

"My janitor-supply house has them."

"Batteries?"

"My auto-supply distributor."

"That broken adding machine?"

"I have an office sales representative."

Then it dawns on the service-station operator—there are no more salespeople. Where will all the things he needs to conduct the business come from? Who will take the orders and see to the deliveries? How will he be able to keep abreast of all the new products available?

"That will teach you a lesson," says the dreamer. "You need salespeople."

Yes, society needs salespeople, because they are the ones who make new ideas and products available to the people who need them. Remember the quote attributed to Ralph Waldo Emerson: "If a man can write a better book, preach a better sermon, or make a better mousetrap than his neighbor, though he builds his house in the woods, the world will make a beaten path to his door."

With no disrespect intended for Emerson, this wasn't true even 100 years ago. People went out beating paths, not to find merchandise, but to sell and distribute it. Even in those days, quality products survived only if people were informed of their existence and value. Certainly, in a less complicated time, there were fewer products on the market. But people of vision, aided by sales representatives, have had an enormous influence on the economic well-being of society.

At some very early time, the inventor of the wheel had to "sell" the idea. Every great idea (service) had to be "sold." Any improvement in the

PROFESSIONAL SELLING
MAKES THE WORLD GO ROUND.

Figure 1-1

quality of life, from fire to the gas lamp to the electric bulb, had to be "sold."

Perhaps the earliest of salespeople were those known as "hawkers." They roamed the streets with packs of merchandise and hawked their wares. Later, there were the peddlers, in the United States frequently referred to as the "Yankee peddlers." The *ped*, the Old English word for a pack in which articles to be sold were stored, was the sign of these people.

The peddlers enriched the life of every community they visited, often carrying the news of other towns, always bringing the buttons and pins and needles that the far-flung pioneers needed. Among them were some who gained great riches based on their early experiences traveling throughout the country. Men like Stephen Girard, the giant Philadelphia banker; Thomas Edison, the great inventor; B.T. Babbitt, the earliest of the soap millionaires; and even the father of John D. Rockefeller—all served their turn as peddlers.

The current version of the peddler, the door-to-door salesperson, is very much in evidence. Companies such as Avon Cosmetics, Electrolux Cleaners, the Fuller Brush Company, and Amway play an important role in our society.

Translated into modern terms, it is the appointed challenge of the salesperson to make people aware of products and services, not only to earn a living, but to constructively add to the quality of life.

WHAT IS SELLING?

There are many definitions of *selling*. All seem to include value judgments, such as one of the best known, which says, "Selling is the transfer of goods or services that don't come back to customers who do come back." This encompasses more than is required of selling. It sets conditions that are useful but not absolutely necessary for selling.

A simplified version of this statement allows for a basic definition, which meets all purposes:

> Selling effects the transfer of products or services from one person to another.

Here we have the main points of the profession of selling. A transfer between two parties! In earlier times, these transfers involved product for service, product for product, or service for service. This was known as the barter system. Society has evolved another way to "trade" products or services—by using money. Thus:

> Selling effects the transfer of products or services *for money,* from one person to another.

It could be argued that *trading* is an inappropriate word, that selling involves a measure of profit. However, the two parties in a barter situation generally feel that they each got the better part of the bargain—that somehow, each profited from the trade. This thought is basic to professional selling. Making a sale implies that both buyer and seller benefited from the exchange, both are satisfied and happy.

The barter system was applicable when a farmer could trade eggs to the cobbler for a new pair of boots. Or when the blacksmith offered horseshoes in exchange for a new saddle made by the village leather craftsman. Modern selling uses money to effect the transfers, and both parties must be agreeable to and content with the exchange.

A typewriter salesman was wrestling with the problem of how to make an exciting approach to a hotel purchasing agent. After thinking about the buyer and getting some background information, he hit upon an idea. He packed a brand new electric typewriter in a box, wrapped it with colorful paper, and tied a ribbon on the top. Unannounced, he walked into the buyer's office and said, "Now is the time for all good managers to come to the aid of their secretary."

By drawing on this unusual way to bring the typewriter to the attention of the buyer, this salesman was trying to effect a transfer of product for money that would be mutually agreeable. With this novel approach, he was able to move through the sale to a successful conclusion. This and the incidents that follow illustrate professional selling.

The day after a devastating rainstorm, an insurance company sales representative bought photographs of the damage in the community from the local newspaper. In the months that followed, these pictures were shown to prospective clients. At the beginning of each interview, the representative asked, "What would you do if your home sustained this kind of beating?" The job of selling home insurance was made easier by the visual display of the storm damage. Again, the salesperson found an original method to bring the product to the attention of the client. The pictures were intended to alert the homeowner to the need for insurance protection against the possibility of future financial losses.

"I'm a question-asker," said the marketing consultant.

"What does that mean?" countered the busy president of a large bank. "I've got plenty of questions," the banker said. "What I need are answers."

"If you engage me as a marketing consultant, I will ask you questions that will lead to answers—answers that will increase the number of dollars the bank is earning. Would you be willing to spend $50 to make $100?"

"What kind of question is that?"

"It's the first in a series of questions that will tell me whether or not you are ready to profit from my experience," replied the consultant.

This person sought to make the interview as interesting as possible while bringing a service to the client.

In these incidents, the salespeople presented the product or service in an exciting, invigorating, and imaginative way. They also exhibited a desire to help the buyer solve a problem. Ultimately, what took place was the "transfer of products or services for money, from one person to another."

IS SELLING PROFESSIONAL?

When did you last encounter a thoughtful, considerate, knowledgeable salesperson? If you think hard, you will remember the time and the pleasure of dealing with a salesperson who really knew and enjoyed the work. This was a true professional.

The word *professionals* designates those who look with pride on their work, who constantly strive to perfect their techniques and improve their capabilities, and who seek to upgrade an admirable career. It is in this context that the word *professional* will be used in this book.

Professional selling demands expertise and competence in at least two areas: the methods, techniques, and objectives of selling; and knowledge of the product or service that is being sold.

The fact that sales training is offered at the college level indicates the high regard educational institutions place on the career aspects of this profession.

People should be taught to sell in a professional manner. That is why the major companies in the United States and around the world have significant sales training departments. The demand for people with *professional* skills is so great that many companies offer newly-hired trainees the equivalent of a full semester of full-time sales training, to prepare them for a future of success.

WHAT ARE THE DIFFERENT KINDS OF SELLING?

Regardless of where people sell, whether they want to travel or prefer to remain in a retail store, the need for professional knowledge is the same. There is, however, a difference in the application of this knowledge. For instance, some salespeople are constantly confronted with the need to call on strangers—people they do not know. This is called "cold canvass," or "calling cold turkey." The salesperson who works in a retail store generally finds people walking through the front door; but there is nothing to prevent the retail salesperson from telephoning complete strangers to invite them in to see a new product, or an old product that has been modernized. Whether you go out to find potential customers or they come to you, the rules for selling are merely applied in a different way.

However, there are a number of ways to differentiate the varieties of selling—all of them correct, and none of them totally complete. This text divides sales activities into four levels: industrial, manufacturing, distribution, and retail. This is an arbitrary division, which seeks to cover the broad spectrum of business life.

Industrial Level

Salespeople working for industrial firms generally deal in basic products—goods that are grown, mined, harvested, or in some way drawn from raw materials which will be used in a manufacturing process to make finished products. This definition is from the point of view of the salesperson and not from the view of the overall economic picture in the United States.

Sales territories are generally large, comprising several states. Sometimes only half a dozen people will cover the entire country, each responsible for a number of sales organizations in smaller territories.

Frequently, travel is of major importance; sales representatives fly from city to city to meet with big buyers as well as smaller accounts. Orders may be large, but they come infrequently. Because timing is significant, an industrial salesperson may call on buyers only by appointment, which is in itself a considerable difference in selling style.

It is not unusual for an industrial salesperson to be away from home all week, returning on weekends. The central office may be in a distant city, and the sales representative may operate a local office or even maintain an answering service and a desk at home.

An aluminum company at the industrial level would operate huge refining plants and facilities to produce sheets, rolls, and rods of aluminum for sale to manufacturing companies. Other examples of industrial sales opportunities can be seen in the operation of a coal mine, a cattle ranch, or even a large farm. Each of these enterprises requires some degree of sales representation.

* Manufacturing Level

A manufacturing firm buys a variety of products, many from industrial salespeople, then cuts, bends, or shapes (manufactures) those products into consumer items. For instance, a company making fire extinguishers will bring together a number of individual products that will ultimately emerge as a complete unit. A processor of frozen food might purchase raw vegetables from a farmer or from an industrial sales representative and then peel, clean, and freeze these products before packing them in bags or boxes.

A good deal of manufacturing or processing is done on the national level. Many more companies serve limited geographic areas. The salespeople representing these firms have large territories, ranging from half a state to several states.

From the salesperson's perspective, this type of selling requires a good deal of travel, usually by car—60,000 to 70,000 miles a year. One-, two-, or three-day trips tend to be the rule. A regional or local office may be supplemented by desk space in the home. Sales calls are made regularly, but spaced out, perhaps once a month or once every six weeks. Each firm establishes its own pattern.

Generally speaking, industrial and manufacturing salespeople deal with professional purchasing agents who spend the bulk of their time placing orders. It is interesting to note that these purchasing agents may not always make the "buying decisions." That is, they may place an order, but the decision to buy from a particular company may be made by another member of the company. Often, the plant engineer actually writes the specifications for a particular product and then turns the information over to the purchasing agent. Competent salespeople will seek to assist the engineer in the preparation of these specifications, thus ensuring their share of the business.

Distribution Level

Thousands of distributing companies warehouse, sell, and deliver all manner of products, from candy and tobacco to food, office supplies, electrical equipment, chemicals, auto supplies, and countless other items consumers take for granted.

The area covered by a distributor rarely exceeds a 200-mile radius. One characteristic of the distribution level is fast delivery service, ranging in time from a few hours to several days. Thus, the distributor must confine deliveries to a relatively small geographic territory.

Distributor salespeople travel 30,000 to 50,000 miles a year but are rarely away from home overnight. This level of selling includes a great deal of close cooperation with the customer, such as making an occasional "special delivery" in the trunk of the car. The sales representatives call on their accounts regularly—twice a week, once a week, once in two weeks, or sometimes once a month.

Since the representative is in close touch with the home office, distributor salespeople are never more than a phone call away from their customers. The advent of cellular telephones finds many sales representatives talking with customers even as they drive around town. And the ubiquitous "beeper" has become commonplace with many salespeople. Many give their home phone numbers to customers, suggesting a collect call any time a problem arises. Because the product line encompasses hundreds and often thousands of items, this salesperson is hard pressed to keep up with changing products. Sales sometimes seem almost routine, and the sales representative is a constant supplier of merchandise to the trade.

Almost every community boasts a number of distribution firms. These may vary from food wholesalers to paper jobbers to warehouses crammed with TV sets and stereo components. Other products that require the services and facilities of a distributor include gasoline, commercial cleaning supplies, office equipment, meat, and literally thousands of everyday products.

Retail Level

On the surface, it seems that the salesperson at this level has the easiest job. After all, the customers come to the store; there appears no need to "solicit" new business.

But some retail salespeople do a superior job. The furniture salesperson who has studied home decorating, the vacuum-cleaner salesperson who knows carpeting, the book salesperson who reads widely, the appliance salesperson who has tested the machines, and even the butcher who treats meat with loving care, regarding every meal as a feast, all add to the dignity of the sales profession.

Another aspect of retail selling is regular hours. For those who prefer to report at 9 A.M. and quit at 5 P.M., this is ideal. All other fields of selling allow salespeople a modicum of personal liberty—and the responsibility for setting their own schedule is often considered an asset. However, just as a good teacher doesn't work only from 9 A.M. to 3 P.M., a good salesperson will spend many hours at home or in the office studying the best ways to present the proposition to prospects.

When you consider the vast number of retail establishments, you can begin to understand the complexity of selling at this level. The person selling jewelry has a different opportunity from that of the person selling toys. Obviously, selling in a retail dress shop differs from selling in a linen-goods store, and all are different from the job of the clerk in the local card shop. Nonetheless, all are involved in selling.

Other Types of Selling

Several areas of the sales field seem to defy description: insurance selling, door-to-door selling, and real estate sales. Actually, they all fit into the distribution level. They have an element of travel, although limited, and they represent the distribution function—that is, the delivery of a finished or complete product or service to the buyer.

Door-to-door selling lies somewhere between the distribution level and the retail level. It is a highly successful and very important facet of selling in the United States. The salespeople are frequently well trained and energetic, and they make more money than many other professional salespeople.

It is also important to take note of real estate selling. This is one of the fastest-growing sales fields in the country today and requires a tremendous amount of technical and legal knowledge. To ensure that this group of salespeople is properly equipped to do the job, tests have been devised and administered by the same organization that produces the College Board tests, and rigid examinations are required by many states.

Many sales experts and teachers draw a distinction between "tangibles" and "intangibles." A tangible product is one that can be seen, heard, tasted, felt, or smelled. Intangibles, which are not perceived by the five senses, include insurance, advertising, and consulting. As indicated earlier, the decision to deal with selling at the industrial, manufacturing, distribution, and retail levels was arbitrary. Within the confines of these classifications, this text will cope with the sales problems and challenges of selling both intangibles and tangibles.

HOW MERCHANDISE FLOWS FROM LEVEL TO LEVEL

Figure 1-2 shows how merchandise flows from one level of industry to the next. It is presented in a simplified form so that you can visualize the selling process at each level. One apple grower (industrial level) may sell to ten packing houses (manufacturing level). In turn, each packing house may sell to 30 wholesale grocers (distribution level), each of whom may sell to 100 grocery stores (retail level). An individual store might serve 2,000 people (consumers).

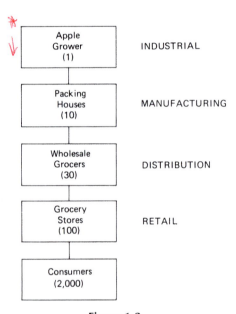

Figure 1-2

Figure 1-3 shows in more detail the complexity of the business scene. The apple grower and the packing house must remain mindful of the many types of customers they are trying to serve. The needs of the restaurants are not necessarily comparable to the needs of the mom & pop stores. Moreover, each level requires a different type of selling.

Obviously, the merchandise and services needed at each level are very different. The packing houses buy cans, sugar, labels, preservatives, maintenance supplies, office equipment, trucks, tires, and so forth, in ad-

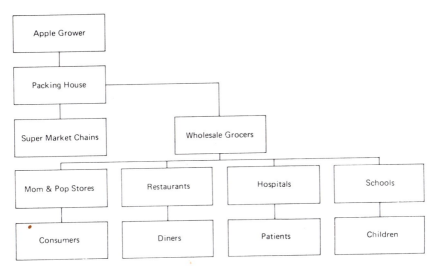

Figure 1-3

dition to apples. At this level, the manufacturer brings together all the materials needed to produce a salable product.

At the distribution level, the wholesaler or supermarket buys from a number of manufacturers (packing houses) to fill out a line of 3,000 to 15,000 items. Also necessary are purchases of operating supplies, such as typewriters, adding machines, pens, pencils, paper, forklift trucks, and electronic data-processing equipment.

You can see that business life is very intricate. At the same time, the opportunities for a successful, profitable sales career exist in a multitude of areas. It remains only for the individual to select that phase of business that has the most personal appeal. The differing personality requirements for salespeople will be discussed in Chapter 4.

There are many exceptions to our categories. However, these classifications cover the large majority of selling situations, each with its own unique characteristics. The point is that even though selling takes place in different places, at different times, under different circumstances, the basic rules, techniques, methods, and objectives are the same.

THE SALES PLAN

A sales manager was working with a new person. As they left the customer's store, the salesman said, "Okay, we'll send you this order. I'll see you next week."

Once outside, the sales manager asked, "Why didn't you thank him for the order?"

"I didn't think it was appropriate," answered the man. "We never did it in the company I was with before."

"How's that?"

"Well, he's getting his money's worth," said the salesman.

"All right," said the sales manager. "Let me explain. Among professional salespeople, it is considered proper to thank a customer for an order. I don't care where you work—as long as you are trying to be a professional, it is part of the ritual. You should thank people for orders."

The salesman was surprised. "Gee, nobody ever really laid it on me like that. I just didn't know that was one of the rules."

To say there are rules to selling means there are broad, all-encompassing, accepted forms of behavior. Within these boundaries is a great deal of leeway for people to express themselves in their own unique styles. The single most important starting point for any person engaged in the profession of selling is the *sales plan*.

Essentially, the sales plan is divided into two parts: the *Base of the Sale*, which consists of knowledge, traits, characteristics, and background material; and the *Heart of the Sale*, which represents the implementation of these elements, the actual face-to-face meeting with the buyer. Each of these parts is covered in detail in this text.

At this point, let us define certain terms and what they mean to the professional salesperson. Every career has a language of its own, including a sales career.

The *proposition* is the product or service you are seeking to sell, including a complete explanation of what the purchase will mean to the person, how much it will cost, when and how it will be delivered, credit terms—everything an individual may want to know before making a buying decision.

A *suspect* is a person who might be able to use your product or service, one who might find your proposition acceptable.

A *prospect* is a person who probably has the need for the proposition and more than likely has the wherewithal to pay for it.

A *customer* is a person who has bought the product or service, one who has accepted the proposition.

In Figure 1-4, you will notice that "prospecting," the verification that a suspect might become a prospect and ultimately a customer, is part of the general investigation that brings the salesperson to seek a sales interview.

It is in the Heart of the Sale that most salespeople fail—that time when they are with a prospect, trying to get an order. Notice that this

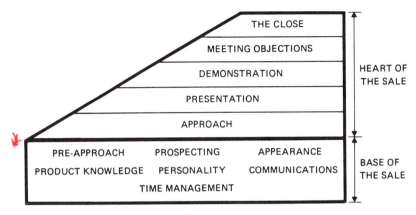

Figure 1-4

segment of the sales plan is viewed as an inclined plane. A successful sale does not move in even, measured steps. You do not automatically glide from one phase to the next.

It is possible to start with an approach and zip immediately to the close. On the other hand, having progressed through the various stages, say, to meeting objections, you might slide back to the presentation. It's a slippery wedge, one that requires the salesperson to be flexible. Moreover, when salespeople get ready for an interview and prepare the statements they will make during the Heart of the Sale, they are forced to consider all those points noted as the Base of the Sale.

All selling—if it is to be professional—must start with a sales plan. One objective of this text is to enable readers to create their own sales plans. As you move through this text, the validity of the sales-plan concept will become apparent, and you will derive strength from its strength. The distinguishing characteristics of a sale do not revolve around the level of industry or the product. They are related to the attitude, desire, skills, and knowledge of the salesperson.

SELLING AS A WAY OF LIFE

Everyone sells—from the parent showing the child the correct way to cross the street, to the businessperson seeking to persuade a client, to the scientist trying to convince a colleague about a new theory. Show, persuade, convince; they are all variations of selling. However, the distinguishing characteristic of professional selling is the application of proven methods and techniques.

Politicians are deeply committed to "selling" their candidates. Managers "sell" their employees by trying to motivate them to higher productivity. The business of selling is not restricted to the traveling salesperson or the retail clerk.

As a life-style, the profession of selling offers many opportunities. First is the assurance that your income will be directly tied to the amount of time and effort you are willing to devote. Regardless of how salespeople are paid, they share somehow in the dollar volume of the sale. (Chapter 16 discusses the many sales compensation possibilities.) They know that more sales mean more dollars of income for the salesperson.

Second is the chance for advancement. An overwhelming proportion of corporate presidents and managers have come up through the ranks as sales representatives. Apparently the drive, the knowledge of how to get along with people, and the learned techniques of persuasion have helped them achieve management positions. One report estimates that over 50 percent of business leaders attribute their success to years of sales success, a time when they utilized a sales plan to enhance their careers.

Third is the independent life-style of professional salespeople. Having passed through training programs and study sessions, they are pretty much on their own. For the outside salesperson, this means setting a schedule and determining how much time to devote to the profession and career of selling.

Finally, professional selling spills over into everyday life. The forward thrust and the positive nature of selling provide salespeople with a healthy attitude toward current problems. They become seekers of solutions; no situation is without the opportunity for success. This usually leads to active participation in community life. Salespeople are noted for their willingness to join and work with social, religious, and service clubs, as well as professional organizations. Certainly a portion of this involvement is an attempt to know the territory better. Either way, selling is a frame of mind that propels people into ever more exciting vistas.

CAN SELLING BE LEARNED?

Today's professional salespeople carry an enormous burden—the challenge of bringing change to society; other ways of effecting change abound, but salespeople can do it daily in selling and taking orders. They do this in two distinct ways. The first is as a problem solver. Often, before skills can be applied, it is necessary to properly identify and isolate the problem. Most people tend to be content with things as they are; they reject change out of hand. One of the techniques of selling is to demonstrate a better way to do something, by first helping the prospect determine that there is dissatisfaction with the current situation.

This leads directly to the second way salespeople seek a measure of self-gratification, one of the most fascinating aspects of selling. The professional salesperson is a creative human being! The business of successful selling is built upon creative and innovative methods of introducing new products. This single phase of selling has attracted some of the most talented minds to the field of selling.

Both problem solving and creativity stimulate many professional challenges in the field of selling. They also raise the question, "Can this type of selling be taught, or are you born with this talent?"

Fortunately, the ability to sell can be learned. Anyone with determination can apply the methods and techniques discussed in this textbook. This is not to say that some people do not have a flair for sales work. You can spot them every day, those whom we identify as "born salespeople." But even those who seem to be "born for selling" must acquire professional techniques if they are to advance. Most people (the author included) who study, practice, and employ professional sales techniques find considerable satisfaction and challenge in the sales field.

Given the opportunity to participate and work within the structure of the sales plan, you will have ample opportunity to express yourself. The many facets of selling can be learned!

SUMMARY

A sale takes many forms, sometimes routine and exacting, other times thrilling and exciting. The atmosphere of selling is varied; however, the essential definition is, "Selling effects the transfer of products or services for money, from one person to another."

It is important for the student of selling to recognize that the degree of professionalism rests with the individual. If you attach significance to the personal and economic good wrought by the business of selling, then it is equally important that your approach to this vital activity be on a professional basis.

Although it is difficult to categorize the many types of selling, the scene can be viewed from the life-styles of the people involved. For that reason, this book will deal with salespeople on four levels:

Industrial

Manufacturing

Distribution

Retail

To broaden this approach to selling, examples will be offered which cover the sale of intangible services such as insurance and advertising. Real estate sales and door-to-door selling are also touched upon.

THE PROFESSIONAL SALESPERSON IS
THE KEY INGREDIENT OF OUR COMPLEX
ECONOMIC SYSTEM — BRINGING
"CHANGE" TO SOCIETY.

Figure 1-5

Paramount to this entire presentation is the sales plan. Every sales-person should have a sales plan, and each phase of this plan should be prepared. In particular, we shall cover the Heart of the sales plan, which includes the following:

Approach
Presentation
Demonstration
Meeting objections
Close

To carry out a successful sales plan, the salesperson needs other knowledge, understanding, and characteristics, which constitute the Base of the sales plan. These include:

Preapproach
Prospecting
Product knowledge
Personality
Human behavior
Communications

Time management

Service

All this knowledge and information will prepare the salesperson for an independent and productive life-style, as well as for a vital role in society. Professional selling can be learned!

How important is the salesperson? We cannot imagine a progressive economic order without the dynamic efforts of professional salespeople. Moreover, the many opportunities inherent in a selling career can lead to a meaningful, happy life.

In some other societies, those which foster a different type of economic climate, the notion of selling is becoming ever more important. The need for someone to carry the message forth is omnipresent. Thus, the role of the professional salesperson continues to grow. In a most prophetic way, the following statement personifies the work of the salesperson: "Until a sale is made, nothing happens."

A SUCCESS STORY

A raw sales recruit was working with an experienced salesperson one day. As they drove down the highway at the close of an afternoon filled with orders, the new salesman asked, "How'd you get into selling?"

"Well, I'll tell you," the older man said. "It was back in the Depression, and I realized that the best way to earn a living was to rely on my own efforts. This selling opportunity came along, and I took it."

"You mean you never had any training?" asked the novice in surprise.

"Not at the beginning," answered the old-timer.

"Wasn't that tough?"

"It sure was. If I had known better, I would have taken some sales courses. As it was, I wasted about five years before I started to read about selling."

"Did it help?"

"Sure did. I began to realize that I had a whole lot to contribute; that my work was important. There's a lot more to this profession than just making money."

"Didn't you ever want to get into management?"

"Oh, I had that chance years ago."

"What happened?"

"I turned it down. First off, I like the idea of making as much money as I can, based on how hard I want to work. Second, I like the work itself; and third, I like the feeling of meeting and selling new people. It's a challenge. What you young people call a 'turn-on.' "

"Wow!" said the new man. "That's quite a speech!"

The old man smiled broadly. "Heck, what more could you want? I do pretty much as I want, earn as much as I need, and still feel that I'm doing something important."

QUESTIONS FOR CLASS DISCUSSION

1. What are some of the advantages of an economic system in which products or services are "sold" as opposed to a system in which products or services are "bartered"?
2. What is the difference between a suspect, a prospect, and a customer? When you enter a store, are you a suspect, a prospect, or a customer?
3. From your personal experience, relate an incident in which you feel the seller did a poor job. Can you recall a time when you felt the selling was professional?
4. Describe how an economic system might function if there were no sales-people. Do you know if any such system exists? What system of exchange is used?
5. If you were a salesperson for a small local printing plant, which level of industry would represent the greatest opportunity for your product? Explain why.
6. Expand on the statement, "A sale effects the transfer of products or services for money, from one person to another." Do you think this statement is valid? Why?
7. What are the differences in the life or working style of the sales representative at the industrial, manufacturing, distribution, and retail levels?
8. Some sales experts believe that a sale moves in even, measured steps. Do you agree or disagree with this point of view? Why?
9. Explain what is meant by the expression, "Until a sale is made, nothing happens."

COMMENTS ON THE CASES

At the close of every chapter will be a case. As you cope with the problems of the people in the case, you will recognize the need for more professional sales skills.

Each case draws on the reading in the chapter. However, the imagination and creativity of the student will extend in all directions. One way to deal with these cases is to list the five most important facts, a single sentence describing the problem, and five specific recommendations to solve the problem.

As these cases are discussed in class, you may not find complete agreement on which facts are most important, what the problem is, or what recommendations should be implemented. This is what makes selling so exciting—the fact that there may be more than one answer to a question.

CASE 1—MARY TURNER TAKES A JOB

When Mary Turner left the coal regions of West Virginia to find a career in Philadelphia, she met with more disappointments than success. Back home she had earned good grades in high school and then gone on to complete two years at a community college. Knowing how to type and take shorthand seemed a good stepping-off point for a career in business.

Mary found that jobs were far from plentiful and the salaries lower than she had expected.

Her roommate had a job with a small company that distributed beauty supplies and equipment to drugstores, beauty parlors, small grocery stores, and supermarkets. An opening in the sales department prompted her friend to recommend Mary for the job. When she applied, the owner said, "Sorry, but we don't need anybody in telephone sales."

Mary was insulted. "How about a regular sales position?" she inquired.

The owner wearily asked, "What do you know about selling?"

"Well," she replied, "I like meeting people, and the chance to travel around the city sounds exciting."

"Our outside salespeople deliver merchandise. That means a lot of lifting."

"How heavy are the packages?" she asked.

"Probably no more than 19 pounds."

"That's no problem for me."

"But you don't know how to sell."

"I'll learn," Mary said. "I need a job."

The owner thought for a moment and then replied, "I'll try you for a month. After that, we'll see what happens."

1. What mistakes did Mary Turner make in applying for a sales job? no experience
2. What did she do right? willing to learn
3. Now that she has the job, what advice would you give her? p. 15

COMMENTS ON THE SALES PROBLEMS

Throughout this text, the pervasive idea is to introduce the realities of selling to the student. In this new edition, "live" sales problems have been included in each chapter. Class discussion of how each problem might be solved will add to your own thinking. There may be more than one way to solve the sales problem. In fact, you might find the second solution better than the first.

SALES PROBLEM 1–HOW TO RIGHT THE WRONG PHONE CALL

In an attempt to reduce the cost of sales, many companies have an active telephone sales force. These people call customers, take orders, and frequently try to sell new products to both existing and new prospects. When calling established accounts, they sometimes err, causing the regular sales rep additional problems.

It happened to John Hardy when he went on vacation. His return seemed to bring more trouble than the benefits he had gained from lying on the beach, soaking up the sun. Hardy had to find ways to placate angry customers.

Here is how three different salespeople cope with the same problem:

Sales Rep #1: I would do some fact-gathering. It's absolutely necessary to ask the customer what went wrong, and then to ask the telephone person what went wrong.

With the customer, I would try to find out what the telephone rep did, step by step. Then I would commiserate with the customer and apologize for the error. Only then would I try to find out what it would take to completely satisfy the account.

The follow-up would be to convey everything I have learned to the salespeople who deal over the phone. They have particular problems and need lots of help from the outside sales rep.

Sales Rep #2: It is inevitable that this kind of problem will arise. It happens because the telephone person is not intimately aware of all that has taken place during the ongoing sales relationship. That is why I would first apologize to the account. The next step is to analyze what happened in an attempt to avoid similar conditions later on. One way to do this is to take orders in advance and have them delivered when you are on vacation or when you can't make the sales call in person. Keeping a good set of records will help.

Sales Rep #3: Diplomacy is what you need to satisfy the customer who feels the telephone squad has created chaos. You must make sure the customer knows you are working hard to see that the same thing doesn't happen again. Talking about it may be all right, but doing something definitive speaks louder than words.

The customer has to be told ahead of time that a telephone person may be calling and just what to expect. And even when you are on vacation, it may be wise to keep in touch with your major accounts to make sure all is well.

COMMENTS ON THE EXERCISES

Each chapter has an exercise that allows students to utilize some of the information they have read. This is intended to reinforce the practical application of academic learning to the realities of the sales world.

EXERCISE 1

"How do you help your customers solve problems?"

Ask this question of an insurance agent, a stock broker, and a distributor sales representative. Get at least three responses from each sales representative.

2

THE HUMAN SIDE OF BUYING

PERFORMANCE OBJECTIVES

After you have read this chapter and completed the Questions for Class Discussion, the Case, the Sales Problem, and the Exercise, you should be able to do the following:

1. Explain why prospects cannot be defined by religious, ethnic, or political groupings.
2. Differentiate between "motivate" and "motivations."
3. Describe the problem-solving aspects of selling.
4. List and explain Maslow's Hierarchy of Human Needs.
5. Explain the four views of the self.

"I'M IN THE MOOD FOR . . ."

The background music is soft and romantic as the woman on the screen looks deep into the eyes of her gentleman friend and murmurs, "You know, my dear, your comfort and happiness mean more to me than the world."

The camera moves off as the couple embraces and pans to a view of a plush living room, replete with fireplace and burning logs. Slowly the picture changes to the exterior of the house and then to a close-in shot as the cellar opens before your very eyes, and there, nestled deep beneath the entwined couple, is a sparkling new gas-powered pump. Emblazoned across the screen is the motto, "Ajax Pumps Bring Love to the Love of Your Life."

"Lights," called out the sales manager. Then, turning to the assembled sales force, he beamed, "How did you like that? Quite a nice film presentation. I'll bet you can sell the heck out of pumps with that kind of material in your sales kit."

A brief murmur filled the room, a low rustle of voices as the salespeople reacted to the film. Then one blurted, "What the heck does all that sexy stuff have to do with our pumps?"

Heartened by this singular outburst, others joined in. "Yeah. Who cares about love on a couch when we're trying to sell pumps." "Can she come with me on my next sales call?" "I'd like to sell her a pump." "That's a sexist approach and it won't work."

"Hey, you characters," snapped the sales manager, "knock it off."

"C'mon, George," said one sales rep. "This was supposed to be a film on the benefits of buying Ajax Pumps. Why don't you give us some product knowledge?"

"I'll tell you why," answered the sales manager. "There are plenty of reasons why people buy merchandise. You can have all the best stuff in the world, and know all about your products, but if you don't have a feel for people and what makes them tick, you won't be able to sell."

"But what's that got to do with romance?"

"Just this. We know our pumps are the best in the industry. What we need now are more insights into what motivates people. When we talked to the ad agency, they came up with the idea of adding a touch of glamour to our pumps. You all know that love and sex make the difference in a lot of selling."

"But with pumps?" questioned one sales representative.

"If sex and love won't do it, switch to prestige. I don't care what buying motive you hit; hit them all if necessary. Find the right button and push it."

"Well, can't we come up with some buying motives that are more realistic?"

"Heck, yes. Don't forget, it would be great if everybody bought merchandise based on the quality and price and service. That's why we have to discover what turns a buyer on. And the beautiful part is that every person you talk to is different."

For a few moments the room fell silent. Then a voice from the rear asked, "Can we use safety?"

"Man, that's right on target for the buyer who is worried about what will happen if the electricity goes off and the person needs light and heat in the house."

"How about esteem?"

"That's a little harder. But you could figure out how a person would accept ownership of an Ajax Pump as a mark of distinction. Why not!"

"Are you trying to tell us that anything can become a reason to buy?"

"What I'm trying to tell you is that what motivates one person may not motivate the next. Your job as professional salespeople is to find out what will motivate a specific individual. There's a human side to this business, and you have to be prepared to deal with human beings."

Once again the room fell silent. The sales manager concluded with, "Next week we're going to see how Ajax Pumps can help a person become part of a group and find happiness with the aesthetic lines of Model 313."

A new salesperson off to one side was heard to whisper, "Wow!"

HOORAY FOR DIFFERENT PEOPLE

For many years, schoolchildren in the United States were taught that our country is a "melting pot." This meant that all the people who have come here from Europe, Asia, and Africa, all the various nationalities from Germans to Hungarians to Siamese, all gradations of religious belief were mixed together and emerged as composite human beings—Americans. Current sociological thinking runs counter to this idea. Instead, although all these diverse people did arrive on our shores, and all became Americans, each group, each individual, has retained its own identity.

You may wonder what this has to do with selling. It is important for the professional salesperson to recognize that people are individuals—each with his or her own set of likes, dislikes, biases, and prejudices. The relationships between this individuality and why people buy are complex and intertwined. In this chapter we shall attempt to point out that the reasons people buy are the same, but they are set in different backgrounds.

You might want to think of it this way. A two-carat diamond is the same stone whether it is in a platinum setting or a silver setting. It may appear different, and it may even appeal to various people in different ways, but the essential stone is the same. Another way of separating the background from the motive or reason to buy can be visualized by thinking of a person sitting at a campfire eating beans out of a can. At the other end of town, another person is sitting down at a table covered with fine linen and crystal. A thick steak and a glass of wine are placed before the diner. Quite different settings. The two backgrounds are really dissimilar. Yet both people have the same motivation. They're hungry!

How Are People Different?

It is fairly obvious that people who have traveled to this country from Europe have a different background from those who have arrived from Asia. Each group is the result of a long history and diverse upbringing. Even individuals in any single group may represent variations of the cultural theme. The idea that the "Scotch are thrifty," the "French are terrific lovers," or the "Orientals are crafty" is the worst kind of nonsense! Professional sellers, because they come in contact with all kinds of people, should be particularly careful to avoid categorizing groups. Instead, they should recognize that there is a French cultural pattern that the French individual may or may not be part of, that some Scots are thrifty, but so are some Russians, Spaniards, and Brazilians, and that craftiness may apply to many different individuals.

Even within the same religion, people are dissimilar. Some attend religious services every day, others once a week, and some only once a year. On the one hand, some people interpret the Bible loosely, and on the other hand, some subscribe to a rigid interpretation. Although many children have moved away from the beliefs of their parents, as we mature we find that a person's religious beliefs are a matter of individual conscience and ought not to be a subject for public discussion or even comparison. The professional salesperson must be able to accept all these differences.

There are other areas in which people tend to be different. Politically, economically, and socially, people are often slipped into specific groupings, such as "conservative" or "liberal." Recent history has amply demonstrated that the lines separating these classifications are so blurred that the use of such terms is inaccurate. Defining a person's political position with these words is an oversimplification. Yet their use is widespread, and the professional salesperson has to be wary of thinking of clients and prospects as either one or the other. One of the most "liberal" businesspeople in the country today is the offspring of an "ultraconservative" family. Millions of dollars of inheritance have not swayed the beliefs of this person. At the opposite extreme are the many people in the lower-middle economic class who are "conservative."

IT TAKES ALL KINDS OF PEOPLE TO
MAKE THE WORLD. THE PROFESSIONAL
SALESPERSON RESPECTS THEM ALL.

Figure 2-1

Given the complexities of the human condition, it is safe to say that the professional salesperson should draw no conclusion based on the ethnic, racial, sexual, religious, national, political, or economic background of the prospect. Rather, the professional salesperson should revel in the differences. Each person represents a unique opportunity.

Physical and Environmental Differences

At any given moment, people undergo a set of circumstances that affect their behavior and therefore their decision to buy or not buy. For instance, a telephone ringing in the middle of a sales interview can disrupt all the well-laid plans of the salesperson. The prospect who realizes that a ringing phone will upset the tenor of the sales presentation may instruct a secretary to stop all incoming calls.

The physical setting can affect potential customers in other ways. An insurance agent was calling on the news editor of a local paper. Realizing that noise and confusion are part of the scene in the editorial office, the agent prepared for constant interruptions. What the agent did not realize was that the prospect would refuse to sign a policy in the full view of all the other news colleagues. Something about the overt act of agreeing with the salesperson disturbed the prospect, and the sale collapsed.

Even the heat and humidity can affect buying habits. Who feels like buying a set of encyclopedias when the sun is streaming in through the window and beads of perspiration are beginning to pop out on your forehead?

A salesperson for one of the cosmetic firms was making a regular house call to demonstrate a new line of powder bases. As she was ushered into the living room, the prospect said, "Worse luck, the air conditioner just went on the blink." As the two sat face to face, the humidity rose, and the salesperson's face began to show creases where the new product had been applied. Needless to say, the prospect was turned off.

If the setting causes people to react differently, what about their personal physical discomfort? What effect do you think tight shoes might have on the progress of a sale? How do you think the prospect might respond to a sales proposition the day after being told a son is flunking out of college? What of the person who spent the previous night "out on the town"? Do you think that person is ready to make a buying decision?

Some of the more obvious physical characteristics that affect behavior are hunger, anger, anxiety, backaches, and, of course, headaches. The list could go on—but the point is that all these things are reasons for and explanations of why people are different, why they behave differently, and even why they react in various ways.

The professional salesperson hopes to have a sufficient number of selling opportunities when the background of the prospect, the physical setting, and the normal aches and pains are at a minimum. However, the descriptions above are of conditions that the salesperson must face. The sooner salespeople accept and acknowledge that differences exist, the sooner they will be able to grapple with those things that motivate the prospect.

WHAT IS MOTIVATION?

Two Cadillac agents were comparing notes. "Did you see that guy who just left? He bought the biggest car we had in stock. Cost him close to $21,000."

"Well, you should be happy."

"I am. But just the other day, I sold the same car in blue to a woman."

"So?"

"She has plenty of dough. Her husband died about a year ago and left her almost $1 million."

"Yes."

"Well, this guy only makes $39,000 a year. He had to sign all kinds of notes to buy his car. It doesn't make sense. What motivates people?"

"You do, baby," laughed the friend.

"No, I didn't do it. I just happened to be here at the right moment."

The question of what motivates people has puzzled salespeople for a long time. Perhaps the best starting point is with some basic definitions that will tend to orient the salesperson as we seek to identify some of the latest thinking on this fascinating subject. Here are some definitions taken from the Random House Dictionary:

> motive—"something that prompts a person to act in a certain way or that determines volition, incentive."

Probably the key word here is "something." This does not make a value judgment, it merely takes note that "something" (a force, an interest, a need, or a desire) has brought about an action. We will be discussing what these "somethings" might be very shortly.

> motivate—"to provide with a motive or motives."

Obviously, anyone or anything might serve to motivate (to provide "something" that will bring about an action). Cold weather motivates people to put on warm clothing—that is, provides a reason to act a certain way even though it does not always produce identical results. If professional salespeople can discover what "something" will bring about an action by a prospect, they will be more successful.

> motivation—"the act or an instance of motivating, the state or condition of being motivated, that which motivates."

Note that motivation has three possible applications with regard to selling:

First, the salesperson can be the motivator; that is, can provide the motive for making a buying decision. This is an active role and one used by professional people.

Second, the prospect, the person who is being affected, can react to the motive being presented.

Third, motivation can describe the motive that was used to bring about an action.

There has been considerable debate on the question of whether motivation (the state of being motivated) is internal or external. Some people hold with the notion that all motivation is internal, that people are "self-motivated." Others think that external forces actually bring about motivation. There may never be an adequate answer to this question.

Therefore, we pose an easier question, one that will allow us to apply the use of motivation to professional selling:

"Do people do things (act) because of what we say, or do we as salespeople merely create an atmosphere that allows them to fulfill their own motives?" The field of professional selling assumes that salespeople can create such an atmosphere and thereby hasten the self-motivation process. The better we understand the "somethings" that motivate people, the better is our chance for success.

One thing we do know: If a purchase is made, if a sale is consummated, there has to be a change in the mind of the prospect. Something has moved the prospect in the direction of buying from us. Finding the correct motive for these diverse individuals we call prospects is an exciting journey. It is in this context that we can explore the human side of buying.

HISTORICAL PERSPECTIVE OF SALES MOTIVATION

Since the entire study of motivation is so challenging, we offer some views of what has gone before—what thinking has pervaded the sales profession, and how that thinking has brought us to the current state of the art.

Rational Motivation

Many experts feel that people are motivated by rational or real reasons when they make a purchase. Based on this thinking, a straightforward approach that relates the virtues of a product or service should suffice to convince or motivate the prospect to buy.

Perhaps the best way to understand this thinking is to consider the professional buyer or purchasing agent, the person who devotes all or almost all the time to the task of making purchases for the company. Generally, a professional buyer will welcome salespeople because of the responsibility to supply products or merchandise for others in the company to either work with or use in the manufacture of other products. Essentially, this person will be seeking the best value for the price, so that the job will be carried out successfully and the company will prosper.

How does the professional buyer reach a decision if two competitive salespeople offer the same value, or even the same product at the same price? A purchase from either of these two salespeople might represent an honest, rational reason for buying. Therefore, the purchasing agent must rely on other reasons for buying, some personal and some emotional. Apparently no two offers are identical, and other factors enter into a purchase over and above the price, service, and quality of the proposition.

Besides the professional buyer, a considerable amount of buying is done by "nonprofessionals"—people like you and me who buy stereo sets and clothes and household equipment. We are "amateur" buyers; that is, we devote very little time to the business of buying. Do we always reach decisions based on the bare facts and the relative value of the product in question? Based on our own individual backgrounds and physical and mental considerations, we each make purchase decisions based on reasons other than price, quality, and service. Moreover, we sometimes make a purchase from a salesperson we do not really like because we want the product that person has to sell.

In defense of the rational motivation for buying, it is important to realize that the customer does, in fact, feel that the purchase decision is rational. "If I decided to buy this car, even though it costs $500 more than a comparable, competitive model, my reasons were good. I like the service I will receive, and the delivery date and colors appeal to me." Therefore, in the mind of this person, a good, rational decision has been made.

Compare these two statements. Are they rational?

Prospect A: I bought an ABC dishwasher because the price was lower than competitive brands and the guarantee is for two full years.

Prospect B: I didn't buy an ABC dishwasher because the low price indicated it wasn't as good as some other brands on the market. Besides, a two-year guarantee is hardly enough for a major purchase.

Both these people are certain they made a rational decision. Each had the same salesperson, the same information, and the same approximate needs. Yet they arrived at different decisions. This example illustrates the significance of the basic differences in people. It is very easy for rational thinking to deteriorate into rationalization, in which the person finds reasons why he or she did or did not do a certain thing. After the fact, the decision is justified.

Emotional Motivation *feel*

Although most people would like to think they make buying decisions based on mature, unemotional reasoning, the truth of the matter is that most purchases are made for emotional reasons. Think of the advertising appeals that link sex with the purchase of a new car. The implication is that if you buy a "Super 8," the women will lounge all over your front seat and make cooing sounds in your ear. Or that if you use "Brand X" toothpaste, all the boys in the high school class will fall at your feet. Or that tinting your hair from grey to black will rekindle the fires of love in your spouse.

People do make purchases based on just these reasons. They allow and even force their emotions to assist in making a buying decision. Although sex is the most obvious appeal, there are others. For instance, sporting goods are usually sponsored by a professional athlete who implies that using certain racquets, clubs, or skis will improve your ability to participate. Physical comfort is high on the list of emotional appeals. That's why bedding manufacturers stress the benefits of a good night's sleep, and work shoes are sold for ankle and arch support.

For the professional salesperson, a better understanding of these emotions and how they can be used advantageously will complement a good sales plan. If the salesperson can satisfy the emotional desires of the prospect, then a selling service has been performed. For example, if the prospect has a strong desire to engage in physical exercise or active relaxation, then selling benefits directed to those desires are perfectly valid. A new car might represent the chance for a prospect to get away to the seashore for a day of swimming. A set of tools might meet the need for physical involvement that translates into a form of exercise. Reverse appeals might also be made. For instance, "After a day of exercise and strenuous activity, why not sit down to a quiet game of chess? These sets are available in three styles. . . ."

Here are some other appeals which are purely emotional. Everyone has a need for some form of esthetic gratification, whether that be painting a landscape oneself or owning an oil painting to hang in the living room. Other forms of esthetic desires are satisfied by owning beautiful furniture, listening to fine music, or attending the opera. Usually, we think of the esthetic values with regard to art, music, literature, and dance.

Some people require that all purchases have the added value of increasing their prestige. Buying a home in the better section of town falls into this category. Belonging to a country club or dining in a particular restaurant also adds prestige in the minds of many people. At the lower economic levels of society, a new suit of clothes, a new TV, or a set of encyclopedias may spell prestige. There is no way to define prestige with regard to all the possible prospects the salesperson will face. What is prestigious to one person may not affect another. However, everyone has some need for meeting this emotional need.

Close to prestige is status. Ownership of certain products adds to the regard with which the rest of society might view a person. Consider the quirks that may occur. In a low-income area, a small imported car is viewed as a smart buy. In a high-income area, ownership of the same small imported car is seen as a status symbol. Many years ago, wearing blue denim work clothes was the sign of a person who made a living doing manual labor. Today, these same denims are the sign of someone who is sufficiently well off to be unconcerned with what people think. Denims have become a status symbol.

One of the oldest emotional appeals is "keeping up with the

Joneses." This comparison between what you have and what the neighbors down the street own has been valid for a long time. The desire to be equal to others is replete with strong emotional attachments. This is also a potent motivator when dealing with professional purchasing agents. After all, they must think, "If a competitor is buying this product, I want to be able to offer it to my own customers." Often a salesperson will confront the problem of whether a prospect wants to emulate a competitor. It's a two-edged sword, and it can be disastrous if the purchasing agent prefers to do his or her own thing without regard to what the rest of the market is doing.

Profit or gain is an emotional motive for making a purchase. It might appear that this is purely a rational reason to buy. However, suppose the prospect has a sufficient supply of the product, and the main reason to buy is the fact that there is a "special" and a saving can be effected. Sure, this may be construed as good business; it can also mean that the motive to make a few extra dollars has taken hold and caused the buyer to make a decision based on emotions and not on reality. Many times, purchasing agents have overbought only to find they lacked warehouse space to store the purchase.

Many people are motivated to buy because they want to acquire products. There may be some hidden factor in their personal background that brought them to this state of affairs. An old story tells of a man who owned 150 pairs of shoes. When he was a little boy, the family was so poor that the only shoes he ever owned were hand-me-downs from an uncle. As a result, he could not control his desire to buy shoes. Sounds silly? Think of someone you know who owns 15 suits, or twelve fishing poles, or 40 ties, or ten hats, or 1,000 books.

Fear is another strong emotional motivator. People buy insurance out of fear. They equip their houses with burglar alarms out of fear. They go every six months for a medical checkup out of fear. They purchase bigger cars out of fear. The list of purchases made because people feel they need some form of protection or security is limitless. Even the purchase of a household hammer might be made out of fear. "Suppose you had to open a crate or hang a picture. You wouldn't want to be without a hammer in the house." Even the fear of smelling like a person has been foisted on the buying public. That's why there are so many scents for after shaving, after arising, after going to sleep, after doing anything.

There is no end to the emotional reasons for buying. Remember, romance, sex, creativity, mental and physical health, curiosity, pride, and arrogance are just part of a lengthy list. In some instances, these may be prime reasons for making a purchase. In others, they may be buttons the salesperson ought to touch while seeking to find the proper wedge for concluding a sale. The professional salesperson should recognize that

EVERY INDIVIDUAL HAS A
FISTFUL OF DESIRES, WANTS,
AND NEEDS. PROFESSIONAL SELLING
SEEKS TO FILL THESE NEEDS.

Figure 2-2

these emotions exist while at the same time remaining aware that they
may be cloaked in the garb of "rational" reasons for buying. People may
not want to reveal the basic emotional reasons they want a certain product. Nonetheless, all emotions can serve as motives for making a purchase. It
is up to the salesperson to discover these motives and relate them to the
product or service to be sold.

PROBLEM-SOLVING MOTIVATION

Another view of the human side of buying suggests that people are
motivated to buy because of the ability and desire of the salesperson to
help solve problems. In fact, many sales trainers and experts feel this is
the most important task of the professional salesperson. In its simplest

form, this can be exemplified by the salesperson who arrives on the scene with a fire extinguisher just as the wastebasket catches fire. Not only is the problem solved, it is solved at the most opportune moment. Now, imagine this salesperson trying to make the sale the day before. The task of warning the prospect that a wastebasket might someday catch on fire is difficult. But what are the chances for success if the presentation is made on the day following the fire?

Since we have already reviewed the complexity of people and the diversity of their backgrounds, how can a salesperson solve problems that are unrecognized? Therein lies one of the great challenges of selling. The insurance salesperson knows that funeral expenses can cripple a household budget. How can that information be conveyed to the prospect as a warning about this problem—which is a certainty? Perhaps the prospect has never properly considered this need; maybe the prospect has never even thought about this need. Nothing is as certain as death. Offering protection against the financial inroads of this eventuality is certainly providing a service and solving a problem.

Other areas of problem solving are not nearly as clear. Take the case of the detergent salesperson with a new product that kills germs on drinking glasses. In making the presentation to a restaurant owner, the sales representative stressed the sanitary aspects of the product. The prospect did not think there was a problem until the salesperson took a swab of a clean glass and demonstrated that the bacteria count was inordinately high. This salesperson had to first identify the problem, alert the prospect to the fact that the problem did exist. Only then could there be an attempt to solve the problem with the product.

Everybody has problems, and most of them are dormant or unrecognized. In effect, the salesperson for cosmetics is saying, "If you use this hair spray, you will avoid the problem of your spouse looking at other people." The tire salesperson likewise is saying, "If you buy these new steel-belted tires, you will eliminate the problem of worrying about blowouts." The paint salesperson is saying, "Our paint will last for ten years, and you will eliminate the problem and expense of repainting the house in five years."

There may even be a time when a salesperson can respond to a prospect who asks for help. A homemaker called the hardware store one day and said, "My bedroom rug is dirty and needs cleaning. What would you suggest?" The clerk replied, "We rent machines for $12 a day and we can sell you a bottle of rug shampoo. For $3 you will have enough product to clean your rug properly in about two hours."

Thus we can see that the professional salesperson is truly a solver of problems. Some of these problems surface by themselves; others have to be uncovered by the alert salesperson. Hidden behind any problem may be the emotional or rational desire to fulfill a need. There is little doubt that when professional salespeople solve a problem, they are performing at the highest level. However, the sense of this interpretation of "motivation" is that the salesperson devotes the most energy toward dealing with a specific problem and only slight effort to the human element, which may deflect the successful solution of the problem.

SELF-CONCEPT MOTIVATION

As scientists continue their study of human beings, new approaches to the human condition are being revealed. One of the most fascinating is the notion of "self-concept." Over the past two decades, more and more attention has been paid to the individual. As we have tried to stress in this work, the individual must be examined as a unique entity. There can be no benefit from categorizing people as a smart part of a larger group. The student of professional selling should be aware of four areas in order to expand a personal comprehension of what motivates people:

REAL SELF is the way you think of yourself. This is your assessment of what type of person you are, what characteristics predominate and what personality traits prevail.

REAL SELF What I think of myself	OTHER SELF What I would be if I were perfect
REAL OTHER What other people think of me	IDEAL OTHER What other people would think of me if I were perfect

Figure 2-3

OTHER SELF is the way you would like to be. It is an image in your mind of what you would be like if you were "perfect." Sometimes this view will translate into goals and objectives; the person will determine to improve, go to school, smile more often, or work harder.

REAL OTHER is the way you think other people really think of you.

Obviously, if the REAL SELF and the REAL OTHER are out of balance, this may prove motivating to the individual; it may be a reason to change.

IDEAL OTHER is the way you think other people would like you to be if you were "perfect."

It is important to note that each of these positions is in the mind of the individual. Every person has these four views of himself or herself: how I am, how I would like to be, how others see me, how others would like to see me. Granted that this explanation is oversimplified, it offers enough information for the professional salesperson to gain meaningful insights. If this view of how people think of themselves is valid, what does it mean to the salesperson?

Understanding the prospect and how the mind works is the sign of a sophisticated salesperson. It indicates an interest in the prospect and a sincere belief that the proposition at hand will in fact be of use to the prospect. Through in-depth understanding of the "needs" of the prospect, the salesperson can demonstrate how the proposition will meet those needs. A basic example might be the person who knows he is not a good athlete (REAL SELF), but who conceives he would like to be a good athlete (OTHER SELF). The clerk in a sporting-goods store, recognizing this need, will suggest those products that will help the prospect meet this need.

As the individual prospect reveals herself or himself during a sales interview, the salesperson has the opportunity to deduce whether that person is moving from one view to another. Here is a conversation between a purchasing agent and a professional salesperson:

"These samples of adhesives are fine. But the price is way beyond what we can afford to pay. You know, we're a pretty big buyer and we get the best prices."

"There's no question about what you say. The rest of the industry looks to you for leadership. That's why an order from you would be so important. You agree the product is excellent. Certainly the price is only relative to the quality of the merchandise."

The salesperson in this exchange assumed that the prospect had a REAL OTHER image as a leader and felt that a better price was needed to preserve that image. Therefore, the response of the salesperson was to recognize that leadership position and still hold firmly to the price.

The salesperson can fortify the prospect by agreeing with the self-concept, or supply the route by which the prospect can escape into another self-concept. Either way, the salesperson is answering a human need, which in a sense is a return to the observation, "We don't sell products, we sell people." The more you know about the human side of buying, the more successful you will become.

The Hierarchy of Human Needs

During the mid-1950s, the psychologist Abraham Maslow devised a Hierarchy of Human Needs. From a business point of view, it is interesting to relate these needs to the process of selling. Here, briefly, are the needs that Maslow described in detail:

Physiological: These are the needs of the body—food, water, shelter, warmth, sleep, sexual fulfillment, and bodily elimination.

Safety: A feeling of safety from physical and emotional injury and a sense of freedom from illness.

Need for belongingness, acceptance, and love: The social need for other people, to be part of a group, to give and receive love in other than sexual ways.

Self-esteem and the esteem of others: Self-respect, a sense of personal worth and adequacy, a feeling of competence, the respect of others, status in the eyes of others, and the admiration of others.

Self-actualization: The need for a person to be everything he or she is capable of being.

Maslow suggested two further needs, but for the professional salesperson, these five are the most important. In his interpretation, Maslow related these needs to motivation. For example, he said that until one need is fulfilled, there is no motivation to the next higher need; that once a need is satisfied, it no longer motivates; and that the pattern of needs is recurring. (Hunger satisfied at 8 A.M. must be resatisfied at 1 P.M.)

How does this information assist the professional salesperson? At the lowest level, we can easily see that trying to sell a prospect who is sleepy or hungry is a terrible, if not impossible, chore. As we move up the scale, the salesperson has the opportunity to capitalize on a variety of human needs. Think about the appeals made during the sale of:

A car—esteem, personal worth, respect. (Note: One of the reasons automobile manufacturers have been hesitant about advertising seat belts is that they appeal to a lower level of needs—safety.)

A life insurance policy—the old appeal to safety has been supplanted by need for love and even esteem; owning the biggest policy on the block is showing the greatest concern for a spouse or a child.

A new heating system—could appeal to physiological needs or safety, or even being part of the group that buys the new product.

The most expensive brand of any product—appeals to the need for esteem by others.

As the sales interview moves along the inclined plane, the salesperson has the chance to discover what needs of the prospect must be filled. It is foolish to continue to mention the low price of a product if the prospect is clearly interested in the admiration of a peer group. It is equally fruitless to relate the safety factors of the transformer on a TV set when the prospect wants to be part of the group that owns oversized screens.

The importance of the Hierarchy of Human Needs is that needs motivate! These are human needs, and they can be directly related to product or service needs. It is the appointed task of the professional salesperson to isolate the merits of a particular product and bring them to the attention of the prospect. It is obvious that the need for a suit of clothes is not the same for the truck driver as for a bank president. The truck driver needs esteem and belongingness, whereas the bank president needs a "uniform" to wear to work each day.

ANALYZING PROSPECT BEHAVIOR

We have attempted to present a variety of motivating forces that exist in each individual, and even to present the views of experts in the field of selling and psychology. But keep in mind that there is no rule as to their application. Other factors prevent or deter the professional salesperson from successfully concluding every sales interview.

Often the prospect is unaware of the true motives for wanting (or not wanting) to purchase a particular product. Why does Mary Smith own 14 pairs of slacks? Does she "need" them, or is there an underlying reason that motivates her to possess so many? Why does Harry Jones buy a new car every three years even though the old one has gone only 30,000 miles? Why do some families own three cars? four cars? Do people buy a dishwasher because the old one broke? Are purchasing agents impervious to the various emotional or human needs we have presented?

Because many people either knowingly or unknowingly hide the reasons why they make purchases, the job of the salesperson becomes more difficult. The search for these reasons is what selling is all about. The salesperson may be prepared to fill a need, but first must come the discovery of what the need is. Frequently, purchasing agents mask their needs as they seek to make a better buy.

The reality of this total picture is that the underlying needs of people are complex. No one reason for making a purchase will suffice. More often than not, people have a number of needs to be met.

As the sales interview progresses, prospects may behave in a number of different ways that provide clues to their needs. Take the case of a skeptical person. During the interview, this person is constantly asking questions, seeking to confound the salesperson. It is hard to convince the prospect that you are telling the truth or to create an atmosphere in which the prospect will accept what you are saying. Every statement is challenged, and it often seems that the effort of the salesperson is in jeopardy. Which need is this person trying to fill? This prospect might be looking for a way out, but we can draw no conclusions here without more information. But the salesperson in this situation has to grapple with the reality that this prospect is skeptical—and then seek to discover why.

Another "acting-out" behavior pattern of prospects is anger or arrogance. This may merely be the style of the individual. The prospect undoubtedly feels that this attitude will in the end get the best bargain. Or it may be a method used to cloak true feelings and needs. The timid or reticent prospect is another one commonly encountered. Then there is the fearful person, the procrastinator, the impulsive buyer, and the hypertense or irritable person. Thus, "reading" the prospect is a problem in itself.

To these and other behavior patterns, it may seem to the student that there are no solutions. On the contrary, the salesperson must draw many conclusions as the sale moves forward. However, there is no way to predetermine what a particular behavior means with regard to a specific individual. Anger in one person may not mean the same thing as anger in another. It is up to the salesperson to "read" these signs and try to position them in the realm of needs.

ANALYZING MOTIVES

Remember that human behavior is very complex and that the professional salesperson should be cognizant of certain guidelines. First, don't categorize prospects. People are unique and should be treated accordingly. The prospect who responds and reacts to praise and "soft soap" tells you only about that particular person. Just because that person buys for a sporting-goods store does not mean that all sporting-goods buyers will respond in the same way. By the same token, the purchasing agent who is miserable and nasty does not represent all professional buyers. Certainly religion, race, and cultural background are not criteria for drawing conclusions about groups of people.

First impressions, although important, tell very little about a prospect. Often a prospect will affect a certain attitude and behavior that is intended to disrupt the sale, to put the salesperson on the defensive. Other prospects pretend to be friendly and kind, only to reveal themselves during price negotiations as tough bargainers. The professional salesperson will hesitate to draw conclusions about anyone after only one meeting.

Actually, people are more alike than they are dissimilar. As presented in this chapter, all people are subject to the same physical, emotional, and psychological needs. Identifying the needs of the prospect and deciding on the best ways to satisfy them is the problem. However, along the way, the professional salesperson must keep in mind the diversity of background and the deep-rooted psychological factors that affect the human condition.

The preparation of any sale should include coverage of all possible human needs, which are motivations to buy. Any product, no matter how complex or how simple, can be presented to a prospect in a number of ways, each designed to appeal to a different buying motive. As the salesperson analyzes the prospect, the opportunity is presented to skim up and down the ladder of needs to find the correct motivational factor for bringing the sale to a successful conclusion.

This discussion of the underlying reasons people feel the way they do, act the way they do, and are moved to make a purchase seems quite complex. It is. However, the professional salesperson considers it a challenge to try to understand the prospect. Toward this end, we present a "magic" formula that will assist the salesperson during the interview:

Expressed in easy-to-understand language, this formula reads, "SALES SUCCESS equals TWO EARS minus ONE MOUTH."

That is, spend twice as much time listening to the prospect as you spend telling about your proposition!

SUMMARY

Everybody in the world is different; people come from varying sexual, ethnic, religious, and cultural backgrounds. To make their behavior more complicated, all people are affected by the environment in which the sale takes place. A hot room or uncomfortable undergarments can have a decided effect on the success of a sale. However, the things that motivate people to buy, the reasons that cause them to respond to a buying stimulus, are all the same.

An examination of motivation suggests that some people buy for completely rational reasons; they need the product. However, even these buying decisions are studded with emotional reasons. What appears rational to one person is irrational to another. It is for this reason that emotional motivation seems the more powerful force. A recounting of the many emotions suggests that people have a number of different needs to be satisfied, ranging from prestige to economy to esthetic gratification.

The idea that salespeople solve problems is completely valid within the framework of the psychological needs of the prospect. The professional salesperson does indeed solve problems. However, these problems often relate to the emotional needs of the prospect as well as the practical needs. The absolute need for a new refrigerator is mingled with the emotional need for color, quality, credit terms, and the price the prospect is willing to pay. Other times, the salesperson must meet the challenges of uncovering the absolute need as well as the emotional need.

Another way of thinking of the human needs that affect purchasing decisions is to consider the self-concept of prospects. How do they see themselves? How would they like to see themselves? How do they think others see them? How would they like others to see them? These personal factors are often more powerful in making a buying decision than the physical need for a product or service.

Finally, the psychologist Maslow has ranked the needs of human beings into a progression, stating that as lower needs are filled, they no longer motivate people to act—or in the case of selling, to make a purchase. Moreover, needs once filled may have to be refilled at a later time.

All these insights into reasons or motives why people buy are important to the professional seller. They are significant as the salesperson analyzes the behavior of the prospect. However, behavior only tells how a person behaves at that particular moment; it does not necessarily reveal motives. It remains for the salesperson to discover and determine what will actually motivate the prospect. The only thing we know for certain is that things that motivate are multitudinous; people are moved individually by different motivating forces. It is the discovery of these motivating forces that makes selling a great and exciting challenge.

A SUCCESS STORY

Disgust crept into his voice as Sam Stetzer closed his briefcase and said, "I'll stop next time I'm in town."

Across the desk, Paula Sterling smiled. "What's the matter, can't you stand defeat?"

"Heck, it's not defeat. I just don't know what will make you move on this deal. It has to be the best offer of its kind in the country. Where else can you get so much for so little?"

"Maybe you haven't touched the right nerve," chided Paula.

"Look," Sam said, a tone of anger slipping into his voice. "I explained the benefits of this proposition from A to Z. You agreed that the quality and price and service were first-rate. What more do you want?"

"That's your job, Sam. Maybe you still haven't touched the right nerve. Just because I agree with the specifics about your product doesn't mean there is enough reason to buy."

"What other reasons are there besides the things I have already told you? If everything is 'go,' what else can I say?"

"Have you thought of appealing to my prestige?"

"What do you mean?"

"Well, wouldn't placing an order for 2,000 pieces make me a very big buyer?"

"Gee, I never thought of that. Well, how about placing an order so you can be the first person in the country to take advantage of this remarkable offer?"

"Good try, Sam. But prestige doesn't affect me. How about safety?"

"I don't get the game, but I'll play along. Why not place an order today and be certain you have saved on the first shipment by having it arrive before the month is out?"

"That's better, Sam. You're beginning to get the hang of this thing. Why not appeal to my sex drives?"

"How the heck can I get sex into a presentation about cardboard boxes?"

"Try."

"Okay. We can imprint these boxes with colorful pictures of bathing beauties. How does that sound?"

"Not bad. How about appealing to my need to feel like part of a group?"

"All right. There are probably ten buyers in the whole country who can make a purchase like this. Because of your company's size and storage capability, you are in a fairly select group."

"Now," laughed Paula, "you have found about five other ways to motivate me into buying. Doesn't that make you feel better?"

"Darn it, Paula, what will make you buy?"

"Why don't you suggest that if I make this purchase, I will free myself from having to worry about boxes for a good long time and I can devote that time to more productive pursuits?"

"Yeah, I guess that's true. Shall I write the order?"

"Yes, I guess you'd better. I have convinced myself that it's a good idea. You certainly are a persuasive salesman."

QUESTIONS FOR CLASS DISCUSSION

1. What is the relationship between a prospect's religious beliefs and the salesperson? Is it ever safe for the salesperson to introduce religion into a sales interview? How about if you are selling a religious item?
2. A good deal of advertising is directed at "ethnic" groups. Is it valid for the salesperson to use similar types of appeals?
3. In addition to religious, sexual, political, economic, and ethnic differences, everybody is affected by physical problems that disrupt the sale. How many can you name?
4. Which statement do you agree with? "People motivate themselves," or, "People are motivated." Explain your thinking.
5. Explain how "problem solving" can be related to motivational needs and desires. Do we all have problems?
6. Scottish poet Robert Burns wrote, "O wad some power the giftie gie us/To see oursels as others see us!" What does this have to do with the notion of self-concept?
7. How would you react to the statement, "Everyone can be motivated"? Is it true? Why?
8. Using Maslow's Hierarchy of Human Needs, write five statements, one for each category, that would help a salesperson sell a $100 fishing pole.
9. Differentiate between "rationality" and "rationalization."
10. We have talked a great deal about how people are different, but can you suggest any ways in which we are all alike? How does this help the salesperson?

CASE 2—THE SELLER WHO WOULDN'T LISTEN

Murray Green arranged the stereo components around the large room in anticipation of a return visit by Joan Ginger, a school teacher. The preceding night, she had called at the store and examined various units. At Murray's suggestion, she was to return after he had hooked up all the sound-making devices so that she would have the chance to hear the music in the store as she might hear it at home. Adding up all the units, Murray realized the total cost was approaching $1,000. "Quite a nice sale," he murmured to himself.

When Joan arrived, he ushered her into the back room and asked, "What kind of sound would you like to hear first? Soul? Rock? Jazz? You name it, we have them all."

"Could we start with something on the quiet side? Perhaps some of the oldies, like Benny Goodman and Harry James."

"Hey, we'll play anything you want. But nobody buys those sounds anymore."

This disturbed Joan. So many people had told her about new styles in music, a combination of fast beat and raucous melodies. There were times when she questioned her own tastes, and now this salesperson seemed totally unsympathetic to what she wanted.

"We just got this new Rolling Stones record. I'd like you to hear what we can do with this music on this equipment. You sit here in the center, and I'll just play with the dials until we find the right combination for you."

"If you don't mind, I prefer Benny Goodman."

"Right you are. You relax and listen to this while I find one of those old-timers. I know we have a few kicking around."

The jangling, blaring sound unnerved Joan. She really wanted to try some symphonies and operas on this equipment, but the condescending attitude of Murray Green had made her feel unwanted. When he returned to the sound room, he was humming and tapping his fingers in beat with the music.

"I wonder," she asked, "if you have *Die Fledermaus?*"

Murray thought for a moment. "Is that a new rock group?"

"No," answered Joan in a tired tone. "It's a light opera by Strauss."

"You see," said Murray, "Those old things don't have the peaks and valleys of the newer music. This equipment was made to catch all the nuances and middle tones of modern music. That's why I want you to appreciate the full range of sound."

"But I know what I like."

"Sure you do. I just want you to know the possibilities with this arrangement of woofers and sound boxes."

"Could I hear *My Fair Lady?*"

"Anything you want," answered Murray.

1. What did Joan Ginger want?
2. What needs do you think she was trying to fill?
3. Was Murray Green meeting those needs?
4. What other needs or desires was Joan seeking to fill?
5. What advice do you have for Murray?

EXERCISE 2

Survey five male students. Ask each to list, in order of importance, three reasons why he purchased his best outfit.

Survey five female students. Ask each to list, in order of importance, three reasons why she purchased her best outfit.

Visit a men's clothing store and ask a salesperson to list, in order of importance, three reasons why customers buy.

Visit a women's clothing store and ask a salesperson to list, in order of importance, three reasons why customers buy.

SALES PROBLEM 2—THE "RIGHT" BUYER

"I don't think I like it. It won't sell," said the owner of the shop.

"I like it; it's just what we need, and I think we ought to order them," said the store manager.

The sales rep was confused. He wanted to make the sale, but he wasn't sure whether to side with the manager or the owner of the shop. Even though he had been told early in the relationship that the manager had the authority to order merchandise, this was the first time he had to contend with out-and-out disagreement from the owner.

Here are solutions offered by three different salespeople:

Sales Rep #1:   First, I'd find out if the owner is familiar with the product in question. Maybe he never saw it before, or maybe he isn't aware of the sales potential of this particular product.

I would also ask the owner what he didn't like about the item; why he thought it wouldn't work in his store. I guess I would also have to understand the relationship between the manager and the owner. Is it friendly? stormy? simply courteous?

In the final analysis, I'd try to sell the owner, because the manager is already sold.

Sales Rep #2:   This happens to me quite often, because the owners tend to bring their own likes and dislikes to the decision-making process.

The ultimate decision about the value of the product is really in the hands of the customer who shops in the store. I'd sit down with the owner and the manager and seek to show how the people who shop in the store will like and buy the product. The point is that the personal taste of the owner should not deter him from making a purchase that will please his customers.

Sales Rep #3:   This has happened to me only twice in my sales career. On both occasions, I got permission to actually approach several customers in the shop and ask them what they thought of a product. This way I was able to convince both the owner and the manager of the value of what I was selling.

The final judge of value still remains with the customers of your customer. They are the ones who decide the relative merit of merchandise. I sometimes find myself selling a product that I myself do not like. That should not stand in the way of making a professional presentation if the product will prove useful or beneficial to the customer.

3

HOW
TO COMMUNICATE
WITH BUYERS

PERFORMANCE OBJECTIVES

After you have read this chapter and completed the Questions for Class Discussion, the Case, the Sales Problem, and the Exercise, you should be able to do the following:

1. List and describe four differences between nonverbal and verbal communication.
2. Explain five methods of nonverbal communication.
3. Describe the three modes of communication—verbal, nonverbal, and alternate.
4. Incorporate nonverbal and alternate communication techniques in a sales dialogue.

CLEANING UP WITH VACUUM CLEANERS

Jack and Joan Carven were walking the aisles of the local department store, shopping for nothing and looking at everything. Behind them trailed 10-year-old Jackie and 8-year-old Susie. At least once a month, the family strolled around the shopping mall and then made their way into the department store, completing the circuit at the lunch counter, where each had a soda and a hamburger.

"Not much change in these stores," Jack said. "They look pretty much the same from one trip to the next. The only thing different is that the displays have been moved around or a few more items are out on the counters."

By taking a circular route around the store on their monthly visits, the family hoped to learn about new products as they spent a few pleasant hours. On this particular Friday night, they were in for a surprise. Just past the jewelry counter, a tall, thin man stopped Jackie and asked, "Want to have some fun? Here. Throw this bag of dirt on that carpet over there."

Jackie looked up at his father, uncertain of what to do. He knew that throwing dirt on a carpet was something kids weren't supposed to do. Yet the fun of making a mess is part of growing up. A nod from his father was all the coaxing he needed, and the contents of the bag were soon spread on the clean blue carpet.

Then the man pointed a long finger at Susie and said, "Here, take hold of the handle of this vacuum cleaner and you can sweep it up."

The little girl shrugged her shoulders. "I don't know how."

"Nothing to it," said the man. "Just push this button and away you go."

As she moved the machine back and forth, the salesman turned to Joan and laughed. "See, if your little girl can do the vacuuming, imagine how easy it will be for you." As he was talking, he handed a brochure to Jack and pointed to a list of the selling points of this particular machine. Then he stepped back, satisfied that he had involved the entire family in the demonstration.

"How does that feel, young lady?" he asked Susie.

"I never did this before."

Still smiling, he handed Susie another bag of dirt and indicated she should throw it on the carpet. Then he pressed the machine into Joan's hands. "You'll be impressed with how rapidly this model works. Think of the time it will save you on cleaning day."

Joan took the handle and awkwardly pushed the machine back and forth. "I guess it's all right," she said.

"I want to try," said Jackie.

"Sure," smiled the salesman. Turning to Jack he said, "Did you notice that this model has a two-year guarantee? That covers parts and service. Any time the little lady has problems, simply bring the machine in for immediate service."

"I don't understand what you mean by 'the little lady.' "

Somewhat taken back, the salesman replied, "Why, I mean that if your wife has any problems with the machine, we will take care of all repairs."

"Oh," was all that Jack could say as he crossed his arms. For the first time the salesman felt he had lost contact with the prospects. He wasn't getting through. A rapid mental review of the interview indicated that his appearance was acceptable, he had smiled a good deal, had had the family participate in the demonstration, had spoken calmly and in a friendly tone, and he knew the machine was doing an excellent job. What, then, was wrong?

"Do you have a vacuum cleaner?" he asked Joan.

She shrugged her shoulders. "Of course."

"Is it a new model?"

"About four years old."

"Do you like the way this machine picks up the lint and cigar ashes?"

"Looks great to me."

"This new machine sells for $249.95. Sight unseen, we will give you a $50 allowance on your old model. Does that sound fair?"

"It's up to Jack," she answered uninterestedly.

"You mean he is the one who does the buying?"

"No, I do the buying. But he does the vacuuming. If he likes the machine, we'll buy it."

With that, the family moved off toward the lunch counter. "We'll talk about it sometime," Jack said.

The crestfallen salesman squirmed; a hot flash ran from the tip of his polished shoes to the top of his neatly trimmed hair. He had done everything right except communicate with the proper person. He had failed to ascertain who would make the decision about a new machine. Basically, he had failed to realize that communication is a two-way street.

WHAT IS COMMUNICATION?

There has been so much use and misuse of the word *communication* that many people fail to grasp its true significance. Communication is the "*interchange of thoughts, opinions, or information by speech, writing, or signs.*" The important point in an *interchange* is that more than one person is involved. When only one person is transmitting information, or thoughts, or data, and the transmission is not being received, then no communication is taking place.

Some people think that television is communication. Actually, it is one method for transmitting a message, and only when there is some audience response or recognition can we be certain communication took place. Think of it this way. Suppose you leave your TV set on in the living room when you are asleep in your bedroom. Has there been any communication? Of course not, because the sound and picture played to an empty room.

Imagine a college professor lecturing to a class. Often the students sink down in their seats and fall asleep. Has there been communication? Or merely someone standing at the front of a room talking, emitting words? Pehaps a better example is the pantomime actor. A message is transmitted through actions and gestures. However, if you close your eyes, no message is communicated.

It is even possible to conceive of two people talking, neither one paying attention to or receiving the messages sent out by the other. A frequently heard expression is, "Are you paying attention to what I am saying?" Parents often yell at their children, "Listen to me!"

For the professional salesperson, it is imperative that communication be recognized as an exchange. The salesperson who rattles on and on about the product is making a speech, not communicating. Also of importance to the salesperson is the idea that the exchange between two people need not be only with the *spoken* word. The written word has a tremendous effect as it communicates. How many times have you heard people say, "I just read this in [fill in your own choice] magazine. It must be true." Only when the magazine article has been read and understood has communication taken place.

There are other, nonverbal ways to communicate. For example, the crying child is communicating something to a parent—perhaps hunger, fear, or a wet diaper. Few communications are as effective as a smile.

How we communicate is the subject of this chapter. We shall discuss methods of communication in some detail, once we have firmly established the fact that communication is more than the spoken word. The professional salesperson cannot accept a narrow definition of communication; it is important to understand that people communicate in a number of ways, and the professional should be in a position to capitalize on all these techniques.

PHILOSOPHY OF SELLING (COMMUNICATION)

It has been suggested, with a good deal of justification, that selling is communicating—that is, the transmission of thoughts and ideas about the benefits and virtues of a product or service to a potential customer. The implication is that a variety of methods and techniques are employed to convey the message so that the receiver of the message, the prospect, will understand and therefore act on the communication. That is why the professional salesperson should seek to combine an ability to communicate with a basic philosophy regarding selling as communicating.

If the professional salesperson adopts a philosophy of work that runs counter to good selling, this attitude will show through during communication with the prospect. For instance, if making money is your prime purpose in being in the sales profession, it will be difficult if not impossible to conceal this feeling from the prospect. Not that there is anything wrong with making money; but it is a goal or objective and not a philosophy. The true professional may have financial reward as a goal but also adopt a philosophy of how to reach that goal. Think of it this way. The pot at the end of the road is money; but the road itself is the operating philosophy. You may reach the pot by taking a number of different roads, but if you select sales as the way to make money, then you should also accept that the road leading to the reward is service to the customer.

One highly skilled salesperson stated a philosophy this way: "When I approach a prospect, I always say to myself, 'What can I do for this person that is not now being done?' It is the kind of question that reinforces my outlook. By bringing service and product to people, I make money."

Another sales expert put it like this: "My business is showing people the benefits they can derive from using my products. The more benefits I show and the better I show them, the more money I will make."

Why is it important for a professional salesperson to have a philosophy? Because this philosophy is communicated in several ways to the prospect. If it is a philosophy that is detrimental to the concepts of professional selling, the prospect will read the signs just as surely as if they are emblazoned on the forehead of the salesperson. The process of communication is so varied that hidden feelings often come through with clarity and sharpness. This fact can work for or against the salesperson. People communicate in a number of ways, and whether basic feelings are hatred, love, or boredom, those feelings will soon become apparent.

Although the purpose of this chapter is to add significantly to the techniques and knowledge of the salesperson, it is important to realize first that communication is a two-way street. Even as you are receiving messages from the prospect, the prospect is receiving messages from you. If your message emanates from a philosophy other than service, the prospect will read you loud and clear.

HOW WE COMMUNICATE

A purchasing agent went to the door of his office to look out at the salespeople waiting to be interviewed. At the far end of the room sat a distinguished-looking man wearing a dark blue suit with thin pinstripes.

He was holding a derby in one hand and a copy of the *Wall Street Journal* in the other. Sitting next to him was a younger man with longish hair, dressed in blue jeans and an open collar. On his lap rested a dark brown briefcase. The third chair was occupied by a dark-haired young woman in a pantsuit. On the floor next to her rested a large black sample case.

Scratching his head, the agent walked to the interoffice phone and quietly asked his secretary, "Are all those people selling?"

"I think so, Mr. Jones," came the reply. "Shall I send the next one in?"

"I suppose so," he answered. "I just can't make out what is going on in business today."

Even though no words had been exchanged and no gestures were made by or among the four people in question, the purchasing agent had already drawn some conclusions. All the people sitting in the outer office had sent a message in the way they were dressed. We have no way of knowing how the buyer received the message; we know only that a message was sent. Obviously, if we described the purchasing agent as wearing sneakers, flare trousers, and a colorful shirt without a tie, we might

MESSAGES ARE SENT WITH WORDS, GESTURES, AND THE WAY WE LOOK.

Figure 3-1

draw the conclusion that the younger man in the outer office was dressed appropriately for this particular prospect. But even that conclusion would be based on our own individual ideas and thoughts about how people should dress for business. The only thing we know for certain is that a message was transmitted and received.

Many people, sales professionals among them, resent the notion that they are prejudged by the way they dress. (The author himself prefers well-worn button-down shirts and comfortable but beat-up shoes.) The point is that whether we like it or not, people do judge other people by the way they dress. With this thought in mind, the professional salesperson always has the advantage, the chance to decide what kind of "message" should be transmitted to the buyer. When a salesperson considers wardrobe as a communicating factor, the selection of what to wear on each occasion takes on a new complexion.

Clothes are not the only thing that enters the communication picture. Hair length, polished shoes, dirty fingernails, smoking habits, and manners also have an effect. These things can be seen from afar; they require no accompanying words to convey the message.

Verbal Communication

One communications expert claims that there is no such thing as purely verbal communication; the spoken word does not exist in a vacuum. Let's trace what happens when a salesperson says something. The verbal message is accompanied by gestures and motions, in addition to the message sent by how the salesperson looks. These three components travel to the receiving party, and on the way, they meet interference in the form of noise and other actions taking place. The receiver, therefore, receives a distorted set of messages. Here is an example:

The prospect is sitting at a desk interviewing the salesperson. As the salesperson speaks, he crosses his legs, hands the prospect a sheet of paper, and then clears his throat. Outside, a siren sounds as engines clang their way to a fire. The sun plays on the far wall of the office. The shoes of the salesperson shine in the daylight.

This relatively simple setting demonstrates the inherent difficulties in transmitting a message to the prospect. Everything taking place requires some of the prospect's attention. If we examine an even more realistic example, the problem becomes magnified. During an interview, here is what took place between a storeowner and a favorite salesperson:

"Good morning, John," said the sales rep, hefting a briefcase onto the display counter. "I have some fresh samples to show you." With that, he opened the case and drew out three colorful swatches. The bright hues caught the eye of the buyer, who ran his fingers over the fine textured materials. At that moment, two people walked through the front door, and the storekeeper glanced around to see if floor salespeople were aware that they were in the store. The whirr of the elevator complemented the gentle hum of the fluorescent lights overhead.

"These look very nice," said the storekeeper. He noticed that the sales rep was wearing a new blue suit, one of the latest plaids. Reaching over, he felt the material of the suit and admired the details. Then, flipping the samples on the counter, he opened the sample case and began to rummage through the other swatches.

"Hey, looking for anything in particular?" asked the salesman. He reached over to help his friend and in the attempt, spilled the contents on the floor. "Darn," he said.

"Here, let me help," said the storekeeper. He bent over to retrieve the samples, and the two men lifted the sample case back onto the counter.

"No problem," smiled the salesman. "I have to rearrange my bag anyhow. These samples you asked for are available for immediate delivery." He handed the three swatches once more to the storekeeper. Another customer entered the store, and the rumbling noises of a bus on the street slipped through the open door.

"Let's go into my office," said the storekeeper. "We can smoke in there."

Now, reread what took place, and imagine how much of what was "said" got through. There were just too many distractions for the verbal message to be properly received.

How does the person receiving a message respond? First, the responding person must allow the various messages (verbal, nonverbal, and alternate) to be received. He or she has to think about them, digest their meaning, and then formulate a reply that will include not only spoken words but gestures and actions. The reply encounters the same kind of interference as the original message. Thus, the response to a message is often a rather garbled version of what was intended.

It is also interesting to note that while the speakers are sending out messages, they are also listening to the messages themselves. This is known as external self-feedback. Even as they hear the words, they have the opportunity to correct or modify the intent of what is being said.

This explanation of communication problems is not meant to confuse the student, but merely to reinforce the thought that communication is a difficult and complex procedure. Under the best of circumstances, probably little more than half of what we say is comprehended by the person to whom we are communicating. Again, we raise the question, what does this mean to the professional salesperson?

Because verbal communication has to overcome so many external interferences, the salesperson must pay rigid attention to what is said, how it is said, and how often it seems necessary to repeat a message. Obviously, saying the same words over and over will have a deadly effect upon the prospect and the progress of the sale. It is incumbent upon the salesperson to find new and fresh ways to say the same thing. It is also important to check with the prospect to ascertain how well the message is coming through.

In brief, spoken words in and of themselves have little if any magic. Just because you say something is no reason to assume that the prospect heard or understood the message. If professional salespeople are to be successful, they must come to grips with the idea that verbal communication has its shortcomings and limitations. If "selling is communicating," then we have to find additional and improved ways to get our message across to the prospect.

Nonverbal Communication

Did you ever wonder how people got along before the invention of language? Surely some early cave dweller was able to convey an expression of love without using words. Body language—nonverbal communication—has received a good deal of attention within the past 20 years as we have come to recognize the significance of communicating by motions and signs. A popular song of the 1950s said, "Your lips tell me 'no-no,' but there's 'yes-yes' in your eyes."

Some communications experts feel that more than two-thirds of all communication is carried out using nonverbal channels. A brief examination of some of this thinking will prove helpful to the aspiring salesperson.

Nonverbal communication is continuous. For instance, a person standing by the side of a road trying to hitch a ride clearly communicates a desire by a long pull of the thumb across the chest. This message goes on for an extended period of time, much longer than the ability to continually yell, "Can I have a ride?" Moreover, it is not as tiring as the need to repeat over and over, "How about a lift?"

Nonverbal communication can indicate two messages at the same time. Imagine a traffic officer signaling "stop" with the right hand and "go" with the left hand. There is no way that verbal communication can accomplish a similar feat. In fact, delivering "stop" and "go" instructions verbally would only add to the confusion.

Nonverbal communication requires little skill. Even a baby who does not yet know words can communicate by grabbing a spoon, smiling, or crying. However, to communicate verbally, both the sender and the receiver of the message have to agree on what they mean by words. "Hood" to an automobile salesperson is the front of the car. To a police officer, it is a gangster. To a fashion designer, it is a covering for the head.

Nonverbal communication may be intimate. Depending on the tone and quality of the voice, one person tells another of love and affection. By intonation and modulation, by a gentle kiss or an arm around the waist, the effect is multipled. Body language conveys messages in a forceful manner.

Given that body language sends out a message all its own, how can the salesperson capitalize on this knowledge? First, by mastering a set of gestures and movements to fortify verbal messages. Second, by "reading" the messages the prospect is sending, both verbal and nonverbal. There are five key areas to observe:

Body Movement.   Repositioning the body during a transitional point in the sales interview tends to emphasize a statement. Moving about gently also tends to relax the prospect. Extreme movements will cause concern and upset the prospect.

Facial Expression.   Frowning when you have bad news only adds to the consternation of the listener. Smiling when you have bad news confounds and disturbs. You may have considered the proper words to use in a given portion of the sale, but have you also considered which facial expression will best accompany those words?

Eyes.   Remarkable as it may seem, eyes do sparkle at certain times. And they are very effective at riveting a person's attention.

Gestures.   It is important to keep your hands relatively free so that you can emphasize important points of the sale when necessary. These movements should be slow and easy, so that they do not become important in themselves, but rather serve to reinforce what you are saying. (Every student has probably had a professor with some nervous habit, such as scratching behind an ear or dabbing the upper lip with a handkerchief. After a while, the gesture becomes more important than the lecture.)

Voice.   Don't confuse the voice with words. How you deliver the words can make a tremendous difference to the listener. The voice can be changed and modified, once you decide how you want to alter the tone, pitch, quality, and intensity.

Caution: Although we know that nonverbal communication is extremely important, we are in no way suggesting that a given motion has meaning of its own. Some experts tell us that when prospects fold their arms, they are becoming defensive and our proposition is in trouble. Because we subscribe to the notion that all people are individuals, the arm folding only tells us that this particular human being has tried to send us a message, but we do not know exactly what it means. The same gesture by different people will have an entirely different meaning. The professional salesperson must be aware that a message is being sent and seek to interpret that message as an additional road sign on the way to a successful sale.

People communicate through words, nonverbal expressions, and even through alternate channels, such as physical appearance. Professional salespeople can train themselves to use these channels to the best advantage. Simultaneously, they have the opportunity to better understand the response message of the prospects.

It is well to remember the magic formula, SS = 2E − M: Sales success equals two ears minus one mouth.

LISTENING AS COMMUNICATION

A very bright young student was asked, "Why don't you contribute more in class?"

Quickly the young person replied, "Because I can say only what I already know. Only when I listen can I learn."

This rather astute observation represents one of the key strengths of professional salespeople—the ability to listen to the prospect and learn what problems exist, or what services are needed. Many highly skilled and professional purchasing agents have been known to remark, "He is a good listener," which translates into the fact that the salesperson has "communicated" a sincere concern to the buyer. In other words, good listening habits can become a way to communicate.

From our earlier discussion of the problems inherent in the communication process, it is understandable that good listening habits must overcome a number of hazards. The same interference messages exist for the listener as for the sender of a message. However, good listening techniques can be learned and applied. Here are some of the important points to good listening:

First, listen with your eyes as well as your ears. Close eye contact with the prospect will impart a sense of attention. Merely by directing your eyes and ears to the subject matter at hand, you will gain a better understanding of what that person is saying, because you will simultaneously read the body signals that reenforce the verbal message.

Second, you should not rush to respond to what the person has said. A slight pause in the conversation never delays the selling process. If a prospect voices an objection, you may take your time answering. This delay gives you time to think and also implies that you have considered what has been said and you are trying to frame a sensible and adequate reply.

Finally, a good listener asks lots of questions. The message inherent

Figure 3-2

in a good question is, "I want to hear more of what you (the prospect) have to say on this subject." Moreover, this is a subtle form of flattery, since generally most people prefer to hear what they themselves have to say rather than what the salesperson has to say.

There are other minor touches that might be employed while listening. You can react or convey a message by facial expressions or body movements. If the prospect offers you a cup of coffee, you do not need to use language to accept or reject the offer. A raised hand, palm flat will at once say, "No, thank you." A smile and a nod of the head does not require the use of words. Thus, the prospect can continue to express desires and wishes while you gain valuable information about this particular human being.

Even as you consider a reply, you have to listen critically to what the prospect is saying. Often people will ramble on and on, barely touching on the true reason they do not want to make a purchase. It is the province of the professional salesperson to untangle the many emotions of the prospect and discover what button must be touched to effect a positive purchase decision.

During a sales interview for a major piece of equipment for a manufacturing company, the purchasing agent slipped into a lecture on the state of the economy. He ranted and raved about "bad times" until the salesperson almost jumped out of the seat. After leaving without an order, the sales rep later met with the sales manager to review what had taken place.

"He nearly drove me nuts," said the salesperson.

"You weren't listening to what he had to say," replied the sales manager.

"I heard every word," said the indignant salesperson.

"You may have heard every word, but you didn't get the message. He was trying to tell you the company was in financial difficulty and he wasn't in a position to make a purchase."

"Well, why didn't he say so?"

"He did. You weren't listening."

This is a very common example, because few people are prepared to admit they are in financial trouble. Therefore, the message will be cloaked in strange attire, and the salesperson will have to see what is hidden beneath the surface.

COMMUNICATION AND MOTIVATION

In the preceding chapter, we discussed the "human side of buying," which has to do with motives and motivation. In this chapter, we are dealing with the problems involved in the communication process. Making practical use of these two concepts certainly presents a challenge to the professional salesperson, one that calls for creativity and imagination. To activate these two characteristics, we shall work through a sales problem.

Linda DeYoung works in a sporting-goods store that caters to upper-income clientele. Often these people will stop by just to look over new stock and perhaps buy a few golf balls and chat for a while. The atmosphere is relaxed and comfortable, which is why the prospects feel secure in stopping by after lunch. However, Linda knew that Richard Osbourn had just been promoted and would be spending more time entertaining prospects on the golf course. In her mind she prepared several messages that would touch on the new motivations affecting Richard Osbourn.

Linda thought that Richard had moved beyond the *belongingness* need and was stretching to the *esteem* need. A new set of matched golf clubs seemed a perfect way to meet that need. Here is how she conceived that the conversation might go:

"Before you leave, Mr. Osbourn, I'd like you to take a look at this new set of clubs." (Gently motion him to follow to the back of the store.)

"Well, I don't really need clubs, Linda. But I'll take a look." (Smile as you walk to the golf section.)

(Slip a wood out of the bag and hold it shoulder high.)

"Please note, this particular club has a little more whip to it. Step over to our driving range." (Lead prospect to the tee and then hand him the club.)

After a few swings Mr. Osbourn says, "It seems very good, but I just don't need another set of clubs."

"Of course not. (Smile) But what about a set of clubs for your customers?"

"Why, when we play, if they don't have a set of clubs, we rent a set from the golf pro."

"Let me ask you a question. (Extend right hand, palm up.) In your new position, will you be playing more golf?"

"Yes."

"Sometimes you are with a client and you decide to play a round of golf on the spur of the moment?" (Look surprised.)

"Yes."

"Now, here's a tough one. (Rub chin for effect.) How do you think your clients will react when you tell them you have a special extra set of matched clubs for them to use at your club?"

"You make a good point," the prospect replied. "But I don't really think it's valid."

(Linda DeYoung anticipated this response.)

(Big smile) "It is a pretty unusual idea, isn't it?"

"Yes, it's different."

"Here's another question. (Rub chin again.) How about if *you* get a sudden invitation to play away from your home course. You can keep these clubs in your trunk and you'll always be prepared."

"Now, that's a fairly good idea."

In this sales interview, the salesperson had laid heavy stress on the significance of owning two sets of clubs. She planned to accentuate her verbal message with appropriate nonverbal actions and gestures. Most important, she related the communication process to the motivations of this particular prospect. By joining the two, she was on the way to a successful sale.

Planning is an important part of selling. In the example cited, it would seem that the salesperson had prepared an entire script or scenario of what was going to take place. That is exactly what happened. To the extent possible, every move, every word, and every gesture was considered as a part of the selling procedure. Here is another example of this type of planning:

Howard Blum represented a carpet manufacturer that specialized in hotel and motel sales. His normal call would be upon the purchasing agent of a large hotel in an attempt to present his line of carpeting for use throughout the property. On this occasion, he has been alerted that the new owners of the Aldine Hotel planned extensive alterations. His background information also indicated that quality would be uppermost in the minds of the new owners.

He adjusted his sample case, discarding a good many worn swatches, and included two samples each of low-, middle-, and high-price goods. In reviewing how he would make his approach, he decided to walk in, spread the six samples before the buyer, and stand quietly aside. Only after the buyer had scrutinized or touched each of the samples did he intend to pick up the two quality pieces and say, "This carpeting will show less wear, and at the same time, it is easier to maintain."

He realized there would be a good deal of interchange, and he decided to use gestures and motions only when he was discussing the more expensive fabric. To add to the dynamism of his proposition, he planned to light a cigarette and grind it into the better sample. About midway in the demonstration, he intended to ask, "Just what is it you want from your carpeting?" He felt assured that his prior information would elicit a response such as, "We want the best possible product, one that will last us for at least five years of hard wear."

Howard Blum did not commit his entire sales interview to written form; he had gone through that process when he was a young salesman. Now, years of experience had taught him to plan in his mind what was going to take place and still retain enough flexibility to change with the tide of the interview. He knew the points he wanted to make, and he knew that he would have to "listen" to the prospect to ascertain whether he was on the right track.

In the final analysis, putting together communication techniques and motivation is a key portion of the sales plan. How the message is to be transmitted and the direction of the target allow the professional salesperson to preplan the many steps along the way. It is not possible to cover all emergencies. That's why the sales professional learns to "listen."

SUMMARY

Communication cannot be construed in a narrow sense. It is the way people transmit messages, and it consists of verbal, nonverbal, and alternate methods. How communications are carried out is affected to a large degree by a basic philosophy of selling. This philosophy will be transmitted in the way the salesperson acts and the methods selected to convey the message.

Even though spoken words are uppermost in the minds of most people when they think of communication, the nonverbal aspects are equally if not more important. In this text, a great deal of attention will be paid to the use of language, but significantly, we take note of the fact that the spoken word is not the only way to communicate. Under no circumstances does the spoken word exist free of nonverbal accompaniment. When the two are mingled together and linked to alternate types of communication, it becomes clear that conveying meaning between people is at the least a knotty problem, one requiring considerable attention.

In addition to verbal and nonverbal communication there exists another channel called alternate communication. This consists of all those contacts which take place that are neither verbal nor nonverbal. The most important of these is the matter of how people dress. Clothes send a message; they communicate with the buyer. Odor sends a message, either pleasant or distasteful. The point is that a message, an alternate message, is being sent.

In the following chapter certain of these aspects of communication are covered in detail. For the moment it is significant for the student to be alert to the notion that the third channel of communication, alternate communication, does exist.

For the professional salesperson, there are two benefits in knowing and understanding the difficulties involved in the communication process. The first is the opportunity to improve personal performance so that a strong impression can be made upon the prospect. The second benefit is a learned ability that assists in "reading" the prospect, in understanding what the prospect is trying to communicate. The more it is possible to comprehend the position of the prospect, the easier it is for the salesperson to find solutions to problems and thereby serve the prospect.

Ultimately, the true professional can create a relation between the communication process and the motivational needs of the prospect to bring about a positive action by the prospect. The sales job, after all, is to sell a product or service. When salespeople use the best possible communication methods to deal with existing motivations, they have coupled the two strongest forces at their disposal.

A SUCCESS STORY

Mike Salerno sat at his desk and studied the can of dehydrated soup mix. "It's a pretty dry story," he said half aloud, and then laughed at his own feeble joke. He knew that somehow the benefits of preparing soup from a dry product could be dramatically presented to the food buyers in restaurants and schools. Slowly a plan evolved and took shape.

Taking a pad of yellow legal paper from his desk drawer, he began to scribble some notes. This is what they looked like:

1. Get a thermos jug. Fill it at home each morning with soup made from the dry mix.
2. Keep a supply of small paper cups and plastic spoons in briefcase. Also paper napkins.
3. Sample approach statements:
   a. "Mrs. Cafeteria Manager, here is soup for six cents a portion."
   b. Maybe start with a question: "How many times a week do you serve soup?" Then open briefcase and take out thermos.
   c. "I made soup this morning in five and a half minutes. Here, taste this." Hand prospect a cup of soup.
4. Since the name of this product is nationally known, I'll save that information till the close of the sale.
5. During demonstration, hand customer soup, spoon, and napkin. Allow time for tasting. Step back and allow plenty of room for prospect to move about. Stand still.
6. After prospect has tasted soup, hold up six fingers and repeat, "Only six cents per portion."
7. Carry sample packages of two other types of soups to demonstrate variety.
8. Study package to verify cooking time and yield per container.
9. Prepare closing statement by referring to special promotional allowance. "If you order ten cases, we offer one case free as a special incentive. You may select any mix of product that suits your needs."
10. Since this is a very dramatic and new product, it will be important to remain as quiet as possible so that the full attention of the prospect can be drawn to the product. Can't afford to distract prospect's attention. Try to move the buyer into office, away from noise of kitchen.

Mike leaned back in his chair and propped his feet up on the desk. He raised the sheets of paper and reviewed them as an actor reviews lines in a play. For half an hour he deliberated, often saying things out loud to listen and make corrections. He stood and went through the motions of opening the thermos, pouring the soup and even practiced how he would wrap every spoon in a napkin, to ensure cleanliness.

When he felt he was ready, he called his wife from the next room and said, "Honey, how about pretending to be a customer for a few minutes? I want to try out this new sales presentation."

QUESTIONS FOR CLASS DISCUSSION

1. Explain what is meant by, "Nonverbal communications are continuous." Can you give two examples?
2. Differentiate between "communications" and "messages." How many ways can "messages" be sent? Describe them.

3. Prepare a sales approach as if you were representing a book publisher, using only nonverbal techniques. Act out this message for the class.
4. Use the word *fire* in these three instances: fire someone from a job; fire a cannon; call the fire department to put out a fire in your kitchen. Was there any difference in the nonverbal methods of communicating this message?
5. Describe the five methods of nonverbal communication.
6. How would you dress if you were selling insurance to a group of bankers? musicians? factory workers? Explain your reasons and thinking.
7. What does it mean when the prospect folds his or her arms across the chest? Is the meaning the same when the person smiles at the same time? How about if the person frowns and folds his or her arms?
8. There are four differences between verbal and nonverbal communication. Describe them.

CASE 3—THE CASE OF THE RETICENT SELLER

For vacation this year, Mary and George Rollins were considering the purchase of a mobile home, one they could use to transport the family around the country. They felt that a trip with the two children would help to make the family closer and could be a lot of fun. The entire family drove over to Robbinstown, where an acre of ground was covered by the latest styles and models. Seated at a long table in one of the mobile homes was a salesperson, sorting through stacks of papers.

"Good morning," said George. "We're interested in learning more about mobile homes. Can you help us?"

"Sure," replied the salesperson. "Why don't you take a walk through some of the homes, and I'll catch up to you as soon as I finish my paperwork."

The family accepted a handful of brochures offered by the sales rep and left the office. "Doesn't seem very anxious to make a sale," said Mary.

"Maybe that's the way these people sell," suggested George. "Real soft approach."

As the family examined the interior of one home, little Amy exclaimed, "Gee, there's even a TV set in here. Boy, that's great."

"I wonder how much water the shower tank holds?" George mused.

"Do you need natural gas for the cooking?" Mary asked aloud.

At that moment the salesperson appeared and said, "This particular model sells for $14,850. However, we have a special this week, and you can make a deal for only $13,000."

"How many does this model sleep?" asked George.

"You can squeeze six in, I think," said the sales rep. "By the way, we also give you 100 gallons of gasoline and a full tank of cooking gas."

Then the sales rep added, "Spend as much time as you wish looking around. If you have any questions, I'll be in the office. Here are some more brochures I found."

Once again the family was left to their own devices. They walked through four models and then returned to the office. "What do you think we ought to know about that blue job on the rear of the lot?" asked George.

"Not much to know," said the sales rep. "If you want, we can take a ride in it."

"No, that won't be necessary," replied George. "I guess we'll just think about it for a while."

"Take your time," replied the sales rep. "I'll be right here if you need any help. Just ask."

Slowly the family strolled around the lot. The kids were very happy climbing through the opened doors and clambering over the mobile units. Mary and George were not happy.

1. Why were Mary and George Rollins unhappy?
2. Did the salesperson know what the family wanted? What *do* they want?
3. What kinds of nonverbal communication might this salesperson have used during this sale?
4. Describe how you would have prepared for this sales opportunity.

EXERCISE 3

Here is a brief dialogue between a salesperson and a prospect. Please add the alternate and nonverbal communication techniques you would use during this exchange.

Sales Rep:	How much profit do you think you could make with this 100 percent wool sweater?
Prospect:	Depends on how much they cost.
Sales Rep:	How many sweaters do you sell each week?
Prospect:	We don't need any sweaters right now.
Sales Rep:	These are packed six to a shipping case. We cover the freight, so your cost is only $13.50 a sweater.
Prospect:	Did you say they were all wool?
Sales Rep:	The best quality.
Prospect:	What's the minimum order?
Sales Rep:	How many shall I ship?

SALES PROBLEM 3—WHAT TO DO WHEN
YOU DON'T KNOW

She was very confused. The telephone caller asked for the nutritional breakdown of the frozen dinner. Not only that, information was requested on the cholesterol level, salt content, and even calcium. There was nothing unusual about the questions, except that she didn't know the answers, and the package was in the freezer on the other side of the store.

Here are the solutions offered by three different salespeople:

Sales Rep #1:   During our weekly sales meeting, this kind of information is handed around by the manufacturer's rep or one of the food brokers. But these sheets of paper are just too complicated to remember.

What I usually do is tell the customer I don't know the answer, but I'll call back in a few minutes. Then I go to the dietician and ask for help.

Sales Rep #2:   The first thing I would do is ask for the person's name and phone number. Then I would flat-out say I don't know the answer, but I would call back before the day was out.

I used to try to keep this kind of information in my head. Then the sales manager told me it was more important to know where to find the answer than it was to know everything. With all the new products coming on-stream, there is no way a competent salesperson can know everything about every product. The important thing is to find the answers as fast as possible.

Sales Rep #3:   Right off, I would tell the caller I didn't have the information. Then I would go to the sales manager and ask that person to call the manufacturer and get the data. This kind of question is coming up more and more as people become more diet- and weight-conscious. Also, many people are mindful of what they are eating, and that's why most food packages do have the information printed along the side. However, there is just too much for any one person to keep in mind. The best thing to do is admit you don't know but say that you will find out.

4

YOUR SALES PERSONALITY

PERFORMANCE OBJECTIVES

After you have read this chapter and completed the Questions for Class Discussion, the Case, the Sales Problem, and the Exercise, you should be able to do the following:

1. Describe the eight characteristics of a "sales personality."
2. Distinguish among the four types of tests or measuring devices commonly given to sales applicants.
3. Assess your sales personality.
4. State five ways to improve your own sales personality.
5. Analyze the sales personality of three salespeople.

HOW NOT TO SELL

Purchasing agent Larry Chapman had a problem. His new assistant was a bright young man, but very excitable. Larry knew that when major purchases are to be made, it is always best to remain calm and not reveal your hand to the salesperson on the other side of the desk. That way, you make the best possible deal for the company. He also knew that salespeople come in a variety of styles and temperaments; some you need, some you can live without. But as a professional buyer, he had to cultivate all these salespeople against a time when he might have to call on them for a fast delivery or a special price. To give experience to his young assistant, Larry arranged to have him sit behind the big desk and observe how purchases are made. Monday turned out to be a perfect day to scrutinize sales techniques.

"Mr. Glenn is here," announced the secretary over the intercom.

"Have him wait just two minutes," responded Larry. Then, turning to his young charge, he said, "The man you are about to meet has been in the business for 30 years. After he leaves, we can talk about his style."

"Good morning, Larry," smiled the big man. "I see you got yourself a helper. How are you, son?" Then he laughed and added, "I don't know why you need any help. There's not that much to do around here."

Larry pointed toward a chair and said, "How many drums of adhesive constitute a truckload?"

"Heck, Larry. You never bought that much in your life. There are 32 drums to a truckload. What are you trying to do, drive my price down?"

Larry smiled. "Sure, George. But you didn't give me a price."

The big man took out a cigar, held a lighted match to the end and puffed heavily. The room filled with purple-blue haze as George reached into his briefcase and pulled out a price book. "Sixty-four dollars a drum in truckloads and $68 in less than truckloads," said George. "Care for a cigar, young man?"

The assistant nervously shook his head and watched Larry. The purchasing agent took an order form from his desk and began to fill in quantities.

"You want the usual six drums?" asked George.

"Yes, I think that will cover us. Listen, I hate to rush you off, but here is the order, and we'll see you next trip."

"Glad to be of service," George said. "Hey, did you hear the story about the . . ."

"See you next trip," Larry interrupted.

The door barely closed when the intercom crackled, "Mr. Shore is here."

"Just a minute," Larry answered. Turning to his assistant he said, "Make some notes for yourself, and we'll talk later."

"Good morning, Mr. Chapman," said Harold Shore. "Watch this." He proceeded to take some adhesive, smear it on a piece of wood, and then press the block of wood against a five-pound metal weight. He then counted to ten slowly, and lifted the wood block, with the metal weight attached. "How's that for strong?"

"Looks good," said Larry. "Is this the adhesive you've been telling me about?"

"It sure is. And here's the best part of all. We can make full-truckload deliveries starting next week."

"What's the price?"

"Sixty-four dollars in truckloads. Is one truck enough?"

"For starters, yes," responded Larry.

The conversation continued, and the salesman alerted Larry to another new product that would be available in the next month. He thanked him for the order, waved to the young assistant, "Good luck in your new position," and left.

"Okay," said Larry. "What do you think?"

"You should have thrown the first guy out on his ear," snapped the young man. "He was a wise-guy, didn't know how to take an order. He sure made me feel like a punk. And he fouled up the air with smoke. If he calls on me, he'll be in big trouble."

Larry laughed. "You're a pretty tough guy. But suppose you were on the other side of the desk. Do you think it's easy to come in here and try to sell me a product? Don't you forget, I've been doing this for years, and these salespeople know I can be plenty hard on them."

"But why buy from cigar-puss?"

"Because he has adhesives and I need him. I need him as a backup when others may not have products. He gets about 5 percent of our business, and the funny part about it is that he doesn't even know what he's missing. I can't stand his attitude—he's overpowering and gruff. But he has merchandise we need. Believe me, if another adhesives supplier walked through the door, I'd drop our cigar-smoking friend in a minute."

"Do you mean there's nobody else around who sells adhesives?"

"Oh, there are plenty of people around. But when everything is equal, then I have to start looking at the seller's personality. Look, I'm a professional buyer. My job is to make the best possible deal for the company, and only at the very end can I worry about whether I like the salesperson or not. I agree, though, it's much easier to do business with salespeople who have a pleasing personality."

There was a dual lesson learned on this fateful Monday morning. A calm purchasing agent succeeds more than one who is tense, and the personality of the seller can spell the difference between modest and sizable orders.

WHAT IS SALES PERSONALITY?

There is a very simple and direct definition of personality. It is "the sum total of the physical, mental, emotional, and social characteristics of an individual."

Stated another way, your personality is a composite of everything you have ever heard, seen, smelled, touched, read, and been exposed to; the summation of all these characteristics has been formed and is observable in a number of ways. You are what you are, and the sales manager cannot change you. The only possible changes are those you wish to implement yourself.

Is there a particular personality that can be described as a "sales personality"? No one is prepared to nail down those characteristics that foretell sales success. That would be the same as saying, "Salespeople are born." There may be some rare exceptions who seem destined for sales careers, but in the main, salespeople are trained. There is no such thing as a "perfect" sales personality.

MEASURING YOUR SALES PROFILE

Many sales trainers flirt with the idea of defining a personality that will foretell sales success. Think of the possibilities: People could take a few tests or examinations and know that their work life is predetermined and that they have the makings and the moves of a professional salesperson. The hard facts of life are that professional salespeople are created and trained.

A training manager was quizzing a new sales trainee one day and asked, "Could you become an electrician?"

"Of course not," answered the young person. "That takes a lot of study and training."

"Could you become a plumber?"

"Oh, no. I understand it takes four years to become competent in that area."

"How about a brain surgeon?"

"My goodness. Everybody knows that it takes ten or twelve years to do surgery, and you have to be equipped."

"Then how long do you think it will take you to become a professional salesperson?"

Stymied, the trainee said, "I don't know. But how do you know I *can* become a professional salesperson?"

The answer is that nobody knows, but there are a number of measurement devices (tests) that can pretty well sketch a picture of what profes-

\sional salespeople look like, what characteristics they possess, and where their interests lie. Large organizations use these measurement tests constantly, and even smaller companies now recognize the advantage of "profiling" salespeople/

Because job applicants will undoubtedly undergo a battery of tests, it is significant for the potential salesperson to have some idea of what these tests will show and prove.

Intelligence (IQ) Tests

It would be wonderful if someone could cast a spell and the idea of IQs would disappear. That's not about to happen, and misunderstandings will continue. Throughout their school careers, students are overcome with the weight of IQ tests. What is it these tests reveal?

Actually, the use of the word *tests* is currently under heavy pressure. A better expression is *measurements.* In other words, IQ measurements tell where a person stands in relation to other people in ability to absorb and learn at that particular moment. Modern educational thinking suggests that, given time, anyone can learn anything. What this means is that a person with a 100 IQ will require more time to absorb information and data than will a person with a 120 IQ.

What does this have to do with selling? As a general statement, anyone with the ability to read this book and understand the concepts presented has the ability to absorb the information required to become a professional salesperson. Are there exceptions? Of course, the salesperson dealing with very sophisticated and technical equipment may need a degree in engineering to cope with certain problems. Although you may not have to understand how an X-ray machine works to sell it, if you are explaining the inner workings to an engineer, you will have to have specific product knowledge.

However, you do not have to know the principles of how an automobile runs to properly present the benefits of auto travel to the prospect. In the same sense, you do not have to understand the theories of economics to represent the loan department of a bank or the securities division of a brokerage house. The insurance agent need not know how actuarial tables are formulated, only that the company does it accurately. The real estate broker does not have to know how to build a house, and the steel sales representative need not be able to build a foundry. Product knowledge can and must be acquired over an extended period of time. The ability to learn the methods and techniques of the professional salesperson demand no particular IQ.

To ferret out sales prospects, one company went to the local high school and offered a $25 bond to the graduating senior who best expressed, "Why I Want to Be a Salesperson." At an open assembly, the president of the company spoke briefly and then made the award. After the program, the company head accosted the winner in the hall and suggested a meeting to talk about a sales position.

"Oh, I don't want to be a salesperson," the high school student said.

"But you wrote the winning essay," replied the surprised president.

"Well, sure," explained the senior. "I want to be a writer."

Although the ability to write may prove a valuable asset to a sales career, it is no indicator of a person's ability or desire to sell. If a sales applicant takes an IQ test, it is usually designed to give some indication to management of the ability to learn. Once again, anyone who can read, study, and understand this text has sufficient intelligence for a successful sales career. Note, however, that even though readers of this text may have the IQ to be successful, they may not have the other characteristics required for success.

Aptitude Tests

Another battery of tests, or measurement devices, gives a pretty fair indication of those areas in which a person is proficient. Interestingly enough, these tests review the past, they reveal the kinds of things you know from what you have done. They are not very good at predicting the future, unless you draw the conclusion that someone who has experience building wood structures will find happiness building houses.

Aptitude tests are a valuable adjunct to all the other measuring devices used. If the past experience of a person fits into the sales profile, it is an additional piece of evidence that can predict sales success. The fact that a person has limited practical experience is no reason to suspect that inputs of training and other knowledge will not make that person a success. That is why most companies have formalized training programs to complement a person's background. Someone applying for a sales position in the complex world of electronics may lack the necessary technical background, but the company knows it can teach a trainee how to deal with the technical problems at the same time the trainee is learning how to sell the products.

What aptitude tests tell is whether the person's background readily relates to the job opportunity. If it does, the chance to get the job increases. Proven ability and knowledge of various fields do have some sort of relationship. Naturally, if the applicant has sold in the past, that knowledge of selling will be of some assistance. This is true despite the fact that some firms prefer to hire people who have had no previous sales experience.

Personality Tests

By definition, personality is a combination of all those characteristics that tell something about a human being. Thus, a personality test details how those characteristics help or hinder that person in his or her dealings with other human beings. For instance, if you exhibit feelings that psychologists refer to as antisocial, it is a fair guess that sales work will run counter to your basic nature or personality.

There is little question that as we try to define the characteristics of a "perfect" salesperson, we will find openness, friendliness, a desire to mingle with people, and inner drive as worthy attributes. And a number of other characteristics help to isolate the sales personality. Among these are an outgoing nature, a willingness to serve others, and a need to win friends.

Personality tests can give a good indication of who you are, where you are, and where you want to be. However, these tests are far from perfect. They tend to complement other investigations into your sales potential.

Probably the question most frequently asked of sales applicants is, "Why do you want to go into sales?"

The most frequent reply is, "I like being with people." This response, of course, is equally valid if you want to be a teacher, an actor, or a minister. Those personality characteristics that best define sales potential also define the necessary characteristics of many other professions. However, when personality tests are used in tandem with the other examinations, interviewers are able to at least eliminate those who by personality, aptitude, and intelligence seem unsuited for sales work.

Interest Tests

Probably one of the most telling of measurement devices is the "interest" test: The job applicant merely ticks off interest in a number of activities, ranging from a desire to be a ship captain all the way down to menial work. Other areas of interest range from sports activities to reading and writing. One of the most popular of these tests incorporates about 400 questions. There are no right or wrong answers, but simply a compilation of how you as an individual feel about certain kinds of work.

You can't beat the test; in fact, there is no reason to even try. There are a significant number of cross-checks that cancel out answers you think might affect the interviewer. If you do beat it, what have you won? Nothing, because the interest tests were created by asking people in different professions what their interests were and then assuming that people with similar interests would perform well and be happy in the same field of work. By gathering the interests of successful people, it is hoped that people with similar interests will do equally well.

Does it work? Psychologists who rely in part on interest tests claim a high correlation between the results. People of similar interests do like to group together—it's comfortable. However, a very thin line divides the interests of a public relations worker, a salesperson, and a politician. In the same way, the interests of an airline pilot, an auto racer, and a locomotive engineer show a close affinity.

When grouped together, these tests and measurement devices do a fairly accurate job of classifying those people best suited for sales careers. However, even when the results of all this investigating are assembled, no clear-cut decision can foretell sales success. All the data merely identify the possible trends and directions. Management improves the odds when selecting a sales candidate by exposing that person to a series of tests, none of which is perfect, each of which has merit, and all of which aid in the hiring process. Anyone going into the field of professional selling will at one time or another take some or all of these tests. They are all investigations into your background and personality that will better pinpoint your chances for sales success.

CONTROLLING YOUR SALES PERSONALITY

Professional salespeople like to argue the "salespeople are born" philosophy. It ranks with the discussion of whether Babe Ruth was a better hitter than Hank Aaron. There is no way to prove either point, and if you could, what about the rest of us who have worked long and hard to perfect our professional life? In other words, there probably are some sales greats who were "born" with the natural talent to transfer product or service between people. At the other extreme are many people who, despite all the training in the world, would never make competent professional salespeople. In between are the vast majority of people, who, with proper direction and effort, can achieve success in the world of selling.

SALES PERSONALITY IS DEVELOPED BY PUTTING TOGETHER A NUMBER OF BUILDING BLOCKS.

Figure 4-1

The essential study of why people develop the way they do, what factors cause them to be either outgoing or secretive, what forces have impinged upon them that have caused them to be the way they are, is not the purpose of this section. People as individuals are the end result of a good deal of living. What we do know are those characteristics, traits, and attributes that make for a healthy sales personality. The implication is that you can recognize these personality characteristics, that you can control your personality, and that you can develop as a sales professional.

⚡ The ability to cope with your own virtues or shortcomings is one sign of maturity. This might well be the one overpowering characteristic of the professional salesperson. You must be able to face up to the reality of what your personal characteristics are, how you can deal with them, and what the best ways are to meet success in selling. The idea of maturity is important, because throughout the careers of professional salespeople, they have to exhibit a huge amount of self-control—control over self. An excellent starting point is with those characteristics deemed important by sales experts.

Physical Appearance

While on a two-week vacation in the backwoods, John Sutton grew a beard. His wife thought he looked good after it was trimmed neatly. At the office, his fellow salespeople kidded him, and the sales manager looked askance. For a month, he withstood the jibes and laughter of his neighbors. Few customers failed to make some sort of comment.

Late one night, while his wife was at a business meeting, John decided to shed his whiskers. In the morning, his wife, who usually did not rise quite so early, purposely got up to tell him about the meeting of the preceding evening. He left for work and returned as usual in time for dinner. Only after dessert had been served did his wife exclaim, "John, you shaved your beard!"

"Hey, that's right," said the two children.

"In case you didn't notice," John pouted, "I didn't have any beard this morning at breakfast. Is that how much attention I get around here?"

Somewhat taken aback, his wife replied, "John, when I look at you, I see the wonderful man I married. How you look on the outside is very unimportant. I know what you are deep inside."

Within the confines of his home, John was held in very high regard. But what had caused him to remove the beard was the ribbing he had taken at the office and the prospect who refused to talk to him because he looked like a "hippie." That's right, there are plenty of people who want salespeople to look neat and trimmed and who resent a beard. This is no sermon on the relative merits of beard-growing. It is recognition of what people out there, your prospects and customers, expect. The simple facts are that many people are "turned off" by a beard. This physical characteristic is one that the professional salesperson can control. (Personally, the author has great admiration for beards. However, it is unwise to place face whiskers in the way of a completed sale.)

Every human being has some physical problem. Glasses used to be seen as a detriment. ("Boys don't make passes at girls who wear glasses.") Today, styles of frames are legion, bifocals are commonplace, and contact lenses are a popular alternative. If you need glasses, take a little extra time to select a pair that add to, rather than detract from, your total appearance.

Barbers no longer merely cut hair. They now shape the hair and create styles that accent your physical characteristics. Bright shiny teeth fit any face and make it more appealing to the stranger. Clean fingernails and scrubbed hands are the sign of a person concerned with looks and cleanliness. The plethora of body colognes keeps people from smelling like people.

All that bodily hygiene that your parents sought to impose upon you as a child is valid for the professional salesperson. Will this sell more product? No, but it will improve your chances of making a good impression. It is one of the characteristics by which you will be judged even before you open your mouth.

Clothes

American productivity now affords nearly everyone the opportunity to wear clothes that are both stylish and attractive. The highest-fashion styles are available in relatively inexpensive copies, so that the well-dressed salesperson is the rule rather than the exception. Clothes, despite claims to the contrary, do make the person. A smartly tailored suit of conservative material is always acceptable in the business office.

One highly successful salesman explained his wardrobe to a friend: "When I make the first call on a prospective client, I always wear a suit with a vest, something quiet in tone and very conservative. After I get to know the client fairly well, I might wear a jacket with contrasting slacks. When I have done business with someone for a long time, I might take a long chance and wear an open sport shirt and a modish pair of trousers."

Among saleswomen, dress codes are equally important. Short skirts revealing shapely legs are great on a date. Nonetheless, they are distracting to professional buyers. Depending on your own particular prospects, pantsuits may be either good or bad. Every salesperson has to study the prospect before deciding what is acceptable attire.

People—prospective customers and clients—do draw snap conclusions from your appearance. The professional salesperson usually decides it is less difficult to overcome a prospect's objections when it is not also necessary to overcome appearances. A sales trainer relates the story of a trip to Atlanta: "I had to appear before about 100 salespeople. So I took along a three-button, pinstriped, vested suit. I felt the audience would be less skeptical of what I had to say when they saw that I was dressed very conservatively. But the following week I had to go to San Francisco, so I wore a light brown suit with tight trousers and a very narrow tie. My job was to satisfy those people in the audience, and I didn't want to have to apologize for how I looked. Whenever I have to make an important sales call, I always consider what the prospect will think of the way I look."

Many young people today have seemingly rejected the notion that people should be judged by the way they look, so they dress in worn jeans, scuffed shoes, and beat-up shirts. They have developed a new version of how people ought to look. But try joining their crowd if you are wearing fancy loafers and creased trousers. In other words, if you want to sell to people who dress in that style, by all means dress to fit the prospect. Advertising people are notably in the forefront of the fashion parade. A vested suit would be as inappropriate in that atmosphere as sandals in the executive suite. Whatever class of people you are dealing with, dress accordingly. When you walk through the door, you should be acceptable by virtue of your dress and what the prospect expects in a professional salesperson.

Voice

In view of all the things over which a person can exercise control, the person intent on a professional sales career entertains the idea of a total self-improvement program. The tone, modulation, and use of your voice can be very helpful in your career. A very successful meat distributor whose main thrust was personal contact with the trade had a thick foreign accent. Over the years, the company developed a long list of satisfied customers. At age 60, this distributor decided his voice left something to be desired, and he went to school. Within six months, he was talking in Oxford English, the beautifully clipped and melodious tones of the British.

On the surface, it seemed he did not need this improvement. But what this man knew was that in his community, there was a class of prospects with whom he had never been successful. He felt that, in part, his heavy accent had kept him from being invited to certain social functions during which friendships were sealed and business arranged. True to his suspicion, people who had formerly had no desire to deal with him found his new voice so interesting that they were now prepared to pay attention to what he had to say. The words and thoughts were the same, but now they were being delivered in a new wrapper, one that the prospects found acceptable.

Professional salespeople can improve their own voices in some very easy ways. The most obvious is to tape a sales conversation, then try to place themselves in the position of the prospect and judge whether they are talking too fast or too slow. Does the pace of the presentation remain constant and dull, or is there variation in the ups and downs of the voice, thereby adding to the dramatic effect?

Voice, as a sales tool, requires constant care. It allows us to attract attention when we raise or lower it. We can retain attention by speaking softly, or make an impression by speaking in stentorian tones. It is the first thing a prospect will discover about you if you call ahead for an appointment, and it rates as second only to the first impression you make when you walk through the door.

Listening Capabilities

Silence, or the use of silence, is probably one of the most neglected assets salespeople possess. Few things can relieve a tense situation like a moment of complete silence. Unfortunately, salespeople by nature and personality are gregarious; they enjoy repartee and conversation. Any lag in the discussion is seen as bad; a steady stream of chatter is considered part of selling.

But the ability to keep quiet can be learned, and it can be utilized as a positive aspect of selling. For instance, when you ask the prospect a question—and there are many times when questions are used during the Heart of the Sale—do you allow time for an answer? These brief respites can force the prospect to give additional and careful consideration to your proposition. But if you rush to answer, then the prospect has little else to do but listen to you. Which is all wrong—*you* should be listening.

If there is one subject in which all people have a great deal of interest, it is themselves. If a salesperson is so talkative that prospects have no chance to express themselves, the salesperson will never have the chance to learn what it is the prospect wants or needs. Since it is a safe assumption that people will disclose themselves, the professional salesperson must keep this thought in mind. Part of the job is to probe the prospect's mind to discover facts that will lead to a successful sale. Another part of sales behavior or personality should be containment, the ability to listen. There are ways to listen that permit the salesperson to extract the meat of what a person is saying without abdicating the essential control over the direction of the sale.

Imagination and Creativity

One of the main purposes of this text is to assist the student in developing creativity and imagination. In part, this will be accomplished by forcing the student to write specific thoughts in a variety of ways. This suggests that there are a number of ways to say or do something. Other techniques will be employed to help the reader become involved and to challenge individual ingenuity. Every person has an unused reservoir of imagination and creativity. It is not enough to admit that it exists; it is important to grapple with the notion.

Many people feel that creativity is a "gift," that some people have it and others do not. This may be true when you consider people of true genius—Leonardo da Vinci, Eleanor Roosevelt, Rembrandt, or Margaret Mead. But millions of other people possess untapped pools of talent waiting to be released. The profession of selling allows and demands that all the imaginative meanderings possible be activated. The opportunity to deploy your creativity is ever present.

The inventive genius of Thomas Edison is invariably coupled with the statement of his interpretation of his success: "10 percent inspiration and 90 percent perspiration." This idea is wholly applicable to professional selling. The more time and effort devoted to thinking of new ways to present your proposition, the greater will be your success. Imagination is also a matter of "sweating out" an idea. The interesting part of this equation is that the more you test your imagination, the stronger it becomes, just as a muscle becomes stronger with use. The unfortunate truth is that a good deal of education tends to stifle free and open thinking. Selling insists on a broad spectrum of new and exciting approaches to problem solving.

Imagination and creativity can be developed; professional salespeople have the opportunity to change personality, to force themselves to be imaginative and creative. There is no set pattern of how this change might be effected. Surely the suggestions and work incorporated in this text are devoted to the premise that the student has vast reserves of ability and imagination that ought to be utilized.

It is not enough to say, "Be creative," or, "Be imaginative." Therefore, here is a practical technique that has worked for others. Seek the *second* right answer. What this means is that you should not be satisfied that you have the best response in a selling situation. Nor do you have the best answer for the customer's problem. Go for the second answer. Force yourself to find multiple ways to answer questions, solve problems, or make sales.

Dependability and Reliability

The behaviors and attitudes of the salesperson are signs to the prospect of what to expect. No one is suggesting that the professional salesperson should suddenly change a desire to wear blue shirts because it will help sell the product. But the way the job is performed conditions the prospect. When a salesperson says, "I will telephone three days before my next sales call," the call should be made. When the salesperson says the price of a product is $4.56, then the bill should read, "$4.56." When the salesperson claims the product is 50 percent polyester, then it had better be 50 percent polyester. It is important to the relationship that grows between a prospect and the salesperson to be nurtured by absolute dependability and reliability.

There is an old and somewhat hackneyed expression: "My word is my bond." Every time a salesperson says something to a prospect, every time a commitment is made, this idea is energized. It isn't necessary to make a pledge on a Bible; thousands of salespeople daily stake their reputations on what they have said, and for the millions of customers who listen to them, that is all that is needed.

Dependability and reliability are forerunners of honesty. When you are honest, it is very easy to make commitments that you can and will fulfill. If you are honest with your prospects, you will demonstrate this attribute by being dependable and reliable. "When John Stratton tells me a delivery will be here by Wednesday morning, I know I can rely on his word. One time he drove 40 miles out of the way with a car trunk full of merchandise because he had made a commitment."

A sales manager always impressed new sales representatives with the idea of promptness, which of course intertwines with dependability and reliability. This manager would make appointments to work with sales-people at strange hours. "I'll meet you at Ninth and Market at eight minutes after seven."

A new representative, struck by the meeting time, stopped one of the old-timers and asked, "Does he always arrange such odd hours?"

"The only thing I can tell you," said the senior salesperson, "is that you'd better be there on the dot. The old man has a quirk about keeping appointments."

At the precise moment, the salesperson arrived, spotted the manager, and dutifully reported. "This is one of the most important lessons I can impart to you," said the sales manager. "You will probably be with this outfit for a long time. Never forget, when you have made a commitment, be prepared to keep it. The easiest commitment to keep is to be on time."

Often, in the course of a business relationship, the salesperson will find that a promise cannot be fulfilled. When that happens, there is only one honorable course of action. Go to the customer and say straight out that you erred. By doing this, you create a further impression of honesty and sincerity and dependability. If you are fearful that the unfulfilled promise will lose the account, you might just as well make a clean breast of it. The customer must be able to rely on you to keep him or her aware of everything that is going on. Sometimes you may have to deliver bad news. That, too, is part of basic reliability.

Smoke Gets In Your Eyes

There is a very simple rule with regard to smoking: Don't!

Here is the rationale. If the prospect doesn't smoke, then your smoking will surely be disturbing. This has nothing to do with admonitions by the various health agencies; it is not a value judgment. Our only concern is that the professional salesperson does not drop a nicotine roadblock in the path to sales success.

If, on the other hand, the prospect is a smoker, you are still best advised to refrain from smoking during the progress of the sale. Why? First of all, your hands should be free to make your demonstration, turn pages in a price book, or write an order. Second, the presence of the white cigarette curling smoke and dropping ashes can be very distracting to the person with whom you are speaking. And you yourself will find a degree of preoccupation with the requirements of smoking. Your mind should be completely devoted to guiding the progress of the sale.

There are other concerns. Smoking does leave an odor and a taste in the mouth. Your breath, when you are close to a prospect, can be offensive. Also, the pollution factor is certainly one the aware salesperson should consider.

Is it ever proper to smoke in the presence of a prospect or a customer? Probably, when the sale is concluded and the two participants want to relax and possibly talk about the weather, an occasional cigarette won't hurt—that is, if the prospect is a smoker. These moments should not deteriorate into gab sessions and more smoking. The distractions of the cigarette still prevail, and a room filled with billowing haze is not terribly desirable. If the sale occupies two or three hours, the heavy smoker may feel pressured to light up. We can only suggest that the pleasure of smoking be measured against the importance of the sale. You decide if a cigarette is worth earning, say, $5, $10, or possibly $50. Perhaps that will make the decision not to smoke easier.

A special word to cigar smokers and pipe addicts: You should *never* smoke in the presence of a prospect or customer. (The author readily admits to chomping on a pipe with much relish and happiness—but never when selling!) Obviously, this does not hold when you are having cocktails at the local country club or in the anteroom at a banquet.

Sex, Religion, and Politics

Bright sun streamed over the stone path leading to the swimming pool. Harold Maul was glad, because that meant he could wear sunglasses, and the prospect would not be able to tell where his eyes were roaming. He felt this was a form of protection. The buyer had requested information about chemicals for the swimming pool, and Harold was nervous. It was his first time at a nudist park.

As he laid his sample before the buyer, Harold noticed half a dozen people coming up the path; all were nude. Exercising control, he continued with his presentation and demonstration. The buyer was impressed; Harold got his order and hastily made his departure. It was more than just another sale—it was distinctly out of the ordinary.

Caught up in the exhilaration of his visit, Harold could hardly wait for his next sales call. "Hey, you know where I just got an order?" he told the customer. "I was out to the nudist colony. You ought to see all those people running around in the altogether."

All his friend could say was, "Oh."

Harold had made two bad mistakes. The first was in divulging the business affairs of a customer. What transpires between the buyer and seller is almost privileged information and should remain confidential. The second was the assumption that the second customer would feel the same way Harold did about nudist colonies. The reactions to nudists range all the way from indifference to hate, from curiosity to jealousy. There is no way to prejudge how people will feel about anything related to sex or nudity.

The obvious solution: Don't raise the subject! It can be as hazardous as talking about politics or religion. There are more religious beliefs than any salesperson can cope with, and the best way to deal with them is to avoid them. Also, prospects or customers frequently try to sound out salespeople on political subjects. Whatever you do, stay away from these topics.

Recently, a front-page story told of a pro football star who was involved in a sexual relationship with a young girl. Did this hurt his career on the playing field? Did fans stop coming to see him play? Some may have turned in their season tickets, but very few indeed. However, this is not true of the professional salesperson. The salesperson who takes a position with regard to controversial subjects jeopardizes a career, or at least the chances for success with a specific account. The proper time to air your feelings on these subjects is in the confines of your home, or on the political platform, or at meetings designed for the purpose of free and open discussion. Certainly the time devoted to a sales career should not be wasted on peripheral topics, particularly those of an explosive nature.

One very devout buyer was in the habit of handing salespeople religious pamphlets after every interview. There was never an attempt to convert anyone, but the distribution of these tracts continued. Finally, after six months, one of the favorite salespeople was questioned, "What do you think of these little messages I pass out?"

Caught, the sales representative replied cautiously, "I read them."

"Do you think you would like to come to a service sometime?" asked the buyer.

"I respect your feelings," said the salesperson. "But I would never try to persuade you to convert to my religious beliefs."

"But don't you try to persuade me to use your products?"

"That's only money," replied the salesperson. "I surely wouldn't want to impose my view of eternity on you."

This was an impossible situation. Ultimately, the two had a falling out. The salesperson felt bad about losing a piece of business but soon discovered that no salesperson could last long with this customer. The buyer had mingled religion with business and made buying decisions based on religious beliefs. This is not to say that the tenets of one's religion cannot be practiced daily. But to seek to impose them on a business acquaintance is bad business indeed.

Politics can be equally treacherous. There is no way to win a discussion, and discussion frequently leads to argument. Any self-respecting salesperson adheres to the rule, "You can't win an argument with a customer." Or, as it is popularly said, "You may win the argument, but you'll lose the account."

PLAN FOR PERSONALITY IMPROVEMENT

Controlling and improving your sales personality is only a matter of observation and practice. How you appear, act, and react are all observable characteristics. Gathered together, they represent your sales personality. If you don't like the way you look to others, you have the opportunity to change.

One of the ways to cultivate better habits that translate into improved sales personality is to learn from experience. All the admonitions not to smoke in front of a prospect may seem meaningless, but the first time you lose an order because you lit a cigarette in front of a member of the Cancer Society in your community, you should get the message.

When you call on the president of a large corporation and your suit is worn and rumpled, you'd better take note not to do it again. If you are making a presentation in the living room of a prospect and the TV is drowning out your voice, you had better learn to ask the prospect to turn the set off. When the day dawns clear and crisp and you feel like a dullard, you'd better learn to tap into your creative juices. If your sales manager sends you a message that a customer complained you didn't make a sales call last week—look out. If your voice at the end of the day is hoarse and tired, maybe you aren't listening enough.

There are other ways to discover your own shortcomings and improve. Ask your sales manager for a critique of your "sales personality." Be prepared for the worst, but accept the comments in the sense in which they are offered. By virtue of experience and training, the manager is probably more acutely aware of those characteristics that make for more successful selling.

The point it, you *can* improve your style and technique. Do what golf pros do. They stand at the driving range for hours at a time and seek to perfect a single stroke. A professional salesperson should do no less.

SUMMARY

Although there is no way to accurately predict sales success, a number of tests, examinations, and measurements add credence to what successful salespeople do and how they act. These sets of data and facts constitute what are generally known as "sales personality." The beginning salesperson will probably be asked to take many of these tests, all in an effort to determine how close the person's characteristics come to the characteristics of successful salespeople.

Every human being is the result of everything that has happened during the period leading to chronological maturity. Salespeople as a class are expected to mature. They exercise a good deal of control over their own lives, and therefore, they have the opportunity to change and improve on those characteristics that apply to the profession of selling.

High on the list of visible characteristics that all professional salespeople should possess is an acceptable physical appearance, one in which virtues are accented and disabilities modified. A pattern of dress commensurate with the class of trade you are calling upon is advisable. If you are dealing with farmers, rough clothes are surely acceptable. If your prospects are college professors, perhaps a tweed jacket, dark trousers, and rep tie are in order, or a cashmere sweater and heavy wool skirt.

The professional salesperson should exhibit listening skills, a true desire to hear everything the prospect has to say. This does not mean that salespeople should enter into discussion about such touchy subjects as sex, religion, or politics. These topics are to be avoided—probably by changing the subject.

Dependability and reliability are hallmarks of professional salespeople. They arrive on time and carry out promises they have made in the name of the company. They don't blow cigarette smoke in the eyes of the prospect. Truly professional salespeople seek to stretch their imagination and creativity, constantly searching for fresh ways to keep the sales time attractive to the customer.

All these attributes or characteristics are things that professional salespeople themselves can control. At all times they have the opportunity to improve on their own sales personalities, questioning and requestioning the impression they make on prospects and customers. This requires a strong measure of maturity, quite possibly the most important characteristic of the professional salesperson.

A SUCCESS STORY

Manny Brown looked at his fingers, which were stained from years of handling tanning dyes. "Funny," he thought, "I know that a salesperson should have a clean appearance, but what can I do about all the dyes I have to handle? No customer has ever complained. Some of them have hands as dark as my own."

This line of thinking disturbed Manny. The more he considered the problem, the less important it seemed. After all, if everybody in the industry suffers from the same problem, why should he be the one to be different? But that notion of being different appealed to him. "Let's get the old creative juices working," he said aloud.

On his first call the next morning, he bounced into the office of the buyer and dramatically announced, "From that same wonderful salesman who brings you dyes with which to tan, we now bring you clean fingers." With that, he bowed from the waist and laid on the buyer's desk a pair of clear plastic gloves. "These, dear sir, so you may examine our new color #4056 and still keep your pinkies pure."

The two men laughed together. "What's the idea, Manny?"

"Just for fun, Tom. All of us in the selling end of this business get our fingers covered with dye. Well, I just thought maybe I would try a few pairs of these plastic gloves and have my customers wear them when we compare shades. How do they feel?"

"I guess they're okay," smiled Tom. "What have you go to show me?"

As the conversation progressed, Manny neatly printed his order, handed the paper to Tom, and with a flourish, dropped his gloves into the waste basket. "Here you are, sir. The gloves we discard."

"Did you hear the president's speech last night?" Tom casually asked.

"Nope," smiled Manny. "I was out buying plastic gloves."

"C'mon. You're kidding," said the buyer.

"Well, yes, I was kidding," said Manny. "But you see my sales manager has instructed me never to discuss politics when I'm out for business."

"You mean you do everything he tells you?"

"Pretty near. You see, he may not be perfect, but he certainly knows about selling. I take almost all the advice he offers. When it comes to politics, I have a stock answer. If you want to talk, we'll get together with a whole gang of people and discuss till you are completely satisfied."

"That's silly. I only asked you if you heard him speak."

"Yes, I heard him speak."

"What did you think about the speech?"

"I'm going to take the fifth amendment. I never discuss politics during business hours."

"Okay," smiled Tom. "We'll stay with business. No more politics."

QUESTIONS FOR CLASS DISCUSSION

1. What is meant by "sales personality"?
2. An old adage says, "You can't make a silk purse out of a sow's ear." What does this have to do with making a salesperson out of an average human being?
3. When sales trainers work with new salespeople, they generally look for eight characteristics. Name these characteristics. Do you think they differ from level to level of selling? Why?
4. How would you dress if you were selling furniture at the manufacturing level? sports clothes at the retail level? computers at the distribution level? soy beans at the industrial levels? Would there be a difference in your attire?
5. Have you ever had an argument with a salesperson? Describe the situation. Who won? Can a salesperson ever win an argument?
6. How would you describe the "perfect" sales personality?
7. Make a list of "sales personality" characteristics. How would you grade yourself on these characteristics using a scale of 0 to 100? Do you think you would make a good salesperson? Why?
8. How do you feel about the expression, "Salespeople are born, not made"? Do you agree or disagree? Why?
9. What are the tests or measurement devices generally used to qualify sales candidates? Describe and discuss each.
10. List the ways you might improve your "sales personality."

CASE 4—JACK HOLT IS CALLED ON THE CARPET

"You wanted to see me?" Jack Holt snarled at the new sales manager.

Looking up from the desk, Sally Griffith stared straight at the slovenly dressed sales representative and said, "I thought it was time we had a long talk."

"What about?" blurted Holt.

"Perhaps the best place to start," said Griffith, "is to ask you what you think we're trying to do as a company. Franklin Furniture has been in business for almost 60 years, and I have the sneaking suspicion that you don't really understand our function in the sales department."

Holt looked surprised. The question struck him as sheer nonsense. The only reason a company is in business is to make money. This whole scene seemed unnecessary. "I'm not sure I understand your question," he said. "Beyond making money, what other reason is there to be in business?"

"You're right when you say making money is important. But my question was, what do you think we're trying to do here?"

"I guess, just plain sell furniture?"

"Okay. I think you're getting closer. You've been here for six years, and apparently no one has bothered to tell you how management thinks. Shall we talk?"

"I don't know why. I'm here to sell and I do that pretty darn well. Last year I was number 3 in the sales contest and number 2 in sales income. What more do you want?"

"Very briefly, I want you to talk nicer. I want you to dress in a clean, pressed suit. I want you to get your shoes polished. I want you to shave in the morning instead of the night bfore. Shall I continue?"

"This is a lot of nonsense. You have no right to tell me how to dress and what to wear. I admit I'm no fashion plate, but I do sell furniture."

Leaning back in the big, black swivel chair, Sally Griffin said, "You don't seem to understand. The policy of Franklin Furniture is to pursue business in a certain fashion, a gentleness toward the customer and plenty of service. This company feels that the way our salespeople look is a reflection on business. We also feel that smart-looking salespeople will do more business. We think that if you looked, acted, and carried yourself properly, you would do even more business."

Slipping a cigar from his breast pocket, Jack Holt touched a match to the end and sent streams of smoke coursing through the room. "I'll tell you," he said. "As long as I do the volume of business that I do, I'll dress the way I want to."

"I'm afraid not, Jack. Somewhere along the line, you didn't get the word about Franklin Furniture. Now you have a choice. You have three months to acquaint yourself with the underlying philosophy of this company. We'll talk again at that time and see if you have a better understanding about what we're trying to do here. The choice is yours—straighten up, or straight out you go."

1. What do you think Jack Holt will decide?
2. Was Sally Griffith too demanding?
3. Should a business house tell its salespeople how to dress?
4. Was there a basic error in Jack's sales training?

SALES PROBLEM 4—KICKING THE "KICKBACK" HABIT

The new sales representative was thrilled; she had opened her first account, and the flavor of the order was exciting. Then the buyer said, "How much do I get?"

Stunned, she looked at him with surprise. "I don't understand," she answered.

"You know what I mean. What's my percentage kickback on the order I just gave you?"

Here is how three different salespeople handled this touchy subject:

Sales Rep #1:   This is a difficult question, one that seems to come up at the end of the year. What I try to do is explain that our company just doesn't give buyers any kind of cash kickback. I would also tell him that there simply isn't enough profit in our line to afford giving money for orders.

It's never worth doing anything like this, because it never stops. Not only that, if you do it with one account, it's sure to get around the industry and ruin your own reputation.

The way I look at it, if you have to buy your business from someone who is basically dishonest, you're better off looking for honest people to deal with.

Sales Rep #2:   I would tell the account that our prices are the lowest they can be, and there is no way to pass along any money. I would try to convince him of my excellent personal services.

I would wait for the fourth or fifth visit before going to the general manager or the owner of the business. Sometimes a buyer is just trying to test the salesperson. I had this happen to me once, and eventually the customer dropped the other suppliers because their prices had to be higher than mine in order for them to be able to kick back 5 or 6 percent of the order in cash.

Sales Rep #3:   The only answer to give to customers who ask for a kickback is to inform them of the quality, service, and wide range of products they are buying.

One thing, if the buyer insisted on being paid off, I would first go to my sales manager before going over the buyer's head. I need the advice of my superior in such delicate matters.

EXERCISE 4

Use the form below to evaluate, on a scale of 0 to 100, the characteristics of an insurance agent, an automobile salesperson, and a clerk in a clothing store.

	Insurance agent	Automobile salesperson	Clothing store clerk
Physical appearance	_____	_____	_____
Clothes	_____	_____	_____
Voice	_____	_____	_____
Listening capabilities	_____	_____	_____
Imagination and creativity	_____	_____	_____
Dependability and reliability	_____	_____	_____
Smoking	_____	_____	_____
Discussions of sex, religion, and politics	_____	_____	_____
Total	_____	_____	_____

There are no right or wrong answers, but you will have an objective measure of these three people. It will give you a better way to evaluate sales personality.

5

PRODUCT
KNOWLEDGE

PERFORMANCE OBJECTIVES

After you have read this chapter and completed the Questions for Class Discussion, the Case, the Sales Problem, and the Exercise, you should be able to do the following:

1. Explain the four benefits of product knowledge.
2. Describe the link between creativity and product knowledge.
3. List seven questions you should be able to answer about a product.
4. Explain the six internal and seven external sources of product knowledge.
5. Convert product knowledge to customer benefits.

STREET SMARTS VS. PRODUCT KNOWLEDGE

Soft piano music reached into the corner of the dimmed cocktail lounge where Tom Bogan and his friend Gerald Haag were having a drink before the monthly meeting of the Professional Purchasing Club. Haag was intent on persuading his friend to air his views at the meeting. "Look, it's part of our job to upgrade the salespeople, even if they don't have enough sense to know they should be more professional. Don't you think it is better for us to deal with people who really know what they are talking about?"

"I'm not so sure," Bogan said. "Our job is to make the best possible buys for our respective companies. If we have to overcome the problem of some salespeople being too smart or not having enough knowledge, that's part of the buying profession."

"Yes," responded Haag, "but if we can upgrade the quality of the selling profession, we help ourselves in the long run."

"That's where we part company. I figure part of my job is to keep the salespeople off guard and, when possible, take advantage of their ignorance to make a better buy for my company."

"You know, we could argue this all night. Let's bring it to the floor and see what the other buyers think."

So it was that Tom Bogan rose to his feet near the close of the meeting and said, "I would like to describe two salespeople who call on me, and to explain a potential problem. The first is a sharp apple who has plenty of 'street smarts.' You all know this type. A good salesperson, plenty of answers but not very much real information. As you might imagine, this person has a bagful of funny stories—not dirty, mind you, but good clean stories. A nice enough person—we go to a ballgame from time to time. I place plenty of business, because this seller is sharp, pleasant, and wears well.

"But when I need hard data and information, I have to ask another salesperson. I'm sure you all know someone like this, someone who just knows merchandise inside out. Sometimes I think the sales manual has been memorized; this person sounds like a walking textbook. Well, this person is nice enough, but there is a lack of zip and zing. There are times I almost have to force the order. Can you imagine being content to sit and talk about products all day and never even try to close a sale?

"Clearly, I need both these people. Now, I contend that I should have both of them, that my job as a purchasing agent is not to train salespeople, but to make the best buys for my company. On the other hand, Gerry Haag thinks that the professional buyer has an obligation to help train the salespeople who call on us. What do the rest of the professional buyers think?"

"Why don't you introduce the two salespeople," one buyer laughed. "They'd make a wonderful couple."

"You can laugh all you want," another interjected, "but this business of product knowledge is fierce. There are so many new things on the market, I just can't keep up. If the salespeople didn't tell me what's going on, I'd be dead in the water."

"Sure. But that's the job of the manufacturer. Let them train their people better."

"Hey, listen, I had to buy a power saw for home the other day, and the dopey salesperson didn't even know what size blades I could use. There's something radically wrong if a salesperson isn't sufficiently interested in the product to know something as simple as that."

"Wait a minute," interrupted Haag. "The question is this: Should we help try to impart more product knowledge to our salespeople? Are we supposed to help the salespeople who are trying to sell us?"

The room became quiet as the members each sought to find an answer to the question. When the president finally asked for a show of hands, most of those present were against helping the salesperson. These buyers felt that gaining product knowledge was basically a part of professional selling and should be no concern of theirs.

This text is devoted to the principles and techniques of professional selling. There is no way this book can impart product knowledge to the individual student. Think back to our earlier portrayal of a sale as consisting of a Heart and a Base. The need for product knowledge is clearly the responsibility of the salesperson and the company. All the training in "how to sell" will be without benefit if the person does not acquire a significant understanding of the product or service to be sold.

Surveys of buyers and purchasing agents over the years have always indicated that salespeople need more product knowledge. This chapter is intended to explore the many facets of product knowledge and the opportunity this knowledge presents for more creative and effective selling.

THE BENEFITS OF PRODUCT KNOWLEDGE

Everybody wins when a salesperson knows all about the product. Most of all, the salesperson wins in being better equipped to bring a service, to solve a problem, and certainly to make money. There are four main areas in which benefits accrue and continue to grow.

Makes Work More Interesting

The person who opts for a sales career should become completely involved. You wouldn't expect a baseball player to go to the plate and only half-swing at the ball. This is your chosen career and profession, and the more you put into it, the more you will derive. Learning about products or services simply expands the salesperson's background. If products don't interest salespeople, they should either study to become interested or find another line of merchandise to handle.

However, once a sales life-style is adopted, it deserves a significant amount of time and attention. The more that products are studied, the more salespeople will find there is to know. Ultimately, they can become expert in some products. For instance, a retail shoe clerk noticed that different shoes tended to take on strange odors. One day, a customer asked why some shoes smell and others don't. This question sent the salesperson on an investigation of the leather used to make fine shoes. Background was acquired by talking with the factory sales representative, reading books, visiting a leather finder, talking with shoe-repair people, and reading the descriptive material the company had sent along. The quest for knowledge became so intriguing that the salesperson even spent time investigating the historical uses of leather.

Now, learning about leather may not seem very exciting—to you. But for this salesperson, it became interesting. There was a measure of happiness and satisfaction in knowing more about the basic product to be sold.

It is important to recognize that even a negative approach can be productive. Whether you like the product or not, an in-depth investigation may reveal facts that prove of interest.

A toy salesperson noted a line of chess sets in the sales portfolio. This sales rep had always thought that chess required a hidden talent—brains beyond the capacity of the average person. One day the sales manager said, "How come you never sell any chess sets? Are you afraid of them?"

This challenge set the salesperson on the road to discovery, reading about the derivation and origin of the game of chess. The sales rep became conversant with the names of chess champions and even learned how the sets are made—some by hand, some by stamping, and some molded. The fascination of the various designs became a game—to discover how many different types of chess sets exist, and even the idea of designing a set consisting of salespeople and sales managers and buyers. This interest stimulated a desire to know more. That is what product knowledge is all about: fascination and stimulation. Acquiring more knowledge about products adds a new dimension to professional selling.

Builds Confidence

Many activities in the study of professional selling serve as "confidence builders." If it seems that salespeople need heavy doses of confidence-building activities, that is absolutely correct. The nature of selling implies that the person will face many difficulties and many defeats, often working alone, lacking the companionship of other salespeople. There is no way to bat 1,000. Inherent in the profession is the built-in certainty that the salesperson will not make every sale. To prepare for the shock of losing sales requires a countermeasure to sustain the salesperson.

Knowledge is strength and sometimes even establishes a person as an expert. A salesperson who can reach that happy point can command not only respect from prospects but the admiration of co-workers. If making sales calls is one way to success, then the acquisition and application of product knowledge is another.

A small hobby shop, located in an out-of-the-way community, is owned and operated by a man who has made a study of model railroading. So vast is his knowledge that people come from all around the country, traveling hundreds of miles just to buy his products. The materials he sells are no different from those available in dozens of other hobby shops, but with the purchase of a product from this man go many tips on how best to build model railroads, small techniques that lead to happiness in the pursuit of that hobby.

Some salespeople become so expert in their field that they turn to selling their knowledge instead of products. An advertising-space salesperson devoted so much time to understanding the problems of the buyers, the manufacturers of plumbing supplies, that he soon gave up his sales career and turned to selling his knowledge to these same buyers. In other words, he learned so much about their business that he became a consultant.

The person who has acquired a solid foundation of product knowledge has something that no one can take away. It is a marketable commodity; it signifies the necessary background to be successful in a given field. The security that goes with this feeling is hard to describe. It is safety of an unusual kind, the assurance that you have something that no one may take from you. Those who ultimately gain this feeling know a type of self-confidence that is hard to rattle. They exude success.

Meets Objections

In the discussion of "Meeting Objections" (Chapter 11), we shall suggest that meeting objections is relieving the prospect of burdens, questions that were troubling. Objections are really questions in disguise, and the task of the salesperson is to meet those objections with solid and knowledgeable answers. Armed with a complete understanding of the product lines or services, salespeople have few fears about meeting objections. They are so convinced of the value of their merchandise that they welcome prospect objections, because they know they can meet them with little trouble.

In gaining product knowledge, professional salespeople simultaneously convince themselves of the validity of their proposition. During a sales interview, they use this knowledge and their own beliefs to convince the prospect that the proposition is worthwhile. Few things are as upsetting to a prospect as asking a question of the salesperson only to hear, "I don't know the answer to that question." If the salesperson doesn't know the answer, which is really the solution to a problem, where can the prospect gain that information? Remember, selling is partly the resolution of problems, and knowledge or information is the only way to reach those solutions.

The following anecdote, a sales attempt by an office-supply salesperson, seeks to bring the value of product knowledge into focus:

"This paper is very heavy and will hold up in your files. Your secretary will have no trouble erasing mistakes, and the weight means you can keep copies for a long time."
"How much does it weigh?"
"Well, I don't know exactly, but it is very heavy."
"Why will it erase so easily?"
"This paper is heavy and erases easily."
"Why?"
"Well, is that really important? It's heavy and it erases very easily."

Had this salesperson studied the merchandise, the answer could have been, "The paper is 25 percent linen, rated 20, which is the heaviest-weight bond paper, and it is coated with a special chemical that makes erasures possible with a normal rubber eraser." Facts and information prove that salespeople know what they are talking about. If you want to be accepted as a salesperson, know your product.

Ongoing surveys of purchasing people have sought to uncover where they gain product knowledge. A number of sources are available: brochures, magazine advertising, mail advertising, and information delivered by salespeople. Clearly, the information gained from salespeople is the most important and dominates other sources of product knowledge. In fact, many purchasing people rely heavily on their sales representatives to bring them all the product news and data.

Satisfies Prospect Needs

Every product or service has a variety of descriptions that translate into customer benefits. The more salespeople know about what they are selling, the better equipped they are to zero in on customer needs. For instance, a recent style in men's suits is a four-piece outfit that includes matching trousers, a vest, and a pair of contrasting trousers. This allows for a combination of sports and business attire. The appeal to the low-income prospect is the multiple uses, several outfits for the price of one. This person benefits by saving money. However, the appeal or benefit to the middle- or upper-income buyer is the chance to increase wardrobe size appreciably. These appeals may sound familiar, but the money-saving aspect may be more important to the first prospect.

A furniture salesperson was trying to impress a prospect with the wearability of a couch. He explained that the fabric was strong, would withstand sunlight, and could be wiped clean because of a protective coating on the material. Over and over he stressed these virtues. But the prospect wanted something inexpensive to use in a cabin in the woods. The couch had to be durable but obviously would not sustain the wear one normally expects. When the salesperson uncovered this fact, he was able to switch the prospect to a less expensive couch that lacked the lasting quality of the first piece of furniture.

Perhaps the classic example is the couple who enter the automobile showroom, are immediately attracted to the new "super-duper" model, and listen while the salesperson goes through the spiel. As the conversation unfolds, it becomes evident that the primary benefit this young couple wanted was low cost per mile. In their minds, the way to achieve this was to buy a cheap used car. Because he knew as much as possible about the "super-duper," the salesperson was able to show the couple that cost per mile would be less in a new car and therefore save them money in the long run.

It is only when the salesperson truly knows the product that there can be a switch in the sales appeal to the benefits the buyer is seeking. There is little sense in stressing low price when the prospect wants quality; there is no reason to emphasize delivery when the prospect wants something specifically designed; and there will be little success in concentrating on durability when the prospect wants variety. Remember, selling is meeting needs and satisfying desires. With a huge supply of product knowledge, the salesperson has the flexibility to discover those benefits that will turn the prospect into a customer.

CREATIVE APPLICATIONS OF PRODUCT KNOWLEDGE

Few professions allow for the flow of creative juices to the extent that selling does. Creativity is required in every phase of the Heart of the Sale. But even before that, the professional salesperson has the opportunity to be imaginative and creative in visualizing the benefits and uses of the product. The basic knowledge about the product must be translated into viable benefits for the prospect.

One salesperson explains it this way: "I examine each and every product we sell and ask myself two questions: What will this do for the prospect that is not being done? How will the prospect benefit by using our products?"

Here are practical applications of imaginative thinking:

A large manufacturer of paper cups produces a number of items for drive-in restaurants. The ten-ounce cold cup is packed in tubes of 500 units. Each case contains ten tubes of cups. A complete description of where the product is manufactured and the composition of the paper used in the process is contained in the sales manual. However, the sales representative knew that merely relating these data to the prospective buyer would hardly be meeting a need or providing a service. Here is what was stressed in trying to create interest in the line: Because the cups are accurately counted at the factory, the prospect can relate cup usage to the amount of soda dispensed. Thus, the product is an inventory-control device. By counting the number of cups used, the customer would know how much soda was used and how much business was done. Through creative thinking, a decision was made to sell the benefit of preventing loss through spillage or theft by using this company's cups.

Moreover, the sales representative realized that different prospects have different needs. Further creative thinking convinced the rep that wide use of the cups would eliminate the need for glass washing and the purchase of glasses to replace broken pieces, and would provide the safety of paper cups against glass or plastic and a saving in glass-washing detergent. Each of these items became a possible benefit that would appeal to a variety of buyers.

Essentially, the sales representative visualized what the product would do for the customer, what service the product would perform that was not being done for the customer already. This required creativity and imagination.

A typewriter salesperson knew that the redesigned electric machine responded faster, the return carriage moved more rapidly, and the solid metal casing meant longer life for the machine. This information was important, but it wasn't very exciting to the secretary who had to use the machine or the buyer who was interested only in price. Here is a list made by the sales rep of some of the benefits the use of this machine would bring to the prospect:

Faster-typed letters
Longer life, therefore lower overall expense
More time for secretaries to do other things
Saving of wear and tear on secretaries
Hardier construction, thus fewer repairs

From this imaginative point of view, the salesperson was no longer merely providing a collection of nuts, bolts, and metal parts. Instead, something was being provided for the prospect that was different, exciting, and beneficial. This made the proposition more appealing to the prospect as well as the salesperson.

Another example of creativity and imagination can be seen in the story about the insurance agent who was told by a prospect, "Insurance is for poor people, the ones who can't afford to get sick."

To which the insurance agent replied, "For you, I sell a college education for your children. For the person in the next block, I sell protection from long-term illness. In the next town, I sell tax savings. Across the street, I sell death benefits."

"Well, that means you have different policies to fit different needs."

"Not quite. The policy is the same. The reason people buy is to fill their own needs. We all have different needs."

Product knowledge, therefore, gives the salesperson the confidence to explore a number of possible uses and applications of products. This suggests a heavy dose of creativity and imagination—to visualize the many ways products help prospects.

One salesperson was so sure of her own basic knowledge and understanding that she used to say to prospects, "The reason you ought to buy from me is me."

"What does that mean?"

"It means that I know so much about my products that having me available to talk to, to answer your questions, is an asset."

"You mean I should buy from you because you know so much about this business?"

"Exactly!"

WHAT EVERY GOOD SALESPERSON SHOULD KNOW ABOUT PRODUCTS

Every product is composed of a number of facets. Nothing is so simple that it cannot be defined in a variety of ways. Everything has a history. Here are some of the things every good salesperson will know about the product line:

Where is this product made? or grown? or assembled? Is the factory in Chicago or Denver? How did it get shipped to its present location? Did shipping affect the price? the quality?

How was it made? Does the manufacturer have a labor union? What kind of machines produced this piece of merchandise? Who designed the product?

What kinds of materials were used to make this product? Are they rare? Do they come from strange geographic locations around the world?

Can you describe the quality of the final product? Will it withstand heat? cold? How long will it last?

Is the product big or small? bulky? Why is it shaped the way it is?

How can this product be used? What does the manufacturer recommend? What have you learned from other customers who have successfully used this product?

Are there any special features that distinguish this product from other, similar products on the market? Why is this product better?

This list is a sample of the kinds of things a salesperson might learn about any product. Just as people generally fear the unknown, increased knowledge about the product has the opposite effect. The more salespeople know, the more comfortable they feel, and the easier it is to convey enthusiasm to the prospect.

WHAT EVERY GOOD SALESPERSON SHOULD KNOW ABOUT THE COMPANY

Along with what the product can do for the prospect, there are many services the company can perform. Therefore, it is imperative that salespeople know and understand many things about the organization they represent. Here is a list of questions salespeople should be able to answer with regard to their company:

How old is this company? Who started it? How many times has the company moved to larger quarters? built bigger facilities?

What are the basic operating policies and philosophies? Have they changed recently? Do I know the company goals for this fiscal year?

Do we have modern production methods? Is the equipment expensive? Where does it come from? When was the last time I walked through the machine shop?

How do we service our products? Do we have a service department? Is installation done locally? If the customer mails a product for repair, how long will it take? Do we charge for this service?

How do we deliver merchandise? Our own trucks? A common carrier? Can we handle a special-delivery order? Is there an extra charge for this? What happens if a product is broken in delivery? Are we protected? Is the customer protected?

What kind of competition am I apt to confront? Are they bigger or smaller? How do our pieces compare with the rest of the industry? How about our quality?

Once again, this is a brief list of the kinds of questions an aware salesperson should be able to answer. Some organizations have sales manu-

THE PROFESSIONAL SALESPERSON
CAN'T HAVE TOO MUCH
PRODUCT KNOWLEDGE.

Figure 5-1

als detailing this information; others transmit it during formal or informal sales training.

INTERNAL SOURCES OF PRODUCT KNOWLEDGE

Because the need for product knowledge and operational information is so important in the complex world of selling, many companies have established long-term training programs. A new sales trainee might devote a few weeks to working in the warehouse to gain delivery knowledge, spend time in the computer center to learn about billing and credit procedures, assist in the repair shop to see how service is carried out, and then work with experienced salespeople.

To acquaint the newcomer with the skills of selling, the company may conduct training classes. One large paper manufacturer runs a "sales school" three times a year at the company headquarters. Follow-up schools are held every couple of years. It is not uncommon for a trainee to study for six months before making the first sales call.

This entire regimen of training and education is intended to better prepare the salesperson to meet the prospect. These companies know that the more knowledge a novice has, the stronger that person will feel and the more positive will be the approach to a sales career. There is no substitute for knowing your business and merchandise.

Here are other ways for the salesperson to become knowledgeable:

The Sales Manual.   Virtually all large companies and many smaller organizations have prepared sales manuals for the instruction of new salespeople. This book may run to hundreds of pages, depending on the company. It should contain all, or almost all, the information the salesperson needs to know and understand in order to answer questions raised by prospects.

The sales manual may include data on the company, sales techniques, and even some company philosophy. However, a separate type of manual will generally offer complete descriptions of products and materials. Company policy will be detailed, and delivery schedules, credit policy, and even how to fill out specific forms will usually be spelled out. In some instances, there will be provision to add "bulletins" and "notices" that are intended to become part of the operating policies. In most organizations, this manual is commonly referred to as the "bible."

Company Training Programs.   Even the smallest companies have some kind of training programs. These may take the form of yearly conventions, attendance at regional meetings, or even the requirement for the salesperson to attend classes at a community college.

There was a time when the newcomer was handed a price book and told, "Go call on a few prospects and see if you can get some orders." With no background information and no training in what to expect, needless to say, most of these people fell flat on their faces and retired from the sales profession. The complexity of products in today's market demonstrates the need for a more formalized program or indoctrination. To meet this need, many smaller companies buy packaged training programs that they use to acquaint new salespeople not only with product lines but also with sales techniques.

It is not uncommon for smaller sales organizations to contact a local college for assistance in mounting a sales training program. Frequently, businesses will seek out textbooks on selling and use these in their own training programs. (Some of you may discover this very textbook being used in professional selling settings.)

Sales Meetings.   Every company, large or small, conducts regular or irregular sales meetings. They are a certainty!

The variety and diversity of these meetings will depend on the sales manager. In larger organizations, these meetings will be a blend of product knowledge, sales methods, and market conditions. Included in the meetings might be lectures, role-playing activities, videotape replays, demonstrations, and occasionally an outside guest expert to bring new thinking to the sales force.

Too often these meetings deteriorate into a discussion of sales figures and monthly reports of what is happening. In the more sophisticated organizations (and this has nothing to do with size), fresh ideas permeate the air, and the salespeople exchange thoughts and product knowledge.

One sales manager related how to conduct a sales meeting: "I never prepare more than a few questions. After the sales force gathers, I may make a few announcements, and then I'll ask, 'What happened with our introduction of new thingabobs this week?' Then I'll go around the room, and every person will have a chance to tell an experience. As soon as that runs down, I'll say, 'What kind of price competition did you run into this month?' By probing in this fashion, I get the salespeople to talk to each other. It's the best kind of training I know."

This is a somewhat unorthodox approach. Many sales managers prefer to conduct a formal meeting during which they tell about new products, new policies, and new methods to sell particular products. Even though these meetings are less imaginative, the salesperson can learn a considerable amount from them.

Other Salespeople.   Few people can offer better insights into product knowledge or sales skills than salespeople from within the company. They have been in the field and are conversant with the types of problems that are almost standard for a particular industry. In many instances, a junior salesperson will work with an experienced person purely and simply to learn about the sales policies and techniques. At the retail level, this is sometimes known as "elbow training." The novice stands at the elbow of the experienced person and learns from seeing and doing.

Sales Managers or Sales Supervisors.   Depending on the size of the organization, the person in charge of training new personnel may be either the sales manager or the sales supervisor. In either instance, that person will spend time in the field, teaching, training, coaching, instructing, and critiquing the new salesperson.

A typical situation might evolve in this fashion: The sales supervisor travels with a new salesperson, observes prospect calls, and then spends time discussing what was done right and what was wrong. This one-to-one type of training is probably the most powerful. The new salesperson gets immediate feedback and can rapidly correct selling errors while gaining product knowledge. The conversation between the supervisor and the salesperson as they travel from place to place is invaluable.

At the retail level, the supervisor may spend time each day with a new person, feeding small amounts of information. At the same time, since the supervisor is always available, the new salesperson can summon assistance whenever confronted by a problem that cannot be answered.

Warehouse People and Service Personnel.   Because they make deliveries and repair and install products, the warehouse and service personnel are a wonderful source of product knowledge. Many skilled and professional salespeople have come from the ranks of the warehouse and delivery teams. The appeal to dress smartly, drive new cars, and call on buyers is very attractive to workers locked into tight schedules. Even as they aspire to improve their positions, they acquire a significant amount of product knowledge, most of which they will happily share with the salespeople representing the company.

EXTERNAL SOURCES OF PRODUCT KNOWLEDGE

The acquisition, use, and application of product knowledge is not restricted to information gathered and presented by the company. Some external sources can provide the professional salesperson with huge amounts of data. There is no better place to start than the local library.

Library.   As a single source of solid information, few people can compare with the librarian. Mention any subject, and a number of pamphlets, books, or magazines will be suggested, places in which to find the kinds of information the salesperson wishes. A good local library will house many pamphlets from the Government Printing Office, along with research books, reference books that will locate articles on any subject the salesperson wants to know about, census data, both local and national, and plenty of other books that may contain the information desired.

A tobacco representative working for a wholesale house decided to become the company expert on pipes. Through the library, the representative was able to find several books written on the subject, a number of articles about the vagaries of pipe smokers, and detailed information about the incidence of cancer among pipe smokers. Another discovery was that pipe smoking has a rich history. Based on this research, the sales representative created a number of imaginative sales presentations and even helped customers with starting a pipe-smoking contest.

No source of information is as convenient as the library, and few people as anxious to serve as librarians.

Conventions.   This is a business institution that draws large groups together on an annual basis. Hundreds, sometimes thousands, of manufacturers and distributors rent space in a hall and display their latest wares. Prospects and customers roam up and down the aisles, seeking the new and the different. Every level of industry seems to have its own convention.

For the salesperson, the attraction of convention time is the chance to mingle with old friends and new prospects, and the opportunity to review some of the recently developed products being offered by the competition. At the same time, every company prepares its own entry of new products and also special convention "deals" for people who stop by the display booth to place an order.

Different people attend conventions for different reasons. Salespeople are there to make contacts and learn about new products. Purchasing agents are there to learn and to see products they cannot ordinarily touch and operate because of their size. Manufacturers are there to stimulate interest in their merchandise. Usually, spouses and family are there to have a good time. Sometimes related groups convene one after another, and a salesperson may be a guest at one show and a worker at the next. In Chicago each year, the International Foodservice Manufacturers Association meets a few days before the National Restaurant Association. Those people who sell to restaurants are already in town and often stay to visit with their friends and customers who arrive after their own meetings end.

Educational Institutions.   If you are a piano salesperson, part of your training might be to take a course in piano tuning. If you sell TV and electrical appliances, perhaps a course in a qualified trade school would be beneficial. And if you are a food salesperson, maybe you can take classes in cooking to help understand the product better.

High schools, community colleges, and universities throughout the country are placing heavy emphasis on career education, which implies what is known as "hands-on" activities. Classes in how to cook, run a drill press, use a camera, write, make pottery, and an endless number of activities are now offered. This bounty is available to the salesperson who is determined to learn more about the business and the types of products the company sells. Most organizations will reimburse salespeople who take courses of study that seem to complement their work life.

Publications.   Trade and industrywide publications are filled with new products and better uses for old products. Although this information is general in nature, it may in fact apply to the products sold by your company. No trade publication would be complete without a few pages devoted specifically to the new products that have just come onto the market.

The world of trade publications is so important that a short list of trade publications is included in the bibliography. They are a continuing source of what is new not only in a particular industry but also in the field of professional selling.

Tags, Brochures, and Operating Manuals.   One of the best sources of product knowledge is the little tag attached to almost every retail product and most other products as well.

A prospect was examining a sweater in a department store one day when she turned to the clerk and asked, "What is this made of?"
"Gee, I don't know," replied the clerk.
"Can I wash it in detergent?"
"Probably."
"Will it shrink?"

"I doubt that it will. It looks very nice."

"How much is it?"

"It appears to be on the tag. It's a very pretty color."

"What size is this?"

"I think it's an 18."

"Oh, look, said the customer. "Here's a tag with a complete description. I'm sorry I bothered you. I could have answered all my own questions."

"No bother at all," replied the clerk. "Glad to be of help."

This is no worse than the distributor salesperson trying to sell lawn-mowers to a hardware store. "How large is the gas tank?" asked the prospect.

"Here's a picture. Looks pretty big."

"Do you have to mix gas with oil to get the proper combination of fuel?"

"Yes, I think so."

"What kind of guarantee comes with this unit?"

"It's a good company. I'm sure you're protected."

This dialogue proves that the salesperson never took the trouble to read the brochure that comes with every piece of equipment, product knowledge that every manufacturer supplies to its distributors. In the case of complex machinery, an operating manual is an absolute necessity, and the salesperson should read and study these manuals to gain product knowledge.

Customers.   Just as the salesperson imparts product knowledge to the prospect, the prospect can transmit knowledge to the salesperson. As one old-time sales manager used to say, "These customers will smarten you up pretty fast." What the manager meant was that, given the opportunity, the prospects and the customers will tell of fresh uses they have found for the products of the salesperson.

Manufacturer Training.   To further the sale, many manufacturers provide film strips, colorful presentation manuals, and cassette recordings of product-knowledge messages. When new products are introduced, it is commonplace for the manufacturer's representative to conduct a meeting to explain the virtues and benefits of the product.

"The world is a great teacher," one sales trainer used to say. He realized that product knowledge and information is apt to be found anywhere, anytime. The only requirement is that the salesperson maintain an open mind and the imagination to accommodate the product to a variety of prospect needs. During the gasoline shortages in the winters of 1973 and 1979, toy stores capitalized on the situation by offering bicycles as a convenient mode of transportation to work, and small cars became fashionable and patriotic. At any given moment, the needs of the buying public may change the benefits that any product has to offer.

PRODUCT KNOWLEDGE IN ACTION

On a chilly Saturday morning, ten salespeople gathered in the meeting room of a large department store. After a few opening remarks, the manager said, "I'm going to ask each of you to come forward, and then I am going to name one of our products. You are asked to speak about the product for one minute without repeating yourself."

This brief exercise was intended to establish three main points about product knowledge: First, the audience would be able to differentiate between the use of "general" language and the reference to specific descriptive material. The idea that a product is strong is not nearly as forceful as the fact that it can withstand 50 pounds of weight. To say a product is guaranteed is not as powerful as saying, "It has been inspected by the ABC Testing Laboratories for eight hours." To describe a product as "fitting an average window" is not as dynamic as saying, "It fits windows ranging in size from 30 to 36 inches."

The second observation of the assembled group was how the performer turned product knowledge into prospect benefits (see Table 5-1). This, after all, was the true purpose of the exercise. A description of the physical characteristics of a product is a pretty routine exercise. How those characteristics help a prospect save time, energy, or money, or how they satisfy a need of the prospect, means that the salesperson has to translate dull information into exciting uses. Think of it this way. A human being is described in terms of height, weight, length of arms, size of biceps, age, muscle tone, and possibly even knowledge. However, when this "machine" is put in motion, it does a great many things that cannot be done by anyone or anything else. Translating these abilities into language and benefits is the express task of the salesperson.

Finally, it is important to recognize the difference between the "amateur" buyer and the "professional" buyer. For the moment, suffice it to say that the major distinctions fall along two lines: knowledge of what is needed to perform a particular service or job, and whether the person is paid or not paid to perform the function of buying.

Being able to speak about any product you sell, stating facts, data, and uses, is the sign of a professional salesperson.

Table 5-1 Changing Product Knowledge to Customer Benefits

Feature	Benefit
One-piece construction	Low maintenance cost
	Safety
	Easy handling
Ball-bearing wheels	Moves freely
	Saves physical effort
	Preserves carpet or floor
32 miles per gallon	Saves money
	Take longer trips
	Saves time (fewer refills)
U.S. Grade Choice	Good taste
	Tender
	Attractive appearance
Water repellent	Protects underclothing
	Avoids dripping on floors
	Looks neat
24-hour service	Convenience
	Reliability
	Security
All-aluminum	Lightweight
	Durable
	Easy to clean
Drip-dry	Saves money
	No ironing
	Speedy

SUMMARY

The ability to acquire knowledge and understand a product means more fun in selling for the salesperson, and at the same time, the work itself becomes more interesting. As people learn more about the merchandise they are selling, they gain a considerable amount of confidence, and this tends to make the work more enjoyable. People like to talk about things they know. If you are armed with knowledge, the task of countering objections offered by the prospect becomes easier to grasp. A goodly amount of knowledge about the line permits the salesperson to design the presentation to fit the needs of the prospect.

Certainly one benefit to the salesperson is the opportunity to apply creativity and imagination to the profession of selling. Once you are armed with product knowledge, the chance to be inventive in transmitting this information to the prospect makes for a more exciting and challenging career. There is no limit to the ways statistical data can be turned into a dynamic expression of needs or benefits to the prospect.

Any interested salesperson can determine specific facts about the product by being able to answer questions such as, Where did it come from? What is it made of? How was it made? Will it last? How is it used? and a whole list of other basic pieces of information the prospect is certain to want to know. Other kinds of information will be of a more general nature, covering such data as service contracts, company policies, delivery schedules, and even how to fill out the proper sales forms.

To gain all this information, the salesperson has access to a number of internal sources of information. Sales manuals, training programs, sales meetings, warehouse and service personnel, and the sales manager are a few of the sources ready to explain facts about products to the willing learner. Further data can be acquired from the local library, at conventions, from the manufacturers, and through taking special courses at educational institutions.

Along every step of the way, the salesperson has the opportunity to translate data and information into exciting language that tends to fill the needs and desires of both the amateur and the professional buyer.

A SUCCESS STORY

As she walked across the hall to the office of the purchasing agent, Faith Marchal could see the scowling face behind the desk. Her early warning system, the fellow who sold janitor supplies, had alerted her to the generally mean disposition of George Pierson. She thought, "I'll have to sweeten him up."

In a quiet, dignified manner, she placed her sample case on the floor next to the waiting chair, dipped into the bag, and slipped two paper cups from the plastic sleeve that protected them from dirt. Beneath each she placed a paper napkin as she poured a pink liquid from a thermos bottle. "Care to join me in a drink?" she asked.

"What is this?" grunted the purchasing agent.

"It's a new health drink specifically made for use in hospitals and nursing homes."

"Why is it pink?" he asked.

"Because one of the base ingredients is pink grapefruit juice, and that color is retained in the final product."

"Then it's going to be too tart."

"Why not take a sip?"

Grudgingly, he lifted the cup to his lips and took a small taste. "Seems kind of sweet for grapefruit."

"According to the formula, there is a small amount of sweetener added."

"Oh, no," he protested. "I'm not going to get involved in any of that additive nonsense."

"You're right to be skeptical," she added. "However, this sweetener has been approved by the three leading medical associations."

"What else does it have in it?"

"There is 6 percent cherry juice, 7 percent orange juice, and 9 percent pineapple juice."

"Well, that makes it nothing more than a fruit drink."

"Correct. Except that we have added a good amount, over two units, of vitamin C."

"That must run the cost up. I'm sure it's too expensive."

"Adding vitamin C does run the cost up. However, when you study the cost per serving, you will find that this new Happy Time Fruit Drink costs no more than a serving of orange juice."

"Who needs it?" snapped the buyer.

"We all need more vitamin C in our diet, and in particular, patients in this nursing home. You add variety to your menu, increase health benefits, and give a little excitement to your patients. Would you like to try two cases?"

"How are they packed?"

"Each case contains twelve cans of 50 ounces."

"What's the price?"

"Ten dollars a case, which means about eight cents per serving. Isn't that reasonable?"

"I don't think we want to add any new products at this time."

"This isn't a new product. It's an old product that has been revitalized to serve a new market. By changing the formula, the manufacturer has recognized your particular needs. This package was designed for nursing homes."

"How come you know so much about this drink?"

"I spent three weeks investigating all the aspects of health drinks and what they can mean to a sick person. I'm convinced this product will help your patients feel better. May I send you two cases?"

"What's your name?"

"I'm Faith Marchal, and I represent the ABC Drink Company. We have almost 50 years experience in the drink business, and we have devoted almost $20,000 to research about the health qualities of our products. We know your problems, and we have designed drinks to help you in your operation."

"Well, I just don't know."

"That's exactly why I'm here. To give you information and facts about Happy Time Fruit Drinks."

"Well, why don't you pour me another taste. If you're convinced, I'm willing to drink to your health."

QUESTIONS FOR CLASS DISCUSSION

1. In what ways does complete product knowledge help the salesperson? Give three examples.
2. How does product knowledge give confidence to the salesperson? Do people have this same sense of confidence when discussing any subject they know intimately?
3. List the four benefits of product knowledge and give an example of each.
4. Demonstrate that the knowledge of how a product is manufactured can become an important facet of a dynamic sale. Give three examples.
5. Carpenter Distribution Company sells a little-known brand of TV sets. What information would help you prepare a vibrant sales presentation directed at selling these sets to retail stores?
6. List ten questions a prospect might ask about automatic electric toasters; about the purchase of a home; about a life insurance policy.
7. List and discuss the internal sources of product knowledge.
8. List and discuss the external sources of product knowledge.
9. Convert the product knowledge about toasters in question 6 to customer benefits.

CASE 5—THE CASE OF THE TIRE(D) SALESPERSON

The sleek, shiny, metallic blue car sat on the dealer's lot, waiting to be picked up by the owner. Responding to the request for fast delivery, the service people had prepared the car in less than 24 hours, and now the showroom salesperson was waiting for the customer to stop by for final driving instructions. This last effort proved to the new clients that once the sale was completed, the salesperson still had an interest in customer satisfaction.

It was a big model, fitted with many extras. The sale resulted from a planned phone call by the salesperson, who was able to interest the prospect in making a trade before the new models arrived. Happily, they struck a bargain that satisfied both the dealer and the customer. Part of the sale included the addition of a hood ornament, fancy hubcaps, and plaid seat-covers. "These are cosmetic effects," thought the salesperson. "I should have sold the prospect those new safety tires."

Exchanging the tires of a new car for steel-belted radial tires was a common practice at this dealership. The advantage to the customer was a better-quality product and additional peace of mind while driving. For the salesperson, there was an extra 10 percent commission on the new tires. As these thoughts were rushing through the mind of the salesperson, the new owner arrived for a driving lesson.

As the two made themselves comfortable in the bucket seats, the salesperson suggested, "Would you like to consider radial tires?"

"Ye gads," said the customer. "Haven't I already spent enough money?"

"I just thought you would want the added security and safety of riding on steel-belted tires."

"What makes them any safer than the wheels that are already on the car?"

"Well, the manufacturer tells us they have fewer blowouts on these new radials."

"Why?"

"I guess it's because of all the extra material they use in the manufacturing process."

"Do you mean to tell me that I spent all this money on a new car and now I have to worry about heavier tires?"

"Well, the radials are just better."

"Can you give me a single reason why they are better? What do I need a new car for if I have to buy tires?"

The salesperson, troubled now that the entire sale seemed in jeopardy, sat quietly for a moment, trying to reassemble the many thoughts that had been expressed. There seemed no way to redirect the sale, which now appeared in danger.

1. Would more product knowledge have helped this salesperson?
2. When was the appropriate time to sell the radial tires?
3. Can you suggest a better way to reopen the discussion about tires now that the sale has been consummated?
4. Where can this sales rep get more information about tires?

EXERCISE 5

Turning "features" into "benefits" draws on the creativity of the salesperson. Make the conversion in the following examples, citing three benefits of each feature:

A three-piece polyester suit
Individual portions of jelly
Delivery twice a week
Oversize type
Permanent-press shirts
Metal picture frames

SALES PROBLEM 5—THE BLOCKED REBATE

To stimulate business, many manufacturers offer rebates to customers. The easy way to do this is to give the rebate directly to the distributor, who in turn offers this special discount to the customer. It's legal. It's effective. But sometimes the rebate is blocked, when an unscrupulous sales rep decides to keep the customer in the dark and simply keep the rebate for the company. This was what Bob Richardson discovered in his territory. Both his company and a competitor handled the same line of products. But the competition was blocking the rebates.

Here is how three different salespeople handled this situation:

Sales Rep #1: I would make a point of mentioning these products to my customers and being emphatic about the rebate. I would go into great detail to explain that the manufacturer was offering a special inducement to all distributors to give the rebate to the customers. Then I would let the customers make their own decisions about who was seeking to take advantage of them.

Part of how I would do these things depends on my relationship with specific accounts. If they were close friends, I would flat-out say that competition was blocking their rebates.

Sales Rep #2: The rapport I have with my customers would determine how far I would go in pointing out that my competition had been dishonest. Basically, I would tell them in a straightforward way just what was happening.

For those customers with whom I am not too close, I would tell them they are entitled to a rebate, and then I would help them fill out the necessary forms. I don't think I would ever accuse my competition of being dishonest. That just doesn't seem professional. In the long run, dishonesty has a way of surfacing.

Sales Rep #3: There are three ways to approach this problem. One is to tell the customers that the competition is taking advantage of them. Lying, cheating, whatever.

Second, simply tell them what the overall promotion is and what they are entitled to, and help them fill out the necessary forms.

Finally, I might go to the manufacturer to verify whether the rebates were going to the customers as was intended, or whether the competition was actually keeping the money for themselves.

6

HOW TO FIND PROSPECTS

PERFORMANCE OBJECTIVES

After you have read this chapter and completed the Questions for Class Discussion, the Case, the Sales Problem, and the Exercise, you should be able to do the following:

1. List and describe the twelve methods of prospecting.
2. Explain the need for a prospecting system.
3. Prepare a prospecting plan.
4. Relate the function of prospecting to the process of actually selling.

THE SMOKING SMOKESTACK

Light puffs of fog drifted in an uneven pattern over the tall pines. Around the curves, Harriet Henshaw caught an occasional glimpse of life, a small cottage or a log cabin secreted in the woods. There was no traffic, but she saw a set of tracks along the side of the road showing where a deer had crossed to the other side. Behind the trees, she spotted a rabbit scurrying to take cover, frightened by the noise of the car.

Henshaw enjoyed this casual commune with nature, something of a special reward for leaving home a half hour early just to drive through the forest alone, discovering new roads to reach the seashore. Her first appointment for that morning wasn't until 9 o'clock, so she had ample time to take a more circuitous route. In the back of her mind was the thought that along the way there might be some new sales opportunity, a place untouched by competition and removed from the rush of the heavily trafficked roads near the coastline.

Today was a new adventure, and the serenity of the tall trees surveying that flat land for miles around set a tone of quietude, not unlike the restful center of a hurricane moving into position to make a dash for the shore line. It was impossible to see beyond the immediate roadside; the high trees tended to blot out the drifting clouds. Then, rounding a sloping curve, she saw a small spiral of smoke inching its way upward. Just as fast, it disappeared from view as the forward momentum brought the car around another curve leading to a thick strand of trees.

"The smoke is too high to be a cabin," Harriet thought. "Maybe the woods are on fire. Or it could be a building, a factory, maybe a school." Always her mind reverted to business, the opportunity to bring services to yet another prospect who was unacquainted with Harriet Henshaw.

Further along she spotted the smoke once more, only now it billowed forth, and she realized that somewhere deep in the woods there was activity. However, the twisting roads seemed to lead away from the smoke; the search was fruitless. Then, dead ahead, standing like an exclamation point in the sky, stood a massive stream of smoke, punctuating the roadbed. She pressed the accelerator to the floor, and the car zoomed over a slight ridge as the road led to a declivity, a hollowing in the trees. There stood a three-story building, looking like a resort hotel carved out of the woods.

She pulled into the long driveway and stared at the hanging sign, "Pine Nursing Home." Here, hidden from view, buried in the wilds far from society was a massive facility that housed 200 patients, all of whom needed medicines, medicines that Harriet Henshaw could supply.

Glancing at her watch, Harriet saw that time was short. She gunned the motor and roared away, off to keep her appointment. On the daily call record, Harriet noted, "There's a heck of a nursing home back in the woods, and I plan to call on them next week. It should make one very big account."

A return message from the sales manager was a little disappointing. It read, "Congratulations. You have discovered a suspect. When this nursing home becomes a prospect, I will be happier. If it becomes a customer, I shall be overcome with joy."

Harriet studied the note. "It's true," she conceded. "All I have at the moment is a name and location. But if I didn't have that much, I would be even farther away from a sale. This is the first step. I know that nursing homes generally buy medicines, the kinds we sell. So maybe what we have is a true prospect. Now I have to turn it into a buying customer."

Sales managers, accustomed to the excitement their salespeople experience every time they trip over a possible customer, are hardened to the facts of sales life. They recognize the importance of a fresh supply of prospects. Some even feel that "suspecting" and "prospecting" may be the most important facet of selling.

WHAT IS PROSPECTING? WHY IS IT IMPORTANT?

Selling is a very human enterprise and brings with it all the elements of living—and dying. Thereby hangs a tragic note, one repeated with unremitting regularity. Customers die! Buyers and friends of many years suddenly pass away, and the salesperson is constantly confronted with the reality of replacing lost business. Harsh as it may seem, natural attrition is permanent. Prospecting, the search for new accounts, is an ongoing part of the sales profession.

Salespeople lose customers, often through no fault of their own. A family owned a small furniture-manufacturing business in the center of a metropolitan area. Next door was a nightclub, a throwback to a past era. Early one morning, a fire erupted in the nightclub and gutted the furniture plant as well. Disgusted and worried, the owner told a fabric supplier, "I have been here for almost 30 years. The idea of starting all over again just doesn't appeal to me. I think I'll collect my insurance and get a job somewhere. Maybe your outfit needs another sales representative."

The fabric salesperson suffered because of that fire. Not only was the sales representative distraught over the consequences of a friend's upset, there was the problem that a huge hunk of business had gone up in smoke. The problem was not quite as upsetting as that of the sales rep who had sold paint to a retail hardware store. The owners of the store had joined a cooperative buying group and now received all supplies and merchandise from a central warehouse. No amount of friendship could combat the thinking of this storekeeper who had made a decision to run the business in a completely different style.

One of the most common reasons salespeople lose customers is that the business is sold or there is a change of buyers. A large corporation may acquire a smaller business. A restaurant owner decides to move to another community and sells the establishment to a stranger. The owner of a service station retires and sells the business. A paper distributor decides to turn the purchasing over to a son. The local school district hires a business manager, and the maintenance person no longer orders brooms and cleaning supplies. In the factory where the salesperson has been doing such a great selling job, the buyer is promoted, and a new person is now making purchases. Business is lost because the new buying authority does not know the salesperson.

Perhaps the customer with whom the salesperson has had such happy relations over the past 20 years goes broke! Yes, many business houses wither on the vine and ultimately close their doors, often owing money to old and friendly suppliers. This is not to mention the customer of only two or three years who goes bankrupt. Then there is also the loss of business because the warehouse didn't deliver an order on time, or the credit manager insulted the buyer, or a truck driver refused to carry packages to the second floor. There are dozens of reasons why salespeople lose business through no fault of their own.

The professional salesperson knows for certain that some business will be lost. It is one of the hazards of professional selling. To meet this certainty, professionals prepare for tomorrow by prospecting today. They always maintain a list of potential customers, new places to sell.

The method of locating these suspects varies with the level of selling. Obviously, the door-to-door salesperson literally starts at one end of the block and calls on every house. The retail salesperson may be content to sit back and wait for prospective buyers to enter the store. However, the industrial, manufacturing, or distribution salesperson has a more limited market, and the search for prospects is more complex.

In an earlier chapter, we differentiated between a "suspect" and a "prospect." A suspect is a person who may have use or need for your proposition. A prospect is a person who probably has use or need for your proposition. Actually, a prospect is a suspect who has been qualified. This means that the salesperson has observed and made an assumption about the potential of the suspect. (A note of caution: It is possible to make wrong assumptions, like the salesperson who did not think the person dressed in overalls had the resources to buy a new Cadillac. Door-to-door salespeople make immediate assumptions about the suspect because in the brief moments of the interview, it will be necessary to "qualify" the person as a prospect. Fortunately, most other salespeople do not have to make such snap judgments.)

The first step in prospecting is to locate, physically and geographically, the names of suspects. The second step is to make some minor assumptions about whether or not they can qualify as full-fledged prospects. (In Chapter

7 we will discuss the preparation for the sale, during which time the sales-person may "disqualify" a suspect.)

With regard to the business of making assumptions, a good deal of discretion is needed. However, a number of assumptions may seem fairly obvious. A commercial building with hundreds of cars around it may have a first-aid station. It may also have a cafeteria, may need cardboard boxes, office supplies, a whole list of products and services. Based on these assumptions, the salesperson might draw an immediate conclusion that this establishment is not a suspect, but a prospect. The distinction between the two is modest. But as we explore methods and techniques of prospecting, this difference will come into better focus.

Nothing is forever. Salespeople absolutely must prospect for new business! No list of customers will remain unchanged; nature and the course of business will nibble away at and destroy the strongest sales foundation.

HOW TO PROSPECT

Two sales representatives were discussing the relative merits of how they each prospected for accounts.

"I never use direct mail," said one with assurance.

"Gee, I have a lot of luck with that method," replied the friend.

"It's silly. The kind of people I want as customers just won't respond to a piece of mail."

PROSPECTING MEANS REAL DIGGING
TO LOCATE AND IDENTIFY PEOPLE
WHO WANT OR NEED YOUR
PRODUCT OR SERVICE.

Figure 6-1

"How do you know?" asked the fellow salesperson.

"I've been in this business for ten years. I ought to know something."

This sounds like the salesperson for buggy whips who knew exactly what kind of whips went best with what types of carriages. Unfortunately, while the sales representative was so busy being certain, they stopped making carriages. Just because a prospecting method failed once is no reason to think it is without value.

Whichever methods of prospecting seem applicable to your particular level of selling, don't rule out the other methods. A great many people have found success using each method, at all levels of business life. However salespeople apply these methods, they should keep in mind their own territory. There is little sense in soliciting prospects in Arizona if you cover Colorado.

Remember, prospecting is the accumulation of names and addresses of probable and potential customers. If you use all or any of these methods, you should have a limitless supply of prospects.

Cold Canvass

There has never been and there will never be any substitute for the cold canvass. It is variously referred to as "cold turkey" or "new-account calls." It is the stopping in at every house on a block, every factory in a development center, or every office in a building. Cold canvass telescopes the process of discovering whether a suspect is a prospect into a few sentences of conversation.

Let's examine what happens when door-to-door salespeople start the day. They arrive at a street corner that was mapped on the territorial chart. They approach each home, keeping a record of who answered and what took place. In some instances, they will be invited in for a cup of coffee and the chance to make a presentation. The wife may invite the salesperson to return when the husband is home. There may be no answer. Or they may have the door slammed in their faces, although this happens very infrequently. In a flash, the salesperson must decide whether the suspect has the power to buy and the money to buy, and really needs or knows about the product. Recent legislation has restricted the efforts of those fly-by-night organizations that have given this type of selling a bad name. Many fine and substantial companies have suffered because of the "get-rich-quick" schemes of less-than-reliable salespeople.

State and national laws with regard to sales contracts now protect the unwary customer. Signed contracts are not binding if the customer changes his or her mind in three days. However, "truth in selling" regulations vary from state to state, and most conform to the federal legislation on the subject. Responsible companies provide their sales departments with complete information on the existing rules. This subject is so varied and complex that each company must mount its own training program to ensure that salespeople do, in fact, conform to the law.

One of the largest electric vacuum cleaner companies in the country, with sales over a quarter of a billion dollars annually, sells only on a door-to-door basis. Cosmetics, cleaning supplies, and food are sold this way. Or didn't you ever think of the person who delivers milk as a salesperson? Architectural landscapers, people who mow lawns for a living, sell this way. Magazines, encyclopedias, and Bibles are sold door-to-door. Even home television movies have been sold on a door-to-door basis.

However, cold canvass is not restricted to those people you see pounding the streets in residential areas. Office-supplies salespeople have been known to cold-canvass office buildings, stopping at every office to find prospects for typewriters, duplicating equipment, pens, and pencils. A classic story tells about the air-conditioning salesperson who cold-canvassed a high-rise apartment building, stopping at every apartment that did not have an air conditioner sticking out of the window. Lack of an air conditioner was the clear sign of a prospect, someone in need of a product.

Cash-register salespeople regularly cold-canvass business districts, with the idea that every retail store is a suspect for the product, one they would like to convert into a prospect. Paper-supply houses start their new salespeople walking up and down the streets calling on stores, some of which may buy rolls of wrapping paper, bags, or twine. Cold canvass is also used by insurance agents, who never know where they will find a likely prospect. Many real estate brokers contact suspects at random to ascertain whether they are in the market to buy or sell a property.

Cold canvass is a lengthy and tedious process. A good deal of territory is covered with few results. It may not be the most productive method, but it has singular applications to every sales field. When wholesale salespeople are driving down the highway and spot a new building, they can cold-canvass simply by walking in and asking, "Do you need my services?"

Many professional people view cold canvassing as the most exciting type of selling. It sets the nerves on edge, requires a complete and dynamic sales plan, and is the only sure-fire way of knowing your entire territory. That's right, no other method will produce as many sales prospects as going to see every suspect in the territory.

Personal Observation

Because of the different levels of selling, suspects may be hidden, or may have to be ferreted out. This means that personal observation—the ability to keep your eyes open—is important, like our traveling salesperson who roamed through the woods and accidentally discovered a nursing home. A salesperson needs a sense of awareness, a sensitivity to the surroundings.

The president of a roofing and siding company regularly walks through the territories of the firm's salespeople, making four-block sweeps, looking closely at the condition of the houses and the general state of repair. This on-site observation is often done with the salesperson while the two talk about the territory. One result of this activity is renewed vigor on the part of the salesperson to get out and find more prospects.

Where personal physical observation is not possible, salespeople can keep in touch with their territories through local newspapers. A caterer in one small community subscribes to 14 local weekly newspapers, searching for the names of newly engaged couples in an attempt to sell a wedding dinner or luncheon.

A salesperson for an electronics firm who sells to stores and businesses in need of equipment said, "One day every three months, I ride through my entire territory without making a stop. It takes almost 300 miles of going up and down streets and out into the country. But I try to take a fresh look at my territory and imagine what I might be missing. Sometimes I spot a likely prospect who has been there all the time."

Sphere of Influence

"If you can sell Sara Jones, you'll pave the way to lots of business," the old pro said.

"What do you mean?" asked the new salesperson.

"Sara Jones is a leader in this community. Now, she won't tell anybody to buy from you, but if you sell her and the fact gets known, you've got it made."

"That stinks," said the new sales representative. "I don't want to have to get my business that way."

"Hey, I'm not making any kind of judgment. There are a lot of people who think that if Sara Jones deals with a person, they would be wise to do the same. It just makes your sale a little easier."

"How come you never sold her?"

"I do," smiled the old pro.

There are people in any community who seem to be at the center of activity. They are known, and what they do matters to others. This is not necessarily a bad thing. Newcomers to any community meet these people first, like the person who came from out-of-state and needed help finding a house. The real estate broker not only found a dwelling but also sent an insurance agent around, told a stockbroker there was a new prospect in town, and invited the newcomer to the local country club for dinner. In this instance, a local salesperson (the real estate broker) was the hub of the wheel and spread the word. A "Sara Jones," the local version of a sphere of influence, might have lunch each day at the local club where she regularly dines with eight or ten other businesspeople. As they discuss affairs, each adds his or her own thoughts, and Sara is the one they listen to most. Get invited to lunch one day, and you will have a natural opening to call on every person present. In the community, Sara Jones may be a club person, or the banker, or the superintendent of schools. Small social groups cluster together, and one person emerges as the natural leader. Such people represent spheres of influence.

In some more sophisticated types of selling, the main people involved in the industry might gather at private clubs or dining rooms. If you are not welcome at these dining places, you just can't make it in that industry. College clubs are another example. If you didn't graduate from Pipsqueak College you can't belong, so you can't mingle with the grads who might tend to favor one another with business. In recognition of the tendency of people to join like-minded people, most of the service clubs around the country (Kiwanis, Rotary, Lions, and Exchange) restrict the number of members from any one industry, thereby ensuring a mix of thinking and opinions.

The professional salesperson must recognize the existence of spheres of influence, whether they be specific people, associations, or other affiliations. Membership in these groups or friendship with the leaders may further your sales career. It is another way of prospecting.

Referral

A satisfied customer is an excellent source of new prospects. After completing a sale, one insurance agent invariably asks the customer for a list of five people who might also be interested in hearing about the proposition. Sometimes this becomes almost a formalized query. "Mrs. Customer, this offer is one that you found favorable and acceptable. There must be other people who would find it equally valuable. Would you please write the names and addresses of five other people on the back of my business cards? Then I can say you recommended I call on them."

For the customer, the successful conclusion of a sale signals a wise decision, something worth sharing with friends. When the salesperson calls on the new prospect, it is easy to start the sale by saying, "Ms. Smith from Downtown suggested I call on you to tell you about this new policy." Ms. Smith may not be a sphere of influence of the proportions we discussed earlier, but everyone has friends; we all belong to small groups. This means an entree for the wide-awake salesperson.

Even an unsuccessful sale can lead to referrals. If the reason for failure to close the sale is valid, the salesperson still has the opportunity to ask, "Even though my proposition did not appeal to you at this time, Mr. Prospect, surely you know people who need our service. Would you be kind enough to give me the names of three people whom I may contact? I will tell them you did not buy and why, but I will explain that you felt they might be interested in my proposition."

THERE ARE A DOZEN DIFFERENT
WAYS TO LOCATE PROSPECTS.

Figure 6-2

A third way to gain referrals is from the recalcitrant prospect, one who claims no interest at all in hearing your proposition. The request might go something like this: "Mr. Prospect, I know you are not interested in my offer at this time. However, would you do me a favor? Let me make my complete presentation, and then I will ask you to suggest four names of people who you feel will be interested in my product." Often, salespeople find that when the presentation is over, the prospect is interested and not only will give names in referral, but will even make a purchase.

Referrals add credence to your sales approach. The recommendation of a satisfied customer will tend to make the new prospect seek to gain the same satisfaction.

The Telephone Book

At a party one evening, Harvey Slade met an electrician who complained that his business could grow if there were more time to contact people who needed service. "The big problem is that whenever I'm out on a job, I can't take phone calls. If I ever hope to get a little bigger, I'm going to need a secretary, and I can't afford a secretary till I get bigger. It's quite a problem."

Ever mindful of a possible lead, Harvey asked if he could call on the electrician to demonstrate a new automatic answering service. Needless to say, the sale was consummated.

Harvey then decided that as a class, small electricians might all be interested in this device. How to find them was a question with an obvious answer. Look them up in the classified pages of the telephone book. There, a list of 22 prospects leaped from the page. Based on this single experience, Harvey developed a fresh approach and demonstration. He let his fingers do the prospecting.

Buoyed by this prospecting success, Harvey decided to group his sales calls by categories. Thus, he attempted to sell all the plumbers, doctors, lawyers, consultants, auto agencies, service stations, and funeral homes. For each he developed a new way of presenting the proposition. When he ran dry of prospects, he took to reading the classified section of the telephone book for ideas.

Another salesperson, who had always used the cold-canvass method of presenting check writers, called on a beauty parlor. During the sale, the representative learned that the prospect wanted two machines, one for personal use at home and the other in the store. Using this information, the sales rep zipped to the phone book and ripped out the page listing all the beauty shops in the city. The new approach was to relate one sales experience to an entire class of prospects.

Another version of this technique is to gain access to the directories published by many small communities listing the names and addresses of all residents. Many contain a cross-reference that will provide the salesperson with a listing by address and then the name. It is always more impressive to approach someone by name.

The classified pages of the telephone book are extremely valuable for the salesperson calling from another city. If you are assigned a new territory, the Yellow Pages of the telephone book represent "instant prospecting."

Advertising

Advertising doesn't sell; only people sell. But advertising is an excellent vehicle for locating prospective customers. An advertisement in the daily papers one day offered "tomato soup for only ten cents." A telephone number and a list of other "specials" accompanied this information. This ad was a "teaser," intended to solicit phone calls that would result in a sales call by a food-freezer company.

A more sophisticated technique from a competitive food-freezer company saw the firm actually taking orders for a limited assortment of products. Then the merchandise was delivered by the salesperson, who tried to further introduce the concept of the food-freezer plan. By investing in sales calls that held promise, this company was trying to prospect selectively and call only on suspects who appeared interested. This was a way of qualifying the suspect.

There are other kinds of advertising that are intended to elicit interest on the part of the buying public. Stockbrokers and insurance people regularly advertise to announce that they are available for consultation and discussion—all of which could lead to a sale. Cemeteries don't generally solicit business, except for the ones that are selling burial plots "in advance of the fact." Also, virtually all real estate brokers are listed in the classified pages of the phone book.

Direct Mail

The use of direct mail is so significant that it is generally considered separately from other advertising. Very simply stated, it is mailing to a list of suspects a form of proposal or a request to have a salesperson stop in for a meeting. Usually the preprinted mailer is sent to a large potential audience. The response rate is very small, frequently less than 1 percent. However, the overall cost of this type of prospecting is rather inexpensive, particularly if the unit cost per sale is high.

A typical mailer might read:

Dear Prospect:
　　If you can answer "yes" to these three questions, we have a proposition that will mean security and benefits for the rest of your life.
　　1.　Can you save $10 a week?
　　2.　Is the welfare of your family important to you?
　　3.　Will you give 15 minutes of time to our exciting proposal? Simply mail the enclosed card for an appointment.

These mailing pieces are written to entice the reader; they are not lies, nor are they deceits. This is a valid way to test the market and arrive at a list of prospects who have some interest in what you have to sell.

A somewhat more sophisticated approach to this technique is used by a consultant in Boston. First, an original letter is written offering services for a specific type of work. Then the letter is autotyped and mailed to 100 suspects. Each letter appears to be individually typed and is addressed to a specific individual. The typing equipment is so refined that the name of the person may appear three or more times in the body of the letter, which adds to the credibility. "If I get a 5 percent response and a 1 percent sales close, I will be way ahead of the game," this consultant said.

Another use of direct mail might best be called "indirect" mail. Hundreds of trade or business publications carry advertisements directed at specific market segments. Virtually all these magazines contain a card that allows the reader to request more information about certain products. These mailers, known as "bingo" cards, are sent to the magazine, which in turn sends the requests along to the appropriate company. Ultimately, these cards are shifted down to the salespeople on the street, who follow up what are supposed to be hot leads.

Bingo cards are a complex system; the information has to pass through a number of hands, and from the time a prospect indicates interest until the salesperson actually calls, weeks sometimes pass. Thus, when the salesperson does call, the person who sent the card off may have long since forgotten any interest. Nonetheless, many companies use bingo cards, and the magazine and publishing industry pays a good deal of attention to the results. A good return indicates that the advertising is being read. This in turn becomes a sales tool for the advertising-space salespeople of the magazine.

Mailing Lists

Those same magazines that offer bingo cards also represent a vital source of new prospects. They sell copies of their mailing lists on a regional, local, and sometimes zip-code basis. In other instances, they may break the list down according to certain categories—company presidents, purchasing agents, salespeople, or warehouse workers. In other words, if you want the purchasing agents in a particular industry all over the country, or in a specific area, the magazine of that industry is an excellent source of information.

A list of 1,800 names of the sales managers of companies in the state of New Jersey cost one salesperson about $75. This sales representative then had the option of calling these people on the phone, writing them a personal letter, or sending out a brochure telling of a new service or product.

Suppose you had a product with ethnic appeal. A good source of information would be the newspaper or magazine that reaches that audience. A mailing list of that nature could prove valuable. How about a list of all the doctors who receive a particular medical journal in your territory? Or the restaurant buyers who receive a food magazine in the eastern portion of the country? Or the teachers who read an education publication in the state of Delaware?

In addition to magazines that sell mailing lists, many agencies specialize in this kind of information. Any list you care to describe can be compiled. The advantage of buying already-prepared lists is that the price per name is cheaper than you can compile through cold canvassing. Any saving in time and effort is a saving in dollars.

Service Personnel

One neglected source of prospect information is the service personnel within your own organization. A salesperson for a plumbing-supply house related this experience to a fellow salesperson:

"Last week on my regular walk through the warehouse, I learned that the shop supervisor from the Ajax Company was leaving to go to the Beta Company."

"Who told you that?" asked the friend.

"One of the truck drivers."

"Well, what's the big deal?"

"Two things. First of all, this supervisor wants to buy from me. As soon as things are settled, I'm going to get a big piece of business. The second is that my monthly cigars have paid off."

"What do you mean?"

"Every month or so, I take a stroll through our warehouse and pass out a few cigars to the truck drivers and warehouse people. When they hear anything that they think will be helpful to me, they pass it along."

The lines of communication among people who work for the same organization are sometimes clogged. In fact, this is one of the prime complaints of industry, the failure of people in the same organization to relate to one another. However, for the professional salesperson, these lines are cleared rapidly when some interest is shown in co-workers and their opinions and assistance are solicited.

Service people are another source of invaluable information. What better clue is needed than the story, passed along by a repairperson, of a worn-out washing machine, or information from a mechanic that the motor of a car is about to fall out? The person who actually services equipment can joggle the memory of a forgetful salesperson and even relate information about competitive products that suddenly appear in the storeroom of a customer.

Other Salespeople

"How do we stand now?" asked the air-conditioning salesperson.

"I think you're one up on me," responded the office-supplies sales rep. "It's about time. I think this is the first time in six months that I owe you."

"Good," replied the friend. "Because the next lead you come up with ought to be a big one. Remember, you had a ball with that new office those lawyers opened last month."

Comparing notes with noncompetitive salespeople can prove a gold mine of vital information. Usually, people who have been selling for years come to know one another from contact in various sales situations. Sometimes a successful salesperson will be asked to recommend a reliable source of supply with regard to other materials. One wholesale meat salesperson had a working relationship with a real estate office. When the broker knew a property was to be occupied by a food store, the meat representative would be alerted. When the meat representative learned that a customer was going to move or open another store, the information would be passed along to the real estate agent.

It is fairly obvious that although competitive salespeople should be cordial to one another, only a cautious exchange of information is called for. If you are happily selling a customer, you certainly wouldn't want to reveal that to a competitor. Despite this warning, many salespeople like to brag about their sales, and this can reveal new prospects to the nimble competitor. Even bad news can be converted to new prospects. One salesperson complained to a competitor about the slow-pay habits of a certain account. Heeding the warning, the alert sales rep called on the prospect and sold a bill of goods after first establishing rigid credit relations. It is dangerous to talk to competitors—and profitable to keep in touch with noncompetitors.

Association Directories

There are more than 2,000 business and professional associations in this country, each servicing a particular segment of industry and society. The size of these associations may vary from a few members to hundreds of thousands. And the associations themselves buy many things, from equipment for their own use to insurance contracts for members, to training and instructional services, to group car rentals, and on and on. Because they are seeking ways to better serve their members, they are likely prospects for all kinds of materials, products, and services.

A sales training consultant was called upon to do some programming for an association. This led the consultant to solicit business from several of the members. Hence, a single business relationship was converted into many new sales opportunities. Ultimately, training films, newsletters, and cassettes were sold to the association and to some of the individual members.

Conventions and Meetings

Over the last three decades, the business of people coming together at conventions has grown beyond belief. Whole new industries have evolved because of the need and fascination that result when large groups unite to exchange information and data. The underpinning of much of this activity is the support of business houses that want to reach a large segment of the market at one time. Display booths that visually portray the wares are staffed by skilled and competent sales personnel. Convention visitors stop, review the products, and sometimes place an order. More often than not, they will leave a request for the local representative to call on them at their office. This method of accumulating prospects is so important that many companies have a special task force to set up and staff convention displays. The names they collect at these conventions are passed along to the territorial sales representatives.

Meetings and conventions are conducted on national as well as on regional bases. For example, the American Psychological Association meets twice a year, usually alternating between opposite geographical sections of the country. The Eastern Psychological Association, which represents only a small segment of the larger organization, meets once a year in its own backyard. For the novice salesperson, the chance to "walk a convention" and visit all the booths, meeting old and new friends, provides a rare kind of excitement. The National Restaurant Show held each year in Chicago draws more than 100,000 food buyers and business owners.

Recently, a smaller version of the convention has become popular. A company large enough to handle it will have its own convention, usually in its own warehouse. Invitations are mailed to many old customers, and each salesperson is asked to add the names of prospects who do not currently buy from the company. The effectiveness of this type of prospecting is highly gratifying. When prospects go to the trouble of spending a day, or half a day, walking through the facilities of your company, you can almost bet they will become customers. Thus, many companies give strong support to the prospecting efforts of the sales force.

WHAT IS THE BEST PROSPECTING SYSTEM?

"Hey, you old turkey," laughed the veteran sales rep. "What's doing up in the north woods?"

"Good to see you, Malcolm," smiled the burly man. "Just came down to our sales meeting. Have to come back to the big city once in a while."

"Did you learn anything?"

"Yeah. Our sales manager is off on a new kick. He thinks we ought to change our prospecting methods."

"We do that all the time."

"What do you mean?"

"A couple of years ago, all the salespeople seemed to be leveling off. The pizazz had gone out. So our manager introduced the idea of changing our methods for finding new prospects. At first it was a drag. Every three months there would be a new plan. Can you imagine me writing letters to prospects?"

"Did it work?"

"Not only did it work, we switch every couple of months now, just for fun."

In large organizations where a pattern of prospecting has been established over the years, the salespeople are exhorted to "do more of the same." However, many companies now recognize the value of stirring the salespeople by training them in new and different ways to sell and to prospect. There is no best way to prospect; whatever method produces results is the one to use. More important than that is the need to change methods from time to time in an attempt to ascertain that the method being used is in fact the best for that particular time and product. What brought success in one year may fail in the next. That is part of the charm and challenge of professional selling—the continued opportunity for revision and improvement.

One of the largest auto insurance companies in the country rarely sends salespeople out to sell policies. When the firm decided to also offer homeowner insurance, it became necessary to contact old customers as well as new prospects. To do this, the company had the salespeople call every old customer, people they had not seen or spoken to for years, to inform them of the additional policies available from the company. The method of prospecting for auto insurance and the method employed for home insurance, both from the same company, were completely different.

If there is one rule to follow in the search for prospects, it is to keep trying fresh methods till the richest lode is uncovered. When that vein runs out, switch to another prospecting technique.

SUMMARY

Visualize the scene: A bright, sunny morning, a salesperson in a sharply creased pantsuit and white blouse, carrying a snappy new briefcase. After six months of sales training, this agent steps into the world ready to do battle. Standing at the curb, the sales representative looks around and then quakes with fright. "Where shall I go? Who wants to buy from me? They didn't teach me how to find people who want to buy."

Maybe we have overdone it. Certainly prospecting is one of the major things any company will impart to its salespeople, new and old alike. Because the search for the suspects who want and need your product is a process unto itself.

One lesson that professional salespeople can always review is the variety of ways to discover new suspects who may become prospects. There is a constant need for new prospects created by forces beyond the control of the salesperson. Fire, death, change of buyer, and the sale of a business can bring about a decline in sales volume. The only certain way to maintain sales levels is to add to the list of prospective accounts. To do this, the professional salesperson has a number of methods. They are:

Cold canvass
Personal observation
Sphere of influence
Referral
The telephone book
Advertising

Direct mail
Mailing lists
Service personnel
Other salespeople
Association directories
Meetings and conventions

None of these methods is perfect. Great opportunity lies in trying them all at one time or another. A mix of prospecting techniques makes for an exciting beginning to a sales career. In the boxing game, there is an expression, "You can't hit 'em if you can't see 'em." In the selling game, you might say, "You can't see 'em if you don't look for 'em."

A SUCCESS STORY

"Why did you agree to meet with this person if you don't want to?" asked the wife.

"I had to."

"What do you mean, you had to?"

"She said it was my last opportunity. This was the last time she would call."

The woman sat quietly, controlling her exasperation. "Let's play this again. You agreed to have her come over and tell you about insurance even though you don't know her, and the reason is that she said this was the last time she would call you."

"That's right," said the husband.

"Well, what would happen if you didn't agree to have her over for a sales talk?"

"She would never call me again."

"Did she ever call you before?"

"That's the funny part of the whole conversation. She said this was the last time she would call me and I better make a decision to have her come over. So I asked her when she had called before, and she just kept saying this was the last time she intended to call."

"Sounds reasonable," said the woman with a note of chagrin and disbelief in her voice.

"Well, you wouldn't want me to let this opportunity slip through my fingers, would you?" demanded the man.

"Oh, no," she smiled. "If she said this was the last time she could call you, I guess you did right. Because if she never called you again, you would never hear from her."

"Sure, and that wouldn't be right," the man said. . . .

"Stop, stop, stop," screamed the sales manager." Do you really expect me to believe that story?"

"I can only tell you what the customer said to me," replied the sales rep. "I'm telling it to you the way they told it to me."

"Did you really tell this guy it was the last time you would call?"

Sheepishly the salesperson said, "Yes, I guess I did."

"What the heck makes you think you can call people on the phone and tell them a crazy thing like that? Is that what you learned from all the training we give in how to find new prospects?"

"Yeah, but you said to go out and find some people to buy insurance, and didn't you say to use your imagination?"

"Okay, wiseacre. But don't try those nutty stunts any more, will you."

"Sure, boss. Do you want this contract, or should I give it to your secretary? Here's a check for the first six-months' premiums."

QUESTIONS FOR CLASS DISCUSSION

1. What causes the attrition rate among satisfied customers? Is there any way to compensate for the loss of customers?
2. What function does prospecting play with regard to the Heart of the Sale?
3. Is it possible to cold-canvass if you are selling automobiles? tape recorders? cinder blocks? How would you carry out this function?
4. Write a brief prospecting plan using all twelve methods of prospecting from the point of view of a book salesperson.
5. Describe how you might prospect for business if you were selling carbon paper; steel ingots; printing inks.
6. Name five people you think represent spheres of influence in this college; among your own personal friends; in the city.
7. How would you adopt a direct mail campaign to find prospects if you were selling venetian blinds? office supplies? drive belts for industrial use?
8. What are the limitations for the "smokestack" method of prospecting? What are the possible benefits?
9. How would you use the classified section in the telephone book if you were selling grocery-store refrigeration fixtures? adding machines? office desks and chairs?
10. How much prospecting should a salesperson do? Is there any certain measure of prospecting effectiveness? Explain.

CASE 6—THE CASE OF THE HELPFUL BUYER

Now that the basic training was over, Faith Sloan felt a sense of fulfillment. She smiled broadly as the powerful engine under the hood of the sports coupe carried her toward the first stop of the morning. The sun was barely peeking over the horizon as she swung the car into the parking lot and prepared to call on Milton Irving, purchasing agent for a chain of hot-dog stands.

Sloan had been with Beehive Distributors for three years and after much cajoling had agreed to take a sales position. The sales manager had recognized in Faith Sloan all those characteristics that make for superior selling and had finally prevailed upon her to take the training program and represent the firm on the street. After a rigorous eight weeks of learning sales techniques and methods, Sloan had quite naturally slipped into the territory left vacant by the death of one of the older representatives.

"Good morning, Mr. Irving," smiled the saleswoman. "Did your order arrive on time last week?"

The buyer looked up and answered, "Yes." Then he leaned back in his seat and said, "You know, Faith, you've been calling on me for a couple of months now, and I've been pretty satisfied. That's why I'd like to give you a little advice."

"How's that?" she asked, a little apprehensive.

"You almost lost my business," he started. "Now, don't get upset. It had nothing to do with you. Just when old George passed away, I felt inclined to switch my business to a couple of other people who have always gotten a fair share of my action. Anyhow, you have certainly shown yourself to be worthy of my business."

Somewhat relieved, Sloan nodded and reached into her brief case for her order book.

"Here's what I want to tell you," Irving said. "I like you and I want to warn you that there must be plenty of people who felt just the way I felt. An old sales acquaintance dies, and a buyer likes to deal with someone who has been around for a while. You'd better line up some new business, fast."

This was a new thought for Faith Sloan, and she was a little put off. For a moment, she sat there and let her idea sink in. "You'd better line up some new business, fast." She thanked Irving for his advice and then flipped open the order book, prepared to write business.

1. Does Faith Sloan have a problem?
2. Where can Sloan line up some new business? How?
3. What did the sales manager see in Sloan that told that she was a likely sales candidate?
4. How many different ways can Sloan prospect? Explain.

EXERCISE 6

Suppose you were looking for a sales position. Convert the following personal "features" into "benefits":

SALES PROBLEM 6—LINING UP FOR REALIGNMENT

Businesses grow. They get bigger, more complex, and more challenging. One way many companies cope with this growth is to redistribute or realign the territories. When this happens, old customers are moved to new salespeople, and the shift in geography is often upsetting to the old salespeople. Nonetheless, redefining territories to gain greater penetration of the accounts is a fact of sales life.

Here is how three different salespeople responded to having their territories realigned:

Sales Rep #1:   This just happened to me, and believe me, it's unnerving. I went from sales of $2 million a year to nothing.

The first thing I did was drive through my new territory, write down the names of all the prospects I could see, and scour the phone book for others. Then I made a grand sweep of the territory, asking each potential customer what was the best time of the day and the week to make a sales call. I never even asked for an order.

Then I checked out the competition. I asked a lot of questions and made a lot of notes. It was starting all over again, but I took it as a great challenge. During the time I was opening new accounts, my company paid me an average of what I had earned the preceding year. I had ample time to redevelop my business, and it was really exciting.

Sales Rep #2:   The only way to approach realignment is to go out and build from the bottom up. I made it a point to visit all my old accounts, thank them for past business, and wish them well with the new sales rep. Also, I told them I was still available for advice and information.

I used the phone book to find where my new prospects were located. That really is the best way. Driving through the new area is also good. From that point on, it was simply a matter of making lots of cold calls. I built my other territory the same way. Instead of sampling old friends, I had to adopt some fresh approaches with people I never saw before. It was terrifying for a few days, and then I really began to enjoy the feeling of achievement.

Sales Rep #3:   One of the first things I did was to recall my earliest days in sales. I remembered all the tough times I had in facing up to the cold call. It was much easier the first time my territory was realigned.

One of the things I missed most was the trust that had developed with my old accounts. I had to reestablish myself with new people. Over the years, I learned the methods that bring people to the point of trusting. It really hasn't been too bad. In fact, I think anyone who calls himself or herself a professional salesperson should ask to have the territory realigned every few years. It's a humbling experience that gives you the chance to grow as a sales professional.

Past experience in one job
This course in professional selling
One accomplishment (athletic, social, or educational)
Your grade point average

Now, explain in detail which six methods of prospecting for an employer you plan to use.

7

PREPARING
FOR THE SALE

PERFORMANCE OBJECTIVES

After you have read this chapter and completed the Questions for Class Discussion, the Case, the Sales Problem, and the Exercise, you should be able to do the following:

1. Explain the purpose of preapproach.
2. Give five examples of personal information that might prove helpful in developing a sale.
3. Give five examples of business information that might prove helpful in developing a sale.
4. Describe the five methods for gathering preapproach information.
5. List preapproach information about two prospective employers.

GET READY, GET SET—BEFORE YOU GO

Strong drafts of cold wind swept down the side streets as Harry Celler forced his way against the crowds toward the massive pillars that supported the doorway. He pulled his coat collar up, twisting slightly as if to ascertain once more that he wasn't being followed. Inside the building, the stuffy smell of overheated corridors and alcoves mingled with the steam from the radiators. Swiftly he turned to the right and made his way to the end of the hall. The room was filled with drowsy old people warming themselves against the chill winter drafts. Harry approached the receptionist at the desk and said, "Do you have a copy of *Linen News?*"

"There should be one on the shelf behind that cabinet. If you can't find it, let me know, and I'll see if we have some back issues in the storeroom."

Deftly, he slipped out of his coat and flung it over a chair. This was, after all, the public library, and people could make themselves at home. He lifted the magazine from the rack and eased himself into a seat. Carelessly he flipped through the pages, not completely certain what he was searching for. Once more he stopped at the reception desk to ask, "May I see about a dozen of the back issues, if you don't mind?"

"No trouble," answered the clerk. "Give me a couple of minutes to dig them out of the back room."

"While you're gone, can you tell me where to find the *Hotelkeepers Guide?*"

"Try the shelf next to the window," answered the helpful librarian.

As Harry settled once more onto the hard chair, the librarian appeared with an armful of back issues, dusty and worn. "These ought to be of some help."

Harry nodded and returned to his study. He was happily taking notes, recording the cost per room for towels, linen usage by occupancy rate, annual average cost for linens in large hotels, and inventory figures showing that the industry was buying slightly less than in previous years. He found an announcement that Barbara Geller had been appointed purchasing agent for the Jersey Hotel chain. Further on in the notice was a description of Geller's background, telling of her previous experience in both the United States and Europe.

Returning the magazines to their place, he nodded to the librarian, making a mental note to bring her a small date- and notebook as a remembrance of all past help. He surveyed the room casually and then moved down the hall and out onto the cold sidewalk. The snap of the fresh air brought him up sharply and he quickly turned toward Main Street and the office of his stockbroker.

The noisy clatter of data-processing machines and the stream of flashing lights that announce the changing sale prices of stocks were in strong contrast to the quiet solitude of the library. "Hi," greeted Harry. "How's the market?"

"Bubbling along," answered the stockbroker. "Looking for a good buy, or are you here for fun?"

The two laughed at the weak joke. "What I need," said Harry, "is the latest annual report on the Jersey Hotels."

"Sure," answered his friend. "You after another big one?"

"Hey, don't say that! You want my competition to find out?"

"You're not doing anything remarkable. You just work hard and are smart at your business."

Harry took the report and slipped it into his briefcase, planning to read it later that evening. "By the way," he started, "you always stay at Jersey Hotels when you travel. Got an opinion about the general conditions of the rooms, the linens in particular?"

"I'd say they are among the best hotels I ever stay in. The rooms are clean, and as far as linens are concerned, they seemed to be using a new floral pattern the last time I was in Detroit. I remember we thought they looked more homelike than the usual stark white towels that most hotels use."

"Thanks," smiled Harry. "I can always count on your opinion." With that, he moved toward the door and once more found himself on the chilly sidewalk, aimed for the parking lot and his car.

The motor hummed smoothly as Harry shifted into drive and eased into the flow of traffic. He circled the hotel three times, slowing as he neared the delivery platform, searching for clues, signs that would help him tomorrow, when he had an appointment to meet with Barbara Geller. Piles of papers and ripped-apart cartons awaited the trash collector. Then he spotted a stack of waste rags, the kind used in the boiler room. He recognized the stripes down the middle; they were worn-out towels. Or were they? Perhaps a better control over inventory would appeal to Geller. It was a thought he would note on his file card as soon as he returned to the office. It might be nothing, or it might spell the opening sentence for the next day. "Ms. Geller, our inventory-purchase control system is designed to save you 14 percent on the cost of your linens."

Harry felt warm, despite the bitter winds. He sensed a security that came from knowing where he was going and how he was going to get there. Tomorrow was a big day—and he was ready.

Professional selling requires a degree of investigation before actual contact is made with the prospective customer. This text subscribes to the notion that all this prior investigation and learning is separate from the face-to-face contact with the prospect. What you know about the prospect before you engage in conversation is a significant part of the Base of the Sale.

WHAT IS THE PREAPPROACH?

If you mentally stretch the process of selling as far as possible and scrutinize each step along the way, you will find something like this: A suspect, a mere name, becomes a prospect when somehow qualified. The most sketchy kinds of information will quickly shift a suspect into the position of prospect: a new car, a rise in income, birth of a child, purchase of a new home. Almost any kind of news may transform a suspect into a prospect.

This transition from suspect to prospect usually takes place during the prospecting stage, because, as we have discovered, the very act of prospecting is intended to confirm the qualifications of a potential prospect. The next natural step in this progression is to discover more about the potential prospect, to identify that person, to add flesh and bones to the bare skeleton of an idea. This is the task known as the preapproach. It leads to the next phase of the sale, the actual approach.

The course of events looks like this: suspect to prospect to preapproach to approach. There are times when all these four elements seem to blend together and become one. As we shall see shortly, the preapproach looms more important in different kinds of selling. However, it is significant for the student of professional selling to be wholly conversant with what is, or should be, taking place. You may always use the preapproach, or you may never use it as we have described the investigation of Harry Celler. Regardless, you have to pass through this segment of the sale, even if it is not recognizable.

As a sale compacts, like a telescope being closed, the separate segments of the sale become compressed into what appears to be a single motion. The preapproach is that period when the professional salesperson gains more and detailed information about the prospect. In our story, Harry Celler went to a library and a stockbroker's office, and even took a look at the outside of the building to search for little signs to help him. You can't know too much about the prospect or the prospect's business.

WHEN IS THE PREAPPROACH USED?

A preapproach is always in order and always used, although often not recognized. It becomes an integral part of any sale of any consequence, depending on the level of selling. Several examples will help the student to comprehend and identify how the preapproach fits into any sale.

Door-to-door salespeople do remarkably little preapproach, generally restricting investigations to a geographic area. They know, or hear, that a certain neighborhood is receptive to the type of product or service they have to offer. They start at one end of the street and work their way to the end of the block, stopping at each house to approach the suspect–prospect. Experience and long hours endow door-to-door salespeople with a "sixth sense" about the qualifications of the suspect–prospect. Snap judgment is almost part of their carrying cases. When used at other levels of selling, this attribute can cause more trouble than it is worth.

Door-to-door salespeople are not deterred by any seeming difficulty. They forge ahead, seeking to make a sale despite whatever odds they meet. They are the original "never-take-no-for-an-answer" type of salespeople. At times, this forward drive and momentum may appear callous, inconsiderate, and even obnoxious. Generally speaking, they are at all times using the very best of sales tactics, which manifest themselves as "high pressure." They lack the time for an in-depth study of the individual homeowner. They know they have only one opportunity to conclude a sale, and they do their best to succeed.

This description of the work style of the door-to-door salesperson may not appeal to some people. However, it is a challenge of a different sort and one to which many people subscribe. They revel in the uncertainty that this type of selling encompasses. It is a rough-and-ready atmosphere, one filled with constant problems and challenges to overcome. A typical day might include calling on 100 or more houses, with only a small number of sales. It is not for the weak at heart. (Note: During the Great Depression of the 1930s, some of the most successful salespeople were those selling silk stockings door to door. Despite the general financial conditions, people still somehow found the money to pay for what was then a luxury.)

By way of contrast, the insurance agent or the real estate broker may do a considerable amount of preapproach work. Understanding the changing financial condition of the suspect is extremely important to the preparation of a skillful sales presentation. Some insurance agents work on a "debit," which means they call every week or every two weeks on the customer to collect the insurance premium. These payments are noted in an insurance receipt book, and the insurance agent has the opportunity to learn all about the family life of the customer. The arrival of a new baby is the signal to suggest another insurance policy, either on the parents or on the child "for a college education." These insurance agents make up the vast majority of insurance salespeople. They work at the bedrock of society and are in constant contact with their prospects. They know their clients intimately, and every change in the life of the client is known to the insurance representative.

Another type of insurance representative is the one who sells family plans or retirement plans. This task is more complex, because the agent will see the prospect once a year, or once in two or three years. Each policy sold will be large, probably for $100,000 or more. In addition, the insurance representative will be expected to know about changing Social Security benefits, tax laws, retirement programs in industry, IRAs (Individual Retirement Accounts), Keogh Plans, and the long-range outlook for college costs and medical problems. The salesperson is an expert in family finanical planning. Thus, the type of prospecting done will be of a more intensive nature. Discovery that a client has changed positions and now earns twice as much money is an indication that more coverage is needed to protect the family. Likewise, a growing family indicates the need for more coverage for education and protection.

Other types of insurance people—those who sell fire, auto, and health policies—are confronted with a similar problem. However, these types of coverage have become so commonplace that they are often sold "over the counter" in retail outlets or through the mail. This does not diminish the opportunity for the vibrant salesperson to gain the knowledge and expertise to be successful in these areas. Remember, advertising doesn't sell; only people sell to people.

Industrial

In this text we have described the business of professional selling by arbitrarily classifying different levels according to the work style of the salespeople. You will recall the industrial salesperson from Chapter 1. The job calls for considerable travel, and the sales representative is often away from home for a week at a time. Orders are usually large but infrequent. This suggests that the customers take a good deal of time in assembling their needs and deciding where to make a purchase. Order placing is a lengthy process and requires a sufficient amount of time to properly discuss the many virtues and problems inherent in any sales proposition.

This level of selling is in direct contrast to door-to-door sales. The professional industrial salesperson will probably maintain a separate file on each prospect and customer. Information will have time to develop, and changes in the life-style or position of the customer will be noted. Because the salesperson may see the buyer only once a month, the intervening time may show significant alterations on the profile card of the client. We will discuss the profile card later in this chapter.

Because the stakes are high and the orders large, the industrial salesperson may prefer to do considerable investigation before trying to get an appointment with a prospect. When salespeople walk into buyers' offices for the first time, they want to know as much as possible about the person sitting behind the desk. An order, although desirable, may take a year to achieve. In many instances, this salesperson will be interviewed by appointment only, so the thought of cold canvass just does not seem to apply.

The industrial salesperson will use a number of ways to uncover more information about the prospect. Time must be spent to develop this information; be in no rush to learn about and study the prospect or the company. There is time to do a great deal of investigation, all of which should help toward a vital and dynamic sale.

Manufacturing

The industrial level of selling and the manufacturing level are quite similar. In manufacturing selling, territories may be somewhat smaller and travel not as extensive, but orders are spaced, and each sales call requires a substantial amount of time to conclude. A regular schedule of sales calls may be carried out without a formalized appointment. However, the buyer will generally know what day of the week or month to expect the salesperson.

The manufacturing representative calls on distributors whose specific problems are completely unlike the problems of a manufacturing concern. Therefore, the professional salesperson needs a different set of data to relate the goods and services to the distributor. Moreover, once a sale has been consummated, a considerable amount of service may need to be rendered. For example, the manufacturer sales representative may be expected to do "end-user" work; that is, make sales calls on the customers of the distributor. In a sense, this helps the distributor salesperson sell products. This effort can be a great assist to manufacturing salespeople, because they can gain insights into the problems of their customers, the distributors.

What this means is an ongoing relationship requiring that the salesperson understand the distributor-customer intimately. Since they will be together so often, and since the salesperson will work with the distributor salesperson, it is important that profile cards be developed. The manufacturing salesperson needs information not only about the purchasing agent; there might also be a file on the salespeople of the distributor. Often a friendly affiliation with these salespeople can spell the difference between success and failure in selling to the distributor.

The manufacturing salesperson has the dual problem of compiling a profile on the customer and on the customer's salespeople. At the same time, this improves the relationship between the manufacturing representative and the distributor. Moreover, when the distributor salespeople can count on a sales assist from a manufacturing representative, they will be more disposed to sell that rep's products. Any background information the manufacturing salesperson can accumulate on the distributor salespeople will prove helpful in making a sale to the distributor's purchasing agent.

Distribution

The life of distributor salespeople is fairly well organized. They make between ten and 20 stops a day, calling on the same people every week or every two weeks. To the extent possible, they become an "adjunct" member of the customer's work force. They may in fact perform many chores for the customer, such as taking inventory, straightening shelves, or writing the orders. To reach this happy point of acceptance, the salesperson and the customer must know each other extremely well.

To keep track of 75 to 100 customers is a near impossibility. So, many distributor salespeople also compile file cards describing their customers. Noted will be a considerable amount of personal information and business information. Using these cards as a model, distributor salespeople will seek to gather similar information about prospects during the preapproach time. However, like the door-to-door salespeople, distributor representatives will often seize the opportunity to do a considerable amount of cold canvassing. When a likely suspect is spotted, they will "telescope" the prospecting with the preapproach and simply make a sales call without further ado.

In many instances, the distributor salesperson will see the makings of a prospect in the construction of a new building. After ascertaining that the new structure will in fact represent a business opportunity, the salesperson will begin a preapproach investigation. Few things are as subject to scrutiny as a hole in the ground where a new store is to be built. The trail may lead from the builder to the real estate broker and ultimately to the prospect.

Retail

Retail salespeople may be content to wait for customers to walk in off the street. This is their privilege. But the professional retail salesperson will also create a profile of information about good customers. Consider the person who sells in a men's store. Any one of the customers may spend from $200 to $2,000 a year for clothes. Two hundred customers represents a fair volume of business. To keep track of this many people requires some set of records defining each customer. A phone call when new stocks arrive can help to generate new business. That is the way professionals will conduct themselves.

A more striking example is the corner grocery store. Think of the potential. A small family will easily spend $4,000 a year for food. A "professional" storekeeper will soon recognize that 300 families, those in the immediate vicinity, can produce over a million dollars' worth of business a year. To reach this goal, the storekeeper must know every customer intimately, down to the last detail, even when little Susie goes to the dentist for braces. As a matter of practical fact, the survival (and it has been difficult) of the corner grocery store revolves around this kind of detail. Anyone who has not had the advantage of meeting grocers who are thus committed has missed being in contact with a rare and disappearing type of professionalism.

Unfortunately, most people think of the "clerk" when they think of retail selling. It does not have to be like this. Retail selling represents all the challenges of any other type of selling. Just because the salesperson remains in the same location each day does not diminish the chance to prospect for new customers and to gather preapproach information to help the sale along.

PURPOSES OF THE PREAPPROACH

You simply cannot know too much about a prospect. An insurance agent had an appointment one night. The opening comment was, "Mr. Prospect, with this new policy, you can be certain you will have the resources to send your child to college." What the agent did not know was that the prospect was single! He had been confused with someone else with a similar name. This agent had failed to carry out the preapproach sufficiently to discover that the prospect being addressed was a totally different human being with completely different problems.

On another occasion, a manufacturer's representative had an appointment with a large distributor. The main thrust of the approach was to demonstrate how the representative would work with the distributor's salespeople to build business. Imagine the chagrin of the representative when the distributor said, "We have revised our entire way of doing business, and we have eliminated the outside salespeople. Our business will all be done by telephone."

Probably more ironic than either of these two examples is the story of the industrial salesperson who called on the Acme Steel Company to sell rolled sheets and rods of steel. "Oh, we're not in the steel business," said the buyer. "That name is a carryover from the business we used to be in. We sell paints and charcoal and other allied items, but we don't sell steel!" A minimum of preapproach investigation would have saved this sales rep from an embarrassing situation.

Qualifies Information

A preapproach investigation will yield satisfying facts that will either move the sale forward toward the approach or stop it dead in its tracks. Suppose the salesperson determines that the suspect in question has a very bad credit rating, one the credit manager would find unacceptable. Either more investigation is required or the salesperson must seek the help of the credit manager. Credit information may tell the salesperson to proceed along certain lines, or it may say that there is no way to accept business from that prospect.

Other kinds of information, such as delivery distance, may disqualify a prospect. The company may not be able to deliver merchandise to that particular location. Thus, the salesperson may have to clear with the traffic manager. An intensive investigation may well unfold information that will strengthen the resolve of the salesperson to turn that prospect into a customer. Perhaps the seller will uncover the fact that the prospect has the potential to purchase a huge volume of products. Or the sales rep may discover that the prospect is related to the rep's grandmother's aunt on the other side of the family. That could be helpful to a sale.

Shades Your Approach

Background information will help determine the best possible approach to a prospect. A good example is the discovery that this account demands superior delivery service. With this fact in mind, a salesperson might make delivery the main thrust of a sales presentation.

Perhaps this prospect is a person who has worked up from the bottom and admires others who have also achieved success despite overwhelming odds. Maybe the buyer likes football. It could be that the prospect never went to college, but the purchasing agent is a Princeton graduate. What is there about this person that can give the salesperson some help in preparing for the best possible approach? The salesperson is free to use any personal information that might pave the way to a successful sale.

Because the approach is so vital to a dynamic sale, the inclusion of preapproach information can set the tone for the entire interview. Take the case of the salesperson who learned that a distributor was drawing detergents from a master warehouse, thereby losing control of small shipments and the ability to turn over invested capital rapidly. The entire sales appeal was developed around the principle that buying smaller quantities effected savings in at least two areas—more control and better return on investment. This salesperson might have preferred to make a completely different approach to the purchasing agent, but preapproach information provided an interesting peg upon which to hang the sales story.

Identifies Problem Areas

A significant portion of professional selling is problem solving. If salespeople know in advance the dimension of specific problems that confront the prospect, they can devise a sales presentation designed to solve these problems. The classic example relates the story of the salesperson about to call on a prospect. Walking past the receiving dock, the sales rep overheard loud voices and complaints that a shipment from a competitor was late and caused a great inconvenience. In a flash, the salesperson redirected the sales proposition toward solving the problem this prospect faced—late deliveries.

Every prospect has problems, some recognized, others latent. Although it is the job of salespeople to help solve these problems, they are helpless unless they know what the problems are. A little imagination and a healthy preapproach investigation can give the salesperson an extra selling edge. In conversation with a noncompetitive salesperson one day, a floor-covering rep heard the story about a food server who had slipped carrying a tray from the kitchen of a restaurant to the dining room. Ordinarily, the sales rep would have paid scant attention to the story, except that the company had recently taken in a line of nonslip carpeting. In the mind of the sales representative, this product seemed a potential answer to people's slipping. After asking a few questions, the sales rep visited a restaurant owner, an old friend, and then prepared a presentation for the restaurant in question. This rep did quite a little preapproach investigating and tried to solve a problem that would effectively carry the sale forward.

Few methods for selling are as successful as solving a problem for a prospect. Preapproach research and investigation tend to identify and isolate these problems.

Keeps You from Making Mistakes

We will offer only one example of how a preapproach investigation can save a salesperson from making mistakes. It revolves around the efforts of a textbook salesperson. This representative was so concerned about personal success that the time required to do preliminary work in discovering more about the prospect was minimized. After a lengthy interview with a college professor, the sales representative could not understand why she would not adopt the text for classroom work.

"Professor," said the sales rep, "I have discussed the merits of this text in detail, trying to show you that I have studied the subject so that I might make a valid presentation."

"That's true," replied the professor. "I am impressed with your knowledge of the subject matter. There is no question that you have worked hard to prepare yourself. I doubt if a semester in my class would prove any more enlightening."

"Well, would you tell me what there is about the book that doesn't satisy you? Perhaps there is some way we can resolve the question in your mind."

"I seriously doubt that."

"Why?"

"Because the book we use in my course is one that I wrote."

Good preapproach investigation would have revealed that vital fact. Enough said!

Builds Confidence

Imagine entering a strange room when the lights are out. You walk haltingly, testing each step for fear of a bulging piece of furniture or the sharp point of a table. Lamps may be balanced precariously on small surfaces; the least bump may knock them to the floor. Everyone fears the dark and the unknown.

A professional salesperson who does not undertake a preapproach investigation is no different from a person walking into a darkened room. The professional salesperson has no need to play the game in the dark. All the methods and techniques to discover many things about the prospect are available. By throwing light on the subject, we suddenly illuminate the darkened room, misplaced pieces of furniture appear, and there is an easy path to the next room. As the salesperson learns more about the prospect, it is possible to move forward with confidence.

A young man was making his first trip to Philadelphia. As the time to leave approached, he told his father, "I'm scared!" He was plainly afraid of the unknown. Only when his father gave him explicit information—where the bus would enter the city, how to get to the street level, where to find a subway, and how many blocks to walk to his sister's house—were his fears allayed. This was a perfectly natural reaction of a human being embarking on a journey for the first time.

No better example can be cited than the astronauts who landed on the moon. They seemed fearless. In reality, they had practiced the landing so many times under simulated conditions that the fear was gone; they knew as much about the surface of the moon as it was possible to learn without actually walking there.

There is nothing unnatural about being afraid of the unknown. It is unnatural if professional salespeople do not arm themselves with data before they make that excursion into the unknown. They can have confidence in direct proportion to the amount of information they have about the prospect.

WHAT INFORMATION IS VALUABLE?

Experienced salespeople learn to show a keen and abiding interest in people. It becomes an important facet of their sales personality—the ability and the desire to ask questions and find out about the people they are talking to, whether in a business situation or in their private lives. When the information they are gathering pertains purely to business, they will keep a system of file cards, noting small pieces of data that may help toward meeting the sales success. This use of a "profile" card system proves invaluable when the salesperson makes an appointment with a new prospect. It is also valuable as a review when the salesperson is calling on old accounts that may not have been seen for some time. The information needed falls into two categories, personal and business.

Personal

Name—The exact spelling, including middle initials. If possible, the name of the spouse, children's names, and birthdays.

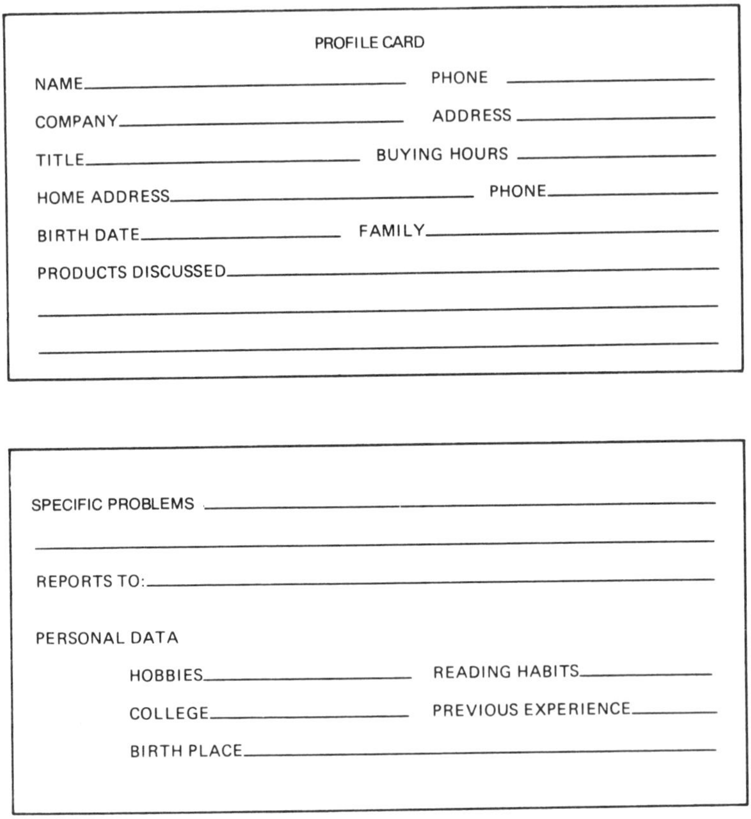

```
┌─────────────────────────────────────────────────────────────────┐
│                        PROFILE CARD                               │
│   NAME_____    PHONE  _____         │
│                                                                   │
│   COMPANY_____    ADDRESS _____          │
│                                                                   │
│   TITLE_____    BUYING HOURS _____           │
│                                                                   │
│   HOME ADDRESS_____    PHONE_____                │
│                                                                   │
│   BIRTH DATE_____  FAMILY_____            │
│                                                                   │
│   PRODUCTS DISCUSSED_____            │
│   _____            │
│   _____            │
└─────────────────────────────────────────────────────────────────┘
```

```
┌─────────────────────────────────────────────────────────────────┐
│                                                                   │
│   SPECIFIC PROBLEMS  _____            │
│   _____            │
│   REPORTS TO:_____            │
│                                                                   │
│   PERSONAL DATA                                                    │
│         HOBBIES_____   READING HABITS_____            │
│         COLLEGE_____   PREVIOUS EXPERIENCE_____           │
│         BIRTH PLACE_____            │
│                                                                   │
└─────────────────────────────────────────────────────────────────┘
```

PROFILE CARDS GIVE A COMPLETE AND
FACTUAL BACKGROUND OF THE CLIENT.

Figure 7-1

Age—Date of birth. You may decide to send a birthday card at some time in the future.

Residence—Home address. Season's greetings are more impressive when received at home, and emergency situations do arise. This information may be helpful when you least expect.

Education—High school, college, and if applicable, postgraduate studies. Names of institutions might prove important.

Buying authority—What is the person's title, and how far does his or her authority extend?

Clubs and organizations—Social, community, and business groups should be noted. Religion is important; you may save yourself a good deal of grief if you find this out without alerting the prospect. (Remember our earlier warnings about religion and selling.)

Best time for a sales call—Does the prospect have a preference, and if so, what is it?

Hobbies—Is there a stuffed fish on the wall or a set of golf clubs in the corner of the office? Find out what are the hobbies and outside interests of the buyer, including spectator sports.

Where the prospect works—In the case of insurance, mutual fund, real estate brokers, and stockbrokers or retail salespeople. The other levels of sales personnel will already have this information.

Peculiarities—Maybe the prospect is left-handed, or bowling is a favorite activity. Does the prospect preach at salespeople, or is the prospect a keen observer of the political scene? What subjects are absolutely taboo in the presence of the prospect?

Anything that strikes the salesperson as an important personal trait or characteristic, any previous work experience that tells something about the prospect, any anecdote told about a youthful escapade; all these things should be noted on the profile card.

Business

Need for your proposition—The prospect may need it more than is realized, and the seller should be aware of that fact. On the other hand, the prospect may not really need the proposition today. What about tomorrow?

Company merchandising methods—In the case of a purchasing agent, what are the merchandising problems, and how can the proposition help to solve those problems?

Inventory policy—Do you know enough about the company you are trying to sell? How do the salesperson's objectives jibe with the prospect's objectives?

Credit—Does the prospect have a credit rating? What is it? Has it changed over the years? Is it getting better, or worse?

Present suppliers—Do you know who the competition are and how they became so firmly entrenched with this account? How many suppliers are there currently, and what is the outlook for the immediate future?

What products the prospect company makes or uses—Do you have full knowledge of the marketing problems and products of this prospect?

Structure of the prospect company—Is this a marketing structure? a management structure? Do you know the name of the president and the junior officers? Who are next in line above and below the buyer? How do they sell their merchandise?

End-users—What do you know about the customers of the prospect? Are you acquainted with the problems of the prospect's customers?

Prospect's position in the industry—Is this the largest or smallest company in the industry? How might this information affect a sales presentation?

Company history—What is there in the background of the prospect's company that might prove useful during a sales presentation? When was the company founded? When did it become a public company?

This profile card of information and data may ultimately become several file cards. It is a research asset. Not only will it help the salesperson to know and understand a prospect's problems; it will also help if the salesperson wants to build other territories and decides to turn these accounts over to a junior salesperson. Maybe the company will come up with a plan to expand into other areas, or maybe the sales representative will be offered a promotion. These file cards afford instant information for someone taking over sales calls. Remember, the sales representative may want to take an extended vacation sometime and will want a substitute salesperson to give the customers the same fine service they have received over the years. These cards will tell a good portion of the story of the salesperson's relations with the prospect who by this time has become a customer.

PROFILE EXAMPLES

Knowing the customer is so important that we have gathered two profiles from the food industry. The first is a profile of a food-service distributor that might be used by the manufacturer or packer of foods. The second is the profile of the customer, which the distributor would adopt for use by the sales force. The distinctions between the two profiles demonstrate the information differences between selling at the manufacturing level and selling at the distribution level.

DISTRIBUTOR PROFILE

NAME _____ PHONE _____

ADDRESS _____

_____

SALES VOLUME $ _____   BUYING AFFILIATION _____

PRINCIPALS _____

_____

_____

MANAGEMENT TEAM

    GENERAL MANAGER _____

    SALES MANAGER _____

    PURCHASE MANAGER _____

    ADMINISTRATIVE MANAGER _____

    OPERATIONS MANAGER _____

    FINANCIAL MANAGER _____

COMPANY HISTORY

    WHEN FOUNDED _____

    EARLY HISTORY _____

_____

_____

_____

GROSS PROFIT _____%   NET PROFIT _____%

WAREHOUSE

    SQUARE FEET _____ FREEZER _____ CUBIC FEET _____

    LOADING DOCK _____

    WAREHOUSE EXPANSION PLANS _____

_____

INVENTORY TURNOVER

CANNED _____		FROZEN _____	
E & S _____		MEAT _____	
PRODUCE _____		COFFEE, TEA _____	
DETERGENTS _____		DISPOSABLES _____	

DESCRIPTION OF SALES FORCE
        DISTRICT SALES MANAGERS _____
                                _____
                                _____
                                _____
        SPECIALISTS   _____
                                _____
                                _____
        SALES REPS   _____

MARKET POSITION

MAJOR COMPETITORS

NATIONAL ACCOUNT COVERAGE

SIZE OF DELIVERY FLEET _____

ANTICIPATED ROI* _____   ROA** _____

GROWTH PLANS

SALES MEETINGS   (PLEASE DESCRIBE DISTRICT AND GENERAL MEETINGS)

SOPHISTICATION LEVEL OF ORGANIZATION

COMMENTS:

---

*Return on investment.
**Return on assets.

CUSTOMER PROFILE

NAME _____   DATE _____

ADDRESS _____

PHONE _____

MANAGER _____

CHEF _____

BOOKKEEPER _____

HEAD CASHIER _____

_____

_____

_____

WHO HAS THE AUTHORITY TO PURCHASE:

    FRESH MEATS? _____

    FROZEN FOODS? _____

    CANNED GOODS? _____

    EQUIPMENT AND SUPPLIES? _____

    COFFEE? _____

    PRODUCE? _____

    DISHWASHING SUPPLIES? _____

    LAUNDRY PRODUCTS? _____

HOW MANY SEATS IN THIS OPERATION? _____   HOW MANY ROOMS? _____

SALES VOLUME $ _____

HOW MANY PEOPLE SERVED AT   BREAKFAST? _____

                                          LUNCH? _____

                                          DINNER? _____

DOES THIS ACCOUNT HAVE A   BANQUET ROOM? _____ SEATS _____

                                      CONFERENCE ROOM? _____ SEATS _____

                                      COCKTAIL ROOM? _____ SEATS _____

                                      EMPLOYEE DINING? _____ SEATS _____

                                      ROOM SERVICE? _____ SEATS _____

WHAT ARE THE THREE MOST POPULAR ENTRÈES ON THE MENU?

    1. _____

    2. _____

    3. _____

WHAT ARE THE THREE MOST POPULAR VEGETABLES ON THE MENU?

    1. _____

    2. _____

    3. _____

WHAT GARNISHES ARE MOST POPULAR ON SANDWICHES?

    1. _____

    2. _____

    3. _____

WHAT GARNISHES ARE MOST POPULAR ON PLATTERS?

    1. _____

    2. _____

    3. _____

DOES THIS CUSTOMER HAVE A SALAD BAR? _____

    NAME THE ITEMS FEATURED. _____

    _____

    NAME THE SALAD DRESSING FEATURED. _____

    _____

WHAT KIND OF PROMOTIONS DOES THIS CUSTOMER EMPLOY?

    1. _____

    2. _____

    3. _____

HOW OFTEN IS THE MENU REVISED? _____

WHAT EQUIPMENT CHANGES ARE PLANNED FOR THE NEXT 12 MONTHS?

FRIALATORS _____		SLICING MACHINES _____	
OVENS _____		DISHES _____	
TABLES & CHAIRS _____		GLASSES _____	
RADAR RANGE _____		TOASTERS _____	
DISHWASHERS _____			

WHAT FROZEN ENTRÉES HAVE BEEN EXAMINED AND TESTED IN THE PAST YEAR?

1. _____
2. _____
3. _____

WHAT DESSERTS ARE MOST POPULAR?

1. _____
2. _____
3. _____
4. _____

WHO HAS THE AUTHORITY TO RECEIVE DELIVERIES?

1. _____
2. _____
3. _____

WHAT IS THE BEST TIME TO MAKE DELIVERIES? _____

WHERE DO THEY USUALLY GO? _____

HOW MUCH TIME DO YOU SPEND WITH SALESPEOPLE EACH WEEK? _____

WHEN WE TALK ABOUT "SERVICE," WHAT DOES THAT MEAN TO YOU?

ON-TIME DELIVERY _____
RELIABLE SALESPEOPLE _____
CONSISTENT QUALITY _____
_____
_____
_____
_____
_____

HOW LONG HAVE YOU BEEN IN THE FOOD-SERVICE BUSINESS? _____

HOW LONG AT THIS LOCATION? _____

WHAT TRADE MAGAZINES DO YOU GENERALLY READ?

_____
_____
_____

HOW DO YOU TRAIN TABLE SERVERS? _____

_____

_____

HOW DO YOU LEARN ABOUT NEW PRODUCTS? _____

_____

DO YOU HAVE A FORMULA FOR MENU PRICING? _____

_____

WHAT WOULD YOU SAY IS YOUR BIGGEST PROBLEM? _____

_____

_____

_____

WHAT DO YOU FEEL IS THE THING YOU DO BEST IN YOUR OPERATION? _____

_____

_____

_____

Sales Potential Forecast

APPROXIMATE FOOD AND NONFOOD PURCHASES $ _____

ESTIMATED SALES POTENTIAL	198 __	198 __	198 __
FRESH MEAT			
FROZEN FOOD			
CANNED GOODS			
PRODUCE			
EQUIPMENT & SUPPLIES			
LAUNDRY SUPPLIES			
DETERGENTS			
DISPOSABLES			
COFFEE			

HOW TO GAIN PREAPPROACH INFORMATION

It isn't necessary to have a detective agency gather the kinds of information the salesperson needs about a prospect, although there have been instances in which salespeople have gone to that extreme, particularly when a large sale was at stake. This accumulation of information is to discover what there is in the personal background or business life of the prospect that could help the salesperson gain a successful interview and sale.

Access to information about people is fairly simple. There are at least five basic sources, which require only that the salesperson pursue the data.

End-Users

This is the term used to describe those people who use the product of the company the salesperson is trying to sell. Another way of saying it would be to refer to them as the "customers of the prospect." They are a fruitful source of information. Who knows better about a company than the people who buy from it?

A manufacturer's representative for an electrical-appliance firm wanted to sell a large retail store. To gain perspective, the representative visited ten private homes in the neighborhood and solicited opinions about the kinds of products the homemakers were using. During this "survey," the representative gained insights into the retail outlet, which was the real interest. The salesperson learned about service-after-the-sale problems, delivery schedules, types of credit extended by the retail store, and the names of several salespeople on the showroom floor. This information was duly noted on a file card. It was purely business information.

Often a company will survey end-users and ask them, "If our product were available in your area, which store would you prefer to buy it from?"—a perfectly valid question. A food manufacturer sent a team of salespeople to call on restaurants, all with the same query: "We are seeking a distributor in this market. Whom do you buy from? What kind of services do you require and expect? How long has that company been in business?" There are a number of questions that customers of the prospect can answer—and the answers will add to the information on the profile card.

Other Salespeople

Professionals of all kinds exchange information. Another salesperson in a noncompetitive field is an excellent source of information and may even have the kind of file cards you yourself use. A fair exchange of information about a specific buyer is considered equitable. What a friend tells a salesperson today can be repaid at some later time.

Short of your having a working arrangement with another salesperson, additional bits of data can be gained during a friendly conversation:

SOURCES OF INFORMATION

END-USERS
OTHER SALESPEOPLE
TRADE PUBLICATIONS
NEWSPAPERS
BUSINESS PUBLICATIONS
OBSERVATION
PERSONAL DATA
BUSINESS DATA

THE MORE YOU KNOW ABOUT
THE PROSPECT, THE BETTER YOU
DEMONSTRATE YOUR PROFESSIONALISM.

Figure 7-2

the best time to call on a person, how old the company is, quirks of the buyer, personal likes and dislikes. Salespeople, like everyone else in society, like to talk about their business and the funny or strange things that take place from time to time. An occasional cup of coffee with another professional can prove quite revealing.

Trade Publications and Newspapers

Every field has its own trade publications. These magazines always highlight personnel changes, success stories, sometimes even bankruptcies. The pages of these business publications are intended to keep everyone in the industry aware of what is taking place. The mention that a certain purchasing agent has been promoted may be the signal to call on that person at the new location or to get over to meet the person who has replaced the purchasing agent. Even the promotion of a person who does not buy from you can be good news. It opens the door to a new sales opportunity.

The local newspapers and weeklies are a significant source of information about the personal life and habits of potential prospects: One person wins a golf tournament, another speaks before the graduating class of a college. Engagement announcements are important not only to photographers seeking a picture-taking assignment; they also mean something for the salesperson calling on the parents of the engaged couple. It is a chance to say something nice, or even something that may be relevant to business.

A teacher was awarded a plaque for superior efforts in the classroom. Imagine the effect when a book salesperson called at the school and said, "I saw the writeup in the paper about your award. Congratulations."

An insurance agent noted to a prospect, "Your picture in the paper with the winning catch in the fishing tourney looked great. Is that the largest fish you ever caught?"

One industrial salesperson went even further. "Here is a plastic-covered copy of the story that appeared in the industry magazine about the speech you delivered two weeks ago. I thought you might want to have a copy to save."

In each instance, the professional salesperson had kept abreast of things in which the prospect was involved and then turned that information into a subject of conversation during a sales interview.

Business and Other Publications

The names of industry and community leaders sometimes find their way into *Who's Who*. Officials in large companies, college professors, leaders in the field of government, health-service officials, and foundations are frequently covered in other prestigious publications. Financial reports at the end of each year spew forth loads of information telling how well or poorly many companies fared that fiscal year.

Credit organizations in every community have reports available on qualified and unqualified persons. Dun & Bradstreet (a well-known organization that collects credit information and financial data) provides in-depth information on the financial standings of thousands of companies around the world, whether they are members of Dun & Bradstreet or not. Local banks may have information files to which your own credit manager might have access. Standard & Poor's publishes business data about companies listed on the stock exchanges. All these sources of information are open to the salesperson to gain background on the company or the person the salesperson views as a prospect.

On-Site Observation

Undoubtedly the best single source of information is the people themselves. That's right, people will reveal all kinds of information during casual conversation. These data should be noted on the file card for future reference.

In the middle of a sales interview, the telephone rang. After the conversation was completed, the salesperson realized there was a good deal of ground to review. But the need to recapture the interest of the prospect seemed more important.

"I noticed your framed diploma behind your desk, but it's too far away to read. What college did you attend?"

"My undergraduate work was at Arizona. Then I took a master's at the University of Tulsa."

"What was your master's in?"

"This may strike you as funny, but I am a biologist by profession."

"That is kind of strange. How did you get to be a purchasing agent for a chain of retail stores?"

"I'll tell you. I worked for three years in my field and then one day discovered I wasn't happy. I went looking for a job. This company was rather new at the time, and it needed people who could make purchasing decisions. I simply transferred my knowledge of buying to a different line of products."

"Do you still keep in touch with your original field?"

"Oh, I play around at home, do a few little experiments. Nothing serious, you understand."

This was wildly improbable information about a strait-laced buyer, but no more upsetting than what happened to a furniture salesperson in the office of a hotel purchasing agent:

"Have you been buying furniture very long?"

"Oh, about ten years."

"What field were you in before that?"

"That's private."

"I'm sorry. I didn't mean to pry. It's just my natural interest in knowing as much about my accounts as possible. You never know when a piece of information from the past will help solve a problem or make a sale."

"Forget it."

"By the way, could you spell your name for me, so I have it accurate in my records—and your home address and phone for emergencies?"

"You can't reach me at night, unless you find a way to get through the prison walls. My cell doesn't have a phone."

"You mean you're a prisoner?" gulped the salesperson.

"That's right. I work here during the day and go back to prison at night."

"You mean this is a work-release kind of job?"

"Exactly."

Now, that's worth remembering!

Basic information, such as the data we have suggested under the personal and business categories, is nonsensitive. Any person will be happy to discuss family, hobbies, needs, desires, company policies and practices, and any other information that will help the salesperson better understand the problems of the buyer. The easiest way to find out what you want to know is to ask. If you do it gently and with sincere interest, you should have little trouble unearthing the life story of the person and the company you are preapproaching.

FORM THE PREAPPROACH HABIT

The admonition to "keep your eyes and ears open" is really too simple for the professional salesperson. These traits are learned; they are the result of practice and attention. The more you listen to what others have to say, the more you inquire after facts and information; the more you seek answers, the stronger you will become. Each piece of information forms a base upon which the salesperson builds, a natural step that leads to the Heart of the Sale. The process of inquiry, once learned and perfected, will become natural.

Along the way, the professional will have to be careful of falling into the "assumption trap"; that is, the rapid formation of opinions based on insufficient information. It is all too easy to make snap judgments about people and ideas. To ward off this possibility, the professional salesperson will make a concerted effort to avoid reaching any conclusions about people or ideas until sufficient data have been accumulated. Salespeople should seek to retain a "gee-whiz" attitude, an aura of surprise that there are still further pieces of information that add to the total portrait of that human being known as a prospect.

This search for background data that will aid in making a successful sale can also be the undoing of some salespeople. They feel compelled to gather enough information to write a biography of the prospect. Somewhere between the two extremes lies the happy medium. When salespeople walk into the office or home of the prospect, they should feel comfortable and know quite a bit about the person they are addressing. It will make the prospect feel good, and it will add to your own sense of what you are about.

SUMMARY

The natural progression before the salesperson reaches the face-to-face contact with the prospective customer includes the confirmation that a suspect is indeed a prospect. To arrive at that point, it is incumbent upon the salesperson to determine facts about this prospect, information that will move the sale forward as the salesperson shows through word and deed some knowledge about the prospect. Very often, the gathering of this information will take place through and with the help of the prospects themselves. This tends to blur the procedure, to imply that investigation before meeting the prospect is not needed. Actually, different salespeople working at different levels of business have differing needs and opportunities to discern more facts about the prospect. Industrial and manufacturing salespeople who call on clients on a monthly or bimonthly basis have a greater need for inputs, and they also have more time to gain the necessary information. Distributor and retail salespeople often find that the best source of information is the prospect.

The purpose of gaining preapproach information is to better prepare the salesperson by qualifying the prospect. It also serves to sharpen the sales approach, identify prospect problem areas, and keep the salesperson from making obvious mistakes. All this gives salespeople more confidence in their ability and in the knowledge needed to complete a sale.

Essentially, two types of information are needed. The first is personal data—name, address, birthday, basic information about where the person comes from, schools attended, hobbies, and so forth. The second category has to do with the requirements of the business the prospect represents: how the firm promotes its products, what specific problems need solving, and how the professional salesperson might relate to those problems.

Various ways are available to the salesperson to find out about the prospect. Among them are friendly salespeople from noncompetitive firms, the customers of the prospect, trade publications and newspapers, and year-end financial reports and related business publications. Undoubtedly, the most effective way to find out about people is to ask them! This last element is most significant, because it should be carried out gently, and the probing should make it easy for the prospect to talk about personal and business subjects, thereby revealing sales opportunities for the salesperson.

If one single point seems overpowering, it is this: The more salespeople know about the prospect, the better off they will be as the sale progresses.

A SUCCESS STORY

Behind the purchasing agent's desk was a colorful coat of arms, one that David Michael had never seen before. He noted a few words on a 3 × 5 card and proceeded with other questions that were on his mind. "Tell me, Mr. Sullivan, when deliveries are made to your loading platform, do the warehouse people help unload the truck? What is your company policy with regard to that?"

"We have a firm policy," responded the purchasing agent. "None of our people is allowed to touch anything on the truck of a supplier company. One of the reasons is that our insurance does not cover our people if they are involved in your work. Another is that we find it saves us a considerable sum of money."

"Good," smiled David. "One other thing. I noticed that deliveries may be made anytime between 8 A.M. and 4 P.M. Does that mean that your receiving dock is open during the lunch hour?"

"Absolutely. We have a carryover crew so that any delivery can be accommodated."

"That's fine. I have certainly gathered considerable information about your operating procedures. From our earlier discussions, I know how you prefer to ship your products and even your marketing plans. I am certainly learning a good deal about you."

"Well, it's always nice to have you visit. But don't you think something ought to happen?"

"What do you mean?"

"You have called on me seven times by actual count. Each time, you ask questions about me, about our company, about my family. But we practically never talk business. Now, I think it's about time we either did business or stopped wasting each other's time."

"Yes, you're absolutely right. Here's a picture of our new wing-tailed widgets. They are strong and inexpensive, and you can buy a modest opening order of 30 dozen. Shall I send them to you?"

"Yes, I guess you'd better."

QUESTIONS FOR CLASS DISCUSSION

1. How can in-depth preapproach research help the salesperson during the approach? Give three examples.
2. If you were a door-to-door salesperson handling a line of copper pots and pans, how might you do some preapproach research?
3. Imagine you are selling real estate. You plan to call on the person who lives across the street. List five specific pieces of personal information it would be beneficial to know about that person before trying to sell him or her a house.
4. Imagine you are selling for a drug wholesaler. You plan to call on the drugstore in your neighborhood. Give five specific pieces of business information you should know about that prospect.
5. How would you develop preapproach information before calling on the women's clothing buyer at a local department store? Would you use the same research sources for gaining information about the owner of the service station where you have your car serviced?
6. Discuss and analyze the five sources of preapproach information.
7. A prospective customer has just inherited a large sum of money. How might this information prove of value to the person selling real estate lots?
8. Read a trade publication. From the lead story, draw five business facts about the company mentioned in the story that might be considered preapproach information.

9. What kind of information would prove of value if you were a textbook salesperson seeking to sell books to the instructor of this course?
10. Write a plan for gathering preapproach information. Use all five methods, and give at least two examples for each fact-finding technique.

CASE 7—THE PROFESSIONAL GOLFER MEETS THE PROFESSIONAL SALESPERSON

Peggy Archer jammed her foot on the brake as she pulled the roadster onto the side of the road. Her eyes blazed with light, as if she had just been struck with a very happy thought. There, off to the right of the highway, loomed a stately but old-fashioned hotel. Sloping down from the wood columns and the carved balustrades was a vast sea of rich grass, dotted with the standing triangular flags that indicated the holes of a golf course.

"Funny," Peggy thought, "I don't have this club listed on my prospect sheet. I was under the impression that every country club in the state was on the mailing list of *Golf Pro Magazine.* They must have a pro shop, and that means another prospect for me."

Smoothly she moved the car forward, gently negotiating the curves that led to the clubhouse. It was still early, and the first golfers of the day were chipping shots onto the putting green, getting in their warm-up strokes. For a moment, Peggy sat in the parked car and considered which samples to carry into the pro shop. But the attraction of the sun glistening on the early morning dew along the rim of the putting green riveted her attention. She got out of the car, opened the trunk, and took a nine iron out of her golf bag. Dropping some balls to the ground, she chipped a few shots, neatly placing them near the pin. The other golfers looked her way, perhaps wondering who this interloper was.

Shortly, she gathered her balls and club, repacked them in the bag, and took her briefcase from the car. She stopped a caddy and asked, "Where can I find the manager of the pro shop?"

A raised finger showed the way, and Peggy circled around to the rear of the building. She stopped momentarily as she arranged possible approaches in her mind, then pushed through the door. There was only one person in the shop, a woman dressed in a new-style golf sweater and knickers. "Good morning," smiled Peggy. "Can you tell me where to find the golf pro?"

A trace of consternation crossed the woman's face. "I'm the golf pro. What can I do for you?"

Peggy winced noticeably. In that brief moment she realized her error.

1. What mistakes did Peggy Archer make?
2. Was there a way to preapproach this prospect? How?

SALES PROBLEM 7—BLOCKING THE MANUFACTURER'S REP

May Wolfe worked for a distributor. She was thrilled to be able to travel with one of the direct representatives of the manufacturer who sold the distributor many different items. On the first call of the day, the manufacturer's rep not only sold items the distributor had in stock; he also sold six items the distributor did not carry.

Now, May was in the difficult spot of telling the customer that her company could not deliver what was ordered. The customer threatened to stop buying from May altogether if the whole order couldn't be delivered.

Here are the solutions offered by three different salespeople:

Sales Rep #1:   I pre-warn the manufacturer's rep before we start the day. I make it very clear that we can only discuss items currently in stock.

If, during the day, some product is mentioned that we don't handle, I usually tell the customer that a two-months' supply will have to be ordered to make it worth our time to bring the item in for a single customer.

Sales Rep #2:   The first thing I do when this occurs is to get back to my sales manager and relate what happened. If I can get my company to bring in items that a good account has seen and wants to buy, I think I have performed a service for both my company and my customer. However, just prior to making each sales call, I tell the manufacturer's rep exactly what the customer is currently buying and alert the rep to stay away from new items.

Sales Rep #3:   Before I even walk through the door, I tell the manufacturer's rep what we are going to try to sell the customer. We plan each call carefully. That's why I have never had this problem.

There have been several occasions when the manufacturer's rep made a sales call without me and sold items we do not stock. When that happens, I offer to substitute something close to the product ordered. When forced to bring in a new product, I usually charge a premium for the extra trouble.

EXERCISE 7

Name two organizations you plan to apply to for a sales position.

Prepare a profile card for each of these prospective employers. Include personal data describing the person who will interview you. Also, record specific information about the business problems, objectives, and opportunities of the organization.

Indicate which preapproach methods you used to gain this information.

8

THE APPROACH

PERFORMANCE OBJECTIVES

After you have read this chapter and completed the Questions for Class Discussion, the Case, the Sales Problem, and the Exercise, you should be able to do the following:

1. List and explain the four objectives of the approach.
2. Describe the twelve different approaches.
3. Complete an approach dialogue, using three or more approaches.
4. Define the "consumer benefit" approach.
5. Prepare an approach dialogue to a prospective customer.
6. Prepare an approach dialogue to a prospective employer.

OPENING GAMBIT

"How would you like to earn an extra $500 this year?" asked the salesperson.

"Who wouldn't?" replied the retail merchant.

"Good. Here's how." The manufacturer's representative went on to present a new line of high-fashion men's suits that would bring the opportunity for substantial income to the prospect.

This brief exchange demonstrates a compelling approach, one that immediately involves the prospect. It starts at the beginning and strikes directly at two buying motives, a desire to make money and the prestige of a higher income. It also elicits a response that leads further into the sale.

The opening 60 seconds of any sale are critical. They are the first physical contact between the salesperson and the potential customer. Mistakes are easier to overcome later in the sale. The opening moments, the approach, must be positive and set the stage for a vital transfer of information between the salesperson and the prospect.

The opening anecdote of this chapter, and those of the five chapters that follow, will trace the progress of this interview as it moves through the various phases known as the Heart of the Sale.

WHAT ARE THE OBJECTIVES OF THE APPROACH?

Each phase of a sale is aimed at certain specific objectives. Language and techniques combine to meet as many of these objectives as possible. Compressed into a sentence, or two or three, should be words that highlight these objectives and help to move the interview forward to a successful conclusion.

To Gain Attention

Few prospects (potential buyers) are sitting back waiting for the arrival of a salesperson. In the case of industrial, manufacturing, and distributing organizations, there may be a single person designated as the "buyer" or "purchasing agent." Part of the job description of the buyer is to purchase merchandise and products to sustain the flow of business. However, in many instances, the buyer will have other responsibilities, including financial matters, merchandising, and warehousing, and frequently this person may also do some selling.

Thus, the salesperson often appears on the scene when the prospect is not in a "buying mood." This means, at every level, a need to gain attention and attract the buyer to what you have to sell.

A purchasing agent had just returned from a conference, and his desk was piled with unopened mail. As he surveyed the work, his secretary announced, "Ms. Green is here to see you." He knew his job was to purchase merchandise, but the distraction of the cluttered desk made him unhappy.

After being ushered in and introduced, Ms. Green sensed that it might be difficult to gain the attention of the buyer. Without a word, she reached into her brief case, took out a plastic dish and placed it carelessly on the desk. It landed with a clatter and the surprised buyer snapped, "What do you think you're doing?"

"I just wanted to show you that our new line of dishes is really breakproof," said the salesperson. "Look, not even a chip."

⋆This dramatic approach is one of the ways salespeople ascertain that the buyer is listening. It is uncommon and risky, but it certainly does gain the prospect's attention.

A PROFESSIONAL APPROACH WILL GAIN ATTENTION AND AWAKEN A NEED.

Figure 8-1

It may not be necessary to resort to this theatrical an approach, but even though larger companies do have purchasing agents, most selling is carried out between prospects who are not "professionals" and salespeople who are "professionals." (Professional buyers are skilled practitioners who study purchasing as rigorously as professional salespeople study selling.) Every person at one time or another is a prospect. So whatever you are selling, it is your task to gain the attention of these prospects.

Sometimes, gaining attention can be as simple as handing the prospect an object to hold. In a sporting-goods store, a prospect was looking at a display of tennis rackets. The salesperson took one off the rack, handed it to the prospect, and asked, "Does the grip on this racket suit you?"

Once the prospect is involved, the level of attention paid to the salesperson's statements will increase sharply.

To Awaken Needs

One of the dynamic aspects of selling is that the need and desire for merchandise or services are without bounds. Fresh ideas, inventions, and revised models of all products all hit the market with fascinating rapidity. No sooner has the prospect become accustomed to a new washing machine than a better model is available.

Changing styles and additional features in automobiles have helped establish a new market each year. Some social critics claim that "pizzazz" in new cars creates a false psychological need and does not add to a person's well-being. But who can measure the thrill and excitement of owners of a new model car as they drive down the highway? Thrills and excitement sometimes represent the needs of particular people. To stimulate these needs, automobile manufacturers continue to design new standard and optional features, such as safety belts, disc brakes, tape recorders, steel-belted radial tires, and air conditioning. These design changes become additional selling points that awaken new needs in the minds of prospective buyers.

Advertising prepares the prospect for these changes, but the salesperson on the floor of the showroom must make the sale. Therefore, alert salespeople study the product line to uncover new features and additional applications of merchandise that will awaken a need in the minds of the prospects.

To Qualify the Prospect

There is a basic need to qualify the prospect. This means that the salesperson must ascertain whether the person is merely a suspect or is truly a prospect for the proposition. Can the prospect afford your offer? Is there a real need for your merchandise? Will your service be useful? Good preapproach investigation will usually answer most of these points. A few well-phrased questions during the approach will aid the salesperson in further qualifying and properly separating suspects from prospects.

> To the person examining vacuum cleaners—"How old is your vacuum cleaner?"
>
> To the purchasing agent who buys—"Do your typists use electric type-writers?"
>
> To the couple examining baby furniture—"Are there any babies in your family?"

These questions pave the way for further conversation at the same time that they qualify the prospect.

Qualification should never be made on the basis of appearances. A well-dressed person indicates nothing to the salesperson other than what can be seen on the surface. Take the case of the salesperson in a Cadillac showroom. A man wearing overalls inquired about a new car. The sales-person showed great disdain and was generally obnoxious. In fact, the prospect owned a fleet of tractor-trailers and was accustomed to working with his hands. The salesperson neglected to "qualify" the prospect, whose grease-stained hands told only that he had not taken time to wash before coming to make a possible purchase.

Money or credit often presents a problem. Many salespeople use a "throwaway" line to get a reaction. With little emphasis, they will say, "I'm sure our normal terms of monthly credit will meet your approval." Yet there is no attempt at this point to spell out the many ways bills may be paid or obligations met.

In another instance, an air-conditioning sales rep became irritated when the manager of a grocery store persisted in asking about window models. The salesperson was certain the prospect needed a five-ton unit. What the salesperson didn't know was that the manager really wanted to buy several units for home use. There was no desire to talk about air-conditioning the store.

Only by asking questions and making statements that allow the prospect to respond can the salesperson determine whether the prospect is "alive." Qualification is ascertaining how or if your product or service is needed. Don't prejudge the prospect!

To Prepare for the Presentation

A successful approach leads to the presentation segment of the sale. Even when salespeople partially fail in an effort to gain attention, awaken needs, and qualify the prospect, they may still succeed by reaching a point where the presentation is in order. Even the most negative response to the approach can open the way for an expanded conversation.

Failing to make an impression on a prospect, one salesperson said, "Look, I know you are not interested in what I've said up till now. But my boss pays me a dollar for every presentation and demonstration I do. Would you allow me to go through my sale, and then I'll leave. Of course, if you have any questions along the way, I'll be happy to answer them."

Another time, an exasperated salesperson said, "I must be doing something wrong. With your cooperation, I'd like to run through my entire sale and then have you criticize what I've done. Will you do that for me? I'd appreciate your help."

These two requests are last-ditch efforts. But they do sincerely ask the prospect for help, a plea that is difficult for the prospect to deny. To meet with ultimate success, the salesperson must move on to the presentation.

HOW TO APPROACH A PROSPECT

A perfect approach will contain elements of all four objectives of the approach. The salesperson should prepare a number of approaches, selecting the two or three that seem most appropriate to the situation. Every person should adopt a style that is comfortable, recognizing that the total approach may well utilize more than one specific approach.

Introductory Approach

This is the most popular technique—and also the least effective, because it rarely meets the objectives of the approach. It envisions the introduction of the salesperson and the company to the prospect:

> "Good morning, Mr. Horton. My name is John Sutton, and I represent the Universal Company. We sell a fine line of couplings and joints."

(To lend a sense of continuity to these examples and the ones that accompany other segments of the sale, we shall refer to the mythical Universal Company. By using examples that demonstrate the many methods and techniques with regard to this singular organization, you will be able to visualize the entire Heart of the Sale. The Universal Company manufactures a number of products, the most important being couplings. A coupling is a device for joining two pieces of shaft or pipe together. For example, you might want to think of the coupling that connects the garden hose to the faucet. Those couplings, which are used to connect two shafts or pipes, are essential in manufacturing and construction. They are available in many sizes and shapes.)

Many sales representatives use the introductory approach because it's easy and because they don't know what else to say. Consider the prospect, busy carrying out a job. The eleven seconds it takes to deliver these lines are generally sufficient time for the prospect to raise a defense network and ask, "What does this bird want?"

This approach meets none of the four objectives of the approach, unless you assume that your name is terribly important, one that every prospect will know. Of course, if you are Arnold Palmer and you are selling golf balls, or Billie Jean King selling tennis balls, then by all means, the use of your name is appropriate.

There are times in retail selling when an introductory approach has value and can be a good way to open a sale. Have you ever noticed the number of salespeople who now wear name tags? This is intended to make the process of making a purchase more friendly and pleasant. Imagine how a person walking into a retail furniture store might feel under these two circumstances:

"Good morning. May I help you?'

Or, "Good morning. My name is Mary Jones. May I help you?"

Even retail stores are trying to introduce more dynamic approaches by their salespeople. This warm show of businesslike concern is effective. It turns a very ordinary sale into a friendly encounter.

There are other times when an introduction is in order. Salespeople who have made advance appointments to see prospects frequently use the introductory approach. In these situations, the prospect already knows who you are; you are merely identifying yourself.

Product Approach

A product approach is an effective and simple way to open the door to further conversation. Every product or service contains virtues. By pointing out these virtues, the salesperson has a wonderful method for opening the sale. If you combine the introductory approach with the product approach, you may open with a substantial statement:

"Good morning, Mr. Horton. My name is Mary Jones, and I represent the Universal Company. This new coupling has a full inch of threads, as opposed to the usual half-inch of threads."

Or (salesperson walks in and lays coupling on the buyer's desk), "This new coupling has a full inch of threads as opposed to the usual half-inch of threads."

As a purchasing agent, which approach did you find more interesting, upsetting, or challenging? The second example got right down to business and sought to immediately awaken a possible need and to attract attention to a feature of the product.

Many people attach great importance to who they are and what they do. The professional salesperson recognizes that introductions at the beginning of a sale waste very valuable time. Get right down to the business of selling.

Let's look at a "wordless" product approach. The same salesperson enters the office and places the product in the hands of the buyer, *without saying anything*.

Now that the prospect is holding the product, what will happen? If the salesperson is standing too close, the buyer might hand it back. More often than not, the prospect will ask, "What's this?" or, "What do you want me to do with this?"

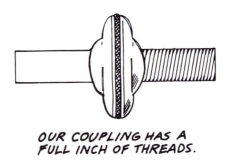

OUR COUPLING HAS A FULL INCH OF THREADS.

Figure 8-2

The salesperson's response: "Notice the full inch of threads. All our couplings offer this extra feature." At this point, the sale has begun to move forward.

Another reason why the product approach is forceful is that when people hold something in their hands, they tend to gain a feeling of ownership. Isn't that what the salesperson is trying to do—to get the prospect to want to own the product?

Consumer Benefit Approach

Probably the strongest approach is the one that tells how the prospect will benefit from the use of a product or service. This represents the resolution of a problem at the same time that it appeals to the emotional side of the buyer.

"This extra inch of threads on our new couplings means you will have fewer complaints from the production department" stresses a benefit. If the buyer can supply the production department with a product that will tend to reduce gripes, that's a benefit.

The sales representative attracted attention by plugging directly into the sale. The need to resolve a specific problem was awakened and the stage set for the prospect to question, "Why will this product do a better job?" Or, "How will this product do a better job?" This suggests that the salesperson can answer a problem.

A comparison will help to show the difference between approaches:

"This improved model of our duplicating machine will produce 40 copies a minute." (Product approach)

"Our new duplicating machine will save your secretary 30 minutes a day for more important work—such as taking dictation." (Consumer benefit approach)

In the first example, the salesperson told about the product. In the second example, the sales representative explored a benefit that the use of this equipment would bring to the prospect.

To say that people buy benefits is an oversimplification of the sales picture. In the final analysis, benefits loom as probably the most important single reason people buy, although certainly not the only reason. The last time you bought a new suit, or a new dress, did you buy the garment that was the most durable for the price? Or did you purchase the outfit that made you look and feel better?

The skillful interpretation of product features into consumer benefits can be learned. Even the price of a product can be used as a benefit:

"Our high-speed manufacturing equipment permits us to sell these paper clips for only $8.40 per gross." (Feature)

"The money you save on our paper clips allows you an extra 10 percent profit." (Benefit)

The benefit is not only the reduced price, but the increased profit as well. The professional salesperson will turn product knowledge into consumer benefits.

Curiosity Approach

This technique is primarily designed to attract attention, to pique the interest of the prospect so that the conversation will continue. As a common defense against salespeople, many prospects will automatically reply, "I don't need any today." Or, "Not today, thank you." However, if your approach can make the prospect curious, you can easily slip into the presentation.

By emphasizing different aspects of a product, it is possible to present your line in a number of different ways. Here are some methods for arousing curiosity:

USE AN APPROACH THAT
EXCITES THE INTEREST
AND ATTRACTS ATTENTION.

Figure 8-3

"Have you ever seen a coupling with a one-inch thread?"

"How much would you be willing to pay for trouble-free couplings?"

"Would you like to solve one of the main sources of complaints from your production department?"

"How many speeds do you think this bicycle has?"

"Push this button. It makes the pulleys go around."

These questions and statements are intended to arouse the prospect—to get that person to want to know more about what you have to say.

Shock Approach

One method used by insurance agents is to show the prospect a photograph of an automobile accident. At the same time they ask, "Are you covered for this kind of trouble?" The use of a horrible photograph is intended to shock the prospect and set the stage for the sale.

There is, however, the possibility that the salesperson might go too far in an attempt to upset the prospect and gain attention. A gory picture of broken bodies could be too distracting to refocus the attention of the prospect on the proposition at hand.

The coupling sales representative might show a picture of a piece of machinery being repaired because the threads on a coupling broke. The effect would be forceful if accompanied by one of a variety of possible statements:

"One out of 20 pieces of equipment break down because of faulty coupling threads."

"Our new long-thread couplings prevent machinery breakdown."

"When was the last time one of your customers complained about coupling threads?"

It is difficult for the prospect to avoid responding to this approach, because the salesperson has touched upon a very real problem.

Theatrical Approach

Curiosity, shock, and theatrical approaches are closely related, but they differ in degree. At the approach phase, the theatrical includes visual aids as a means of attracting attention and awakening needs.

A food-distribution company organized its sales force to produce a show-like effect when presenting a new line of entrées. They worked in teams, and one salesperson donned a chef's hat and carried in a steaming tray of manicotti, chicken Kiev, and egg rolls. The sight of two people walking toward an unsuspecting purchasing agent was more than enough to attract attention, while the odors awakened pangs of hunger.

The coupling sales representative carried an assortment of couplings that had been gathered over the years. Neatly mounted on a heavy panel were a number of broken parts that had failed in actual use. This kind of display proved interesting to the prospects who had similar problems. The desire to look at and touch these damaged parts was overpowering.

Question Approach

One of the most valuable techniques in the salesperson's kit is the question. People are more interested in themselves than in anybody else. Given the opportunity, they like to talk about themselves, thereby revealing interests and problems.

Questions should center on the business at hand. Too many salespeople are afraid to ask questions for fear of getting the wrong answers. When questions are used during the approach, the purpose is to get an answer—any answer. With time and practice, the questions can be altered to produce answers that better serve the purpose of the approach.

Which of these questions are the most dynamic and best geared to meet the objectives of the approach?

"Do you have any problems with the threads on your couplings?"

"How would you like to avoid some of the aggravation that occurs when the production department complains about broken couplings?"

"When was the last time one of your couplings broke?"

"What are you doing to minimize machinery breakdown?"

"If you had a choice between couplings with a half-inch thread and those with a one-inch thread, which would you buy?"

The second and fifth examples meet the requirements of the approach. They both awaken interest and lead to a further explanation of the purpose of your visit. Notice that the questions elicit the desired responses.

Another virtue of the question approach is that it helps to identify the problems that the salesperson can resolve. In the same way that a professional quarterback probes the opposing line at various places to determine weak points, the professional salesperson tests prospects' needs and problems by asking questions. This can be seen in the following series of questions posed by a concerned sales rep:

"Does this new style appeal to you?" asked the clothing salesperson.

"No. I prefer a more conservative suit," replied the shopper.

"Do you like two-button or three-button jackets?"

"Two-button."

"Here. Is this shade of brown to your taste?"

"Not quite. Do you have something darker?"

The answers to each question caused the salesperson to change tack slightly. Each change advanced the progress of the sale. Regardless of the level of selling, the professional salesperson uses questions to uncover the needs, desires, and problems of the prospect.

Bonus Approach

The added inducement of "something extra" is a valid and substantial way to open a sale. To introduce new products or promote old products, manufacturers have "specials," which make buying a little more attractive. Some salespeople prefer to save these inducements till later in the sale, hoping to use them in the close. Others feel that "specials" are the most important reason for buying.

Both these lines of reasoning are valid. There is no single answer, except what suits the individual salesperson. However, salespeople often get in a rut and always reserve the use of a bonus for one specific moment. This is a mistake, because as sales situations vary from prospect to prospect, so, too, should approaches. Also, as we shall discover later in the Heart of the Sale, repeating an offer in other language adds to your selling efforts.

Here are some bonus approaches:

"With every twelve gross of paper clips, you will receive one gross at no charge."

"To introduce our one-inch thread couplings, you get an extra 10 percent discount."

"This month, you get air conditioning at half-price with the purchase of a new car."

"If you buy 30 cases of new-pack pears, we will give you an advance billing. You won't have to pay for them for 60 days."

All these specials are incentives to buy now. They are intended to generate a volume of business when the seller feels the need to move merchandise. When used at the very beginning of the sale, they attract attention.

Survey Approach

There are two aspects to a survey approach. One is an actual survey by the salesperson, and the other is the use of survey statistics.

In the first instance, the salesperson offers to study how products are used, whether they function well, or whether the service offered is really needed. The survey approach might sound like this:

"Our company would welcome the chance to survey your use of joints and couplings. There is no charge for this service, and when we have completed our work, you will receive a complete report."

"Part of our service, Mr. Prospect, is to examine your present situation to see if you need our products. May I have your permission to set up an appointment with the production department to review your present methods of operations?"

"Shelf space in a supermarket is very valuable. Why not allow us to survey your present use of space and give you a full report?"

"There have been a number of changes in the various insurance programs we offer. If we can have all your policies to study, we will be in a position to assess where you are today and where you want to be tomorrow."

Presumably, the end result of this type of effort will show ways in which the salesperson's product or service can solve a problem or fill a need. It means the devotion of time and consideration on the part of the salesperson and an additional sales call to discuss the findings. There is no assurance that a sale will be consummated, but agreement by the buyer is a tacit acknowledgment of a receptive interview following the survey.

The second application of the survey approach is to make the prospect aware of studies and information that might apply to the prospect's company. The reasoning is that similar companies or individuals have similar problems and needs. If the survey has been completed by the seller's company, there should never be a reference to the sources of the information. That would be divulging confidential information. Clients who participated in the survey should remain nameless. But studies made by government agencies or trade associations are considered public knowledge.

"We recently conducted a survey of the entire machinery industry. One of the biggest problems is the length of threads on couplings. Is this true of your company?"

"A study by the machinery manufacturers shows that couplings with short threads tend to break under stress. Our company has designed a coupling with a full one-inch thread."

"Here is a survey of a company in the Midwest that has problems much like your own. It has a lot of trouble with couplings. Does this agree with your own situation?"

"Last year, the Restaurant Association made a study of the eating habits of customers. You can see from this list of favorites that hamburgers are certainly the most popular item."

"A government study of pesticides ranks our combination of chemicals in the top five. Would you like to see the report?"

Thus, surveys and the accumulation of factual data offer a powerful way to open a sale.

Declarative Approach

Opening with a statement of provable facts can be a potent approach. However, because the information is true and valid does not mean that the prospect will accept it. People tend to believe what they have always believed, and the presentation of facts may not be sufficient to move them. It is important to be prepared for some kind of rebuttal. This is good, because the prospect then becomes involved in a relevant discussion, which leads deeper into the sale.

"We sell more paper clips than any other company in the industry."

"Insurance coverage that takes care of hospital bills is the most needed protection today."

"Couplings with one-inch threads last longer than couplings with half-inch threads."

"When we have had enough time to demonstrate our new couplings with the one-inch thread, the whole industry will be buying them."

Each of these declarations might prove disturbing to the prospect; they may appear unacceptable. But do they strive to achieve at least some of the objectives of the approach? The answer is, "Yes!" They do tend to awaken a need, and surely all tend to set the stage for the presentation by raising questions in the minds of the prospect, questions that the salesperson can resolve as the proposition is presented.

Flattery Approach

A number of salespeople like to say something nice to the prospect at the outset of a sale. How you do this—the sincerity implied in the tone of your voice and in what you say—can be effective. But the use of flattery limits meeting the objectives of the approach. For instance: "Your new factory really fits the landscape. The architect must have spent a lot of time working out the details." Certainly any buyer will want to hear this type of compliment, but does it advance the sale? Not very much. Here are some other, more telling uses of the flattery approach.

"I just walked through your machine shop. Those new pieces of equipment really look great. Our new couplings should fit right into your maintenance plans."

"As I walked up the path, I noticed the new rosebushes. They certainly add to the appearance of your home. Then I got to wondering: Who would care for the garden if you were hospitalized for a long time?"

"Anyone who wears stylish clothes like that wool suit you have on today will appreciate our wide selection of ties."

"I've been past your home. It's quite impressive. Can't you just imagine this new station wagon parked in the driveway?"

The key to using flattery is whether you really mean what you are saying or whether you are saying the same thing to every prospect. Nothing is more ineffective than the use of artificial or labored compliments.

Referral Approach

Often a successful sale will pave the way for an introduction to other prospects. A satisfied customer will usually be prepared to suggest the names of several other people who might be interested in your proposition. Increasing your list of prospects by asking for these referral names is an excellent way to expand on your sales universe. Using this background in your approach can immediately set a friendly tone to the sale interview.

A simple, "Mary Jones told me you might be interested in our new encyclopedia offer," might create some resentment in the mind of the new prospect. Therefore, when you use a referral approach, you should consider a variety of ways to convey the information. For instance:

"When I showed these couplings to the people over at Ajax, they thought of you. That's why I'm here to demonstrate the strength of our new couplings."

"Mr. Prospect, John Buyer told me that you and he have the same problem—your couplings tend to break. That's why he suggested I stop to talk with you about our latest design."

"Good morning, Mr. Smith. Your colleague from the State University said you were searching for a new sales text. I'd like you to review this new work and let me have your opinion."

"Good evening. This pension plan is similar to the program Mr. and Mrs. Carpenter just bought. They gave me your name as a couple with similar needs and desires."

In other words, making a sales call because someone else has alerted you to a potential customer can give you access to a more responsive prospect. However, you should never assume that a referral is any less complex a sale. All you really stand to gain is a little more attention at the outset. From that point on, your proposition must stand on its own merits.

HOW MANY APPROACHES SHOULD YOU USE?

There is no magic to any one approach. The sales rep says something. The prospect either responds or does not respond. The salesperson tries another approach, seeking to ferret out some common ground with the prospect, an opening through which to further develop the sale. The entire process generally doesn't last more than a minute or two. At the end of that time, the salesperson either has been dismissed or is into the next phase of the sale. It's a trying, challenging, exciting moment.

A good salesperson, no matter how professional, is often nervous during the approach. Tension is a sure sign that you are properly keyed up to do your very best. Here are some examples of how the complete approach dialogue might evolve:

Salesperson: Good morning, Mr. Prospect. My name is John Sutton, and I represent the Universal Company. We sell a fine line of couplings and joints. (Introductory approach)

Prospect: Yes. (Abrupt)

Salesperson:	Our company would welcome the chance to survey your use of joints and couplings. There is no charge for this service, and when we have completed the work, you will receive a complete report. (Survey approach)
Prospect:	Heck, I thought you had immediate solutions. I don't have time for surveys. (Negative)
Salesperson:	Would you like to solve one of the main sources of complaints from your production department? (Curiosity approach)
Prospect:	I have so many complaints. Which one would you like to solve? (Interested)

This conversation lasted 40 seconds. Although it is not a very dramatic or exciting presentation, it did finally lead to a point where the salesperson was communicating with the buyer.

Salesperson:	Mr. Prospect, how many of these one-inch thread couplings do you think we produce each day? (Curiosity approach)
Prospect:	Who cares? (Annoynace)
Salesperson:	We recently conducted a survey of the entire machinery industry. One of the biggest problems is the length of threads on couplings. Is this true of your company? (Survey approach)
Prospect:	Well, we do have some problems with threads. But it certainly isn't our biggest problem. (Argument)
Salesperson:	How much would you be willing to pay for trouble-free couplings? (Question approach)
Prospect:	Not much, I can tell you that. (Show-me response)

This conversation lasted 29 seconds. The buyer seemed very negative. Still, within this brief time, the essential problem has been isolated. If the new couplings are anywhere near the old-style couplings in price, the sales representative may be on the way to a sale.

Salesperson:	One out of 20 pieces of equipment breaks down because of faulty couplings. (Shock approach)
Prospect:	So what? (Not very shocked)
Salesperson:	This full inch of threads on our new coupling means you will have fewer complaints from the production department. (Consumer benefit approach)
Prospect:	I never pay any attention to those idiots. (True??)

Salesperson:	Every time a coupling breaks, the production department has a fit. If I can show you a way to avoid some of that aggravation, would you be interested? (Question approach)
Prospect:	Not particularly. (Uninterested)
Salesperson:	To introduce our one-inch thread coupling, we are offering a special discount of 10 percent. (Bonus approach)
Prospect:	Will that make them any cheaper than the regular couplings? (Aha, a price buyer!)

It took 37 seconds to arouse this buyer and bring the conversation to the second phase of the sale.

This kind of success is not assured merely because the salesperson has evolved a number of approaches. But the odds for success shift to the side of the salesperson for two reasons. First is the preparation to travel a number of avenues to find the main road, the one the buyer has hidden from view. Second is the refusal to accept defeat at the first stumbling block. Buyer resistance is to be expected and anticipated. Preparation for this certainty is the best way to overcome obstacles.

In buying and selling situations, the person buying will have a limited number of statements to make. The professional salesperson can anticipate what that person will say and prepare to respond with a professional approach. The key is for the salesperson to know that many things can be said at this critical point in the sale, and to be ready with a number of responses. It means preparing several approaches before actually facing the prospect.

ADDITIONAL TIPS ON THE APPROACH

Other aspects of the approach, such as dress, attitude, and personality, were dealt with in Chapters 3 and 4. However, several additional approach considerations need to be examined at this point.

Who Does the Buying?

Whatever you are selling, first determine who has "buying authority." Talking with people who do not have any authority to make a purchase is a futile effort. The title "Purchasing Agent" does not necessarily signify buying authority. A PA may be only the person who carries out a specific function—placing orders from a predetermined source.

There is nothing wrong in asking who does the buying, or, "Who makes the decisions on where to buy?" In the case of a husband and wife, "Do you take care of the insurance, Mr. Jones?"

One of the worst mistakes made by salespeople is to present a proposition to the wrong person. It is imperative that you talk with the person who has the authority to buy!

ɤ Correct Use of the Buyer's Name

If at any time you plan to address the buyer by name, be certain you have the correct pronunciation. Unless the name is "Jones," assume nothing. Smyth might be pronounced "Smith," Gabbler might be pronounced "Gabe-ler," and who knows how to pronounce Papierowicz? (Pap-ear-o-witz).

Ask a secretary, the office clerk, or anyone around how to say the prospect's name properly. As a last resort, ask the prospect how the name should be pronounced. One way to do this is to take out a pad and pen and ask the person to spell the name so that you will have it as a permanent record. Invariably, the prospect will spell it and say it for your edification.

♦Business Cards

Never offer the prospect your business card as you make an approach. The idea that your name is printed in bold type is of very little significance at the beginning of a sale. Moreover, business cards are great for nail cleaning and ear scratching, two endeavors that detract greatly from your sales efforts. Also, once the prospect has your business card, you have lost that person's attention.

The proper use of a business card is to leave it with the prospect after the sale or at the conclusion of the interview. Your parting remark might be, "Here is my card. You are free to call me collect to answer any questions you may have."

Receptionists often ask for business cards to send in to the purchasing agent. Some salespeople purposely don't carry cards for fear of being stopped before they actually face the prospect. Instead they will send in a message that they just ran out of cards and are waiting for a new batch to come from the printer. This idea may sound like heresy, but your observations of what happens to business cards will prove revealing. Whenever possible, save them till the conclusion of the interview.

SUMMARY

The approach is the first face-to-face contact of the salesperson and the prospect. The approach has four main objectives:

To gain attention
To awaken needs

To qualify the prospect

To prepare for the presentation

Every approach should seek to reach one or more of these objectives.

Twelve methods are available to the professional salesperson for making a dynamic, interesting approach:

Introductory approach

Product approach

Consumer benefit approach

Shock approach

Theatrical approach

Question approach

Bonus approach

Curiosity approach

Survey approach

Declaration approach

Flattery approach

Referral approach

Be prepared to use as many approaches as necessary to bring the sale to the next phase—the presentation. Ability to roll with the punches and bounce back with another approach is of paramount importance. Along the way, the professional salesperson should:

Be sure to speak with the person who has "buying authority."

Be certain of the correct pronunciation of the prospect's name.

Seek to use the business card at the close of the interview.

A SUCCESS STORY

Mac was a salesman for a distribution firm selling office supplies and equipment. One of the new products in the line was an automatic copying machine for small offices. To his chagrin, the secretary had insisted he send his business card into the buyer's office. A message came back, "I can give you only five minutes."

All his work in creating a vibrant sales plan seemed wasted; he required at least 15 minutes for a complete sales interview. As he walked through the door, he realized he needed a fresh approach.

"Mr. Prospect," he said. "I appreciate that you can only give me five minutes of your time. However, it will take me only 2½ minutes to copy those six letters on your desk."

The successful sales interview lasted 30 minutes.

QUESTIONS FOR CLASS DISCUSSION

1. Write a consumer benefit approach for the sale of a new automobile. Then write one for a new set of tires. How many different consumer benefits did the class prepare? Discuss.
2. How does advertising prepare a prospect for a new product or service? Can advertising carry out the sales function?
3. What is meant by the expression, "professional buyer"? Contrast the buying habits of the "professional buyer" with those of the public in general.
4. Write a curiosity approach to gain the attention of a prospect if you were selling ballpoint pens; filing cabinets; shag rugs.
5. Which of the following characteristics would aid you in qualifying a prospect: the prospect's appearance or accent, or the size of the prospect's car? Explain.
6. How could you use a product approach to sell insurance? advertising space in a newspaper?
7. Write a dialogue including survey, shock, and consumer benefit approaches from the point of view of a seller of tape recorders.
8. Explain the objectives of the approach.
9. Construct a sales approach using the question technique only.

CASE 8—SEYMOUR FLINK MAKES A BAD BEGINNING

Thirteen days didn't seem very many to Seymour Flink. He felt that he needed more training and field experience before he was asked to attempt a cold-turkey sale. But there was no stopping the sales manager, who insisted, "Practical experience is the best teacher." How could he fight that kind of logic?

"One last word of advice," said the sales manager. "When we get inside the store, don't worry. The worst thing that can happen is that you won't get an order."

"I can't help feeling nervous," complained Seymour.

Quickly they slipped out of the car and walked toward the door of the A & J Sporting Goods store. Once inside, Seymour cautiously asked a clerk, "Where is the manager?"

A pointing finger showed the way to a glass-enclosed office where a man sat hunched over long lists of figures. Knocking gently on the door,

Seymour watched as the man slowly lifted his head and then motioned the two men to come in. "Yes?" he said.

Seymour, unnerved by the name in front and wary of his sales manager behind, moved foward, extended his hand and said warmly, "Good morning, Mr. . . . I'm sorry. The man outside forgot to tell me your name."

"I'm Jonathan Burns," came the reply.

"Well, Jonathan, good morning. I'm Seymour Flink, and this is my sales manager, Harry Jones. We represent the Marine Printing Company, and we have some new styles of letterheads that might work for you."

"What do you want with me?" asked the man.

"Well, these letterheads seem like the kind of interesting . . . I mean, we'd like to sell you some letterheads."

"Oh."

"Would you mind if I start all over?"

"Not at all," the man laughed.

"Our letterheads are only $9.75 a ream imprinted. We can put any design you wish on each page."

The man sat quietly. He looked coolly into Seymour's eyes and said nothing.

"We also have envelopes to go with the letterheads."

"That's nice," said the man. "Why don't you leave your business card, and I'll tell the office manager."

"Don't you do the buying?" asked Seymour in surprise.

"Excuse me for interrupting," the sales manager said. "Would you mind if we just bid you good day. My young friend here is new at the selling game. We'll call again after he has more experience." With that, he took Seymour by the elbow and steered him toward the door.

1. Why did the sales manager want to leave the store?
2. What error did the sales manager make?
3. Was Seymour Flink prepared for the sale?
4. Can you write approach statements that might help Seymour next time around?
5. What errors did Seymour make?

EXERCISE 8

Based on the exercises in the earlier chapters, you have developed product knowledge and preapproach information about your future job potential.

As you get ready for your job interview, you should prepare twelve different approaches. To help in this process, write how the dialogue might evolve, using the various approaches from this chapter.

SALES PROBLEM 8—AFTER THE SHOW IS OVER

It's a new and growing phenomenon of selling, the trade show. For Harry Throckmorton, it had been his first experience. The flow of customers at the two-day session was great, and many of his accounts stopped and placed substantial orders. In fact, it was hard for him to realize how important these yearly events were to his company.

Now, the week following the show, he wasn't sure whether his customers would want to see him on his regular calls. Here are some thoughts presented by three different salespeople:

Sales Rep #1:   On my first call after the show, I would follow up on the items each customer had ordered. I would verify that they were satisfied and that the merchandise was everything they expected. If there were any problems at all, I would certainly attend to them.

After I made sure all was well, I would suggest other items that were similar to or complementary to the specials that were ordered at the show. Not only that, I would still be after the regular order.

Sales Rep #2:   This just happened to me, and some of the show orders are still being delivered. Quite frankly, my people were overloaded, so I sat down with them to figure out how to move the excess inventory and turn the good show buys into profit for my customers.

Usually, show specials move rapidly. Still, there is the question of crowded stockrooms. And there is still the need to keep selling the regular products the customers order each week.

Sales Rep #3:   I have experienced several shows, and in one way, they are a pain. I simply continue to try to bring new ideas to my customers and new products as they are available. To do this, I make extra use of the marketing tools my company subscribes to, things like weekly specials and product brochures.

Many times, after a show, the customers lose track of the little things they have to buy every time I call. It's very important for me to keep track of these things and not let taking a smaller-than-usual order become a burden. After all, I want the customers to buy from me long-term, not just during a show.

(Some people have difficulty thinking of themselves as a "product." You might find it easier to think of yourself as a "machine" that provides services for the prospective employer.)

Here's another exercise. Prepare six approach statements to use in a retail selling situation if you worked in a shopping mall selling men's (or women's) clothing.

9

THE PRESENTATION

PERFORMANCE OBJECTIVES

After you have read this chapter and completed the Questions for Class Discussion, the Case, the Sales Problem, and the Exercise, you should be able to do the following:

1. Describe and explain the four objectives of the presentation.
2. Give seven methods for making an effective presentation.
3. Complete a presentation dialogue using three or more confidence-building methods.
4. Contrast the three ways to handle competition.
5. Differentiate between a canned sales talk and a prepared sales plan.
6. Prepare the presentation phase of the Heart of the Sale for use during a job interview.

DEVELOPING THE OPENING GAMBIT

(This is the next phase in the Heart of Sale, which began, in Chapter 8, with the approach.)

"You certainly carry a good line of stylish men's suits. However, when you add our line of high-fashion garments, you will have something out of the ordinary to offer your customers," the manufacturer's representative said.

"But how is that going to make me more profit?" asked the merchant.

"First, our reputation as a quality house will attract your customers. Second, we offer you an extra discount on initial orders. Third, our advertising program helps to promote your business. I'm sure you will agree that our company has an excellent reputation."

"Sure, you're known. But how does that get me extra business?" questioned the prospect.

"I can tell you from personal experience with other stores like your own that there is a healthy demand for our high-style suits."

"Can you prove that?"

"Yes. Here are two testimonial letters from stores well out of your trading area. I also have sales data from other outlets. All my information remains confidential until a customer gives me the okay to use it. After all, when you deal with me, I respect your confidence. After you have handled our line for six months, I'll ask your permission to relate your experiences to other, noncompeting stores."

The onrush of an exciting approach is meant to attract attention and awaken needs. At the same time, it can be too fast a pace for the prospect. Therefore, the presentation phase slows the pace of the sale and establishes the salesperson and the company.

One old-time sales representative likens the presentation to "getting a foothold," as opposed to the approach, which is only a "toehold." It is the time to expand on your opening remarks, to give them added validity and believability. Remember, in the approach you are only about one minute into the Heart of the Sale; the next minute or two devoted to the presentation will launch you into the actual demonstration.

WHAT ARE THE OBJECTIVES OF THE PRESENTATION?

The presentation restates the facts used in the approach and at the same time permits salespeople to properly identify and introduce themselves and their company. This need not be an introduction by name; rather, it is an introduction by deed, history, fact, and experience. For instance:

"Our company is 102 years old." Compare this: "In over a century of manufacturing stylish clothes, we have gained a good deal of practical experience."

In the second example, the emphasis is on experience gained over a long period of time. The first example merely states a fact. How you tell your story can be as important as the story itself. More important, these stories should meet the objectives of the presentation.

To Establish the Disadvantages of the Present Situation

People continue to do things as they have always done until they discover (or learn) better ways to accomplish their goals. Almost every great invention or discovery faced untold opposition because people wanted to believe what they had always believed. Today, we accept the fact that the world is round. Yet in 1490, Columbus had to do a massive "selling" job to convince Queen Isabella of that fact.

People scoffed at the idea that a carriage could be propelled forward by a machine and not by a horse. In fact, manufacturers of buggy whips refused to accept that their product would no longer be needed.

When frozen foods were introduced, only a few food stores would consider stocking these products. Yet today, we recognize that frozen foods represent the fastest-growing segment of the food industry.

The only assumption that a salesperson can safely make is that prospects are reasonably satisfied with the current condition or situation. If they were not satisfied and happy, the profession of selling would not be a vital part of our economy, because prospects would seek out new products and services themselves. It is the salesperson who presents to the prospect the advantages of a product and at the same time indicates the disadvantages of the product currently in use. This is accomplished in part during the presentation.

A note of caution: It is always better to stress the virtues of your product or service. Avoid condemning what the prospect is currently doing or the product that has already been purchased, because this earlier decision by the prospect may have been a good decision—at that time.

To Be Accepted as the Salesperson

How many times have you heard, "He's a great guy, once you get to know him." Well, there just isn't enough time for the prospect to "get to know" the salesperson during the early moments of the sale. First impressions are important!

A salesperson can do certain things to ensure immediate acceptance. They revolve around appearance, attitude, tone of voice, and general behavior—all those subjects involved with communication (Chapter 3).

From the discussion about sales personality (Chapter 4), we know how important these attributes can be. One sales rep for a meat-distribution firm always stopped at a flower shop for a white carnation. It became his insignia. Only on special occasions would he alter this pattern and buy a red carnation to wear in his lapel. He chose always to dress in a conservative fashion, because he felt this would be acceptable to all possible customers. "I don't want anybody to turn me off because of the way I look," was his attitude.

This is a perfectly natural analysis. What this man was saying is that after the prospect got to know him, how he dressed was not very important, but at the beginning of a sale, he felt he had to look just right.

In terms of the general attitude of the salesperson, a serious demeanor is always acceptable. It's safe. Loud, raucous laughter is acceptable to only a few people. Off-color stories are generally out of place. You can always tell a humorous story later in the sale, but the reason you are there, and the proposition at hand, are serious business and should not be treated lightly.

It's interesting to note that all the traits parents demand of children apply to salespeople. Clean fingernails, neat clothes, combed hair, polished shoes, brushed teeth, and a smiling face are among the first things people see when you meet them. Some companies are so insistent on these visible signs that periodic checks are made of all the outside salespeople. One company won't permit its salesmen to wear anything but white shirts, and the saleswomen may not wear pantsuits.

To Have Your Company Accepted

Most prospects will have a "nothing" attitude about the company you represent, short of having had a good (or bad) experience at an earlier time. They may even have difficulty relating to such an inanimate object as "a company." Many firms of national import are known by their reputations. IBM, Xerox, and General Motors are all widely known today, but 40 years ago, there was no Xerox. To a large extent, the popularity of these national companies was built through the efforts of superior sales forces that represented them in the field.

By far the majority of business houses are relatively unknown beyond their area of specialty. This means that sales representatives must find ways to demonstrate that their firms are the kinds of companies with which the prospect will want to do business. By alluding to certain aspects of your company, you can achieve the desired effect.

"One of our 16 trucks passes your door at least three times a week." The implied size of your firm, "16 trucks," will impress the prospect.

"Last week we sold over 400 of these new, high-style ties." Any store that sells that many ties in one week must be doing something right.

"Our company just built a new 50,000-square-foot warehouse just so we could expand our line to serve the trade better." That's a pretty big building.

There may come a time when the prospect wants to know more about your company, its history and background. But the second or third minute of the sale is not the time to get bogged down with details that do not move the sale forward. That is why small nuggets of information should be tossed out to give at least an inkling that the prospect will be dealing with a successful concern.

To Prepare for the Demonstration

The final objective of the presentation is to open the door to a demonstration of your product or service. A review of the many steps you have taken in the sale leads directly to a display of your wares. You have attracted attention, awakened needs, qualified the prospect (during the approach), sought recognition of the disadvantages of the present situation, and gained personal acceptance and the acceptance of your company (during the presentation). Now you are ready to actually show what you have to offer.

No sale moves in perfect order. Any of the aforementioned points might be missed or improperly covered. The crucial questions are, "Is the prospect ready for the demonstration?" "Are YOU ready for the demonstration?" "Have you built enough confidence to proceed to the next phase of the sale?" "Do you have the information you need to relate your product or service to the prospect's needs and desires?"

HOW TO MAKE THE PRESENTATION EFFECTIVE

Now that the prospect has recovered from your energetic approach, it is time to begin developing a healthy relationship built on mutual trust and confidence. Uppermost in your mind should be the thought that a sale results in satisfaction to both parties. One of the best ways to ensure that dual gratification is to create an atmosphere of respect—for you and your company. You do that with what you say and how well you listen during the presentation segment of the sale.

Keep Your Claims Conservative

People in selling should be excited about their products or services. This excitement should show in how they present themselves and their product, not in the claims they make about the product. To gear himself for the day's efforts, one salesperson used to look in the mirror each day and say, "Harold, be enthusiastic!!"

This same salesperson avoided the use of superlatives in the sales talk. He tried never to say:

"We have the best . . ."
"Our company is the biggest . . ."
"Surveys show we sell the most . . ."

Not that these facts weren't true; but he understood that even verifiable facts may not be acceptable to the prospect—some things are just too immense to believe. Our couplings representative knows that the company produced 5 million units last year. But the prospect who buys 100 or 200 pieces at a time will find this figure too staggering to believe. Therefore, any claim in this area should be modest, one that the prospect can easily accept.

"Our experience in the manufacture of couplings is extensive. We produce thousands of units each week."
"Because we mass-produce one-inch thread couplings, each unit is precision ground."
"New, sophisticated equipment has tripled our production."

In each of these examples, the salesperson has implied or suggested that the company is a major factor in the coupling business. But how would you react if the salesperson had said, "We sell more couplings than anybody in the industry," or, "Our company is the biggest in the field," or, "New equipment has run our production up to over 5 million units a year."

Each of these statements raises a question in the mind of the prospect. "More couplings than what other companies?" "Bigger than whom?" "Five million units?" (This company is too big for me to handle.)

If you want people to believe you, tell them honest facts that are believable. It may be necessary to tell less than the whole story at this time. As the prospect develops confidence in you, there will be more willingness to accept more of what you have to say. It is always easier to make small claims and increase the size later. It is very difficult to make large claims (even though they may be true) and have them accepted.

Show Respect for Your Company

Always remember: You are the company, and the company is you. When you speak disparagingly about your company, it sets in motion a train of thought in the mind of the prospect:

The person doesn't like the job.
There is dissatisfaction with the product.

There is unhappiness with the company.
If I place an order, will I be satisfied with the salesperson?
Probably not!

Even some very positive demands of your company can have a negative effect, depending on how you present them. For instance, compare these two statements:

"My sales manager insists that I lug around this entire product list even though only 10 percent of the line is important."
"I always have our complete product list available so that every customer will have the chance to review overall requirements."

If you were the buyer, how would these two statements affect you? Obviously, the first is the reaction of a carping salesperson who resents unusual orders. The second statement means that the sales representative respects the instructions of the supervisor and is mindful that one part of the job is to satisfy the prospect. Can you imagine the effect on a smoothly

WHEN YOU SHOW RESPECT FOR
YOUR COMPANY, THE PROSPECT GAINS
CONFIDENCE IN THE PROPOSITION.

Figure 9-1

running interview when the salesperson says, "I have to run out to my car to get the catalog"?

A salesperson can verbally and visually show respect for the company in a number of ways:

"We're (the company and I) very proud of the success of our new one-inch thread couplings."

"In addition to the new one-inch thread couplings, we have a number of other machine-tooled products. Here is our new catalog, complete with photographs and prices."

"Let me point out some of the features of this insurance program our company originated and developed."

"My sales manager had this same air conditioner installed at home to verify that it will do what the company says it will do."

If you don't show that you believe in your company, how can you expect the prospect to believe?

Use Factual Reports

Every industry has its own sources of factual data. Trade associations gather information on the most minute details of every industry. Salespeople are expected to be conversant with the workings and activities of these associations. The constant outpouring of reports and data can and should be used as sales aids.

There are also one or more trade publications (business magazines) in every industry that relate experiences, new methods, and business aids. Periodically, these magazines take industrywide surveys and often scrutinize small segments of the field to which they are devoted.

A third source of broad-based data is the Government Printing Office (Washington, D.C. 20402), which produces an enormous amount of material relating to every phase of life, society, business, and government. Whatever field of selling you are in, the GPO has booklets and pamphlets with statistical data on it.

Some large organizations do market research on their own, digging beneath the surface to better understand the demands, requirements, and future needs of their customers.

The salesperson who draws on these sources of information and help demonstrates to the prospect a sincere concern with the industry. At the same time, the salesperson can bring significant data to the attention of the buyer, who might otherwise be too busy to keep up with the changing market. In short, the salesperson has the opportunity to be a fount of valuable information that the prospect will recognize as meaningful and useful.

During the presentation, salespeople use this background material to show that they are conversant with the industry. Ultimately, the information will build confidence, because the salesperson's knowledge of the field is deep. Here are some examples of the use of factual data:

"According to *Restaurant Business* magazine, people prefer breaded veal cutlet to spaghetti and meat balls. That's why I want to show you these frozen cutlets."

"Our entire sales force attended the trade show in Atlantic City last month. That was the first time we displayed this new one-inch thread coupling."

"Here is a pamphlet I just received from the Government Printing Office, describing some coupling tests. Note the difference in strengths."

"In the last issue of *Automotive Fleet,* there was an article about the virtues of long-thread couplings."

"The government just completed a major study of pollution in small streams. It really shows a need for our new control unit."

Some salespeople pride themselves on knowing not only their own product line but also how their company fits into the entire industry. Projecting this image is an important facet of building confidence and gaining acceptance as a valuable source of supply and information.

Explain Guarantees

Guarantees are one of the most abused sales aids—particularly when used to develop confidence and respect. Virtually every product or service carries some kind of guarantee. Prospects usually pay little attention, because they are uncertain what the guarantee means.

"We guarantee this dishwasher for 18 months" says nothing.

"We guarantee all moving parts in this dishwasher for 18 months" says more.

"We guarantee all moving parts in this dishwasher for 18 months, and only charge a nominal service fee to replace broken parts" says a good deal more.

When the salesperson introduces the company and the guarantee, a complete explanation should detail the kind of protection the prospect can expect. If the guarantee comes in written form, all the better. If it is not written, then the prospect must accept the word of the salesperson. The significance of placing reliance and trust in a salesperson is apparent. Your word is important.

Although guarantees can be touchy subjects, they also represent an opportunity for the salesperson to make a strong impression on the prospect. They also provide the chance to demonstrate the advantages of dealing with that representative's firm:

"These one-inch thread couplings are guaranteed not to break under any circumstances for twelve months. We will replace all broken units."

"Here's how we guarantee these new one-inch thread couplings. You can use them 24 hours a day under the toughest conditions, and we will replace any that break. This is good for 24 months. If any coupling breaks in six months' time, we will survey how it was used and then replace the broken part. That way, we can avoid future problems."

"Under normal usage, this washing machine will last ten years. However, we guarantee the motor and the drum against any kind of usage for one full year."

"Sunlight will affect these drapes eventually, but we have a color comparison chart, and if they should fade within two years, we will replace them."

The points made in these statements are specific and believable. If the prospect has any question about them, it can lead to further discussion, which will explore the advantages of your proposition at the same time that it builds confidence.

Cite the Reputation of Your Company

How do you get across the idea that your company has a good name? Just saying it doesn't make it so. The salesperson has several ways to refer to the firm as a substantial, reliable, noteworthy organization. These references might be in the area of size, history, community service, or position in the industry:

"After seven years of research and study, we have finally produced a one-inch thread coupling that withstands severe punishment."

"The president of our company served on the board of the industry convention. In fact, he delivered a speech on the effects of couplings on machinery breakdown."

"Did you notice the picture of my sales manager in *Modern Nursing Home* magazine? She just received an award from the company for 25 years of service."

"Our design department has come up with more than 30 improvements in materials in the past ten years."

"*Business Week* magazine did a cover story on the computer industry, and our company got some excellent mentions."

Each piece of information adds to the total understanding of your company. Little by little, the salesperson can increase that fund of knowledge, so that finally the prospect has a good solid regard for the company.

Present Testimonials

Satisfied customers sometimes write letters of recommendation based on the performance of products or services. These testimonials have a varying effect, depending on who said what, and to whom the salesperson shows the testimonial.

When Lee Trevino, the golfing great, claims that a certain pill relieves his headaches, the public accepts this as a paid statement. On the other hand, when he says he uses a particular brand of golf clubs, that has a greater effect. When TV personality Barbara Walters speaks on behalf of a certain perfume, the effect is far less than when she tells about some of the famous people she has interviewed.

In both instances, the appeal is to the "less-than-professional" prospect. The purchasing agent for a hospital will remain unaffected by Trevino's statement about headache pills, and the golf pro will be unmoved by his use of Brand A golf clubs. However, more people will be affected by Trevino's statements than by a similar testimonial by John Doe, and women who wish to emulate Barbara Walters might switch to her perfume. Department-store purchasing agents, on the other hand, would be little affected by her words, other than to consider their effect on the buying public.

A sincere testimonial explaining how a product helped solve a problem can impress a professional buyer. Some buyers might even respond to the fact that a national company buys and uses your products. Others will be unaffected.

Letters of testimonial that were not solicited by the company tend to be more effective. Here's how they can be used during the presentation:

"When we first came out with the one-inch thread coupling, we asked for comments from 20 customers in different parts of the industry. As you can see, they generally favor the longer thread."

"This letter explains the success XYZ Company has had with our one-inch thread couplings."

"Here's an unsolicited letter of recommendation from the Giant Manufacturing Company. They buy a good many of our couplings."

"We had this testimonial reproduced in an ad for our trade magazine."

One major drawback to the use of testimonials is that it asks the prospect to take time out to read something. This disrupts the forward progress of the sales interview. One way to avoid this is to note that the testimonials exist, and offer to show them at a later time. Once they are in the hands of the prospect, you have lost complete attention.

Cite Personal Experiences

Every salesperson has more contact with more prospects and customers than a nonsalesperson has. Salespeople are exposed to a greater variety of problems and difficulties than is any individual prospect. Thus, the prospect who says, "My situation is different from everybody else's," is not taking full advantage of the useful information the salesperson possesses.

How can any one prospect be "different" to the professional salesperson who has dealt with hundreds of "different" prospects? As a matter of fact, the "I'm different" excuse is a brushoff.

How you offer information based on your experiences can be a delicate matter. It is safe to assume that the prospect is reasonably happy with the way things are going. Being told there is a better way can almost be an insult. Therefore, it is important to suggest new ideas and products in a gentle fashion, so that the idea seems self-conceived by the prospect.

"Last week, a customer told me that couplings wear longer when a drop of oil is placed at the joint each day."

"The new couplings are packed in a wood crate instead of a cardboard box. Several customers wrote the company and said they use the crates as storage bins."

"A few of my clients think of their Social Security benefits as a base for their retirement program. Then they buy insurance for a larger income."

"Many of my customers fry in vegetable shortening because there is less absorption. It prevents the french fries from getting greasy."

No one likes to be criticized for buying the wrong product or to be told that it isn't being used properly. The professional salesperson has a good deal of background in how to get the best use out of products, but great care must be exhibited when trying to express these thoughts to a prospect.

THE PRESENTATION DIALOGUE

Over and over we have stressed that the professional salesperson is flexible. This attribute is necessary because selling deals with individuals, each of whom is different. By preparing to meet these differences and being equipped with a number of ways to meet unfolding situations, the salesperson should be ready with several responses during any portion of the sales interview.

Each of the following presentation dialogues is a follow-up to the approach dialogues offered in Chapter 8:

Salesperson: Our experience in the manufacture of couplings is extensive. We produce thousands of units each week. (Conservative claim)

Prospect: We don't really use that many couplings. (Negative)

Salesperson: In addition to the new one-inch-thread couplings, we have a number of other machine-tooled products. Here is our new catalog, complete with photographs and prices. (Respect for company)

Prospect: Okay. Leave it and I'll examine it when I have time. (Brushoff)

Salesperson: Here is a pamphlet I just ordered from the Government Printing Office, which describes some coupling tests. Note the difference in the strengths. (Factual data)

Prospect: You seem to have a lot of information on couplings. (Interested and attentive)

Salesperson: After seven years of research and study, we have finally produced a one-inch-thread coupling that withstands severe punishment. (Reputation of company)

Prospect: Well, a coupling is just a coupling. (This buyer is now involved.)

Salesperson: These one-inch-thread couplings are guaranteed not to break under any circumstances for twelve months. We will replace all broken units. (Guarantee)

After 68 seconds, the interview has reached firmer ground. Even though the buyer was not receptive, there is a growing acceptance of the salesperson and the company.

Salesperson: Here's how we guarantee these new one-inch-thread couplings. You can use them 24 hours a day under the toughest conditions and we will replace any that break. This is good for 24 months. (Guarantee)

Prospect: Yes, but who said the price was good? (Demand)

Salesperson: Here, I'll show you the price list.

In 13 seconds, this prospect is ready to talk business. It might be possible at this point to jump right to the quotation of prices and close the sale. Although the salesperson is aiming for a demonstration, the main purpose of any sale is to get the order. If the prospect is ready, try to close the sale.

Salesperson:	Because we mass-produce one-inch-thread couplings, each unit is precision-ground. (Conservative claim)
Prospect:	I think I read something about them in one of the magazines. (Mild interest)
Salesperson:	The president of our company served on the board of the industry convention. In fact, he delivered a speech on the effects of couplings on machinery breakdown. (Reputation of the company)
Prospect:	No, I'm sure I read it in a magazine.
Salesperson:	We had this testimonial letter reproduced into an ad for our trade publication.
Prospect:	Well, it sounds reasonable. But we've been dealing with the ABC Company for twelve years. (Objection—competition)
Salesperson:	*(acknowledges the existence of competition)* If any coupling breaks in six months' time, we will survey how it was used and then replace the broken part. This way, we can avoid future problems. (Guarantee)
Prospect:	I get a good guarantee from my present supplier. (Objection)

Without realizing it, the sales interview has passed to the meeting-objections phase, or has simply encountered a smoke screen. This does not mean that the salesperson will not have to go through the demonstration. It means that the sale is becoming more complex, and the prepared professional salesperson must be flexible enough to deal with problems as they arise. Each of these sample dialogues presents a different way to move the interview toward a successful concusion. The salesperson and the prospect must continue to communicate if there is to be a transfer of product or service.

SPECIAL OBSERVATIONS DURING THE PRESENTATION

A prospect and a salesperson are two distinct individuals. What happens between them is unique—something that may never be repeated in exactly the same way. But experience suggests that certain things happen during this specific phase of the sale that require some comment and examination.

Always have several responses during a portion of a sales presentation.

Competition

The knowledge that the prospect is already buying a product or service is a sign that there will be competition with which the salesperson must contend. There are three attitudes or positions the salesperson may assume when dealing with competition:

A Friendly Word.   Dismiss the competition with a smile and say, "Nice company." Pay as little attention as possible when the prospect mentions a competitor. For instance, "Yes, I know them," or "Yes, I've heard of them." Thus, you acknowledge their existence without committing yourself one way or the other.

Handle with Care.   If you must deal with a competitor's product, do it gently. Don't smile as you point out disadvantages. Be serious, but not nasty. Suggest that the opposition has tried its best, but your company has produced a superior product.

Frontal Attack.   Salespeople often say something negative about a competitor. Try in every way possible to avoid falling into this trap, for it is surely a trap. The natural reaction of the prospect is to come to the defense of the person or company attacked. While you are explaining why your competition is "bad," the prospect is telling you why the competition is "good."

Dealing with competition is like walking on eggs. You must tread lightly, seeking never to completely disturb what exists, at the same time that you try to impress the prospect with the need for a fresh egg in the basket. Many salespeople become very defensive at the first mention of competition. It takes considerable training to be able to cope with competition on an unemotional basis.

Interruptions

The ringing telephone can have the most disruptive influence on a successful sales interview. Just as you are beginning to reach some common ground with the prospect, the phone rings. When this happens, move out of your chair toward a spot where you are presumably out of hearing. Show the prospect the courtesy of not listening to the conversation. An offer to leave the room is certainly appropriate.

If you decide to stay, reread your sales material or busy yourself with some work that will indicate you are not paying attention to the talk. Then when the call is completed, retrace your own conversation with the prospect. Don't return to where you were; start a sentence or two earlier and repeat your last two or three statements. This is necessary in order to redirect the attention of the prospect to the proposition at hand.

When to Change the Subject

The professional salesperson guides the sales interview along a predetermined path. When trouble looms, change the subject. You can do this by taking note of a photograph on the buyer's desk, or by asking a question:

"I noticed you have a set of golf clubs in the corner. Are you a golfer?"
"The last time I called, you were in Chicago. Did you fly?"
"Did you catch that fish mounted on the wall?"

This technique has saved the day for many salespeople. After a few moments of conversation, you can return to your own sale; only now, take a different tack, avoiding the problem that caused you to change the subject in the first place.

Challenging Statements

Some prospects tend to be aggressive and make statements that challenge the salesperson. These should be handled gently; answered softly. If you have done something wrong, accept the blame. Don't argue. Allow that the prospect is always right, only suggest that there may be an acceptable reason for any disagreement.

"I'm sorry the delivery was delayed. The next time, I'll personally check with the shipping department."
"I tried to reach you by phone, but the lines were jammed."
"It's unfortunate that the vases were broken when the shipment arrived. I'll call you first thing in the morning, as soon as I have checked with the office to see how to handle this claim."

It is always best to retreat slightly, and then return to your sale. Overaggressive prospects often try to rattle the salesperson. The best response is a soft voice, adherence to the facts—and even a smile.

The Canned Sales Talk

Many years ago, the profession of selling received great impetus with the introduction of the canned sales talk. A completely prepared sales interview was memorized by the salesperson for use in making a sales presentation. The advantages of this system have helped many companies achieve great success.

Although we have no argument with the philosophy and practices of the canned sales talk, the purpose of this text is to assist people in preparing

ALTHOUGH CANNED SALES PRESENTATIONS
HAVE THEIR PLACE, PROFESSIONAL
SALESPEOPLE PREFER TO CREATE
THEIR OWN.

Figure 9-2

their own sales interviews. Each system has its proper place. The reader who joins an organization that uses the canned sales talk will receive good training in how to apply the many principles involved. It is a significant part of the selling parade.

It is the contention of this text that salespeople are stronger and more flexible, interested, and motivated when trained to creatively prepare their own sales plan.

SUMMARY

The presentation is the time to fortify the advances you have made with a dynamic approach. The presentation has four objectives:

To establish the disadvantages of the present situation
To have yourself accepted as the salesperson
To have your company accepted
To prepare for the demonstration

During the presentation, you should try to establish as many of the objectives as possible. They are all intended to build confidence and respect for you and your company. Seven methods and techniques are applicable during the presentation:

Keep your claims conservative.
Show respect for your company.
Use factual reports.
Explain guarantees.
Cite the reputation of your company.
Present testimonials.
Cite personal experiences.

Along the way, take note of certain problem areas. In general, they should be dealt with in a genteel fashion:

Always treat competition with care and feeling.
Do not put the prospect in the position of defending your competition.
Be prepared to handle interruptions.
When confronted by a big problem, change the subject.
When something is wrong, accept the blame gracefully.

In one sense, the presentation is a cooling-off period during which the salesperson secures the ground gained as the rsult of a dramatic approach. The confidence gained in these moments is the platform for a thorough demonstration.

A SUCCESS STORY

Harriet Leader wanted the Alpha Company account very badly. She knew her sales plan was strong, but something was missing. One day she walked around the outside of the Alpha plant, looking for ideas that would set her professional style on the right path. As she passed the receiving platform, she heard the warehouse manager arguing with a truck driver making a delivery.

Here is a chance, she thought, to stress the excellent service of her company—a service that included delivery by the company drivers in their own trucks. However, she didn't want to appear too obvious, so she decided to slip the information into the presentation portion of her sales plan.

After her snappy approach, the buyer asked her to sit down. She began, "Among other things, Mr. Buyer, our company has six shipping docks, where we load orders on our own trucks."

"Everybody has shipping docks," smiled the buyer.

"That's true," said Harriet. "But for the last 20 years, we have been sending company drivers on all deliveries."

"So?"

"It's part of our policy," said Harriet, "to ensure pleasant, courteous delivery."

"What about your product line?" asked the buyer.

"I'd like to show you our line," she responded, reaching for her briefcase. "But I'd like you to keep in mind that all our merchandise will be delivered when you want it and placed where you want it, by our own delivery people."

It was a good point to establish—one that Harriet knew would build confidence and respect and help her nail down an order.

QUESTIONS FOR CLASS DISCUSSION

1. How do you explain the fact that most people are satisfied with their present sources of supply? Can the salesperson turn this to an advantage? How?
2. Have you ever been "turned off" by the way a salesperson spoke to you? Describe the situation.
3. If you were trying to sell someone on attending this college, what kind of confidence-building statements would you prepare?
4. Someone has just told you another college is better than this institution. Give three possible ways to reply to this statement.
5. What is the difference between a canned sales talk and a prepared sales plan? Which do you prefer? Why?
6. How does a new-model typewriter cause dissatisfaction in the mind of the prospect? Is this equally true of new houses? the latest fashion designs?
7. Name three sources of information about the real estate industry; electrical-appliance field; machine-tool industry.
8. Describe an instance when you had to rely on a guarantee. Were you satisfied?
9. Have you read any testimonials recently? What effect did they have on you? Why?
10. If you were the sales representative for Prentice-Hall, how would you convey confidence to college professors interested in using this text in a sales course? Write three confidence-building statements.

CASE 9—SAM KAYE DUPLICATES THE PRESENTATION

The slim black briefcase rested on the desk of Thelma Marks. Its shiny exterior caught the sun streaming through the window. Sam Kaye was 35 seconds into his sale when he said, "Inside this black case is a piece of equipment our company has been working on for seven years. Now, that's a long time to develop a single product, don't you agree?"

"Mr. Kaye," said the buyer. "Whether I agree or not isn't very important. You started out by telling me you had a product that would save our company money. Now, let's not delay any longer. My time is valuable, and I have a number of things to do today."

Sam opened the case easily and folded out an inner flap that formed a tent. Then he slipped a heavy cardboard layer from the other side and flipped a switch. "This unit has been modified so that you can use it with batteries or the conventional electrical outlet. Our engineers worked two years to miniaturize the circuits to make a portable copying machine."

"A copying machine?" asked Ms. Marks incredulously.

Now Sam stood erect. "You know we have made the larger office copying machine for 22 years, Ms. Marks. We're one of the biggest in the field. Each year, we produce more than 8,000 units. That's why our people spent so much time working on a smaller unit, one you can actually carry to appointments and to places where an electrical outlet might not be available. Have you ever traveled with one of your designers and found you wanted to make a copy of a drawing on the spot?"

"That's really not much of a problem."

"Last week in Detroit, I was with a buyer who always seemed in need of copying blueprints out in the field. This briefcase-size unit fits into the car trunk very nicely."

"I just don't see how it will help me."

"We did a survey of all the users of our big machines, and the results show that 70 percent of them wanted some kind of smaller, portable unit. This agreed with a survey made by the Copying Machine Association. They found that 69 percent of the users wanted a portable unit."

"I believe what you say."

By this time, the machine had warmed up, and Sam Kaye inserted a sensitized sheet of paper. "I have here a copy of these two surveys. I'm going to make a copy for you."

1. Did the approach and presentation overlap?
2. How was Sam Kaye going to save money with this machine?
3. Will this copier work while flying in a plane?
4. Has the presentation overlapped into the demonstration?
5. Can you think of any other selling points?

EXERCISE 9

People often say to a prospect (or a prospective employer), "You can have confidence in me."

Although this is an important characteristic, the prospect (or potential employer) needs more proof than a simple statement. It is during the presentation phase of the Heart of the Sale that the salesperson (or job applicant) seeks to establish confidence.

SALES PROBLEM 9—GOOD TASTE IN SELLING

Anthony Thomas is a key sales rep for a food-manufacturing company. Recently, the company designed a new frozen entrée that was planned to be a big seller in the retail markets. The salespeople were given samples of the product to take home to test on their families.

The Thomas family, including their three children, agreed that the new entrée was terrible. "How can you sell this stuff?" asked Anthony, Jr. "It's awful."

Here is how three different salespeople reacted to this problem:

Sales Rep #1:   I think you have to give the product a chance. The opinion of one person and his family should not be the deciding factor as to the value or use of the product. The sales rep should take the product to several customers and have them test it and examine the value. Not only that, the sales rep should not try to influence the customer.

If the customers reject the product, the sales rep should take it back to the sales manager and report the reactions out in the field.

Sales Rep #2:   No matter how strongly the sales rep feels about a product, it is necessary to sell to the needs of the customer. The responsibility of the salesperson is to inform the customers about all available products and let them decide if they can use them.

If there is the slightest possibility that the product may be useful to the customer, then it is the clear task of the salesperson to present it in the best possible light.

Every account is different, and it isn't fair for the salesperson to allow his prejudices to come through. There is a market for all kinds of merchandise. I wouldn't limit myself to only selling things that meet my taste requirements.

Sales Rep #3:   I always try to be up front with my customers. Therefore, I would tell them right out that I don't like the taste of the product. My relationship with my customers comes first.

However, I would try to sell the product, because my company went to considerable effort to bring the product along. But I would not oversell it. I want my customers to make the decision themselves. After all, there are probably many things that don't meet my taste requirements that most people would truly enjoy. I guess the point is that my job is presenting merchandise to customers. I'm not supposed to be a critic of taste, whether that be in food, or clothes, or cars, or even music.

Examine yourself, and utilize the seven methods available as you develop your relationship with the prospective employer. Remember, you have these seven ways to convey why the interviewer should have confidence in you—and to ultimately want you to work for the company.

Give three ways to convey honesty in how you do business.

10

THE DEMONSTRATION

After you have read this chapter and completed the Questions for Class Discussion, the Case, the Sales Problem, and the Exercise, you should be able to do the following:

1. Discuss the three objectives of the demonstration.
2. Plan a demonstration, including the necessary dialogue.
3. Prepare at least five pulse-taking questions.
4. Use the five senses in a demonstration.
5. Analyze and discuss the importance of physical location with regard to a demonstration.
6. Prepare the demonstration phase of the sale as you would use it in applying for a sales position.

THE NEXT MOVE

"Here is a preprinted form on which you can compute the gross margin of profits," smiled the salesperson. "We all like to know how many dollars we can make." With that, a printed form and a pen were slipped in front of the prospect.

Tentatively, the prospect examined the sheet of paper and said, "According to this, your suits sell for $200."

"That's right," replied the sale rep. "Now let's look at what these suits cost you. First, deduct 40 percent, which is the regular wholesale discount. The suit costs you $120."

Jotting down the figures in the appropriate space, the prospect asked, "Then we get an extra 10 percent rebate?"

"Exactly," responded the salesperson. "And there is no delivery charge on orders for three dozen suits."

"It sounds very good, but I'm paying only $90 for suits right now, and I sell them for $150."

"All right. Let's put the figures down in the next column. Competition offers the same basic 40 percent discount—no extra discount—and charges $6 for delivery. Our garments throw off 46 percent profit to you. Not only that, by spending a little extra time selling, you make $38 more gross profit. Isn't that worth shooting for?" [See Table 10-1 for preprinted form.]

"I don't know if we can sell a suit for $200," said the prospect.

"I'm glad you mentioned that," said the salesperson. "It's a very important part of our program. Here, slip into this jacket, feel the material, and take a look at yourself in the mirror."

This highly skilled and professional salesperson used two methods to demonstrate the offer. First, the prospect was shown how much gross profit

Table 10-1 Price Comparison Form—ABC CLOTHIERS

	Ours	Brand A
Retail selling price	$200	$150
Regular 40% discount	80	60
Wholesale cost	120	90
Extra 10% discount	12	0
BASE COST	108	90
Add delivery cost	0	6
Total cost	108	96
Dollar profit	92	54
Percentage gross profit	46%	36%
EXTRA DOLLARS GROSS PROFIT	$ 38	—

could be made, allowing the prospect to do a good part of the computations; and then the salesperson used a visual test of the merchandise. Moreover, as the product was compared, the salesperson drew on the senses of touch, sight, and hearing while keeping a ready finger on the pulse of the conversation.

During the demonstration stage of a sale, the salesperson has the opportunity to completely review each and every aspect of the offer. It is part of a very natural progression of events from the approach (gain attention, awaken needs, qualify the prospect) to the presentation (recognize the disadvantages of the present situation, acceptance of the salesperson and the company) and now a fuller explanation of the features and values of the proposition.

WHAT ARE THE OBJECTIVES OF THE DEMONSTRATION?

A good deal of selling is repeating salient points in different words. For instance, an approach might mention the suction power of a vacuum cleaner. During the presentation, this feature might be further used to help develop confidence in the product and the company. Then during the demonstration segment of the sale, a more complete explanation of this feature might be in order. Later in the sale, this feature may become part of the close.

Thus, the ability to present the same idea in a number of ways aids the salesperson in meeting the objectives of any phase of a sale. When the features of the product are presented during the demonstration, they are intended to meet three objectives:

To Show the Benefits of the Proposition

Prospects react to different stimuli. What appeals to one person may have no effect on another. Basically, there are three elements in any sale: price, quality, and service. These elements may be presented in any order and to whatever extent seems advisable under any given set of circumstances. Ultimately, the salesperson must deal with each of these elements, explaining why the proposition offers the best combination of them—the best value for the prospect.

Price, or the cost of merchandise, has always seemed paramount in the minds of most salespeople. If, in fact, this is a benefit of your proposition, then explain it in detail as our clothing rep did. Almost all buyers are interested in the price of merchandise. But this unique feature may be expressed as a cost of doing business, as an advantage over competition, as a source of profit, or, quite frequently, as a bargain.

John Tabor felt that "lowball" prices were the most effective way to sell. His total approach to the business of selling concentrated on price. However, he used a variety of avenues to make his point. "Here's a brand new set of disposable dishes," he explained to the purchasing agent of a hardware store. "A complete service for eight costs you only $12.90."

"That price sounds a little high," said the prospect.

"The retail selling price is $18.90, which means you make a 37 percent profit."

"Do you think they'll sell?" asked the prospect.

"Other brands cost as much as $15.90 and sell for about $22.90."

"I just don't know."

"The truth of the matter is, this is a heck of a bargain."

Price is a many-faceted concept that can be related in a number of different ways—as a way to profits, in comparison to competition, or simply as a bargain.

The quality of a product is another benefit that requires demonstration. Ease of use, long life, reliability, and sturdy construction all suggest that the salesperson must find a way to express the fulfillment of these needs for the prospect.

In stressing the quality of couplings, the salesperson said, "All our couplings are forged from a combination of steel, carborundum, and vanadium. Each metal adds strength and durability to the product. We have aimed for a tensile strength of 250 pounds per square inch and a torque factor of 7. You can expect long life and consistent performance from these new couplings."

The service element attached to any product might range from speedy delivery to a full supply of replacement parts to free repair service. In the case of the coupling representative: "Our regular delivery takes only six days from the time you place the order. In addition, our factory maintenance person will show your shop supervisor how to lubricate the parts. And in the event of an emergency, we will special-deliver replacement parts in two days."

All these elements take place within the context of another extremely important factor to which prospects generally react. Does your product or service add to or detract from the dignity or prestige of the prospect? Are there features that will appeal to the emotions of your prospect? The salesperson should analyze the proposition, searching for a way to demonstrate these "plus" benefits. Every person will have a different reason for making a purchase. For a complete discussion of these motivations, this might be a good time to reread Chapter 2, "The Human Side of Buying."

A salesperson for a linen manufacturer was showing a line of oversize napkins to the owner of a fancy restaurant. Several pieces were draped over a table as the represntative pointed out the close-weave fabric and explained why the price was a few pennies higher than competitive brands.

"Okay," said the restaurant owner. "But my napkins are very good, and I don't need such a big napkin."

"Won't you feel better knowing that your customers are using the most handsome napkin in the industry?" asked the salesperson.

"Why should I?" questioned the prospect.

This was the response the salesperson wanted. "Because everything you use in your restaurant is of the highest quality, from the dishes to the oven to the food you buy. By using these napkins, you have one further opportunity to prove to your customers that this is a fine restaurant. You want your customers to know about the quality you use, don't you?"

The benefit the salesperson was trying to demonstrate was the feeling of satisfaction the buyer would have in using the best possible product.

The reverse of this procedure can be seen in an appeal to the "smart" buying habits of the prospect in another situation. "Why pay more for a car because of the chrome trim? Our economy model gives you the same horsepower, the same transmission, the same power steering, and the exact same dimensions in every regard. The only thing different is the trim. A wise buyer like you will derive all the mechanical benefits and spend fewer dollars."

To Deal with Competition

Competition exists in several forms, and the demonstration segment of a sale is the most likely place to meet and beat these forces. First, there is the direct competition from other salespeople who are selling the same product or service. Second is the indirect competition from salespeople who may sell your type of product as an adjunct to their regular lines of merchandise. Third is the alternate competition from every other company, agency, or obligation that siphons off the money the prospect might spend with you.

Direct competition from similarly engaged salespeople is rather obvious. During the demonstration, salespeople have the opportunity to show why their product or service represents a better value. A machine may be bigger or stronger or carry a guarantee of long life. If appropriate, these kinds of visible features should be dealt with one at a time. It is not necessary to mention the other brand. Rather, salespeople should indicate in a positive fashion the various merits of *their* product.

Handling the indirect competition that arises when a company sells your product as a sideline suggests that the salesperson stress service, reliability, and delivery, as well as the specific benefits and features of the product. As stores, distributors, and manufacturers seek to expand their share of the market, they add different lines of products, but they may not be prepared to offer the same good service as an organization that specializes in that product. Recently, supermarkets have taken in many nonfood items, such as ladies' hosiery. Is this a good place to buy stockings? The prospective customer has to make that decision. However, when a salesperson enters the picture, the point can certainly be made that other ladies' garments are part of the service offered in a store devoted primarily to that business.

The last competing factor is more subtle and sometimes is the biggest deterrent to successful selling. How many times has a salesperson been stymied by the response, "I'd like to give you an order, but I have to pay my income taxes next week." This kind of alternate competition is very common, and it is real.

Here are some examples of the kinds of alternate competition for the available dollars the prospect has to spend.

"If you really want to know why I can't buy a car right now, it's because I just bought my wife a mink coat."

"We can't spend any money now, because I am the only one working; my husband is studying for his college degree."

"This deal on suede jackets is great, but we're building a new storeroom, and we have to reduce our inventory so we can store the building supplies."

"You know, I really want that oriental rug, but my kid just got braces on her teeth. The dentist bill comes first."

Mink coats? New storerooms? College educations? Braces? What kind of competition is that? Every dollar that the prospect has to spend is like a magnet attracting all kinds of salespeople and services. Therefore, every salesperson must be prepared to show why the proposition should come before all other demands being made upon the prospect. Everyone is competing for business.

To Present Your Offer Clearly

Every product or service, no matter how simple, requires a good deal of explaining. Few products are designed with only one purpose in mind. Even if they are, imaginative customers discover new uses and pass the information along to salespeople, who in turn have more selling features to demonstrate to the next prospect.

Alert salespeople will pose several questions about their products to themselves, and then seek the answers. How was this product made? What did it cost? When can we deliver the merchandise? What does it do? Who else uses this kind of product? These beginning questions will suffice to convince the salesperson that there is a great deal to know about the proposition. In essence, the salesperson cannot have too much product knowledge. The investigation into the uses and adaptation of the merchandise should be endless.

A factory bought a good deal of cleaning compounds from a janitorial-supply representative. It also purchased case upon case of steel wool. The sales representative could not visualize a need for this and finally one day asked the purchasing agent, "What do you do with all the steel wool?"

"We use it to stuff holes," came the reply.

"Stuff holes?" asked the salesperson.

"Yes. This is an old building, and there are a lot of holes—rat holes. We stuff them with steel wool."

If this sounds like a strange application of product, consider the manufacturer of aluminum storm windows who used to buy canisters of nonstick frying compound from a wholesale grocer to use on the sliding surfaces of the windows. Or the hardware store that bought dozens of men's shirts as presents for employees and customers.

It is the mission of the salesperson to expose the prospect to as many potential uses for products as possible. In addition, the prospect must get a clear description of what can be expected by way of service after the sale. How many times will a serviceperson call to train the buyer in how to use the product? When will the guarantee run out? How are the bills to be paid? Where do replacement parts come from?—and a myriad of other details. All this information should be spelled out during the demonstration in clear, precise language. The prospect is entitled to know everything about a product.

HOW TO MAKE A DEMONSTRATION

Just as in other segments of the sale, certain techniques are available to ensure maximum results during the demonstration. Each of these methods should strive to accomplish the objectives of the demonstration, to show the benefits of the proposition, to deal with competition, and to present the offer clearly. Inherent in this phase of a sale is the temptation for the salesperson to "lecture" or "instruct" the prospect. The use of interesting ways to explain your proposition is urgent, because how you effect the transfer of information can be as significant as the facts themselves.

Be Theatrical

When used in the demonstration, the theatrical technique means language, actions, and props programmed for effect. Each gesture—opening your briefcase, standing away from windows that might cast bright sunlight in

AN EXCITING DEMONSTRATION
IS LIKE A THEATRICAL PRESENTATION.

Figure 10-1

the face of the prospect, how you display your wares, the tone of your voice—every move must be carefully planned just as if this were a stage presentation. In fact, it is just that. You and your product are the central attraction, and your every movement will have an effect upon the prospect.

Generally, the salesperson will have a little more time to reveal the details of the proposition, now that the interest of the prospect has been aroused. This does not mean that there is time to waste, only that you must make good use of the five, ten, or 15 minutes at your disposal.

To properly set the mood for the demonstration, the coupling sales rep drew a neatly pressed white cloth from a briefcase and spread it on the buyer's desk. Carefully, the rep placed one coupling in the center of the cloth and extended a collapsible pointer to its full three-foot length. Pointing at the thread, the sales representative said, "Careful tooling has allowed us to develop three-sixteenths of an inch depth for the full one-inch length of the threads." Moving the pointer along, "At this opening, the edges are rounded on the inner surface as well as on the outer surface."

Easily, the salesperson went through a complete description of this unit, stopping periodically to ask questions of the prospect and to re-explain any points that seemed unclear. The performance was repeated twice, each time with the showing of more couplings and detailing of each one.

Continuing with this planned theatrical demonstration, the sales representative then offered the pointer to the purchasing agent and asked where more information was needed. Apparently the demonstration had been sufficiently clear, and the pointer was once more in the hands of the salesperson. As the pointer clicked shut, the sales representative prepared to meet objections and close the sale.

What made this demonstration out of the ordinary was the use of a white cloth and a pointer, and the way the salesperson had predetermined every move and statement. Because the demonstration was not new, the sales representative was able to act natural and indicate through words and actions a keen interest in what was happening. Had the sales rep not used this touch of theater to display the product in the best possible fashion, the demonstration would have been ordinary and flat.

This planning for effect can be applied to any product or service. As the creative juices flow, the salesperson can adapt any likely form to present the demonstration in the most attractive setting. The background may be dramatic or low-keyed, depending on the product to be offered.

Take the case of a jewelry salesperson presenting diamond rings. If 20 rings at a time were laid out, the prospect would have difficulty examining each shape for its own intrinsic beauty. Contrast this mode of demonstration with the salesperson who places a single ring on a square of black velvet. The diamond takes on added luster because the subdued background shows it to greatest advantage.

There is a classic statement by Elmer Wheeler, one of the great salespeople of all times. He said, "Don't sell the steak, sell the sizzle." This concept applies equally well in several phases of the sale. When considered under the theatrical technique, what does it mean?

Imagine a man and a woman sitting in a restaurant, waiting for their dinner. With a flourish, a waiter in a tuxedo appears with a magnificent sirloin steak on a sculptured gold service dish. Pretty impressive. Now imagine the same scene, only this time, the steak rests on a metal plate on the gold service dish. The steak has been cooked on the metal plate, and as the waiter approaches the table, drops of fat from the meat sizzle on the hot metal plate. There it rests, in front of the diners, literally (or at least, so it would seem) cooking before their very eyes. Before he even cuts into the meat, the man exclaims, "Gee, this looks good."

The reaction of this customer is very positive and in fact accepts the idea that the steak is going to taste good before the first bite is in his mouth. The substance of the theatrical technique is to present your proposition so that as many features, virtues, and benefits as possible will make an impression on the prospect without the need to say anything. As you then add language to your demonstration, the force of what you say will be magnified.

Add Senses to Your Proposition

"I think I have the perfect formula for a demonstration," smiled a salesperson.

"Hey, share it with us," said the happy sales manager.

"You see, I use all six senses to make an impression on the prospect."

The sales manager looked puzzled. "Six senses?"

"Sure," said the salesperson. "The prospect hears what I have to say, sees the product, touches it, tastes it, and even smells it."

"But, that's only five senses," snorted the sales manager.

"Well," chortled the salesperson, "I figure if I can get all those five senses into a demonstration, the prospect will have the sixth sense—sense enough to buy from me."

If this sounds a little convoluted, it really isn't. Evey product or service can be experienced in a number of ways. The professional salesperson will study the proposition until suitable ways are devised to inject different senses into the demonstration.

Here's an example of a cracker salesperson who employs all the senses. A standard demonstration includes opening the sample case and placing six individual packs of crackers side by side on a white paper napkin. After the prospect looks at them for a moment, the salesperson zips open a garlic-flavored pack and says, "Smell that aroma." Then the prospect is offered a cracker to eat.

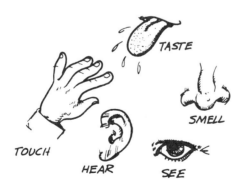

PLEASE GET US ALL
INTO THE DEMONSTRATION

A DYNAMIC DEMONSTRATION
WILL USE ALL THE SENSES.

Figure 10-2

Again the sales representative dips into the sample case, bringing forth a brightly colored cracker basket. After a mound of assorted crackers is piled in the basket, it is placed on a nearby table, and the sales representative asks, "Doesn't that look attractive?"

In this brief display, all five senses were used to get the prospect deeply involved in the proposition. Crackers of course, lend themselves to the utilization of all the senses. What about other products? The coupling salesperson used sight, hearing, and touch. Another sense could have been added: "Our couplings are packed in a special lubricating compound that has no odor."

To further illustrate the use of the senses, an insurance agent might use a fine leather binder to hold the demonstration materials. As the package is handed to the prospect, the salesperson could take note of the smell and the smooth texture of the leather. Or, opening a new policy, the salesperson could cause the paper to crackle. Other involvement might include having the prospect hold the policy or handle a pen and paper.

The more times more senses can be introduced into the demonstration, the better is the opportunity to bring a sale to a successful conclusion. A prospect who has been exposed and sensitized in a variety of ways should acquire a feeling of "ownership" in your product.

Use Tests

Money—the cost of a product or service, and the profits to be garnered from a purchase—is all-important to the professional buyer. It becomes more important when the prospect computes the dollars involved. This is a "test" of the reason to buy.

Take the instance of a door-to-door encyclopedia salesperson whose set of books costs around $500. After the sales rep explained the many benefits and features of the encyclopedias, the matter of cost had to be reviewed. "Here," said the salesperson, handing the prospect a piece of paper and a pen. Let's figure out the cost of this wonderful collection of knowledge. Mark down the price of a pack of cigarettes each day—about $1."

The prospect was guided through this exercise and then told to figure out what this would be in one week's time. "That's it," said the salesperson. "For the price of a pack of cigarettes a day, you can own the complete set."

This "test" could be carried further. Moreover, the actual work was completed by the prospect. Remember how the clothing sales representative had prepared a preprinted form for the computation of gross profits? That was a far more complicated set of calculations but served in the same way to involve the prospect.

Whenever possible, the prospect should perform the test of how the product is to be used. A salesperson for a floor-cleaning product handed the prospective customer a one-gallon can of cleaner and said, "Spill a little on the floor."

A strangely shaped blotch of cleaner resulted, and the sales representative described the harmless chemical composition of the product and even touched a drop on the tip of his tongue. "Doesn't taste very good," laughed the salesperson, "but it won't hurt anybody, either. Take a sniff and you'll detect a faint lemon odor."

Next, the prospect was handed a clean swatch of cloth and told, "Just lightly wipe up the cleaner." What remained was a sparkling clean section of floor. The prospect was so impressed that a little cleaner was poured into a troublesome corner to test the cleaning strength of the product.

Once involved in this manner, the prospect was in the early stages of being "self-convinced" to buy. No descriptive words could have had the same effect as the buyer's own ability to use the product effectively. Moreover, the interest of the prospect in a specific problem (the troublesome corner) was an arrow pointing toward a sale.

The idea of test-driving a new car is an example of this technique. How about the vacuum-cleaner salesperson who dumps ashes on a rug and then sweeps them up? Wouldn't the demonstration be more effective if the vacuum cleaner was handed to the prospect with the suggestion, "Here, you do it, it's very easy"?

How about the hardware salesclerk who offers the prospect a nail and a block of wood, saying, "Drive the nail with this hammer. See how you like the feel." Or the roadside fruitstand where the salesclerk cuts pieces of juicy melon for the weary traveler to taste. Or the furniture salesperson who says, "Just lie down on this mattress to see if it suits you." There are countless ways in which salespeople allow the prospect to test merchandise.

Obviously, some highly technical machinery is difficult to test. In these cases, salespeople frequently arrange for the prospect to visit the plant or to see the equipment at a showroom or in actual operation at a noncompeting plant.

The professional salesperson rarely leaves a sample for the prospect to test at some later "convenient time." If the product does get tested later, the salesperson has no control over the testing conditions. Moreover, the opportunity to explain what is supposed to happen and how the prospect can benefit from the use of the product is lost completely.

A food sales representative had given a package of breading mix to the chef in a restaurant. When the representative returned the following week and asked after the mix, the chef said, "Oh, we ran out of bread crumbs last Thursday and I used your mix."

"How was it?" asked the sales representative excitedly.

"Oh, it worked all right," answered the chef.

"Well, can I have an order for a couple of cases?"

"No," came the response. "We haven't really had a chance to test it. Why don't you leave me another sample?"

This is typical of what happens when a salesperson does not care enough about the product to insist that the demonstration take place on the spot, or at some time when both the prospect and the salesperson are present. However, there are other situations when the salesperson must leave the sample. The textbook business, for instance, allows the representative of the publisher to send examination copies to teachers. Then the sales representative is supposed to follow up the sample and try to make a sale. Whenever possible, tests should be carried out by the prospect in the presence of the salesperson.

Ask Pulse-Taking Questions

Professional salespeople are constantly checking to see if their demonstration is clearly understood and to verify if the prospect is ready to buy, therefore eliminating the need to continue showing the product or service. In effect, this is part of the basic philosophy of selling, to "always be closing" the sale. Anytime during the sale that the prospect seems ready to make a positive decision is the time to stop selling and take the order.

This opportunity occurs most frequently during the demonstration. As the details of the proposition unfold, the salesperson finds it necessary to confirm that the explanation is getting through to the prospect. The best way to do this is to ask simple questions. "How do you like the way this floor cleaner lifts the dirt right off the tile?" A positive answer indicates that the salesperson is reaching the buyer, who may or may not be prepared to make a decision at this point.

Try not to ask the prospect, "Do you understand?" because that implies that if a person doesn't understand, it is a sign of either stupidity or lack of attention. Questions should be directed at specific points and aimed at getting a positive or affirmative reply:

"What do you think of these bone-free anchovies?"
"Did you notice how easily the wax is applied?"
"How do you feel about peas at eight cents a portion?"

Some sales experts refer to pulse-taking questions as sending up a "trial balloon," or making a "trial close." They give the salesperson additional insights into the current feelings of the prospect, and, although they are not a full attempt to get the order, they signal that the prospect is either ready or not ready to sign the order. In either case, the salesperson has better directions in which to aim the sales conversation.

The salesperson who goes through a lengthy demonstration and doesn't ask questions of the prospect is apt to put the potential customer to sleep. Only by the prospect's reactions can the salesperson know whether or not the message is getting across. Here for instance, is how a demonstration interview, complete with pulse-taking questions, might sound:

"The fibers of this rug are washed three times before the actual weaving takes place. This ensures that when the weaving is completed, there will be a minimum of shrinkage. Notice how the sky blues blend with the muted greens. What colors appeal to you?"

"Green is a nice color."

"You'll be glad to know that the greens in this rug are derived from natural roots; they are not artificial in any way. Over here we have a rug with predominant green overtones and undertones. Do you prefer green as the major theme?"

"No, just enough to combine with the other colors in our living room."

"Good. Then this first piece will not dominate the room. It will work with virtually any grouping of furniture. Does this 9 × 12 seem the correct size for your room?"

"Actually, I think we could use a larger covering."

During this conversation, the salesperson used a statement-and-question technique, checking to see if the information was reaching the prospect and then changing the direction of the sale slightly as the prospect revealed likes and dislikes. The salesperson's essential purpose is to join with the prospect in finding solutions to problems. The best way to do this is to take the pulse of the prospect, find out what excites and interests that person, and then explain how the product meets those needs.

Use Comparisons, Similarities, and Exaggerations

A great many salespeople are lured into making comparisons between their product and a competitive brand. Even though there may be times when this cannot be avoided, the less you mention competition, the better. Therefore, it is wise to prepare ways of defining your product that will heighten the features and benefits in the mind of the prospect. A salesperson can improve verbal presentation in three ways: through comparisons, similarities, and exaggeration.

Rather than comparing a product point for point with a competitive product, you may wish to liken it to another successful product that is known for specific virtues. Often a salesperson will refer to a product as "the Cadillac of the industry." This simply means that the buying public accepts the merchandise as the very best in the same way that the public accepts the Cadillac as a standard of excellence. Many other comparisons are equally effective:

"Our couplings are like Mack trucks, tough and durable."

"One advantage to our couplings is their size—small, like a VW."

"We sell more couplings than McDonald's sell hamburgers."

These comparisons give the prospect a measure for properly positioning your product or service in terms of quality, price, or service. Another way to identify and define your product is through the use of similarities:

"Our vacuum cleaner is quiet as a mouse."

"These couplings are light as a feather."

"Note the yellows in this material—bright as sunflowers."

Finally, the salesperson may use claims that are so exaggerated that the prospect merely gets an impression or a feeling and does not question the validity of the statement:

"This rug will last a thousand years."

"The couplings are as strong as ten horses."

"Insurance is peace of mind."

Language is one of the tools of selling. Spicing it with comparisons, similarities, and an occasional exaggeration makes a sales demonstration more interesting. Preparing these statements and expressions beforehand gives the salesperson more confidence and allows for a more natural demonstration.

PRODUCT KNOWLEDGE AND SETTING HELP THE DEMONSTRATION

The demonstration is an exhibition of some or all of the features and benefits of a product or service. In one sense, it is a major production in which the merchandise to be sold is accompanied by a complete explanation of what the product is and what it will do for the prospect. To the extent that it is theatrical or spectacular, it can have a strong effect on the potential buyer. Several aspects of the demonstration require further comment.

Product Knowledge

As the salesperson moves through the demonstration, basic knowledge about the product will be transmitted to the prospect. If the salesperson is not prepared with answers to questions, the prospect will lose confidence. Obviously, the more the salesperson knows about the product, the easier it will be to make a dramatic demonstration.

The whole idea of product knowledge is so important that we devoted a complete chapter to the various ways salespeople can become better informed (Chapter 5). Suffice it to say that the salesperson's company will invariably supply volumes of information and facts concerning the product line. These will be coupled with training sessions and a variety of practical applications of the merchandise. In a nutshell, the salesperson cannot know too much about the proposition.

The Setting

During the approach and the presentation, the salesperson may find that the physical location is uncomfortable. Many times a prospect will be met in the front office of a building, the selling space of a store, or the entryway of a private home. Depending on the amount of space required for an adequate demonstration, a request that the prospect and the salesperson adjourn to a more comfortable setting might be appropriate.

Perhaps the dining room or kitchen table of a prospect's home seems the best place to properly display books, or utensils, or insurance policies. If the demonstration leans heavily on the actual testing of a product in the shop or factory, then this should be the site for the sale to unfold. On the other hand, the boardroom of a major company may provide the quiet needed for concentrated attention.

In trying to find an appropriate setting, the salesperson should have some idea of the atmosphere that will be most conducive to the demonstration. A simple request to move to another part of the house or building should do the trick. If the buyer insists that the demonstration take place in a setting that will not afford the most advantageous climate, the salesperson may have to decide to delay making the demonstration. This is purely a subjective decision and not one easily reached. Uppermost in the mind of the salesperson must be the thought that a less-than-perfect demonstration may be worse than no demonstration at all. Returning on another day may be preferable to a demonstration that must overcome the physical surroundings.

Even in the theater, the backdrops and the props add to the total production. The same is true in selling. To perform in a setting that detracts from your stated purpose is to risk all.

BEWARE OF OVERSELL

In a well-planned sale, every eventuality is considered beforehand. Thus, the salesperson generally has more ammunition than needed. This leads to the hazard of overselling the prospect—and talking yourself out of an order.

This intensifies the need for pulse-taking: attempting to ascertain when the prospect is convinced to make a purchase. Going beyond this point opens other areas of discussion, which may have an adverse effect upon the prospect. Moreover, once this time of positive decision has been reached, the salesperson should secure the order and change the subject.

Among professional salespeople, the problem is sometimes expressed this way: "After witnessing the demonstration, some salespeople are so impressed with what they heard that they buy the product back."

SUMMARY

By the time a salesperson is into the demonstration phase of a sale, the prospect has evinced sufficient interest in the proposition to want a complete explanation of the product or service. The objectives of the demonstration are to show the benefits of the proposition, to deal with competition, and to present the offer clearly.

Since a demonstration is like a stage show, the salesperson has a number of modes, techniques, and methods to effect a forceful and dramatic presentation. Included are the use of a good deal of theatrics, full involvement of the prospect through the use of all five senses, product tests, taking the pulse of the prospect, and the use of exciting language to highlight features and benefits of the proposition.

An effective demonstration relies heavily on product knowledge, a fund of information the salesperson should have ready for use. There is no limit to the depth of knowledge that a salesperson will find beneficial; the more a person knows, the better that person will be prepared.

Regardless of how well a demonstration is organized, it requires an appropriate setting to be fully effective. Physical space, proper lighting, and a certain amount of privacy are necessary for a demonstration to have full effect.

As the salesperson proceeds through the demonstration, every attempt should be made to determine whether the prospect is prepared to make a decision, being careful not to oversell the product, thereby losing the order.

A SUCCESS STORY

"Mr. and Mrs. Jones," the insurance agent said, now that they were seated around the dining-room table, "there are two main policies that seem to have attracted your attention. I will review the important points of each and then compare them with you."

Pointing to a blue loose-leaf book on one side and a red loose-leaf book next to it, the insurance agent explained what was in each book, devoting about two minutes to the presentation. "At this point, I have sketched in two plans. Which one would you like to consider first?"

Mrs. Jones held a finger toward the red book.

"Fine," said the sales agent, flipping it open to the first page, where a series of large, easy-to-read numbers offered the chance to detail the benefits of the policy. The agent asked Mrs. Jones to turn the page whenever she and Mr. Jones were ready. There were only eight pages in the book.

"Now that we have covered one policy, what do you think of the benefits?"

"I don't know if they are big enough to see us through in the case of an emergency," said Mr. Jones.

"Okay. Let's turn to this other plan and see if we can remedy that situation."

This time the sales agent went through the blue book, repeating fresh details and checking the reactions of the two prospects.

"I can't really decide," said Mrs. Jones.

"The red plan offers you the protection of a fortress against the worst possible disaster," suggested the salesperson, "whereas the blue plan is like a faucet; money runs as you need it. What coverage do you feel you need the most?"

"I'm not sure," said Mrs. Jones. "But the way you have demonstrated the differences, we may need them both."

QUESTIONS FOR CLASS DISCUSSION

1. A salesperson for steel ingots told a prospect during the approach that a special price was in effect. How might this information be used during the demonstration segment of the sale? Write two statements for use during the demonstration about this special.
2. How many benefits can you think of with regard to the sale of an electric sewing machine? How would you use them and bring them to life in the demonstration?
3. A travel agent was trying to convince a prospect to take a foreign vacation. However, the prospect said it was more important to paint the outside of the house. How would you demonstrate the value of the vacation? Write the demonstration dialogue.
4. How would you get the five senses into a demonstration if you were selling books? advertising? real estate?
5. Write five pulse-taking questions to verify that the things you did in question 4 were completely understood by the prospect.
6. As you think back over purchases you have made recently, do you recall any in which a full demonstration was completed by the salesperson? What was your reaction to that performance? How might it have been improved?
7. Have you ever been persuaded to make a purchase when you knew there were other pressing demands on your money? What changed your mind?

8. If you were selling cash registers, where would you prefer to conduct the sales interview? How about computers? insurance? adding machines? miniature calculators?
9. Plan a demonstration for the sale of a man's suit; a woman's dress; a baby's layette.
10. Consider the differences in the types of demonstration used at the retail level, distribution level, manufacturing level, and industrial level of business.

CASE 10—MS. DRAKE DEMONSTRATES DARING

Knots of spectators moved forward into the display room. Soon the chairs began to fill, and Denise Drake felt a slight nervous tremor as she prepared for the demonstration. Getting past the purchasing agent was child's play compared to trying to sell an entire audience of people who would have to use her company's products. The gentle murmur was reduced to a chilling quiet as she stood before the microphone.

Ms. Drake had been with the Sweetness Company for three years. During that time, she had made an enviable record calling on purchasing agents for large stores. This was her first experience in dealing with a group of small users, each of whom might throw a roadblock in the path of a successful sales attempt. Earlier in the week, she had amply demonstrated the virtues of the product line, but the head purchasing agent had asked if she would be prepared to give an equal demonstration to all the buyers in the chain.

Even as the audience turned to Ms. Drake, she decided on a new method to make the demonstration; it was to be a daring departure from the usual way of doing things. "Members of the Thurston Company," she started. "Usually I prefer to demonstrate our products under different circumstances. A quiet office or a test kitchen seems the best place. However, since we have a new opportunity, we are going to have each of you do the actual demonstrating. This will clearly show the ease and simplicity of our products. I will stand off to one side and give the directions, and each of you will carry out the demonstration. Everyone present will have a chance to handle the products and make decisions. Shall we start with the people in the front row?"

The first person moved to the work table as Denise said, "If your first assignment was to prepare potato salad, which aluminum tray would you select?"

An array of disposable aluminum pans and trays stretched across the work table. As the participants walked toward that table, Denise asked each of them to make a decision as to which unit best suited the work at hand.

SALES PROBLEM 10—HELPING CUSTOMERS IN TROUBLE

Jack agonized over his accounts. One in particular seemed to need his help. He noticed, for example, that the usual orders from this buyer for dresses, skirts, and blouses had fallen off. The customer tended to "cherry-pick"—that is, to buy only those items that were lower in price. The old idea of quality and style had fallen by the wayside.

Then, bills to this firm were being paid more slowly than usual. Always an extra few days, sometimes a week, elapsed before the check arrived. And Jack had noticed that the store was not as clean as he remembered. Something just seemed wrong.

Here is how three sales reps reacted to these conditions:

Sales Rep #1:   I have noticed over the years that when customers are in trouble, they begin to shop around for prices. They also have trouble keeping their accounts current.

If these signs appear all of a sudden, I go right in and have a talk with the manager. I lay it right on the table and try to get inside the manager's head, to find out where the real problem is.

However, if I'm still the major supplier, I chalk it up to the business being a little off.

Sales Rep #2:   It all depends on how close I am to the account. Basically, I would want to meet with the manager or the owner and have a chat. It may be a minor problem. Then again, I may discover, as I have in the past, that management has given up and what I'm observing is the beginning of the end. If the customer is having cash problems, I keep in close touch with my credit department. Sometimes it's best to put them on a C.O.D. basis right away. This sometimes helps the customer pay closer attention to the business.

It's important to try and figure out just what is wrong. If bill payment slows, it's a sure sign of trouble.

Sales Rep #3:   Before making any move, I would question myself: Have I been paying enough attention to this account? Does the customer know I am a competent salesperson who can help in many ways besides taking orders?

Next, I would check with my credit department and get a strong fix on how bill payments have lagged. I would also watch closely to see if any new suppliers have begun to sell this account. And I would talk to the employees of the store, sort of find out what the morale level is. Only then would I arrange to meet with the manager to discuss ways in which I might be of service.

After each had made a choice, she asked, "Why did you pick that particular tray?" The participants rapidly came up with reasons for their choices, and those in the audience were quick to challenge their colleagues. The conversation flowed back and forth as questions were answered, not only by Denise but also by other members of the group.

After each person had made at least two trips to the front of the room, Denise questioned, "What do you think we are going to do with all these trays and pans now that the cooking process has been completed?"

"That's easy," the group chorused. "We'll throw them away."

1. What do you think of Denise Drake's demonstration?
2. Did she really take a big chance?
3. Can you think of any ways to improve the demonstration?

EXERCISE 10

Products tend to be easier to demonstrate than services are. Still, service to the prospective employer is really what the job applicant has to "sell."

If this sounds strange, consider this possibility: A person applies for a job as a truck driver. Is the employer impressed with physical size, or with an accident-free driving record? The former is easy to see; the latter must be demonstrated. To carry out this demonstration, the applicant has five techniques, all of which have been discussed in this chapter.

Your assignment is to use all five methods to "demonstrate" yourself to the prospective employer as you seek a sales position.

11

MEETING OBJECTIONS

PERFORMANCE OBJECTIVES

After you have read this chapter and completed the Questions for Class Discussion, the Case, the Sales Problem, and the Exercise, you should be able to do the following:

1. Explain the four objectives of meeting objections.
2. Write examples for each of the six methods for meeting objections.
3. Write a dialogue for meeting objections.
4. Define meeting objections as a "question-answering" time.
5. Prepare to meet objections you will encounter when applying for a sales position.

SUITING THE STOREKEEPER

"This is a good-looking jacket," admitted the storekeeper. "But I just don't think my customers will pay $200 for a suit."

"Oh," was the only reply by the sales representative. For a moment the two just looked at each other as the sales representative waited for a more substantial objection.

"Besides," said the storekeeper, "the quality of merchandise these days is pretty uniform. All the manufacturers are producing fine-quality garments."

"You're absolutely correct," answered the sales representative. "Did you count the number of stitches per inch on the seams? and did you notice the tuck in the lapels?"

"What's the big deal, ten stitches or twelve stitches? We practically never have problems with seams coming apart."

"You agree then that the quality is well worth the price?"

"Yes, but I still can't sell a $200 suit."

"That's exactly why I'm here, to show you how our advertising program will pave the way and how I will be available to instruct your salespeople in the best way to upgrade your customers into a finer garment."

"Who wants to upgrade them? I'm happy selling them what we have at present."

"Do you like the idea of making all those extra dollars?"

"Yes, that does have some interest."

Meeting objections is answering questions. The prospect says something, offering a reason for not making a purchase. The salesperson responds, trying to change the negative attitude. Back and forth goes the conversation, until all questions have been answered and all fears have been quieted. For many salespeople, this is the highlight of the sale—a chance to exchange opinions, thoughts, and ideas with the prospect. The professional salesperson knows that meeting objections is the prelude to getting the order, that any sale of any consequences must meet objections.

OBJECTIVES OF MEETING OBJECTIONS

To the beginning salesperson, any objection to the proposition is an insult. This person fails to understand why the prospect can't or won't accept what has been said or demonstrated. Objections are seen as a personal affront, an unwillingness by the prospect to be convinced by the salesperson's way of thinking.

To the salesperson with limited experience, objections detract from the ability to move along and see more prospects. They are a bother that delays

WHEN THE PROSPECT OFFERS AN
OBJECTION, IT IS A ROAD SIGN
TO CLOSING THE SALE.

Figure 11-1

the salesperson from spreading the word about the proposition to other prospects.

But to the professional salesperson, objections are road signs to success and point the way to a sale. They are a great help in isolating problems and identifying the needs and desires of the prospect.

One way to cope with objections is to convert them to questions. Here are several common objections and how they might be restated by the salesperson as questions:

Prospect:	Your price is too high.
Salesperson:	What you really want to know is why my product commands a slightly higher price.
Prospect:	We don't need any today.
Salesperson:	I guess what you're really interested in is our delivery schedule for future shipments.
Prospect:	Our company has done business with ABC Distributors for ten years.
Salesperson:	If I understand what you are saying, it is that you want to know what we have that is distinctive and valuable for your operation.

This technique of converting objections can change the course of conversation in a positive direction. It also helps to better define just what is on the mind of the prospect. It converts general objections to more specific ones that the salesperson can answer.

As the sales interview moves along, sliding up and down the inclined plane that represents the Heart of the Sale, objections may crop up at any moment. One philosophy of meeting objections is that it should be postponed until the presentation and demonstration are completed. In effect, this says, "When I have told you my story, I'll be glad to answer your questions." The underlying thought is that during the demonstration, all possible questions will be answered, and therefore few objections will be forthcoming.

Another point of view suggests that any question in the mind of the prospect should be dealt with immediately, so that the prospect may be sufficiently relaxed during the remainder of the sales interview to pay attention to what you are saying.

Because selling involves at least two people of widely varying backgrounds, beliefs, and feelings, the true professional will remain flexible, sometimes meeting objections as they arise, other times delaying the answers. To help the salesperson decide when to meet objections, there must be a clear understanding of the objectives of this segment of the sale. Based on this understanding, the salesperson will be able to recognize the urgency of meeting objections.

To Allay Prospects' Fears

A sale, any sale, disrupts the usual course of events for the prospect. Even the person bent upon purchasing a new car will undergo pangs of fear about an increased insurance bill, taking on monthly payments, choosing a color that will satisfy the entire family, trade-in value of the old car, or having to pay more money for gasoline. Despite the fact that this person wants a new car, many seemingly insignificant problems arise, any one of which can spoil the sale.

This becomes much more upsetting when a salesperson appears with a new proposition about which the prospect knows very little. The natural reaction of the prospect is to set up a system of defense against this new proposal. Objections are offered to cover the fear the prospect is experiencing over the possibility of incurring additional obligations or changing a way of life.

Take the example of the purchasing agent for a toy-distribution firm. For eight years, this agent bought dolls from three different manufacturers. Now, a new salesperson for a fourth manufacturer is trying to introduce a new line of dolls. Assuming that the price is acceptable and the dolls look good, what problems exist in the mind of the buyer? Do I need another supplier? Can I meet the credit terms? Will the delivery schedule aid or hurt our operation? How much will it cost our company to do the bookkeeping for another account? If I buy from this new company, will my orders with my established suppliers diminish? Who wants another source of supply?

These same problems exist even if the new salesperson has a better price. The whole idea of buying from a new supplier sets in motion a chain reaction of thinking that professional salespeople characterize as "fears" in the mind of the buyer. The easy way for the prospect to avoid these problems (fears) is to offer objections—reasons why a purchase should not be made.

Moreover, when a prospect is dealing with an established source of supply, these same fears exhibit themselves in yet another way. An illustration of this can be seen in the following conversation:

> "George, this late-model typewriter will save a lot of time for your secretary," said the sales representative.
> "You're right. But my secretary is happy, and I don't really want to spend the money right now."
> "With our trade-in allowance on the old machine, the cost of an electric typewriter will only run about $15 a month."
> "Well, my secretary is so used to the old machine that I hesitate to make a change."

There is a hidden reason why this prospect doesn't want to buy a new electric typewriter, even from an old friend. Changing typewriters will somehow affect the operation of the office, create a problem that could be avoided, or maybe establish a precedent for all other secretaries in the company to demand electric typewriters.

These fear-laden objections may be hidden or out in the open; they may be valid or invalid. Regardless of whether they are visible and understood by the salesperson, they stand in the way of completing the sale. Under any circumstances, those objections are real to the prospect and must be handled by the salesperson.

Selling starts with the same basic assumption that a change is going to take place and that the prospect will have a natural reluctance to make that change. This concept must be paramount in the minds of salespeople, so that they will always be gentle with the prospect's feelings. Once salespeople realize that they are affecting not only the practices of the prospect but also a basic inertia, they will be better equipped to meet objections.

Any change in buying habits is a tacit admission that the new proposition offers advantages not contained in the purchase of the older products. For the prospect to make this transition is something of a trauma. At the same time that the prospect pursues the improvement implied in the new product, a concession is made that what was done in the past was partially wrong. Hence, a major objective of this phase of the sale is to make this transition more palatable to the prospect by allaying fears and by showing that the last purchase may have been a good decision, but the next purchase (from you) is a better decision.

To Answer Valid Questions

No matter how complete, how all-encompassing, or how detailed your demonstration might be, the prospect will have questions. These appear to be objections—reasons for not making a purchase. Realistically, these questions represent hurdles for the salesperson to surmount as the sale moves toward a conclusion. Objections are a plea for information that the prospect needs in order to make a decision.

Perhaps the best way to demonstrate the value of questions (objections) is to consider the prospect who has no questions:

After completing a demonstration, an insurance agent was very proud because every point had been covered and the prospect seemed to be paying close attention. The agent then tried to stir the prospect by asking, "Do you feel the benefits from this policy sound reasonable?"

The prospect nodded.

"Have I clearly explained the proposition?"

Again, a silent nod of the head.

In desperation the sales agent asked, "Do you have any questions?"

"No," came the response.

At this point, the insurance agent was in a "win–lose" situation. There was nothing further to say, short of asking for an order. The chances for success seemed slim. This is without a doubt the most difficult type of person to sell. Because of noninvolvement by the prospect, the salesperson had few indicators of which benefits should be expanded upon or what troubles bothered the prospect. If the sales interview had evolved in a slightly different way, the chances for success would have increased tremendously:

"Do you think the benefits of this insurance plan sound reasonable?" asked the salesperson.

"Not really," answered the prospect. "Why do I have to wait two weeks before collecting?"

"I'm glad you raised that question," responded the salesperson. "Obviously, I didn't go into sufficient detail to satisfy your interest. Let me review the salient points and see if I can resolve the difference in your mind."

If the salesperson can answer this question (objection), one more barrier is removed from the path to the successful conclusion of a sale.

Notice that in the response, the salesperson is already setting the stage to close the sale—"to satisfy your interest."

The need for objections is so great that many salespeople purposely eliminate certain important points in their sales demonstration, hoping to force the prospect to raise an objection, or they make exaggerated claims that will cause the prospect to question what they are saying. By changing the idea of "meeting objections" to "answering questions," it is easy to see that this vital phase of a sale can prove most exciting.

To Answer Invalid Questions

Some questions are not valid; they are raised merely as a subterfuge. These may be considered as meaningless; however, they contain the seed of a problem that must be dealt with if a sale is to result.

Many prospects are loath to reveal the true reason they do not want to buy. Still, they feel compelled to raise issues and excuses in the hope that they can sidetrack the salesperson and avoid the necessity of saying no. One of the most important reasons people seek this refuge in objections is a lack of financial ability to pay for the product or service, which in itself is a perfectly valid objection.

Another reason people raise invalid objections is that they are ashamed to admit that they did not understand a portion of the demonstration. How many times do parents, teachers, and salespeople ask, "Did you understand what I said?" Many people are reluctant to answer that kind of question for fear of appearing ignorant.

There are many reasons people raise invalid questions and objections: They have already bought a similar product, and they don't want to hurt the salesperson's feelings. Tomorrow they are leaving on a vacation. Yesterday the husband and wife had a fight. Today it is raining. The list of things that upset people is endless, but the upset is real!

Despite the fact that an objection is invalid, the salesperson is best advised to treat it as a valid objection while seeking the real reason the prospect will not buy. The salesperson should accept all objections at face value and meet them in the best possible fashion.

To Prepare for the Close

If a sale is moving according to the pattern indicated, rising along an inclined plane to the climax, then the last step before the actual close of the sale is meeting objections. Now the whole story has been told, the prospect has raised questions that have been completely answered, and the salesperson is prepared to ask for the order.

Although it may be necessary to slip back into some presentation characteristics or to repeat certain parts of the demonstration, the prospect should be ready to make a positive decision. This is a prime objective of meeting objections—clearing the road for the close of the sale.

TECHNIQUES FOR MEETING OBJECTIONS

Questions are the lifeblood of selling, whether used by the salesperson or directed by the prospect. When salespeople ask questions, they are probing to find prospect interests or problems that they may help to solve. When prospects ask questions (make objections), more often than not they are after more information.

Sometimes a prospect will offer an objection in the form of a statement. ("We can't sell $200 suits.") The salesperson should accept this as if it were a question. ("How can we sell $200 suits?") The only difference is that some people appear to be defensive or seem resentful that you want them to do something other than what they have been doing. This is generally a difference in the way people express themselves, not a personal attack on the salesperson or the proposition.

Direct Denial

This method of meeting objections is presented first because it is the one most commonly used, although not necessarily the most effective. Salespeople normally react to a negative statement or question by defending their position. However, the logic behind a forceful statement by the prospect is sometimes aimed at upsetting salespeople and backing them into a direct denial, which would then give the prospect ample reason not to make a purchase.

After a complete demonstration of a lawn mower, the prospect said, "My neighbor has one of these machines and claims it chops the grass instead of cutting it."

"That's not true," snapped the salesperson. "I've sold hundreds of these machines, and we guarantee they do a good job of cutting the grass."

This kind of answer is a slap in the face to the prospect. It says that you disagree in a very direct but totally unsympathetic way. This shows one of the hazards of the direct denial: It places the salesperson and the prospect on opposite sides of the fence. Moreover, as the discussion continues, the prospect soon begins to defend a point of view in opposition to the one held by the salesperson.

Another illustration of the direct denial was the case of a food salesperson demonstrating a new blend of fruit juice to a buyer. After explaining the advertising program, delivery schedule, and discounts, the salesperson very dramatically pulled a thermos jug of chilled juice from a briefcase. Some juice was poured into a paper cup and handed to the buyer, who sipped it slowly.

"Ugh. This stuff is awful," groaned the buyer.

"Here, let me taste it," answered the salesperson, pouring a second cupful. "Why, that's a very smooth and delightful combination of flavors."

"Not to me," blurted the buyer. "I think it's terrible."

Here is the beginning of a disagreement that is almost impossible to resolve if the solution rests on the validity of "my taste versus your taste." How do you measure taste? If other people are asked to sample the product and they agree with the prospect, the order is lost. If they agree with the salesperson, the prospect is cast in a bad light and will resent having a personal opinion questioned.

From these two examples, it appears that a direct denial to an objection is a dangerous method. It is!—unless the salesperson uses a lowered tone of voice and adds a note of deep concern and interest, using some nonverbal means of communication. Another way to use the direct denial is with a laugh and a smile. "Oh, you don't really dislike this juice." (ha ha)

It is very difficult to characterize this method without expanding on nonverbal means of communication (a subject covered in detail in Chapter 3). Language takes on a completely different meaning and connotation when accompanied by gestures and expressions. Needless to say, the direct-denial method is best reserved for specific instances when the salesperson feels it will have a positive effect upon the prospect.

Too often, salespeople assume that they must defend their product or their company. Although this is an admirable trait, using the direct denial might not be the best way to achieve this goal. The prospect who expresses dissatisfaction is not necessarily making a personal attack; the objections may be intended to disrupt your entire sales plan. Direct denial seems the most natural way to react to the prospect, but it is also the most dangerous.

The true test of the direct-denial method (or any method, for that matter) is whether it meets the objectives of this phase of the sale—to allay fears in the mind of the prospect, to answer valid questions, to answer invalid questions, and to prepare for the close of the sale. Seldom can the direct denial meet these objectives.

Indirect Denial

Closely related to the direct denial is an indirect denial of an objection. This generally entails citing a similar objection by a third party, and then explaining how the objection was answered. The point here is for the salesperson to direct comments at the resolution of a similar problem for another prospect, thereby avoiding a direct conflict with the immediate prospect.

In the case of the lawn-mower salesperson, the response might have been, "You know, last week someone offered the same comment, that the mower chopped more than it cut. We took the machine outside and found that the grass had grown so high that there was a bit of a problem. But we took care of that by adjusting the blades."

Or the salesperson might have responded by saying, "We've sold hundreds of these machines, and I never heard that criticism. Let me review the details of raising and lowering the cutting blades to see if I can solve this problem."

In both these instances, the salesperson had denied that the mower wouldn't work properly, but in a way that avoided directly saying that the prospect was wrong. The indirect method suggests that others may have had a comparable problem, but that it turned out to be without basis in fact.

Here are some other applications of the indirect denial:

"These couplings are much too expensive for our purposes," said the buyer.

"That's interesting," replied the sales representative. "When we first showed them at the convention last April, many buyers felt that way. We were able to show that they didn't really cost any more than comparable products."

"I don't think these couplings will last any longer than the old-style couplings."

"One of my customers on the West Coast felt that way," said the salesperson. "After they had been used for three months, the buyer told me they had saved hundreds of dollars in downtime."

"I know that my tastes reflect the tastes of our customers, and this fruit drink is unacceptable," said the purchasing agent.

"We have a number of accounts who felt that way initially," answered the sales representative. "After displaying the product for a month, they discovered a high rate of repeat buyers. Their customers are similar to your customers."

"The pictures from this camera just aren't sharp enough," complained the prospect.

"Gee," smiled the salesperson, "A man was just in and he told me how pleased he was with the quality of his photographs."

Citing a third party as a source of knowledge has its pitfalls. If the person quoted is an expert, more credence can be attached to the opinion. On the other hand, the prospect may resent comparison to what is conceived to be a competitor. For example, if you were selling a product to the Ford Motor Company, would you tell Ford about General Motors' success? Is Safeway concerned with Super Valu? How will the private restaurant owner react when you mention that Howard Johnson's is using your product?

At best, the indirect denial is an immediate reaction that gives the salesperson time to regroup thoughts and ideas. What the salesperson must avoid is the tendency for this method to polarize opinions. To whatever extent possible, salespeople must ally themselves with the prospect to meet objections to the proposition.

Boomerang (Judo)

By definition, both these words (*boomerang* and *judo*) describe an activity in which the forward thrust is turned back on the user. In selling, this is known as "making an objection a reason to buy." (During the close phase of the sale, this technique is sometimes called a "trap" close.)

Certain key words identify this method for meeting objections. They sound a note of agreement and then seek to resolve the problem. The salesperson's response starts out, "That's exactly why I'm here." This tells the prospect that together you will find the answer to the problem. Here is how this technique evolves:

"Your lawn mower chops the grass instead of cutting it," snarled the prospect.

"That's exactly why I'm here," answered the salesperson. . . .

". . . to show you how the blades operate."

". . . to demonstrate all the features of this machine."

". . . we'll cut some grass together and see what happens."

Once the salesperson accepts the objections as questions and gets in the habit of joining the prospect to solve a problem, the boomerang method is very powerful. Here is another illustration of its effectiveness:

"Your couplings are obviously very strong. But the added expense is too great to overcome any possible savings," said the prospect.

"That's exactly why I'm here," said the sales rep. "Let's figure out the cost on paper. . . ."

". . . to demonstrate the savings in time and money."

". . . to examine your situation and come up with reasonable solutions."

These responses by the salesperson are not perfect, but they do accomplish three things. First, they keep the prospect and the salesperson together, both looking for reasons that make a purchase desirable. Second, they divert a negative objection in a positive direction. Third, they bring the sale half a step nearer to the close; solving the problem removes a barrier to making a purchase.

There is no magic to the expression, "That's exactly why I'm here." There are other, equally effective ways to get across the same point. For instance:

"I'm glad you brought that up, because . . ."

"You certainly have raised an important point . . ."

"I'm glad you reminded me of that . . ."

All these methods are intended to first agree with the prospect, "to take the wind out of the sails." From that moment forward, the salesperson may elect to return to a specific segment of the demonstration to clear up any misconceptions, or may use further examples to answer questions (objections) raised by the prospect.

Compensation

If the salesperson believes that objections are really questions in search of answers, then the compensation method serves to satify that need. This technique admits to the validity of the objection and then offers features that make up for any deficiency. Here is an example:

> "Your price is too high for this adding machine."
> "You may be right that the price is higher than other machines in this class, but we offer you a full year's supply of paper, which more than offsets the increased initial cost. In the long run, you get more for your money."

To some extent, the compensation method is a tradeoff of features. Each product has values of its own, and these are compensating factors that can be used when meeting objections. Many salespeople repeat the objection made by the prospect and then mention other benefits or features. Repeating an objection reinforces the idea in the prospect's mind, and some salespeople prefer to immediately respond with the compensating factor. Here is how the two conversations might evolve:

> "Why should I buy couplings made with carborundum when other couplings are so much cheaper?" said the purchasing agent.
> "You say that couplings made with carborundum are more expensive," replied the salesperson. "But in the long run, they are stronger and less likely to break."

> "Why should I buy couplings made with carborundum when other couplings are so much cheaper?" asked the purchasing agent.
> "Because in the long run, they are stronger and less likely to break."

In both these examples, the objection to a higher price was countered (compensated for) by the promise of longer life. There are a number of other ways in which the compensating principle can be effective. Here are some objections and a variety of possible responses:

> "Your price on typewriter ribbons is much higher than the competition."
> "You say our price is higher than competition, but did you take into account that our merchandise is delivered in 24 hours?"

"We have very muted tones in our home. These drapes are simply too bright."

"The colors in this fabric are bright. But imagine how these drapes will bring added life into the room."

(alternate) "Imagine how these drapes will bring added life into this room."

"You deliver only once a week, and I need merchandise more frequently than that."

"True, we deliver only once a week. However, the superior quality of our products makes them worth having in stock."

Once again, the salesperson must exhibit flexibility in deciding when to restate the objection. When you reread the examples offered above, it is obvious that each salesperson must select a style that best suits the particular prospect.

Someone always raises the question, "How do you respond to a prospect when competitive prices, quality, and service are identical?" The answer, as stated by a professional buyer: "When price and quality are the same, service begins." Thus, many skillful salespeople rely on their professional traits and characteristics to meet objections:

"It's true our price is no better than the competition's. But when you buy from our company, you're assured of a dedicated salesperson."

"Our delivery is as good as that of every other company in the field. But as your salesperson, I work extra hard to keep you satisfied."

"All the manufacturers of these products handle quality merchandise. The only thing I have to offer is 15 years of experience."

Compensating factors come in a myriad of forms. "There are a number of excellent ways to teach selling, but this book is the most direct."

Questions

Whenever salespeople feel they are in trouble, they can revert to asking questions. During the approach, questions are intended to arouse interest. When used during the demonstration, they illuminate problems. As a technique in meeting objections, the question puts the burden of proof on the prospect. Just because a prospect offers an objection is no reason to assume it is justified. Moreover, even if it is a true and valid objection, the prospect may be able to answer the question, which would place the prospect in the position of selling the product.

To avoid upsetting the prospect, questions should be asked in a gentle, inquiring way. There should be no threat in the tone of the salesperson's voice.

"There's no sense going any further. We have too many reports of your failure to make deliveries as scheduled."
"Who said that, Mr. Prospect?"

"This living-room chair is very nice, but I don't like the legs."
"Oh. What don't you like about them?"

"We can't wait till Thursday for deliveries."
"Why do you say that, Mr. Prospect?"

"Carborundum in couplings tends to make them brittle after a while. Cuts down the length of service."
"When did you have experience with carborundum, Mr. Prospect?"

"Your reputation as a company forces me to say we can't do business together."
"Where did you hear about us?"

"Look. I just don't need any more insurance. I have plenty of coverage."
"How do you know?"

Here are six examples offered to demonstrate the easiest and most forceful questions—who, what, when, where, why, and how. Any objection can be met with a properly framed question that starts with one of these words.

"We don't have any equipment breakdowns because of couplings," said the prospect.

"WHO reports breakdowns?"
"WHAT do you mean by breakdowns?"
"WHEN do you ask about breakdowns?"
"WHERE do breakdown reports go?"
"WHY don't you have breakdowns?"
"HOW do you know you don't have breakdowns?"

Given that these questions will add a measure of discomfort to the prospect, they must clearly be asked in a quiet fashion, as if they are an attempt to seek out further information. Ultimately, the goal is for the prospect to answer the questions and therefore meet the objections. Once an objection is exposed to scrutiny by the prospect, it diminishes in size and importance.

In what appears to be a strange phenomenon, people do respond to questions. Frequently they will reveal the most intimate details of their lives if the questioner displays a sincere interest. Some few prospects will resent any intrusion into their business or private life. However, many more prospects welcome the opportunity to discuss themselves, and this represents an excellent chance for the salesperson to find the keys that open the locks to sales.

Pass-Up

Sometimes objections are time-fillers, meaningless comments not worthy of reply, that the prospect throws out because time is needed to consider the proposal. Generally, people cannot remain silent; they like to talk. When caught up in a conversation, they rarely take time for a moment of reflection. Instead, they offer objections that are seemingly without substance.

Probably the most overused objection is, "We don't need any." If you can think about this for a moment, you would have to agree—how can you need something you don't fully understand? Another overused objection is, "I'm not interested." Here comes a salesperson with a new or different proposition that could possibly make a considerable difference in the life of the prospect, and the rejoinder is, "I'm not interested." How can the prospect be interested in something about which little is known? Both these responses are seen by the prospect as ways to avoid talking with the salesperson.

However, the salesperson must be flexible enough to recognize and identify what appears to be a meaningless objection, and the salesperson should be able to distinguish between an invalid objection and the "brush-off." In the former, the prospect is trying to conceal the reason for not buying. In the latter, the prospect is trying to get rid of the salesperson. There are times when objections should not be answered—they should be passed up. In these instances, the salesperson merely changes direction and returns to a further description of the product or service.

DIALOGUE FOR MEETING OBJECTIONS

Each phase of a sale advances toward the objectives of that particular segment of the sale. This is equally true when meeting objections. The following dialogue might take place after a demonstration:

> *Prospect:* I appreciate your time and effort in showing me these new couplings. But they don't fit into our plans at the present time.
>
> *Salesperson:* What did you find most interesting about the demonstration? (Question)
>
> *Prospect:* Your entire presentation was interesting. But we are well satisfied with our present supplier.
>
> *Salesperson:* I'm sure your present supplier has served you well.

However, our new couplings offer you the assurance of superior service. (Compensation)

Prospect: Because of the good service, we feel a sense of responsibility to our suppliers.

Salesperson: That's exactly why I'm here. To offer you a superior product and a promise of equally good service. (Boomerang)

Prospect: It just doesn't seem right.

Salesperson: (Pass-up) Would you like to place a small order, etc. . . . (goes into a close)

Thus it can be seen that the salesperson has a variety of ways to meet objections—all of which may be brought into play. Here is another example of how objections might be handled:

Prospect: Thank you for explaining this insurance program. We just don't need any more coverage at this time.

Salesperson: That's exactly why I'm here, Ms. Prospect. To prepare for your future needs. (Boomerang)

Prospect: Good. When we're ready, I'll call you.

Salesperson: When do you think that will be? (Question)

Prospect: In a year or so.

Salesperson: You mean you recognize that you will need more coverage next year? (Question)

Prospect: Yes, I guess so.

Salesperson: It's good that you brought that to my attention. By planning for next year, we can reduce the cost of the premiums. (Boomerang)

Prospect: What do you mean?

Salesperson: If you buy today, the cost will reflect the current market conditions, not the increased costs we know are going to appear over the next twelve months.

Every objection or group of objections properly handled can lead to a more positive attitude if the salesperson uses the techniques available to deal with these questions.

HAZARDS IN MEETING OBJECTIONS

The professional salesperson will usually revel when meeting objections, like a pitcher throwing strikes, trying to save the game. It is a time of excitement and high drama, emotional, and even bearing a sense of serious entertainment—a few moments when both parties to the sale are performing at their best. Maintaining the conversation at this level requires awareness of specific problems that tend to mar this phase of a sale.

Arguments

Any prolonged interchange can deteriorate into an argument. Professional salespeople don't argue! They reason, rationalize, explain, and otherwise try to convince the prospect that their proposition is sound. Arguments are "win–lose" situations—they offer no reasonable hope for a positive solution.

On the other hand, free and open discussion, devoid of bitterness and rancor, leaves the door ajar for the salesperson to return at some later time. This should be a minimum objective of the salesperson, a chance to present the proposition for further consideration.

Probably the easiest way to circumvent arguments is to change the subject. Although salespeople should not dominate or control the interview, they most assuredly should be able to bend it away from trouble and toward a less emotional area.

One sure sign that the conversation is turning into an argument is the raised voice. If the prospect jumps out of the chair and starts pacing up and down, the salesperson would do well to leave quietly.

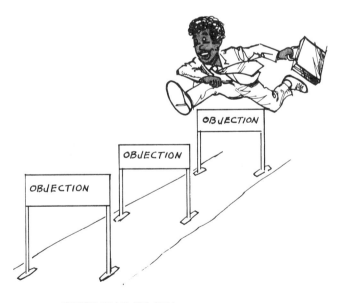

EVERY SALE OF ANY
CONSEQUENCE WILL
CONTAIN OBJECTIONS.

Figure 11-2

Extraneous Issues

Even as the salesperson can be instrumental in guiding and directing the conversation, the prospect has the option to do the same thing. Therefore, it is important for the salesperson to keep the target objectives clearly in mind. Talking about baseball, gold, politics, and the weather detracts from the salesperson's attempt to get an order. At the same time, the salesperson must show respect by at least taking note of the subjects the prospect finds interesting. When the prospect gets off the track, sit quietly and listen. As soon as the prospect has finished, reintroduce the reason you are there—to present your proposition. You may have to slide down the inclined plane of the sale and start in the middle of the demonstration or presentation. This is another reason the professional salesperson must remain flexible.

The Silent Objection

Of all the situations faced by salespeople, none is as trying as the silent treatment. Mostly, this is uncovered during the objection-meeting segment of the sales interview. Visualize if you will a relaxed, smiling prospect, nodding the head at everything you say or do. Finally, you probe. "Any questions?" A smiling reply, "No."

All you seem to get are simple "yes" or "no" answers. Nothing to really sink your teeth into, no juicy objections to deal with—just smiling nods of the head.

Some people adopt this attitude out of need; they are socially inadequate and do not relate well to other people. On the other hand, some skillful purchasing agents use this technique to upset and unnerve the salesperson. Telling the difference is almost impossible. The whole idea does signify the importance of involving the prospect in your complete sale. The salesperson who doesn't let the prospect say anything is doomed to failure.

One way to gain a better reaction is to do something dramatic—drastic. Spill a sample of product "by accident." Yell—scream—talk in a whisper. Change the subject, demand an answer! Obviously, these solutions contain a large degree of risk. But if you haven't been able to get a reaction, you have little to lose.

SUMMARY

Meeting objections is the fertile segment of a sale, which allows the salesperson to answer questions and join forces with the prospect in removing barriers in the way of a successful relationship. In fact, many salespeople welcome objections as indicators of how to best meet the needs of the prospect.

There are four objectives to this phase of a sale:

To allay the prospect's fears
To answer valid questions
To answer invalid questions
To prepare for the close

To accomplish these objectives, the professional salesperson has six techniques or methods available:

Direct denial
Indirect denial
Boomerang (judo)
Compensation
Questions
Pass-up

These methods may be used in a number of different ways, all of which are intended to answer questions and problems that are hindering the completion of the sale.

During the interview, the saleperson should avoid arguing with the prospect. The job is to use a variety of methods to resolve questions in the mind of the prospect. To do this, a salesperson must guide the discussion and shy away from extraneous issues. When confronted by a person who fails to react, it may be necesary to use drastic means to involve the prospect.

Meeting objections is a time when salespeople should try to align themselves with the prospect as they search for answers to questions.

A SUCCESS STORY

Spaced neatly in front of the buyer were five table settings of disposable dishes. Their multicolored surfaces glistened in the bright sunlight streaming through the window. Sam Thayer smiled as he said, "They are all very interesting, but I'm afraid they are too expensive to use in the employees' cafeteria."

"You're now using regular dishes," said Joan Stein. "Do you have any idea how much it costs to wash them?"

"The person who cleans up performs other tasks, so we need help anyhow. We figure the cost is negligible."

"What about breakage?" asked Stein.

"Very reasonable. In fact, less than 1 percent."

"One of my customers in Chicago told me the same thing. Would you be good enough to tell me how you arrived at that figure?"

"Well," said Mr. Thayer, "it's really none of your business. However, we know our inventory in dishes, and we keep track of all replacement costs."

"In other words, if your inventory runs $10,000 and you spend $100 in replacements, that would be 1 percent?" asked the saleswoman.

Mr. Thayer looked a little perplexed. "Yes, but we spend more. How come you know so much about replacement costs?"

"Because your business is my business. What happens to you affects me," replied the salesperson. "Of these five sets, which do you think is the most attractive?"

"I kind of like the blue one. But they're too expensive."

"They are expensive only if you consider the basic cost. After all, you would eliminate the need to wash dishes. How much does that cost each year?"

"I could look up the figures."

"Why don't we do it together?" suggested the salesperson.

"Yes," said Mr. Thayer. "Why don't we do it together?"

QUESTIONS FOR CLASS DISCUSSION

1. How does the question method of meeting objections force the prospect to defend the proposition? Explain.
2. The prospect told the meat-distributor salesperson, "We're very happy with our current source of supply." Write four boomerang responses to this objection.
3. Can you recall any sale in which you were the buyer when the salesperson adequately answered an objection you raised? Can you identify the method used by the salesperson to meet your objection?
4. Explain the rationale of saying that a salesperson ought not to defend the proposition when it is attacked by the prospect. Can you think of any sale when the salesperson felt compelled to defend the proposition? What were your feelings at that time?
5. What compensating factors can you think of that would justify the higher price of a particular brand of blue jeans? Prepare three responses using these compensating factors.
6. Imagine a dialogue between yourself and a salesperson trying to sell you a new stereo outfit. Offer four objections and the responses the salesperson might make.
7. How many hidden objections can you think of that would cause a person not to buy? Remember, a hidden objection may be either valid or invalid.
8. If a prospect raised an objection that the cost of a product was more than could be spent, how would you meet that objection? Explain in detail.
9. Write a 50-word explanation of the meaning of prospect objections.

10. How would you use the indirect-denial method of meeting objections if the prospect said, "I don't like your company"?

CASE 11— THE LONG ROAD TO SOLVING OBJECTIONS

All during the sales training program, Alan Jones had been cautioned about the need to call on prospects more than once or twice. When it came time to call back on those prospects who had turned him down in the first place, he was wary and skeptical. Even though he was skilled at creating strong approaches, when the prospects raised objections, he collapsed in fear. "After all," he reasoned, "I told them everything there is to know about the quality of our paints. That alone is sufficient reason to make them want to buy."

Mindful of his weakness, the sales manager spent some time with Alan and encouraged him to use questions the next time he had to call on a prospect who had refused to buy. On this Monday morning, Alan stopped to see the purchasing agent for the Roundtree Shop, the largest apparel store in town.

"Good morning, Mr. Jones," said Ms. Tower unhappily. "I thought I had made our position clear on your last call. We don't want to buy paint from you."

"Last time I called, you said our price was too high. Is that correct?"

"Yes," answered Ms. Tower.

"I have been somewhat troubled by what you said. Would you mind telling me why you think our paint is too high?"

"Because it costs a dollar a gallon more than other brands."

"Are there any considerations other than price that you ought to think about when buying paint?"

"Mr. Jones," started the buyer, "paint is very unimportant to us. This is an apparel store, and we buy only a few hundred dollars worth of paint a year. Why should we spend more than we have to?"

"A good question. But since you spend only a relatively small amount, why shouldn't you buy the very best?"

"We paint the store four times a year to conform to the seasons. We don't need anything that is too good."

"Why?"

"I just told you. We paint four times a year, and all we want to do is cover the walls."

"Doesn't the paint have to do a good job to cover the walls completely?"

"Of course it does."

"That's exactly why I'm here. To present you with a paint that will seal the colors and stop them from bleeding through."

"We are already using a paint that stops bleeding."

SALES PROBLEM 11—PRICE CUTTING AND PROMISE BREAKING

Shock was the easy way to describe what George Skrat felt when the sales manager screamed, "There's no way we can sell merchandise for that price! No way!"

Skrat had offered to sell the new lawn mowers to the Acme Hardware store for $10 less than the regular price. He knew there was a big push to meet the quota from the manufacturer, and he also knew that the company was having a big year. So he decided to cut the price.

In the past, his decisions to shave prices had been allowed. But the sales manager always cautioned him to sell by the book. On this occasion, he had promised Acme a real deal. Now he had to go back and tell the buyer he couldn't fulfill the promise.

Here is how three sales reps felt about price cutting:

Sales Rep #1:   I guess the sales rep should never have made a commitment without checking first with the office. But since he did, he'll just have to go right back to the customer and tell him he made a mistake.

Then he will have to show the customer why his lawn mowers are worth the extra money. Probably he should try to emphasize quality.

Personally, I resist the idea of cutting prices. If my company sets the price, I just have to believe in its integrity.

Sales Rep #2:   The easy way to cope with this problem is to go right back to the customer and explain that I can't live up to my promise, that my sales manager just came down hard on the idea. Then I would add that we can save him money on other products in the line—that if I could get the complete order, there would certainly be sufficient savings on other items to compensate for the mistake on the lawn-mower price.

If the buyer says he can get the same or similar products elsewhere for a lower price, I would probably question my sales manager to ascertain whether we're getting the best deal from the manufacturer. Either way, I would tell the customer that I would find other ways to save him money.

Sales Rep #3:   Number one, the sales rep has to tell the customer the truth. If you can't go right back to your customer with a firm explanation, you will lose credibility.

Maybe there are other products in your line that represent a real saving to the customer, and these can offset the mistake you made in cutting the price. The important thing is for the rep to admit he made a dumb mistake in offering to cut the price in the first place. Price cutting always leads to bigger problems—like breaking promises.

1. What other ways can Alan Jones use to meet these objections?
2. Has he antagonized the buyer?
3. Is there a hidden objection?
4. What could he have done differently?

EXERCISE 11

Job applicants are typically asked a number of searching questions. Those seeking a sales position must often overcome some very trying "objections." To prepare for this possibility, write six responses (using the methods and techniques described in this chapter) to overcome each of the following objections, which you might encounter during a job interview:

"We don't need any salespeople just now."

"Your educational background hasn't really prepared you for a sales position."

"What do you know about our widgets?"

"We can't afford to pay for your college education."

You might want to rephrase these objections, turn them into questions, before preparing your response.

12

THE CLOSE: PART I

PERFORMANCE OBJECTIVES

After you have read this chapter and completed the Questions for Class Discussion, the Case, the Sales Problem, and the Exercise, you should be able to do the following:

1. Describe the two objectives of the close.
2. Write closing statements for each of the twelve methods to close a sale.
3. Explain the significance of "asking for the order."
4. Close the job interview in a professional manner.

A HAPPY ENDING

"How many salespeople do you have on the floor?" asked the factory representative.

The storekeeper thought for a moment and then said, "During the week, we have three, and on those nights we're open, we generally have six people."

"That means you have about ten salespeople who will need some instructions on how to sell these higher-priced garments."

"Wait a minute. We haven't agreed to buy any."

"Of course, I understand. But when we take an order, we back it up with considerable service. I have to plan my personal schedule to ensure that you have all the ammunition you need to be successful."

"Are you trying to pressure me?" asked the storekeeper.

"Certainly not," replied the salesperson. "Perhaps I got ahead of myself. You see, we have reviewed the dollar and percentage benefits of our line. Is that correct?"

"Yes."

"When you had the jacket on, you liked the feel of the material. Is that right?"

"Yes, it was soft and comfortable."

"Did you like the idea that I would spend some time here, training your people how to sell these suits?"

"Sure. That's a great idea."

"Don't you think this is the best time to order for the fall?"

"Not necessarily," said the storekeeper sadly. "We just changed our fixtures around, and the back room is loaded with shirts and overcoats. We don't have any room."

"I can appreciate that. But let me explain what we can do. Our normal delivery is in two weeks. Because you have this problem, we'll deliver in four weeks. In fact, that way I can arrange my time to work with your people before the merchandise arrives. How does that sound?"

"Well, four weeks is better than two weeks."

"Would you prefer a range in sizes from 38 to 44? Those are the most popular."

"How many colors do you think I ought to have?"

Our sales representative began writing in the order book, noting the selection made by the prospect. At the conclusion of the discussion, the order book was turned toward the storekeeper. "Will you please initial here." The sale was completed.

When should a salesperson seek to close the sale? There is a very simple answer, as simple as A, B, C: ALWAYS BE CLOSING! That's right, whenever the prospect appears ready to buy, or whenever you think the prospect is ready to make a purchase decision, try to close the sale. Some sales trainers and experts teach their students to look for signs—a lifted eyebrow, a relaxed facial expression, or a moderated tone of voice—as the giveaway when the prospect is ready to place an order. Others feel that there is a perfect "psychological" moment when the prospect will happily affix his or her name to the order form. Both these theories are correct.

However, the professional salesperson recognizes that many prospects are professional buyers who are adept at hiding their feelings. That, after all, is their job. Rather than relying on overt signs, sales professionals will try to close the sale the minute they walk through the door. That is why, during the entire Heart of the Sale, the professional salesperson will constantly ask questions. Remember, there are questions in the approach, the demonstration, and the meeting-objections phases of a sale. We will use questions again during the close. These questions are intended to obtain favorable reactions from the prospect and may at any time lead to the closing of the sale.

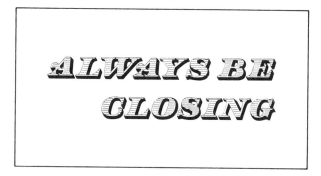

Figure 12-1

OBJECTIVES OF THE CLOSE

Some beginning students of professional selling seem repelled by the idea that salespeople ought to try and close the sale immediately. "Doesn't that make them high-pressure salespeople?" they ask. The answer to this question is found in the definition of "low-pressure" selling. There is no such thing!

All selling is of the high-pressure variety, in the same sense that all baseball players try to get a hit when they come to the plate. All quarterbacks try to complete the pass and score a touchdown. All basketball stars weave and dash through a maze of opposition with the singular thought of sinking a basket. Golf pros don't try to miss putts. Racing-car drivers don't but the brakes on around a turn. Tennis players don't hit the net on purpose.

Salespeople always try to close the sale. In that sense, there is only high-pressure selling.

Some professionals, whether they be athletes or salespeople, are more relaxed in their manner and give the appearance of not being under pressure. When Hank Aaron, the home-run king, strolled from the dugout, people in the stands wondered whether he would make it to the plate. But the opposition pitchers knew they were in for some high-pressure hitting. When Chris Evert Lloyd eases onto the tennis court, the fans know that her nerves of steel will not fail, even though she appears calm and collected. In the same fashion, salespeople, professional salespeople, are always trying to close the sale, even though they give the appearance of relaxed unconcern. Inside they are anxious, nervous, and tense.

The close of a sale is so important that many experts agree, "A poor closer is a poor salesperson, a good closer is a good salesperson." You may lack many attributes of the professional salesperson yet be a good closer and find success and happiness in the sales profession. But no amount of training, practice, knowledge, or capability will make you successful if you don't know how to close a sale.

To Get the Order

The first and obvious objective of the close of the sale is to get the order. This is the culmination of all the time and effort required to reach this point. In addition to all the work that composes the Base of the Sale, for the last ten, 20, or 30 minutes you have been facing the prospect and trying to explain and convey the merits of your proposition.

At the outset, you attracted attention, awakened a need, presented yourself and your company in a favorable light, demonstrated clearly and completely what you had to offer, fended and met objections to your proposition. This is the payoff. This is when you actually write up the order. It is a happy time, because it represents the concluding episode of a lengthy, involved, and complex procedure known as selling.

To Prepare for the Next Order

There is a second and equally important facet to the close of the sale—to prepare for the next order. Many salespeople are so content to have succeeded in finalizing a sale that they neglect to look ahead. There may be an ongoing service that the salesperson must render (see Chapter 15), and in many instances, the salesperson will have to call again to get repeat orders. Few sales do not contain the thread of a lasting relationship. The automobile salesperson may make a sale to a particular customer only once in three or four years. The insurance salesperson may make a sale only when a new child is born, or when the customer reaches a different career stage, one requiring greater coverage. The real estate broker may sell only one house to a given family in a lifetime. But for virtually every other kind of selling, there is the element of more business to come.

Few sales are one-shot affairs. Even the person who sells a set of encyclopedias should leave the prospect in a satisfied frame of mind. The salesperson can always come back to ask for the names of other prospects. If the customers are convinced that you sell a good product, they will be glad to assist you.

In many instances, a prospect will place a small order in an attempt to get rid of the salesperson. Truly professional salespeople will often refuse these "sops," as they are known. They are a salve to the conscience of the buyer, who wants somehow to reward the salesperson for the efforts expended.

After a long demonstration, a prospect said to the salesperson, "Look, I am happy with my current source of supply. The only thing you have that I can use is a couple of cartons of straws. If you want, send me those."

There is a divergence of opinion here; some salespeople would take the order, anticipating an opening wedge for future business. Others might refuse because it is not enough business to make any real difference and the prospect has already said that this will be the extent of the ordering. The professional salesperson has to decide whether there is some hope for business in the ensuing weeks and months. Thus, the close really has two objectives: to get the order, and to prepare for future orders.

TECHNIQUES FOR CLOSING A SALE

As they move toward the close, some salespeople experience a sinking sensation—they are afraid of a refusal. This is quite natural. Having presented the proposition in a clear and effective manner, answered a number of questions, and apparently satisfied the interest of the prospect, many salespeople feel the job is completed, that the prospect should recognize the validity of everything that has been said and offer to make a purchase. To "ask" for an order seems somehow belittling.

Other salespeople sense a feeling of guilt, that they have overemphasized the virtues of their proposition and that the truth of the matter has been "bent." If this is the case—if you resort to lying or distortion—then perhaps selling is not for you. But this should not be confused with the enthusiasm you feel for your proposition. If you believe in your company, if you have studied your line of products and truly feel they are as you have represented them, then this sense of guilt will fade. As one salesperson said, "Mr. Prospect, whether you buy or not, when I leave here, you will know that I have been honest and truthful. That's important to me. My integrity will get me plenty of sales."

By far the biggest reason salespeople fail at the close is they are not sufficiently aware of the many vital ways available to close the sale. Over and over, surveys of professional buyers have indicated that the largest single weakness in salespeople is not being able to close. This has caused sales managers and sales trainers to emphasize and reemphasize the close of the sale. Remember, "A good closer is a good salesperson. A poor closer is a poor salesperson."

Close with a yes, Yes, YES

All during the sale, the professional salesperson will try to ask questions and make statements that have a positive or affirmative tone to them. Any question can be rephrased to bring out positive aspects. For instance, "When you die, your widow will receive $500 per month for the rest of her life." At best, this is not a pleasant thought. Why not say, "You can provide long-term security for your family, $500 a month for your wife."

If you keep your language on the positive or "yes" side, the prospect will begin to think positively toward your proposition. Here is how the coupling sales representative sought to have the buyer respond positively:

> "Did you notice how deep the threads on this coupling are cut?"
> "Yes."
> "You said you use about 200 couplings every month?"
> "Yes."
> "Fewer complaints from the production department would surely make your life more pleasant?"
> "Yes."
> "May I send you a two-months' supply of couplings?"

We hope that at this point, the prospect will continue to say yes.

Does this close always work? Of course not, but it does get the prospect thinking positively and prepares the prospect to make a purchase. Here's another example:

> "Mrs. Prospect, you said your room is painted light green."
> "Yes."
> "And you agreed that this material blends nicely with that shade of green?"
> "Yes."
> "You also said that 15 yards would more than cover your needs?"
> "Yes."
> "Shall I wrap the material for you?"

Once again, we hope the prospect will continue to answer yes. Although we have no assurances, it is one way to close a sale. If the salesperson can get the prospect to say yes three times at the conclusion of the interview, the odds that the prospect will say yes to a request for an order go up tremendously.

Removing the Stumbling Blocks

Experienced salespeople build in a reason why the prospect cannot or will not buy. They allow that objection to remain unanswered until the close of the sale. By removing the stumbling blocks, they then draw the sale to a successful conclusion. Obviously, the stumbling block has to be something the salesperson can remove at the appropriate moment.

> "Mr. Prospect," said the coupling salesperson, "I know you have agreed with everything I have said."
> "Not quite," said the purchasing agent. "You told me the minimum order was 400 units. We just don't buy that many at one time. Sorry."
> "Do you mean that if I can get an order through for only, say, 200 pieces, you would place an order?"
> "I don't know how you can do that."
> "Well, I want your business. Let me call my office right now and see if I can get an okay for 200 pieces."

This company may or may not have a minimum order. The sales representative may have decided to deliver the smaller order in the trunk of the car. Or the buyer may have misunderstood the size of the order and the salesperson permitted the misunderstanding to remain till the close of the sale. Here are other examples:

> "That suit fits you except for the cuffs and the sleeve length."
> "But you said it would take ten days for alterations. I need a new suit for next Friday, when I leave for the Coast."
> "Let me call the tailor over to measure you and see if we can rush this job through."

> "You've said a number of interesting things, Ms. Smith. But the size of the down payment for a new car is more than we can handle right now."
> "Do you mean that with your car and $500, the sale is in question?"
> "That's right. I don't have the $500."
> "How much do you have?"
> "Probably no more than $300."
> "I'll take this offer to my sales manager and be back in 30 seconds. In the meantime, who don't you sit behind the wheel of the car and become acquainted with the instrument panel."

> "These four-drawer filing cabinets will fit neatly into that corner over there."
> "The only rub is that our budget is shot. I have no money to spend for the next month."
> "Okay, here's what we'll do. Give me your order today; that will ensure that you get the best price. I'll simply hold the order a few days, and it won't be delivered till the fifth of the month. Then you won't have

to process the bill till the end of the month. That way you'll have the cabinets and you won't disturb your budget."

Often a prospect will refuse to buy because of a specific reason—one that the salesperson can remove with ease. However, the professional salesperson may decide to wait till the close and allow the prospect to have only one remaining objection. Once this is removed, a sale is assured. Some astute salespeople establish a stumbling block in the opening remarks of a sale. "I know you can't afford this, Ms. Prospect. But I want to tell you about it anyway." Or, "This policy is probably more coverage than your family needs. However, you ought to know that it is available." Or, "We don't make deliveries in this territory on Tuesdays. Any other day of the week is fine." They create a problem or a stumbling block that they can remove during the close of the sale.

Assume the Order

Salespeople who have confidence in themselves and in their proposition radiate a sense of assurance during the sale. It is almost natural for them to assume they have the order. In the larger sense, all professional salespeople should conduct themselves as if to imply that they are going to get an order. However, there are certain expressions, language, and actions that characterize the assumptive close.

A salesperson was presenting a line of office supplies to the head bookkeeper of a manufacturing company. After the opening remarks, the sales representative drew an order book out of a briefcase and laid it on the desk. As the conversation progressed, certain items that seemed of particular interest to the prospect were noted. At the close of the interview, the salesperson flipped the book shut and smiled. "Okay. I have a note of those things you want."

Dangerous? You bet. Because the salesperson has assumed the order without actually asking the buyer. Another way this might have been handled is for the salesperson to ask, "How many of each of these items do you think you need?" Not quite as dangerous, but it certainly takes a bit of nerve.

What we are stressing is the slight variation in language that tends to assume an order rather than directly asking for it. The coupling representative could easily say, "Since you use 200 units a month, that seems an appropriate amount to ship." As the interview draws to a close, the salesperson might have said, "I understand your shipping department is closed on Wednesdays, so we'll make our delivery on Thursday." This was not actually asking for an order, but sensing that a move in this direction will be accepted by the buyer.

What happens if the buyer objects? Nothing. You merely retrace your steps, repeat something to which the prospect has already agreed, and try for a different type of close. Just like the quarterback who finds that the team can't gain ground through the center of the line, you try an end run.

Close on a Secondary Point

Any purchase requires that the prospect undergo a change of mind and make a decision. It is much easier to make a small decision than to make a large one. It is easier to tell a salesperson what color car you like than it is to say you want to buy a car. A decision on the delivery date for a new washing machine is easier than deciding to make the purchase. The method of payment can be an easier choice than the decision to buy a living-room suite.

This understanding is very important for the professional salesperson. The simplest items are complex. Take the two youngsters who conducted a lawn-mowing service. Rather than ask their prospective customers if they wanted the lawn mowed, they asked if the prospect preferred to have the lawn cut high or low. Sometimes they asked if weeding was to be done every week. Other times they asked if the prospect wanted the lawn seeded at the end of the season as well as the beginning. In effect, they rarely asked if the homeowner wanted the lawn mowed; they closed the sale on a secondary point.

Every conceivable sale has a number of angles and edges, each of which represents a secondary point upon which a sale may be consummated. In a retail store, the secondary point could be, "Shall I gift-wrap this sweater?" At the distribution level, the salesperson might say, "Would you prefer to have a morning delivery or an afternoon delivery?" At the manufacturing level, the sales representative might ask, "Do you buy truckloads or carloads?" At the industrial level, the secondary point could be, "We'll ship this material now, and I will call you two weeks before my next stop to ascertain that your inventory position is in balance."

Here are some further examples of closing on a secondary point:

"Our couplings are normally packed twelve to a case. Is that acceptable?"
"We can drop-ship part of your order to each of your three plants."
"Is this a gift purchase?"
"Do you plan to charge this item?"
"Does the merchandise get delivered in the basement or in the kitchen?"

Often, closing the sale on a secondary point relieves the prospect of having to make a major decision. It is always easier to make small or minor decisions.

Reduce the Choices

A cracker saleperson had prepared an interesting display for a restaurant prospect. There on a red velvet cloth lay twelve individually wrapped crackers, each with a distinct flavor and taste. As the sampling progressed, the prospect had trouble reaching a decision. "All these crackers are good, and they're all different," said the prospect.

The salesperson removed six of the samples and then asked, "Of these crackers, which three do you prefer?" By reducing the decision-making aspect of the sale, the salesperson was able to assist the prospect in making a selection. It was an excellent way to close the sale.

To a certain degree, reducing the choices resembles closing on a secondary point. But the difference is obvious. Products on the market today are usually available in a variety of colors, sizes, and shapes. The multitude of styles and colors of new cars would stagger Henry Ford, who made the famous statement, "You can buy any color car you like—as long as it's black." The salesperson has a great opportunity to capitalize on this aspect of our productive genius. "Would you prefer the blue car or the green car?" is a near-perfect way to close a sale.

By continually reducing the number of choices to be made, the salesperson nudges the prospect along the path of making a purchase. Often the question relates not to the proposition of whether to buy, but to personal preferences.

"These couplings can be packed in units of twelve or cases of 72. Which is more convenient to you?"

"Our trucks reach this territory on Mondays and Thursdays. Do you care which day we deliver?"

"These shoes are available in red and brown. What color outfit do you plan to wear?"

"Green beans come in five-sieve and six-sieve. Which do you think will look better on the plate?"

"Would you prefer to pay cash for this sewing machine or charge it?"

The very basis of selling implies that a change will take place and the prospect will have to make a decision. It is the task of the salesperson to guide that decision-making process and help it along. One valuable way to do this is to reduce the number of options. Ultimately, when the choices have been narrowed, the prospect has helped you to close the sale. A prospect decision to buy requires a yes or a no. The decision to buy the "red one or the purple one" improves the odds for a favorable decision.

The "Standing-Room-Only" Close

Did you ever notice how much more desirable a movie is when there is a line of people waiting to get tickets? Have you ever been impressed with the increased value of a possession once you knew it was of limited edition? Do you get a thrill out of buying the last can of peaches on the shelf? If you have had any of these experiences, then you know the effect of the "standing-room-only" close.

The professional salesperson will use this close on a number of occasions, when the facts permit. Because the professional will not resort to deception or lying, there will be no distortion of the truth. In all good honesty and judgment, the salesperson may say to a prospect, "There are only 112 cases of Mandarin Orangettes in our warehouse. Why don't you give me your order today." This sales rep has the interests of the prospect in mind while trying to close a sale.

Newspaper ads often scream the announcement that there are only "three days left to buy!" It's true. A special sale, a new shipment, an odd lot, a distressed group of merchandise, or a closeout of products can be utilized as a "standing-room-only" close.

For the professional salesperson, this is a skillful way to close a sale:

"Mr. Prospect, our vacation starts next week, and the production lines will be down. If you order couplings now, you will be assured of prompt delivery."

"We can't seem to keep these couplings in stock. They are selling very rapidly. Can I have your order today?"

"There are only two pairs of brown trousers in that style left. Shall I wrap these for you?"

"Model changes go into effect next month. That's why we have only three cars on the showroom floor. Of course, you will pay last year's prices. Quite a saving."

"My allotment of calculators for the month was only ten. I have two left. Do you want them?"

There is a touch of scare buying when the salesperson uses the SRO method, but the facts ought to bear out the claim. Moreover, even in these times of plenty, there are still shortages. Prices do fluctuate, and a wide-awake salesperson will share this information with the prospect. If this technique is overused, it will soon become apparent to the prospect. The integrity of the salesperson and the company are often on the line when claims are made about rising prices, product shortages, or special discounts.

Special Discounts

A special inducement to "buy now" is similar to the bonus approach. Remember, this approach brought to the attention of the prospect a price discount or a "free" deal. Just because you used this in the approach is no reason to avoid using the same information to close the sale. What could be more attractive to the buyer than the chance to save money by making an immediate purchase?

A young couple was shopping for a refrigerator. They had their minds set on a black box, one that would match the decor of their new kitchen. Unfortunately, the salesperson had only white and red refrigerators on the display-room floor. "You are convinced that all the features of this particular model will meet your needs. Is that correct?" asked the salesperson.

"Yes," said the wife. "But we really want a black unit."

"We don't have the color you want. But here's what we'll do. This box sells for $335. If we can send you the one on the floor, it will cost only $295. How does that strike you?"

As they reviewed the offer, the couple realized that for less than $5 worth of paint, they could convert the box to the color they desired. The discount was too good to pass up.

Here are other inducements to purchase immediately:

"Mr. Prospect, I know you don't need any couplings today. However, if I can get your order, I can offer you one dozen free couplings with every ten dozen you order."

"I have until the end of the week to take orders for couplings at this special price. May I have your order today?"

"We have made a special arrangement with the manufacturer to give 50 pounds of detergent with the purchase of this washing machine."

"If I can have your order today, we will extend the billing date till next month. You won't have to pay for this shipment for 60 days."

"When you buy a drum of floor wax, we have our service representative come by to instruct your workers how to use the product."

Despite the fact that certain information has already been discussed, such as a "one free with ten" deal, the prospect may have missed what you said. A salesperson should not be fearful of repeating what has been said earlier. Any number of studies reveal that people hear only a small percentage of what has been said, so the professional salesperson should not hesitate to redefine the proposition in terms of a special discount.

Summarization

During a sale, a good deal of conversation has taken place. A great many facts have been thrown at the prospective buyer, and it may have been necessary to examine a complicated piece of equipment. As the close of the sale draws near, one valid way of reaching a successful conclusion is to recap or summarize all that has been said. Naturally, you will emphasize those aspects of the product or service that the prospect seemed to like, and soft-pedal those that were accepted in a negative manner.

"Mr. Storekeeper, I have shown you our entire line of briefcases. You recognized the differences among the three price ranges. At the same time, you realize that a full display of merchandise will be attractive to your customers. With the advertising material and rack we supply, you can make an excellent point-of-purchase display. And if you order the minimum quantity, you can still get the best price, which includes an early shipping allowance. Two weeks after you receive the merchandise, I will stop in to help set up the display and suggest further orders. And, of course, we will send along a handful of educational pamphlets for your customers. We do a number of things to help ensure your success. That's why today would be a good time to place an opening order."

Since there is no single "right" way to close a sale, and since it is advisable to fortify the prospect with a significant amount of information, the summarization close is valuable because it reviews the high points of the proposition. As the review is under way, the prospect may raise other questions that trouble and stop the sale. If at the completion of your summarization it appears you are no closer to a decision, then it is appropriate to ask, "Is there any facet of our product that I have not completely explained?"

If the prospect says, "Yes," you will know what further explanation is required. Having removed this obstacle, you can proceed to ask for the order. On the other hand, if the prospect says, "No," the next natural question is, "If you understand everything I have said, how many may I send you?"

Summarization is the opportunity to remind the prospect of all the virtues of your product or service. It provides both the salesperson and the prospect a chance to relax and think about all the aspects of the sale. It ties all the loose ends together.

Ask for the Order

It might seem that with all the techniques for closing a sale, it is not necessary to ask for the order. In every method described, the business of asking for the order has been implied. This may not be strong enough. Frequently it is advisable to straight-out say, "May I have an order?"

Often salespeople are afraid to ask this question, because they assume that a negative response means the end of the sales interview. Not so! A negative answer more often than not means you must slide down the inclined plane that is the Heart of the Sale and re-present or redemonstrate your proposition. "No" has a great many meanings, and the salesperson must assume it means, "I need more information before making a decision."

Another reason this method is important is that closings are usually a combination of techniques. A summarization close will be ineffective if the last sentence does not actually ask for the order. The "yes, Yes, YES" close might end with, "Shall I send you eight widgets?" One closing technique is not enough. When you have been rebuffed by a prospect, this is the time to reach into your bag of methods and come up with a different close, one the

THE PROFESSIONAL SALESPERSON ALWAYS ASKS FOR AN ORDER.

Figure 12-2

prospect finds more acceptable. In the final analysis, you have to find the key, the soft spot, the weak point in the defensive line that will allow you to score. This is why each of the techniques for closing a sale has been expanded to better explain the methods available to you.

How do you ask for an order? Very easy, just ask.

"May I send you ten cases of couplings, Mr. Prospect?"

"How many dozen couplings shall I send you?"

"Is this the dress you want?"

"Shall I write up your order for this sewing machine?"

"You agree this is the policy you need, Ms. Prospect. Shall I fill out the forms?"

The validity of asking for the order is that the prospect needs help in reaching a decision. You can offer that help in many ways, and one of them is to simply ask for the order.

Emotional

One of the fascinating things about professional selling is the interchange between two human beings, diverse personalities brought together for their mutual benefit. People are complex and interesting—and each is unique. Some will respond to an emotional appeal during the close of a sale. This appeal may affect how people view themselves or how others will view them, or even offer some form of physical comfort or well-being.

Perhaps an example will spell out the distinction among these various emotions. A salesperson for a stereo outfit had reached the close of the sale. Having reviewed all the merits of the offer, the salesclerk decided to use an emotional close. Here are several things that could have been said:

"When you are sitting in your den, the soft strains of this stereo will mean hours of pleasant relaxation."

"Think of the pleasure you will get when your friends share the wonderful sound of this equipment."

"This unit will last a long time. It may be the kind of thing you will pass along to your children when they get married."

"Won't you be proud to own this turntable?"

Each of these appeals is made not to, or about, the proposition itself, but rather to the effect ownership will have on the prospect. This close is very similar in content to the consumer-benefit approach. Remember, that approach described what ownership of the product would do for the prospect, not what the product itself would do. We know that a stereo set will make beautiful music. Who would suspect that it would make a person relaxed, proud, or filled with pleasure?

After all the details and functional data about a proposition have been explored, an emotional appeal can be powerful. For instance:

"Once you sign this insurance contract, you can feel secure that your family is protected."

"Ms. Harrison, driving down the street in this new four-on-the-floor sports roadster will make all your neighbors envious."

"This suit will make you feel like a millionaire."

"Owning a home on this block will automatically put you in the country-club category."

As we have discovered earlier in this text, many decisions to buy are made on an emotional basis. People do not always buy the strongest, heaviest, most powerful, or least expensive item. They buy what pleases them and satisfies a vast array of needs, many of them emotional.

Close on an Objection

During our discussion about meeting objections, we indicated that solving a question in the mind of the prospect is a very natural time to ask for an order. When coupled with a close, it is sometimes referred to as a "trap close." Don't be put off by the language—it merely means that the prospect raised a point that you have resolved and is now in a position to make a positive decision. After all, if you removed an objection, nothing stands between you and closing the sale. The prospect has set the trap; you have sprung it.

The sequence of events goes something like this: The prospect makes a statement. You meet the objection and follow through with a request for an order. You have turned the objection into a reason for buying. For instance:

"Your couplings are too high-priced."

"I'm glad you raised that point. You have agreed that the strength of these new couplings will save you considerable downtime. That saving more than compensates for the slightly higher price of our couplings. Isn't that a good reason to buy them now? Why don't you try a minimum order?"

"This suit just doesn't look right on me."

"You're right. Let's have our tailor measure your arm length and then fix the collar. Then it will be a perfect fit, and you can probably pick it up next Friday."

"Why are these couplings only packed in boxes of 72? That just doesn't fit our needs."

"That's exactly why I'm here. We can offer you any amount you wish, because we sub-pack them in dozens. Would you like four dozen to each of your storerooms?"

"Sorry, Mr. Salesperson. We just don't have any shelf space for your merchandise."

"I noticed that on the way through the store. When we take an order, we also send in a store engineer to help you arrange your products in a way that will allow for the inclusion of our merchandise. Give me a small order, and we will have this person arrange to be here within three days of delivery."

This explanation of how to close on an objection is a natural forward progression up the inclined plane of the Heart of the Sale.

As each objection is met, removed, or satisfied, the salesperson should ask for the order. The logic is that the prospect thinks you are boxed into a position from which you cannot maneuver. However, by solving the problem, you have positioned yourself to ask for an order. An answered objection is a perfect reason to buy.

Offer to Alter the Proposition

Not every product can be altered, but the proposition can be altered to satisfy the prospect. A couple was shopping for a new clothes dryer. They found a model that seemed to suit them, except that the dimensions were two inches more than the opening into which the machine would have to fit. Because the sale was important, the salesperson went to the home, found that the washer next to that space occupied three inches more than needed, and offered to have a serviceperson make the necessary adjustments. The proposition was altered to include an extra service.

Here's a story about a person buying a new car:

"One reason I am hesitant is that the car costs more than I intended to spend."

"We have shaved our price to the bone," replied the salesperson. "However, maybe there are other ways to make our offer more attractive."

"What do you mean?" asked the prospect.

"Do you use snow tires?"

"Of course. It's the law in this state."

"Well, when you order this new car, you're going to have the immediate expense of new snow tires. How about if we take your rear wheels off and replace those tires with snow tires? That way you won't have any additional expense till sometime in the spring. Even then, you will only have to buy one regular tire. In effect, you will be spending fewer dollars."

By altering the proposition, this salesperson was able to consummate a sale. The prospect spent only as many dollars as could be afforded, had the added protection of snow tires, and was generally satisfied.

One of the most common ways for salespeople to alter the proposition is to date bills ahead. This means that an order placed on December 15 could be dated for delivery January 1 of the following year. That way, the prospect would not have to pay for the merchandise till the following month. Even billing for one month ahead represents a considerable advantage. Here is an example taken from the food industry:

"I can use 1,000 cases of peaches, but we have no budget, and I simply can't place an order."

"According to what you have told me, 1,000 cases will last you three months. Now, our normal credit terms say you must pay for merchandise in ten days. However, 1,000 cases is only half a carload. If you buy a full carload, 2,000 cases, we can give you extended credit terms. You pay the first third in 30 days and the balance in two monthly installments."

"That way, I would only be paying for 667 cases in the first month, which is less money than I would have to spend if I bought 1,000 cases. I'll take it."

By altering and re-presenting the proposition, this salesperson was able to increase the size of the order while satisfying a prospect.

There are other ways to alter a proposition:

"The sale on this sofa and chairs doesn't start till the 15th of the month. Give me your order today, and we will enter it on the 15th."

"We don't usually carry pancake flour in larger quantities. However, I will take your order based on delivering two 100-pound bags."

"I can see your point, Ms. Prospect. This contract should include an option for you to regain control of publication rights after five years. Our attorneys will make the necessary changes."

Simply because a product comes from the factory in a certain form, or agreement always include certain points, does not mean they cannot be changed. It is the job, the opportunity of the professional salesperson to be aware of what changes will effect a sale. The salesperson should, of course, have prior knowledge and understanding of how far authority extends. In most instances, professional salespeople have a great deal of latitude in altering the proposition to make a sale.

(Because the close of any sale is of such importance, the concluding section of this portion of the text—the summary and a success story—will follow in the next chapter.)

QUESTIONS FOR CLASS DISCUSSION

1. Many people feel that once an order has been placed, the sale is over. Is this true? Why?
2. The Heart of the Sale, that time when the buyer and seller are face to face, moves on an inclined plane. When is it appropriate to close the sale? Explain your reasoning.
3. What stumbling blocks would you erect during a sales interview that could be removed during the close if you were selling hand tools to a manufacturing plant? if you were selling adhesives to a packing plant? if you were selling canned soda to a food distributor?
4. Differentiate between high- and low-pressure selling. Give examples of what you conceive to be high- and low-pressure selling.
5. Have you ever been a buyer in a situation in which the salesperson tried to apply high-pressure tactics? How did that person's attitude differ from other sales situations in which you have been involved?
6. Give three examples of the "standing-room-only" close from the point of view of a computer salesperson; from the point of view of a wallpaper salesperson.
7. How would you use a "close" during the approach segment of a sale? Give three examples.
8. Discuss how a "bonus" approach can be converted to a "special discount" closing. What might the prospect's reaction be to hearing this two-pronged effort?
9. Analyze in detail the following close: "I'm glad you raised that point, Ms. Prospect. It gives me a chance to explore the differences between the X-100 model gas heater and the X-200 model." What kind of close is this?

CASE 12—THE CASE OF THE MISSING CLOSE

Now Gerald Dormer began to stutter. Uncontrollably, his voice wavered and the words that formed in his head dissolved in his mouth. He tried to force his attention to the matter of getting the words together, but nothing seemed to work. He stared at the prospect in front of him, a professional buyer who was on the verge of placing an order. All his mind could grasp was the positive conversation that had taken place.

The beginning had been great. "Ms. Harrison, look at this." These opening words, accompanied by a grand flourish as he lay two samples of water-repellent material on the desk, launched the sale. As the buyer looked at him, he added, "You can design your own sportswear with our new assortment of fabrics. How does that strike you?"

Somewhat surprised, Ms. Harrison asked, "What do you mean, design our own sportswear?"

SALES PROBLEM 12—HOW TO BLOCK A PASS

Nicky was taking her usual order from the buyer. They had done business for about a year, and the relationship was highly professional. Before she left, the buyer said, "You know, Nicky, doing business with you is a pleasure. Maybe one night we can have a drink together."

It was a surprise to Nicky. She tried never to think of her customers in any way other than business. After selling for five years, she had had very few passes that needed blocking. Still, from time to time, one did float by.

Here is how three sales reps responded to this situation:

Sales Rep #1:   I've been selling for close to 20 years. During that time, many women have suggested we meet after work. I have never agreed.

Oh, we may kid around a little. But we always know where to draw the line. Mixing work and pleasure just doesn't work. Not only that; 99 percent of your customers will lose confidence in you if they discover you play around.

Sales Rep #2:   From the very beginning of a business relationship, I try to let the customers know that going out with men buyers is just not something I will do. I let them know it is against company policy.

Quite a few times, men have made suggestive passes. I fend them off and then come back next week as if nothing had happened. I just think that's the professional thing to do.

About 90 percent of my accounts are men. Quite frankly, the vast majority are most interested in business.

Sales Rep #3:   Sometimes I just laugh and ask if I can bring my husband and kids along. Other times I thank them for thinking that highly of me, but it just isn't part of how I do business.

I always try to maintain a professional attitude. Usually, if I conduct myself like a sales professional, the customers respond in kind. I can be a person's friend. I can meet with them in groups or at business functions. But that's as far as it goes.

I just don't consider myself one of the commodities I'm selling. I wouldn't lower myself just to make a sale.

This fast start sent Gerald into a lengthy display of models and fabrics the buyer could select, each a unique pattern and each garment emblazoned with a design of the buyer's own choice. The interesting aspect of this offer was the chance for Ms. Harrison to utilize her own flair for mixing and matching colors, picking those combinations that would appeal to the customers who bought from her ski shop.

Gerald was excited about the notion of "customizing" orders for individual stores. It was a new idea, and his vision was shared by Ms. Harrison. As he reviewed the prices and quantities, she agreed with virtually everything he said. Deftly he answered all her questions (objections), and she had literally moved to the edge of the chair, anxious to make a purchase.

This was the point at which Gerald froze. His mind went blank and his words were garbled. He sat mumbling incoherent sounds, hoping for a way out.

(Please help Gerald by writing at least six different ways this sale might be closed.)

EXERCISE 12

Well, here you are, almost at the conclusion of your job interview. Please review all that you have said and done during the approach, presentation, demonstration, and meeting-objections phases of this interview.

Now, prepare twelve ways to close this sale—that is, twelve ways you might ask for the job.

Students typically feel that when they have presented themselves and their credentials, prospective employers will offer them a position. You can demonstrate your sales ability by closing the interview (sale) in a professional manner.

13

THE CLOSE: PART II

PERFORMANCE OBJECTIVES

After you have read this chapter and completed the Questions for Class Discussion, the Case, the Sales Problem, and the Exercise, you should be able to do the following:

1. Write a closing dialogue.
2. Contrast high- and low-pressure selling.
3. Write five departure statements.
4. Analyze what is meant when the prospect says no.
5. Complete a closing dialogue during a job interview.

GOOD-BYE—BUT NOT FOREVER

John Thomas prepared to leave the clothing store. Neatly he wrapped his samples and packed them into his traveling case. Gently he slipped the carbon paper of his order book between the fresh blank forms in preparation for his next sales call. He eased the signed order form into a special section of the briefcase and handed a copy to the storekeeper. "Thank you for the order," he said.

"When did you say this merchandise would arrive?" asked the store-keeper.

"You may expect delivery within ten days," smiled the salesman, snapping the lock on his briefcase.

The two men stood appraising one another, each content that the exchange had been one of mutual benefit. The storekeeper was satisfied he had made the best possible purchase and would soon have an expanded line of high-class suits to sell to his customers. The salesman was excited over the thought of having yet another fine store displaying his merchandise.

"My next trip into this territory will be in six weeks," smiled John Thomas. "Before each trip I usually send along a postcard to alert you to my arrival. In the meantime, here is my business card. You will notice my home phone number is listed, and you are welcome to call me collect if you have any questions. Once again, thank you for the business."

With that he hefted his briefcase and pushed his traveling case, which was on rollers, out the front door to his car.

As he sat behind the wheel, the salesman mentally reviewed all that had taken place. Only 40 minutes had elapsed, and during that brief time, all his twelve years of experience had been tested as he brought his background to bear on the Heart of the Sale. "Funny," he mused, "it sure takes a lot of knowledge and study just to make what seems like a simple sale." His effort had been concentrated just as the point of a thumbtack makes its way into a piece of wood. He realized that all that he was and all that he knew were similar to the head of the thumbtack. His memory flitted back over the conversation, and he took note of the many times he tried to close the sale. "It's true," he thought. "My sales manager is right. There *are* ABCs to selling." With that, he turned the ignition key and eased his way into traffic. His mind was already on the next call.

If there is a single lesson that sales trainers and experts seek to impart to new salespeople it is to "Always Be Closing" the sale. There is, perhaps, a corollary to this idea. That is, when you get the order, thank the prospect and leave. Some salespeople prepare lengthy and poetic descriptions of their products or services and feel compelled to deliver orations about their proposition. They seem impressed with the sound of their own voices.

Others prepare excellent demonstrations and want the prospective buyer to see the entire show.

However, the professional salesperson knows that the purpose is to get the order and prepare the prospect for the possibility of buying again in the future. Once the prospect has made a decision to buy, close and leave. Or, as one expert said, "Close early and close often."

HIGH VS. LOW PRESSURE

Our earlier and short explanation of the distinction between high- and low-pressure selling undoubtedly left many students in dismay. Therefore, it seems appropriate at this point to expand on the notion that there is no such thing as low-pressure selling. It is in relation to the close that this idea really takes hold.

During a training session, one group leader said, "The proper stepping-off point to teach professional selling is the close. Now, I know this is contrary to the opinions of most experts. But if we can teach salespeople how to close a sale, that may be all they need to know. Everything a person ever learns, every part of that person's life, all the experiences of the individual are concentrated in those few minutes we call the close of the sale. I don't know why we don't teach selling from the close, and then go on to the other refinements."

The point this expert was trying to make was the overwhelming importance of being able to close a sale. At the same time, it is obvious that if a salesperson is constantly seeking to close the sale, high pressure is being exerted. That's what selling is all about—trying to get orders. Hence, by definition, all selling is high-pressure.

Just as the professional ballplayer makes the difficult catch look easy, the professional salesperson makes the difficult sale appear to take place in an open and friendly atmosphere. However, friendliness and openness do not preclude high pressure. It is the appearances that count.

The salesperson who calls on a prospect already possesses a good deal of drive and ambition. That's part of why people enter the selling field. A person who enjoys the work (and if you don't, you ought to find another occupation) will be anxious to make the right impression and will know that the measure of success is directly tied to the number and volume of sales. You must not take a lighthearted approach. This is serious business; your livelihood depends on your ability to close sales.

More than that, the professional salesperson has studied the proposition and recognizes that a benefit is being brought to the prospect. Few salespeople succeed if they do not believe in themselves and their company. In the main, people are honest, and salespeople are honest. If they were not,

Figure 13-1

then the wary buyer would be able to spot any insincerity. Certainly, some people are able to convince others they are honest while beneath the surface they are charlatans, but this is not a characteristic of professional salespeople.

Another, somewhat hidden aspect of the forward momentum of the professional salesperson is understanding the importance of selling in the economic structure of society. Salespeople perform a service by bringing new products to the marketplace. If the profession of selling did not exist today, someone would have to invent it! No amount of advertising, promotion, or publicity will sell products or services. Those things may prepare the public for new ideas, but only people sell people.

There is, however, a great distinction in the life-styles of different salespeople, and this often gives the impression of a difference in drive. For instance, a stockbroker must be extremely careful in trying to convince a prospective customer to buy a stock. The basic training for stockbrokers suggests that the best relationship is one in which they merely serve to "guide" or "service" the customer. They downgrade the idea that they "sell" stocks and bonds. Rather, they build a degree of confidence that they will carry out the purchase for the client. This frequently appears to be a very soft sell.

On the other hand, door-to-door salespeople sometimes adopt the attitude that they may never see the prospect again and therefore should apply all kinds of pressure. Even this notion is not entirely true; many fine national organizations field massive sales forces based on repeat business. (The Fuller Brush Company and Avon are two prime examples of door-to-door selling that rely on repeat orders.) But the vision of salespeople peddling pots and pans, or dictionaries, or magazine subscriptions is omnipresent. In truth, these salespeople do frequently exhibit a good deal of pressure.

Not as apparent is the pressure used by those salespeople in the distribution industries. They often call on their customers every week, and they are after an order on every call. Because the distribution industry relies so heavily on full trucks of merchandise, the pressure to get orders with regularity is great. Compare this with the people who sell for large manufacturing companies, whose orders may be less frequent but much larger in volume. When an average order fills a rail car or an entire truck, then delivery schedules are less important and the sales pressure appears to be less. It isn't really less; it simply appears to be less.

If you have ever visited an auction gallery and related the methods of the auctioneer to the profession of selling, you will rapidly recognize auctioneers as salespeople who use plenty of "pressure." That is because they have a sense of urgency. If you escape from the audience, they may never see you again; hence the appearance of high-pressure tactics.

There are pressure points in all types of selling. Some are more visible than others. To assume that salespeople do not use high pressure is to assume that their individual desires for success are less. It is also to assume that the batter at the plate doesn't really want to get a hit, or that the racing-car driver doesn't really want to win, or that the surgeon doesn't really want to complete the operation successfully.

Don't confuse the appearance of low-pressure selling with the reality that all selling has its moments of high pressure.

DIALOGUE FOR CLOSING A SALE

As the close of a sale draws near, professional salespeople consider a number of ideas, several ways to bring this phase of the sale to a happy conclusion. They know there are a variety of ways, twelve at least, to convince the prospect to say, "Yes, send me some." They are also aware of the fact that no single method is foolproof and that chances for success are greatly increased by using more than one method to get the order. Once again, professional salespeople resort to probing, always seeking to find the best solution. Where to attack? What to say that will bring about a positive response from the prospect?

Let's take a look at our coupling salesperson as the sales interview draws to a conclusion:

Prospect: Why don't you arrange to see me on your next trip?

Salesperson: I certainly will. By the way, did you notice how deep the threads on this coupling are cut? (yes, Yes, YES)

Prospect: Yes.

Salesperson: You said you use about 200 couplings every month?

Prospect: Yes.

Salesperson: Fewer complaints from the production department would surely make your life more pleasant.

Prospect: Yes.

Salesperson: May I send you ten dozen couplings, Mr. Prospect? (Ask for the order)

Prospect: It's true, I have agreed with most of what you have said. But my budget won't afford a purchase this month.

Salesperson: I only have till the end of this week to take orders at this special price. May I send you some? (Special inducement)

Prospect: That still isn't going to help my budget.

Salesperson: Our minimum order is twelve dozen units. If I can have your order today, I'll hold the billing till the end of the month. That will meet your budget requirements. (Alter the proposition)

By successfully meeting all the problems that loom in the mind of the prospect, this salesperson has paved the road to an order. Here's another way this same situation might have been handled:

Prospect: Why don't you arrange to see me on your next trip?

Salesperson: I'm glad you mentioned that. Our plant is going on vacation next week, and we'll be out of couplings till they get moving again. Wouldn't it be better if I took your order today? (Standing room only)

Prospect: Well, I'll just have to take my chances.

Salesperson: You examined these couplings and noticed the deep threads. Then you agreed that our price was only a mite out of line, but that was compensated for by the fact that these pieces will last a whole lot longer than the ordinary couplings. The packing is standard in the industry, and our delivery is excellent. With the normal good credit terms we offer, why not place an order today? (Summarization)

Prospect: I still think I'll wait.

Salesperson: I understand. But look at it this way. Our couplings will save you a good deal of grief, because you will have fewer complaints. Why not place an order today and buy yourself an extra couple of weeks of peace and quiet? (Emotional)

Trying a number of ways to close a sale does not mean you will always be successful. All you have done is to give it the "old college try" and improved the odds in your favor. If a salesperson tries three, four, or five times to get the order and is not successful, then a quiet retreat is advisable. But before you are prepared to accept defeat, you should become thoroughly conversant with the various methods to close the sale. Here is yet another example:

Prospect: You seem like a pretty nice person, and I guess your company is okay. But I just don't need any new typewriters.

Salesperson: When do you think you will be in the market for some new equipment?

Prospect: Probably in about three months.

Salesperson: May I suggest this? Why not place your order now, take advantage of the special price, and we can ship them in three months? (Alter the proposition)

Prospect: How do I know the price won't be better in three months?

Salesperson: That's easy. We'll note on the purchase order that any decline in our price will automatically accrue to your company. How many units do you think you can use? (Ask for the order)

Prospect: I'm not certain I like the way this whole thing sounds.

Salesperson: I can understand what you mean. How about if we ship you six pieces and date the bill ahead till next month? That way you will have plenty of time to operate the typewriters before you even have to think about paying for them. (Alter the proposition)

Prospect: Well, I hadn't planned to make a purchase for several months.

Salesperson: That's why we're making this special offer. You can have your equipment and still not be concerned about the bill. (Secondary point)

> *Prospect:* But my secretaries don't know how to use these new-fangled machines.
>
> *Salesperson:* That's exactly why I'm here. I'll be back two days after the machines are delivered to train your secretaries. Do you think six units will be enough? (Close on an objection)

The professional salesperson moves along the inclined plane of the Heart of the Sale pursuing a successful conclusion. The thrust is forever upward, where the reward is a signed order form.

SPECIAL CONSIDERATIONS WHEN CLOSING

Every phase of a sale has unique aspects, none as significant as the close. Errors of omission or commission made during the early segments of a sale may be repaired or overcome as the sale moves forward. But the close is the end of the line, and to the extent possible, all the loose ends must be drawn together. If the sale were a dramatic presentation, which to a large degree it is, then the close is comparable to the climax. It is a very exciting time.

Your Attitude

From the viewpoint of the prospect, a number of things have happened. First, there was attraction to what the salesperson had to say because that salesperson evinced interest and concern. The prospect learned how the salesperson could satisfy a need that was barely recognized. New ideas and thoughts were thrown at the prospect—ideas that implied peace of mind and a fresh approach to work or life-style. Objections were adequately met, and the prospect witnessed an exacting demonstration of the proposition. Now, as a last step, the prospect is about to be asked to spend money or make a commitment to something that only an hour ago was foreign to his or her mind. Is it any wonder the prospect seems a little nervous or distraught?

From the viewpoint of the salesperson, a number of things have happened. Methods and techniques professional salespeople employ have been utilized. With words, gestures, and products, the salesperson was able to attract attention and awaken a new need where none existed. Inside, the salesperson felt a slight electric charge of excitement, a sense of power to effect change in another human being. Now, the moment of truth. The salesperson has nimbly deflected objections and answered questions. There is a taste of victory. It is time to close the sale.

These two positions are not overdrawn—they are as real as yesterday's sale. Even though we cannot control the feelings of the prospect, we ought to recognize that the prospect is going through a metamorphosis, a wrenching change. As with all change, the salesperson should be prepared to treat the prospect gently so that there is no rupture, so the sale does not suddenly come apart.

But as a professional salesperson, you can control your own actions. Your attitude should always be one of expectancy and anticipation. We know that some professional salespeople cannot control how they feel, nor should they want to. The vision of victory is heartening and one to be enjoyed. However, you should control your behavior. Your voice should not rise to a fever pitch, and your movements should remain calm. The professional salesperson should not signal the prospect by word or deed the excitement being experienced. One sign of a true professional is a calm outward appearance.

No sale is concluded until a close has been effected. Therefore, as the prospect and salesperson move nearer to that point, the salesperson should demonstrate a serenity, a quiet grace indicating that survival does not depend upon this order. The professional salesperson should be as gracious in winning as in losing. It is imperative that the time of the close be as professionally handled as any other segment of the sale. The salesperson's attitude must reflect confidence and assurance. There should be little, if any, show of excitement.

Why not? For one thing, the prospect will become skeptical of a salesperson who gets excited, because it telegraphs the message that sales are few and far between. If that is so, why should the prospect want to join such a limited group? Or if the salesperson seems overanxious, the prospect may withdraw while considering a request for more price concessions or more free goods. In the mind of the prospect, the thrill of closing a sale should be a routine activity. Also, in consideration of the tenuous position of the prospect, any aberrant behavior will cause further upset.

If anything, as the close draws nigh, the salesperson should become *more* reserved and controlled. The order should be taken in easy stride.

The Third Party

Few things are more disruptive to a sale than the interference of a third party. Once a triangle has been formed, your chances for a successful close are reduced immeasurably. Here's what can happen: The newcomer and the prospect take the same side of the fence, and you have to convince twice as many people that your proposition is valid. While you are answering the questions of one party, the other is thinking ahead to ways to confound you. The odds against success are great.

If the newcomer takes your part in the sale, the prospect will feel overpowered. Even though the prospect may like your proposition, being backed into a corner, as so often happens, will cause the prospect to fight rather than switch. Once the prospect feels like the underdog, there will be plenty of resistance to your overtures to close the sale.

There is a third possibility. The newcomer may say, "I am not going to interfere. I'll just sit here quietly and listen." Seems fair enough. But now you are performing before an audience on which you can have no effect unless you play to that audience. When you are dealing with a single prospect, you have an audience of one. You can get feedback from the prospect, test comprehension, plumb feelings. The uninvited guest off to one side participates in the conversation without saying a word. By the lighting of a cigarette at a particular moment, a crossing of legs, yawning, or smiling, a message is conveyed to you and to the prospect. These are part of the interference messages covered in Chapter 3. The mere presence of another human being can easily destroy the close of the sale.

The best solution to this problem is to find a quiet, secluded place to conclude your business. Remember the small private office each of the salespeople occupied the last time you purchased a car? Even when they call at home, insurance agents like to sell in the kitchen. If the prospect wants another opinion—look out.

There may be times when you have to sell a husband and wife. During the sale, you should be able to ascertain the relative buying authority each possesses. Or in a business, you may have to deal with partners. Frequently one of the partners will remain silent till the very end of the sale and then disrupt the proceedings. That partner may be trying to upset your close and get you to make a better offer.

A relatively new concept at the industrial and manufacturing level is the "buying group." Purchases are made by a committee, and the salesperson must present products to a round-table of experts. At best, the salesperson must be prepared with product knowledge and information; the use of professional selling techniques is almost impossible. There are too many faces to confront at one time. Selling to committees is generally reserved to the experienced and old-time salesperson. It takes a particular kind of courage to face a committee. (The subject of group selling is so important that an entire chapter, Chapter 14, has been devoted to all the methods and techniques that can be employed.)

When a third party appears on the scene, whether invited or not, the salesperson should try to move to an isolated area, to be alone with the prospect. It may even be advantageous to leave off the sale and chat about the weather or the ball game, hoping the interloper will soon depart. As a last resort, you might decide to call back another day.

What Does "No" Really Mean?

A sales manager was conducting a meeting one Saturday morning and asked the assembled sales force, "What does it mean when a prospective customer says, no? Often they will say, 'I don't need any today.' Just what does that mean?"

The salespeople sat quietly for a moment, and then the answers streamed forth.

"It means the person doesn't want to make a purchase."

"It means they don't need anything that day."

"It means the buyer doesn't like the salesperson."

"It means the buyer doesn't like the company."

"How about, 'I want you to convince me.' "

"Maybe the prospect needs more information."

"Probably had a fight with her husband and she's taking it out on the salesperson."

"I'll bet it wasn't her husband, more like her boyfriend."

"One time I ran into that problem. You know what was troubling the buyer? His feet hurt. When he took his shoes off, he gave me an order."

The salespeople all laughed over the protestations of the person who claimed sore feet as a turndown to an order. "It's true. We had just taken a turn through the factory, and when we got back to the office, I could tell the prospect was fidgety and nervous. Then I had to go through my whole pitch, and I couldn't figure out what was wrong. The prospect kept trying to get me out of the office. Then I noticed the new shoes. Well, I didn't want to embarrass anyone, so I said that my shoes had just come back from the shop

OFTEN, PROSPECTS WILL SAY
NO TO A SALESPERSON
BECAUSE THEY DON'T KNOW
WHAT ELSE TO SAY.

Figure 13-2

and they pinched my toes, and would there be any objection if I loosened the laces. With that, the prospect said, "Let's both take our shoes off and get comfortable."

"Preposterous!" snapped the sales manager.

Not really. Prospects have said no because they had another appointment, were expecting a phone call, or were worried about a sick child. There are so many reasons why people say no that the professional salesperson has to assume that the "no" is a request for more information or a better understanding of the proposition. There should, of course, be some sensitivity to this extraneous "no," but by and large, a negative response is a plea for more time to consider what has been said. It is a signal that some piece of information is not clear, or possibly that the prospect needs more time to consider the offer.

From the seller's point of view, a "no" should not be a stopper to the progress of the sale. It is a flag waving that indicates the need for another effort to close the sale. This is not to suggest that the salesperson be obnoxious and overstay the welcome. As long as voices are calm and controlled, the salesperson should plow ahead and seek to close the sale. "No" means a number of things, and the salesperson ought to try to discover what is behind the negative expression. But it should not deter the professional from making another stab at closing the sale.

Don't Be Afraid to Repeat Yourself

Part of the charm and excitement of a snappy sale is the use of vivid language and powerful words. They do have their place. From any number of surveys, we know that people hear less than we say and understand little of what we mean. That is why it is incumbent upon the salesperson to repeat information about the proposition.

Think back to the sales approach; we indicated that the same piece of information might be stated in several different ways. This in no way detracts from the effectiveness of the sale. As a matter of fact, we encouraged the use of the best information at the beginning, because we wanted to attract attention and awaken needs. You can't accomplish those two objectives unless you employ your best efforts. The same attitude should prevail at the close of the sale.

An offer of "free" goods was deemed a likely approach, but it is also a good way to close the sale. A customer benefit that ensures "happiness" is equally valid at the close of the sale. Placing a product in the hands of a prospect implies a sense of ownership at the opening of a sale. The effect is doubly powerful at the close.

There are a limited number of things, you may say about any proposition. But there are limitless ways to describe those attributes. That is why the professional salesperson will not hesitate to rephrase approach statements into dynamic closing statements. Here are some examples:

Approach:	Do you prefer five-sieve green beans or six-sieve green beans? (Question)
Close:	What sieve green beans do you prefer, five or six? (Reducing the choice)
Approach:	Our couplings are cut deeper and therefore do not break. This means fewer complaints. (Customer benefit)
Close:	Why not buy yourself a couple of weeks of fewer complaints and peace of mind by ordering our couplings today? (Emotional)
Approach:	Good morning, madam. These skirts are on special today at $6.95. (Bonus offer)
Close:	As you can see, we have only a limited selection of these skirts. Why not buy them at the special price? (Standing room only)
Approach:	I represent one of the largest manufacturers of plastic-based paint. (Declaration)
Close:	I know you will be happy with these colors, because you are dealing with one of the largest companies in the industry. (Assumptive)

By sliding up and down the inclined plane of the Heart of Sale, the professional salesperson has the opportunity to tap into any piece of information that seems to apply at the moment. You should never be afraid of repeating an earlier statement. But to keep the sale alive and vital, you should use fresh language.

How to Say Good-Bye

Once the order has been signed, the salesperson should depart. Easy as that sounds, many salespeople find themselves standing around, uncertain of how to take their leave. Here is the simplest way: "Thank you for your order, Ms. Prospect. I will call on you in three weeks."

That's all it takes. But many people feel they are obligated to carry on a further conversation: ball scores, family life, weather, politics, ad infinitum. It is not expected, and you should not indulge yourself. You are there for business; the business has been completed, and you should leave.

A sales trainer was instructing a group of novice salespeople, and one of them said, "When I left an account last week, I thanked the prospect for the time and just cut out."

"No, no, no!" screamed the trainer. "You never thank a prospect for time. Your time is just as important to you."

"I don't understand," said the crestfallen beginner.

"Look," snapped the trainer. "You are there to try to bring prospects a service. Why should you thank them for their time? They have as much to gain as you. It was nice of you to call."

"Well, should I thank the prospect?" asked the salesperson. "Especially if I don't get an order?"

"Thank the prospect for attention, courtesy, the use of the office, interest, anything but time. How are you going to feel when you discover that you make more money than the prospect makes? That would mean your time is more valuable than the prospect's. Would you still thank the prospect for time?"

"Yeah, well, that's right," said the salesperson. "If the prospect treats me nicely, I can say, 'Thanks for the kindness.' That's important too."

Under any circumstances, when the salesperson is ready to leave, there should be some offer of thanks. We hope it will be for an order. But when the business of taking the order is over, clear out.

SUMMARY

The close of the sale is the final segment of the Heart of Sale. It is a time when the ABCs of selling (Always Be Closing) come vibrantly to life. A large degree of excitement is present at this moment, and the salesperson should try to conceal any personal anticipation and happiness that a sale is about to be successfully concluded. There should be concern with the two objectives of the close, to get the order and to prepare the prospect for future orders.

To accomplish these two objectives, salespeople have at least twelve techniques or methods for closing a sale at their disposal:

Close with a yes, Yes, YES
Remove the stumbling blocks
Assume the order
Close on a secondary point
Reduce the choices
The "standing-room-only" close
Special discounts
Summarization
Ask for the order
Emotional

Close on an objection

Offer to alter the proposition

The best way to use these methods and techniques is in combination. The salesperson tries a number of ways and a number of times to close the sale, and may even repeat some of the things said earlier in the sale and rephrase them to make a vital closing statement.

As the sale draws to a conclusion, the salesperson should become accustomed to the idea that prospects often say no. This may or may not apply to the proposition at hand, and the salesperson should not let this response stop any attempts to close the sale. You should avoid the natural conflict when a third party is present, recognizing that it is very difficult to deal with two people during a sales presentation.

By maintaining a calm exterior, the salesperson dispels the idea that making a sale is a unique experience. When the time comes to leave, depart forthwith, remembering to thank the prospect for courtesies extended. The professional salesperson will not dawdle and thereby jeopardize the sale. When it is time to go—GO!

When is it appropriate to close a sale? Whenever the salesperson thinks an affirmative response is possible. Because you can't be certain about the prospect's frame of mind, you should try to close early—and often.

A SUCCESS STORY

"How much space do you need?" asked Marsha Allen.

"Hey, I didn't say we needed any space," replied the media buyer.

"Sorry," said Ms. Allen. "When I showed you the readership survey, you seemed impressed with the results. After all, our magazine reaches a lot of people."

"The problem is this. We're going to launch a huge campaign, and we're going to spend an awful lof of money. When I make the decision which way to go, I have to be certain my client will get the most for the money."

"How do you plan to measure the most for the money?" asked the salesperson.

"First off," said the space buyer, "we have to decide on actual dollar expenditures. Then we have to examine how many people will see particular ads. Then we have to stack this up against our objectives. In other words, how do we measure who is reading what?"

"That's a good point. If you refer to the detailed analysis we discussed when I was making my presentation, that sheet right on your desk, you will see we have a large readership and a heavy pass-along readership. Did you notice the high recognition factor among our readers?"

Before replying, the prospect picked up the sheet once more and glanced at the long list of computerized figures. "These look good, but how accurate are they?"

"Do you know the Swift Survey Company? They prepared the study as an independent project. What do you think of them?"

"They're pretty good," allowed the prospect.

"How long have you done business with our publications?"

"About six years."

"How well do you know me?"

He looked at Marsha Allen and said, "Okay. You win. You're right, I do know you and your company, and you have got a good package here. I give up. I'll sign."

"You made a good decision," Marsha smiled. "Shows how sharp you are."

QUESTIONS FOR CLASS DISCUSSION

1. When is the best time to try to close a sale? Explain what is meant by the right "psychological" moment to close a sale.
2. Can you recall the closing statements made by a salesperson? Describe the situation and comment on the validity of that salesperson's attempts to get the order.
3. Write a dialogue for closing the sale of a new car. Use at least three different closes.
4. Write a dialogue for closing a sale for a living-room couch. Use three different closes.
5. You have just successfully concluded the sale of a set of encyclopedias. Write three statements you might use to conclude the interview as you leave.
6. Can you think of any sales situation in which it is appropriate to thank the prospect for time devoted to the interview? Explain.
7. Discuss the possible meanings of the word *no* when used by the prospect. Is this a meaningful way for the prospect to refuse to buy? Why?
8. Explain the differences between "high-pressure" and "low-pressure" selling.
9. Explain how an approach statement can be converted to a close. Give three examples.

CASE 13—THE UNCLOSED CLOSE

George Peters and Jim Sullivan had been closeted for over half an hour. Spread across the purchasing agent's desk were nine samples of floor coverings, each of a different quality. The conversation had been pleasant, and the shared information had kept both men riveted to their seats. Each time Jim implied an order, George had demurred. "I just don't think I'm ready to buy," he said.

As he approached the close, Jim felt the need for some dramatic way to bring the sale to a conclusion. "Is there any other information you need at this time?" he asked.

"No," smiled George. "You have told me all I need to know at this time."

With that Jim began to pack his briefcase. Casually he laid his order book on the edge of the desk as he neatly wrapped each and every tile and placed it in the correct slot in his bag. The room was quiet except for the rustle of tissue paper. Jim obviously had a great deal of respect for his samples. Finally, all nine tiles were packed and Jim sat back to light a cigarette. He said nothing.

"Okay," said George. "What's your game?"

"I don't know what you mean."

"Why haven't you asked me for an order?"

"Say, I'm sorry. Which floor coverings shall I send you? Perhaps a roll of each would be best."

"No. Send me the red, green, and . . . What other colors do you have?"

"Here, let me show you," said Jim, unwrapping the samples and placing them once more in front of the buyer. "You can make your selection from these."

"Okay," said George smartly. "Next time don't put your samples away so fast."

"I won't," said Jim.

1. Would you categorize Jim Sullivan as "high" or "low" pressure?
2. Explain your opinion.
3. What other closes could Jim have used?
4. Why did George Peters almost "force" Jim to take an order?

EXERCISE 13

After the interviewer finished describing the salary, bonus, and expense allowance, the job sounded more attractive than ever. Even though you tried unsuccessfully to close (asking for the job), you now have another opportunity. Please complete the following dialogue:

Interviewer: You sound pretty good. Give me a call in a couple of weeks.

You: (Assumptive close)

SALES PROBLEM 13—THE FUMBLED PLAN

Putting the plan together took Ron three nights of heavy work. It was a variation of a merchandising idea he had used with an account in another city. Basically, it meant that the retailer would have to engage in some advertising, sales training, and promotion work. After selling the concept, he asked for and received a rather large order for merchandise. But what had begun as a great plan soured when the customer didn't carry out all the details. Now, Ron was on the spot. Even though it wasn't his fault, the customer was going to hold him accountable.

Here is how three sales reps felt they might be able to smooth over such a difficult time:

Sales Rep #1: The only thing Ron can do is apologize because the plan didn't work. It's best to go right to the customer and explain that under other conditions, this merchandising program had been successful.

Not only that, Ron has to convince the customer that he deserves credit for bringing in fresh ideas. If they don't all work, it only means they have to both try harder.

Sales Rep #2: I would tell the customer that this program had worked elsewhere. Then I would supply the names and phone numbers of other, noncompetitive accounts who met with success. I would want this customer to call the others.

In certain instances, I have even had accounts call a competitor to ascertain that a promotion I planned for them had been successful.

Sales Rep #3: I would be very tactful. If it was a manager who ran the promotion, as opposed to the owner of the business, I would be extra careful about going over his or her head. You can't tell a boss that one of the employees did something wrong.

Probably, I would want to have a conference with the top manager and say that something went wrong. "Let's discuss what I did wrong, what you did wrong, and how we can make it better in the future."

If I got another crack at introducing a big promotion, you can be sure I would ride herd on the project from the beginning to the very end. No way would I allow it to fail again.

Interviewer:	Not quite sure.
You:	(SRO close)
Interviewer:	That's a chance we'll have to take. Who are you talking with?
You:	(Stumbling-block close)

Interviewer:	Sounds reasonable.
You:	(Summarization close)
Interviewer:	It all does make sense, but do you think you could re-spond to the many disappointments that go with selling?
You:	(Close on an objection)
Interviewer:	You certainly are persuasive.
You:	(yes, Yes, YES close)

(Of course, you could continue with at least six more closes.)

14

GROUP SELLING

PERFORMANCE OBJECTIVES

After you have read this chapter and completed the Questions for Class Discussion, the Case, the Sales Problem, and the Exercise, you should be able to do the following:

1. Explain the WOLIPPP system for group selling.
2. Identify the three methods to control the group sale.
3. Prepare a group sales presentation.

THE HIGH-HORSEPOWER SALES DELIVERY

Jimmy Bank nodded his head. "I agree that I do the buying, Bob. But you know that I have nothing to do with trucks."

Robert Peerson leaned forward and said, "True, but you can set up the meeting with the buying committee. This is a major purchase, and somebody has to get the ball rolling. Since you have known me for many years and accept my reputation as an honest seller, won't you help me get the meeting?"

"It might prove advantageous to me at the buying end if we had trucks that could carry 475 cases instead of only 400 cases. Do you think you can make a presentation that would prove that?"

"Jimmy," the sales rep said, "you have hit the nail right where all nails ought to be hit. If I can convey this information to the buying committee, we'll have one very big sale. Can you set up the meeting?"

Convinced that his friend had some valid points, Jimmy Bank did set up the meeting. Of course, he realized there was an element of risk, which is why he only took this much trouble for those salespeople in whom he had huge confidence. He and Peerson had done business together for almost twelve years, and he knew the sales rep had an excellent reputation. Thus, he felt no qualms about arranging with the branch manager, operations manager, controller, and delivery manager to gather at 10 A.M. the following Thursday.

The conference room was arranged beforehand—a flip chart, an overhead projector, and notepads positioned around the table. Peerson had prepared a full agenda, which would take just over one hour. The participants knew they would be asked to spend that much time. They also knew that time had been set aside to review the proposal and to ask questions.

"Why was I asked to attend?" questioned the controller.

"Good point," said Peerson. "If we gain some agreement on this purchase, we shall want to know how best to handle the financing and depreciation. You are the best person to answer those questions."

"What about me?" quizzed the branch manager. "Can't this decision be made and then brought to my desk?"

"Glad you raised that question," responded Peerson. "There will be a great saving to the branch, and it may require a slight change in overall direction. Each of you should be involved in this decision, because each department will somehow benefit by making a change in the truck fleet."

With those preliminary statements out of the way, Peerson began his formal presentation. Deftly he used the overhead projector to demonstrate figures of interest to the branch manager. Sprinkled throughout the presentation were advantages and benefits for the delivery manager. Of course, all the points had to appeal to the controller.

After each five-minute segment, Peerson tested the audience with some pulse-taking questions to ascertain their understanding and agreement. He moved around the table in an attempt to confirm his complete control of the session. On one occasion, he sat down and encouraged the assembled group to speak out. They all seemed to defer to the controller, acting as if he had the authority to spend the money, or at least to give them permission to spend the money.

Finally, when the questions tapered off, Peerson went around the table, once more gaining acceptance of his proposition. Only the branch manager held back, and then he looked toward the controller, who winked approval.

"Then we agree," closed Peerson. "We can clarify the details as to size and delivery dates, but we have a go-ahead. Thank you, gentlemen."

As the room cleared and all shook hands, Jimmy Banks helped Peerson gather the used material in a heap. "Good show," he said to his sales friend.

"It's always fun to have group meetings," Peerson smiled. "You're right. It really is a show."

THE NATURE OF GROUP SELLING

Selling is selling, whether on a one-to-one basis (best known as personal selling), or when it takes place in front of a group of people. The essential need to cover all aspects in the Base of the Sale and then deliver the Heart of the Sale in a professional manner exists in both situations.

During a group sale, there will usually be three, four, or more people in the audience. It is imperative to recognize that each of these people may have a different agenda, different reasons for attending the sales session. For the salesperson, this recognition will demonstrate itself in the regard shown for the individuals and the fact that on occasion, each will be addressed personally.

Every professional sale requires a considerable amount of planning. Certainly this fact stands out in the foregoing chapters of this book. The more time that is devoted to planning all the phases in the sale, the greater are the chances for success. Group selling is simply more complicated. There are more questions, more objections, more personal problems, more strange voices, more disrupting influences, more of everything that makes selling so exciting.

To say that group selling requires more planning is to state only part of the opportunity. There are significant differences, and these we shall cover in detail. All group sales take place within the context of the sales plan, the absolute need for careful review of the Base of the Sale and the Heart of the Sale.

A Sign of the Future

One-to-one selling, as the terminology indicates, is the sale that takes place between two people. This type of selling will continue to grow and, in fact, will remain the major area of professional selling. When you consider all the sales transactions that take place each day, the number is staggering. In the main, these are conducted between two people.

In the fields of industrial, manufacturing, and distribution selling, group-selling efforts have increased. Although the size of the group-selling market cannot be measured or evaluated, there is strong indication that in the future, many purchase decisions will be made by groups of people rather than by individuals. The rationale for this thinking can be seen in the effect on the organization of any purchase.

When a furniture store purchases a new line of living-room furniture, the purchasing agent may select the colors, sizes, and styles. However, the person in charge of the storeroom is involved in preparing for the space, the controller has to know how the billing will take place, the advertising director has to be able to properly promote the new products, and the salespeople on the floor may have to be trained in the methods to sell the merchandise to the ultimate consumer. Obviously, if the furniture store is small and privately owned, the owner-manager may be the person who makes all these decisions.

There are other reasons why group selling will increase. When several people examine a proposition, they can often detect questions that would go unnoticed by one person. They might also identify advantages and benefits that were not noticed by the salesperson. A key reason that group selling will expand is that the members of the organization who have to work with the material or service being purchased are claiming more authority with regard to purchase decisions.

Group selling is generally reserved for the older, more professional, more experienced salesperson. However, any sales professional will recognize the need for group-selling sales skills in the presentation of insurance policies to a husband and wife, the sale of automobiles to families, the sale of a house, or even the sale of a set of encyclopedias. Even though personal selling will dominate the sales profession, group-selling skills will grow in importance.

THE SPONSOR

Following a detailed presentation of a new food product, the purchasing agent said, "I like this item, and I think we can make money with it. In fact, I'm so convinced that I'm going to take it to the purchasing committee."

"You mean you can't make the decision to buy?" asked the forlorn sales rep.

"Oh, no. All I do is reorder merchandise when we are running low. To add an item to our shelves is a major decision—one made by the buying committee."

This brief conversation identifies a very important person, if not the key person, in a group sale. Someone has to bring the sales representative and the buying committee together. This person is called the sponsor.

Who might this sponsor be? It is likely to be someone you are already selling. It might be the buyer or purchasing agent for a small (or large) business who does buy noncritical items. However, to add an item to the list of approved products that the buyer may order from you may require the approval of a higher authority, such as a buying committee.

The sponsor may also be the person who interviews salespeople and then directs them to the proper person to get the order. For example, some organizations have a head buyer who directs salespeople to buyers of particular lines of merchandise. On the other hand, a lesser buyer may direct the seller to the head buyer, who makes some major decisions. In either circumstance, the salesperson is talking to someone who is generally a customer. This person becomes a sponsor as the sale moves towards the buying committee.

Here are some further examples of potential sponsors:

A sales rep selling audiovisual equipment to a college mentioned to the purchasing agent that the company also handled security systems to track deliveries at the storeroom door, and that it also installed TV monitors at critical stations around the building. The buyer was acquainted with the equipment of the seller and was a good customer; however, security was not her responsibility. Initially, she wanted the sales rep to call on a couple of other people. Because the buyer and seller had a good business relationship, the seller asked the buyer to find out who did make that kind of purchase, and requested that she set up a meeting with the appropriate people.

A sales rep with a new style of jeans wanted to display the product at a rather large women's specialty shop. Since the person who normally placed orders knew the sales rep, she offered to bring the new line to the attention of the store manager. Both the sales rep and the buyer recognized that adding an additional line of stylish jeans might upset the overall marketing plan for the store. Together they agreed that the best presentation would be to the manager, the advertising person, and the department manager. Therefore, a group sales call was arranged.

A food sales rep showed a new frozen entrée to the food-service manager in a restaurant. Although the chef had the final say as to the quality of the product, the owner had to be consulted, and even the headwaiter was involved in the sale. The thinking was that the manager had to consider the image of the restaurant, the chef had to decide if the handling of the product was acceptable, and the headwaiter had to inform the public through the table servers (salespeople).

In each of these examples, drawn from medium-size businesses, the sales representative had to make a major presentation to a group of people. It might appear that selling the various products to three or four people separately might be better. However, the usual response is, "If Harry likes it, it's okay with me." Or, "I'd rather hear what everybody else thinks before going ahead." When people are sold separately, indecision is the rule.

Now that the sponsor has arranged for a group sale, the sales representative has accepted a huge responsibility. The sponsor took a risk, perhaps seeking to make a name or establish a reputation, and has taken a chance by placing faith in the presentation of the salesperson.

For the sales rep, there is the opportunity not only to conclude a sale but to make a hero out of the sponsor. This, quite naturally, will lead to other group-sale opportunities. To do this requires more planning than does a one-to-one sales effort. It is a show being produced for a small audience.

THE WOLIPPP SYSTEM

"Any time you put on a show, you have to have WOLIPPP," said the older timer. "W-O-L-I-P-P-P!"

"That's a funny way to spell wallop," said the sales rep.

"It sure is," snapped the old timer, "until you know what it means."

This mnemonic device is intended to stir the imagination of the salesperson and ensure that all steps are taken to bring the group sale to a successful conclusion. Each letter represents a step or an activity that will lend to that assurance:

"W" Is for Who and What

The direction of any sale is aided by the prior knowledge of some personal and business information about the prospect. When there are three or four prospects, as in a group sale, it is crucial that this information be gathered beforehand. A list of names and titles is essential, as well as some data on the authority of each of the people present, how long they have been with the company, and their particular interest (or lack of interest) in your proposition.

Since you have now joined forces with the sponsor, this is the natural place for you to begin gathering information. Do not assume that a title such as Chief Engineer means that the person is in fact an engineer. Every title has

YOU GOTTA HAVE 'WOLIPPP'
TO WIN GROUP SALES.

Figure 14-1

to be analyzed and explained by the sponsor. Among the data you gather will be some personal leanings or foibles that may represent deep background. This information should be stored away and used only for your personal understanding of why some people act the way they do.

To help during the presentation, the list should be in front of you and laid out as the people are seated, clockwise or counterclockwise. Also, it is important to verify how the names are pronounced and whether first names are acceptable. It is always safe to use the titles Mr. and Ms. (or Mrs. or Miss).

It is apparent that the initial step in preparing for a group sale is to do the necessary preapproach work and to gain as much knowledge about the audience as is possible. Included in this advance work will be the accumulation of knowledge about the business as well.

"O" Is for Objective

Few things are as difficult for salespeople as stating an objective for a sales call. Yet this may be the single most important part of the plan, because it will dictate what to say and how to say it. It will also provide a way to measure the degree of success of the sales call. For instance, many group sales are intended to merely gain agreement to carry out a preliminary piece of work before facing the issue of making a purchase. Thus, the objective of the group sale might be to gain approval for a survey.

Here are some other possible basic objectives, each stated in a single sentence:

"At the conclusion of this presentation, we shall ask for a sample order of $2,000."

"Our objective this morning is to gain approval for the installation of one small computer on a trial basis for one year."

"At the close of this presentation, we shall seek one test order for each of the seven regions in the company."

Inherent in the statement of the objective is the counsel of the sponsor in helping the salesperson aim at the proper target. This once more links the goals of the sponsor and the salesperson.

With clearly stated objectives, the salesperson can select the proper methods, materials, and presentation tactics to gain the result. Moreover, they offer the salesperson the best possible way to start the meeting.

Normally, the sponsor will introduce the salesperson, who can then simply say, "The reason for this meeting is to ask for a sample order for $2,000." Telling the group why they have been asked to come together is perfectly natural. In fact, it is almost imperative so that they may begin to think along those lines. This is a business meeting and not merely a social call. The presence of all the people indicates a sincere interest in what the salesperson has to say. This is not a sale in a conventional sense.

In personal selling, a lot of attention is paid to the approach, because in most instances, the buyer was otherwise occupied. In group selling, the "buyers" have come together for the specific purpose of considering your proposal, so they have a pretty good idea that you will make a sales presentation. That is why it is helpful to tell them why they have come together. Because they are an audience, you will need other ways to gain attention. (We'll talk about this under "L.")

The rhythm of the group sale is not unlike that of other kinds of selling. You tell the prospect what you are going to say, you say it, and then you tell what you said. In group selling, you state the objective, tell (show or demonstrate) the group why the objective is valid, and then seek agreement with the objective. It is always much easier to close the sale when the group knows what you are trying to accomplish.

"L" Is for Leader

A group of people will take on a character all its own. Each group has a leader; this person may be the one who asks a lot of questions, or the one who asks no questions. He or she may be the person with ultimate authority, or the person with perceived authority. As you observe the audience, you should be able to detect who the real leader is. Members of the group will defer to that person, glancing furtively, or openly seeking approval of an opinion.

As a general rule, the highest-level manager will be the true authority in the group. However, this is not always the case, since some lower-level managers, by dint of their personality or ability, may actually be able to exert a huge degree of control. From the viewpoint of the salesperson, these things should become evident as the meeting progresses.

Although there will be a leader of the group, the salesperson is the leader of the meeting. This control is significant, because the salesperson controls the pace and flow of the meeting. There are three effective ways to maintain this control: sitting, strolling, and questioning.

When the salesperson stands in front of the group, he or she dominates the meeting. The physical height and the chance to move about demonstrate that the salesperson is in charge. At some moments during the meeting, the salesperson may decide to sit down, which effectively relinquishes control of the meeting. Standing once more reasserts leadership and regains control of the meeting.

The second way to exert control is to stroll around the room or the table. As questions are raised from the floor, a person on the other side of the table may interject a response. This cross-discussion can prove very disruptive to the progress of the sale. Moving from the head of the table and strolling to one side of the room will effectively refocus control on the salesperson. Since the salesperson is the only one who is mobile, any movement or gesture will concentrate the attention of the group.

The third way to maintain control is to serve as a funnel for all the questions. Frequently in a group discussion, one person will direct a question to another. When this happens, the discussion leader has lost control. To regain control, join the conversation and say, "I guess what you want to know is how many widgets there are in a case? That's a valid question, and I'm certain Marian can give us the answer." Often the salesperson, who should be able to answer all the questions, will purposely redirect a question to a member of the group. This serves to involve the group, make the person responding feel more positively about the proposition, and also tell the salesperson how committed the respondent is. In other words, control or leadership does not mean dominating the conversation so much as it means being the person who directs conversational traffic.

"I" Is for Identifying the Dissident

Every group of people will have at least one dissident; no matter what is said, this person will be against the proposition. The "perpetual pessimist" is everywhere.

The dissident may be the key to the successful sale. This person will raise the most difficult and trying questions. Also, this person will attract the most attention. If you can satisfy (sell) this person, you will simultaneously satisfy the other members of the group. If the person is only trying to be disruptive, you will gain the support of the other members of the group, who will resent the interference. In other words, you can still make the sale without the approval of this person. By raising questions, the dissident really plays into the hands of the salesperson.

By definition, the dissident is a troublemaker. This means the professional salesperson must draw on all the skills available to overcome objections. (Chapter 11 was devoted to this particular phase of the Heart of the Sale, and all these techniques can be employed to cope with the dissident.) Here is an example of how the salesperson might deal with a dissident:

There were five people in the group, the sponsor and four managers. Thatcher was causing the most trouble, raising questions and generally interfering with the forward motion of the sale.

"What makes you so certain we can save money if we use thingabobs instead of widgets?" she demanded.

"That's an excellent question," said the sales rep. "How much are you paying for widgets?" (Boomerang)

"We can get widgets for $30 a dozen, which is a darn good price."

"How much will thingabobs cost?" (Question)

"That's why I'm asking the question. You said the price was $35 a dozen."

"You are right on target. The reason the unit cost is higher is that thingabobs last 30 percent longer. Thus, we charge 15 percent more for 30 percent longer usage." (Compensation)

Even though this is part of a group sale, the principles and techniques of professional selling are much in use. As we have said in earlier chapters, objections are really road signs on the way to concluding a successful sale. Locating and identifying the dissident in any group, and dealing with that person in a professional selling manner, will prepare the group for a close.

"P" Is for Plenty of Literature

As the session drew to a close, the sales representative restated the objective, to be allowed to make a survey of four distribution centers before submitting a written proposal. The last piece of information was a formal request outlining how the survey would be conducted. He started handing each member of the group a three-page document when he realized that the group had grown to nine people—the president of the company had slipped in to hear the presentation. There were only eight copies of the outline.

Many salespeople find themselves in this predicament when conducting a group sale. The simple solution is to have much more material or handouts than you will ever need.

A couple of other points concerning these handouts: If you do distribute reading material, samples, or brochures, you will lose control of the audience. They will be distracted by looking at the handout. If you intentionally pass out some material for reading, stop talking and allow the group time to digest the information. Then, when they have refocused their attention, you may rise in your position as the leader of the meeting and pose questions to ascertain that the group is once more on track.

Some salespeople prepare a brief outline of what is going to take place during the presentation. They actually review the outline first, before making the presentation. The rest of the handouts, pamphlets, reports, surveys, or computerized data are held to the conclusion of the meeting. Some sales presentations may last for several hours, although this is doubtful. In the event that the meeting is this long, the salesperson should prepare for a natural break in the proceedings so that group members may stretch and otherwise relieve themselves.

The objectives of the meeting will dictate the need for material or handouts. Equipment needs—such as overhead projectors, extra bulbs, extension cords, pens, chalk, and scratch pads—should be listed beforehand and double-checked just before the presentation. Having sufficient literature for handouts is one sign of professionalism.

"P" Is for Poll Taker

As the formalized segment of the presentation draws to a conclusion, it is necessary to "test" the group, to ascertain their understanding and agreement. In a one-to-one selling situation, this is known as "pulse taking." In a group sale, it is sometimes called "poll taking."

Since each member of the group is in attendance for a different reason, the salesperson should be prepared to pose questions that relate to specific individuals. Here are some sample questions:

"How will the addition of widgets to the inventory affect storage space in the warehouse?" (to the operations manager)

"What things should be stressed when demonstrating widgets to the machinists in the plant?" (to the production manager)

"Are there any alterations in the billing procedure that will make the flow of paper better?" (to the controller)

These questions involve different departments, each of which is concerned with the sales proposition. As these questions are answered, the salesperson is effectively taking a poll and gaining consensus. The opinions and feelings expressed clear the way for asking for the order, the final phase in the Heart of the Sale.

"P" Is for Pounce

Even though the group sale has a clear objective, one determined by and with the sponsor, it should not be limited. Even if the objective is met, the salesperson may decide that the climate is favorable to seek an even larger order. This is known as "pounce."

In one situation, in which a sales rep was trying to sell training programs to three regions of a manufacturing company, the time seemed ripe to strike for a total order. Despite the original statement of the objective, the salesperson asked for an order for all seven regions. Not surprisingly, she got the order.

An "ounce of pounce" is a characteristic of all professional selling. The fact that a group of people has been assembled to hear the presentation is no reason to desert professional selling techniques. On the contrary, they are *more* needed. The desire to close the sale and gain a larger piece of business is an important part of successful selling. In the wind-down phases of a group sale, it is quite natural for the salesperson to ask for an even bigger order if the timing seems right.

Fresh sales opportunities can rarely be predicted. The professional salesperson will be alert to recognize and pounce upon these opportunities.

SUMMARY

Selling to a group of people has challenges not usually encountered in personal (or one-to-one) selling. Although each requires the full use of all the methods and techniques described in the Base of the Sale and the Heart of the Sale, group selling offers more challenges. That is why special attention should be paid to the complex interworkings of dealing with a number of people at one time.

There is ample evidence that the scope of group selling will increase. As business continues to become ever more complex, the decisions to add lines of merchandise or introduce new products will be made by interested parties within the organization. Certainly this is true in the industrial, manufacturing, and distribution areas.

The chance to make a sales presentation to a group starts with one person—a sponsor who is in a position to arrange the meeting. The sales representative will be responsible for making a good impression, because the sponsor is taking a risk in setting up the meeting. Probably the sponsor will be someone with whom the salesperson is already doing some business, or he or she may be a person who knows the salesperson and is willing to make the necessary arrangements.

IN A GROUP SALE THE NEEDS
AND DESIRES OF EVERY PARTICIPANT
MUST BE MET.

Figure 14-2

In addition to all the preparation required of a big sale, other factors are significant when you are facing a group. The WOLIPPP system is merely a device to make sure that the presentation is properly planned. This approach stresses:

"W" for who and what (of the audience)

"O" for objective (of the sale)

"L" for leader (of the audience)

"I" for identifying the dissident

"P" for plenty of literature

"P" for poll taker

"P" for pounce

These seven characteristics of a successful group sale are interwoven with the prework planning that composes the Base of the Sale and the Heart of the Sale.

A SUCCESS STORY

"She's a devil," thought Sam Acker. "Oh, she is competent as an office manager, but a devil nonetheless."

He leaned forward in his seat, studying the faces of the management group assembled to consider the purchase of a complete system of file folders and binders. For three years, he had been successful in selling coordinated binders to the sales department and the shipping department. Now he wanted to extend this coordinated effort throughout the entire company. It meant increasing his volume by four times if he was successful. The main obstacle at the moment seemed to be Mary Murphy.

Acker knew Murphy from past experiences in trying to sell her binders and file folders. Once in a while, he had been able to sneak in an order, but it was never anything substantial. When his firm, the Three-Ring Binder Company, expanded its printing capability, the idea of selling the Continental Corporation all its binder needs became exciting. If Acker could introduce his products to the shipping, personnel, and office managers, he could put together a price that would save Continental a lot of money and ensure rapid delivery.

The purchasing manager, Harold Robbins, had arranged for a group sale, and Acker had made a dynamic presentation. In less than 50 minutes, he had covered all the salient points and was now waiting for the group to examine some of the new styles and colors. Throughout the entire presentation, Murphy had raised a number of senseless questions—at least they seemed senseless to Acker.

As he sat there thinking about Mary Murphy, Sam Acker realized he wasn't really listening to her questions. She was sending some kind of message, but he wasn't hearing what she was really saying. Her concerns were cloaked. He knew he needed complete agreement to make this program work, so he decided to take a poll.

"George, how do you feel about these binders in the sales department?"

"No particular feeling. If the rest want to go along, it's okay with me."

"Good," said Acker. "Thelma, how about in your area over in personnel."

"I like the idea. When can we start?"

"Just as soon as we get some further feelings out on the table," said Acker. "We know that shipping is satisfied, so that leaves the office. What are your thoughts, Mary?"

Murphy looked sharply at Acker. "Why do we need uniformity? Besides, I like to order my own materials."

"Mary, you have raised two crucial points. First, the uniformity does two things. It gives you all a professional look, and it saves money because of mass buying. But the more important point you raised is controlling your own purchasing. How do you think we can resolve that issue?"

"By not buying from you."

"Sure, that's one way. Is there any other way?"

"By still ordering independently."

"That's exactly why I'm here. To arrange for a master agreement in terms of uniformity, and then to ascertain what kind of ordering cycle each of you will find convenient. What will make you happy?"

"I want someone to see me every two weeks to take an order."

"If I call on you every other Monday, will that be satisfactory?"

"You will still give us the same binders at the lower price?" she asked.

"Yes."

She thought for a moment. "I'm in."

QUESTIONS FOR CLASS DISCUSSION

1. What risk does the sponsor take in arranging a group-sale meeting?
2. How would you handle the dissident in a group sale who said, "This meeting is a waste of time"?
3. Cite three examples of group selling.
4. If you represented a uniform company, what might be your objective during a group sale in a restaurant? at a meatpacking plant? at a retail store?
5. Describe three techniques that will ensure your leadership role during a group sale.
6. What is meant by "poll taking"?

CASE 14—A DISPOSABLE AFFAIR

For Ray Jarns, it was the biggest opportunity of his career in selling. Here, settled in a small hotel in Chicago, sat the purchasing agent for Hotels Incorporated and the three general managers—Throckmorton from Chicago, Thurston from San Francisco, and Thomas from New York. All had agreed to meet with Jarns at the request of the P.A.

"It's really very nice to be here today," Jarns started. "We have some exciting things to talk about. Our new line of disposable tableware and flatware is really nifty. What we would like to do is match the needs of your three properties and make one big order. Won't that be nice? You'll all look alike."

Throckmorton moved uneasily in his seat. "What is it you want from us?" he asked.

"We'd like you to go along with our plan."

"What plan?" asked Throckmorton with disgust. "What's the purpose of this meeting?"

Jarns was a little surprised. "Why, I want to demonstrate these new disposable items so they can be used at your hotels. For example, these new cups are excellent for room service. They circumvent the need for washing."

Thomas interrupted. "We already have disposable cups around our swimming pool, which saves us a lot of trouble when somebody drops one on the concrete. No more cut feet."

SALES PROBLEM 14—PROGRAM SELLING

Frank heard about program selling at a sales meeting. It was the first time he realized that it was possible to sell everything—or almost everything—to a customer.

In the past, he had always adopted the attitude that there was plenty of business for everybody, that he didn't have to get it all. But this new concept the company was pushing did seem to make some sense. That was why he decided to present it to the Holiday Ranch Hotel. He knew that he would have to call on the housekeeper, food-service director, maintenance staff, and office manger. That would be the only way to get all the paper and janitorial business.

First, he had to clear the idea with the general manager.

To his chagrin, the general manager turned him down. Then, three months later, he discovered that another paper house was going to get the bulk of the business, on a program basis.

Here is how three salespeople reacted to this unfortunate turn of events:

Sales Rep #1:   I just went through this experience. It's tough. I decided to keep calling, take whatever business was left over, and wait till the other company makes a mistake.

I have also decided to confront the general manager and ask him what I'm doing wrong, why I didn't get a crack at the program sale. After all, I was the one who asked for the chance.

Sales Rep #2:   It seems to me that Frank sold the program idea, but his competitor "closed" the sale. He should have been ready to strike for the close before he even introduced the idea.

At this point, he should not drop the account. He should try to identify those products he feels strongly about and try to continue selling them to the customer.

Apparently, the sales rep didn't really know about his competition. This may be the time to study what the other people are doing, to find ways to recapture this account and to prevent losing others.

Sales Rep #3:   If the account was planning to use me as a backup supplier, I would do my best to give them the same loyal service I had provided in the past. I would stay very alert to what was happening and wait for the right moment to try to sell my program.

I have had this happen to me. A competitor came in and wiped me out on product and price. When I had been out for a while, I returned to make sure the service level was where it was supposed to be. What I discovered was that the competition had got lax and even raised prices. That's the time to come roaring back with a fresh approach to your own program.

"That's good," said Jarns. "It's part of what we have in mind in bringing you this complete line."

Thurston turned to Thomas and asked, "Where else are you using disposables?"

"Well, we use them in the take-out section of our coffee shop, but never in the main dining room."

Throckmorton interjected, "We've had a lot of luck with disposables late at night, after the dishwashers have gone. We also use them for special snacks during cocktail parties."

Thomas asked, "Have you ever thought about using disposables for some of the inexpensive banquets—bowling parties and stuff like that?"

"No," said the other two managers. "But it might be worth looking into."

Jarns cleared his throat and said, "Well, you can see, gentlemen, the obvious advantage of installing a more complete disposable system would really be helpful."

"I still don't know what you want from us," demanded Throckmorton.

Jarns looked forlorn and beaten. He glanced at the P.A. as if seeking some help. Scattered around his work table were piles of cups, saucers, plates, and flatware. He gestured feebly and smiled.

1. What advice and counsel do you have for Ray Jarns?
2. How would you add WOLIPPP to this presentation?

EXERCISE 14

Downtown in the business district is a five-story department store. Of the 300 employees, about 200 are directly involved in sales.

You are the Prentice-Hall sales representative in the area, and you have a meeting with the department heads from the furniture, toys, jewelry, appliances, and men's clothing departments. This session was arranged by the training director, who thinks every salesperson should go through a training program using *Professional Selling* as a basic textbook. However, there is not sufficient money in the training budget to purchase the books, and the training director thinks that the department managers can come up with the necessary dollars.

Map out your plans for a group sale.

15

SERVICE AFTER THE SALE

PERFORMANCE OBJECTIVES

After you have read this chapter and completed the Questions for Class Discussion, the Case, the Sales Problem, and the Exercise, you should be able to do the following:

1. List and explain the benefits to the salesperson of service.
2. List and explain five characteristics of the customer that help determine the amount of service to be rendered.
3. Prepare a "service plan" from the point of view of a retail salesperson.
4. Prepare a "service plan" from the point of view of a manufacturer's salesperson.

SERVICE SELLS

"Pull into that diner up ahead," said Harry Jackson. "We'll get a cup of coffee and review this last interview."

Ronald Bank guided the car into a parking spot. He was disturbed over the need to review the sale. It had been an excellent interview—at least that was what he thought. From the beginning, he had controlled the sale, moving through the approach, presentation, and demonstration with ease. When it came to meeting objections, he had fielded every challenge, using all the techniques and methods he had learned during the sales training sessions. To top it off, he had neatly presented three types of closes, finally getting an order well in excess of expectations. The idea of reviewing what had taken place seemed unnecessary. Even though he had been on the job only three weeks, he felt secure that the interview was close to perfect.

As the two men settled into a booth, Harry said, "I want to compliment you on the way you handled yourself. You did a fine job."

Heartened by the praise, Ronald asked, "Then why did you feel the need to review what happened?"

"Hey, we learn from the good things we do as well as from the mistakes we make. I just wanted to reinforce in your mind some of the things you said and some of the things you promised to do. Since this was so successful, you can derive double beneifts. Let me ask a question: Why do you think you made this sale?"

Ronald rubbed his chin as he considered an answer. "Probably because I followed all the plans and thinking that took place before we actually went through the door. I spent a lot of time creating a dynamic sales plan, and it worked."

"You said a couple of things during the interview that made quite an impression on Mrs. Silvers. Did you notice how she picked up her pencil when you started to talk about our inventory control program?"

"Well, yes, I noticed her pick up the pencil. But I didn't attach any importance to it."

"Exactly. But remember, I was watching while you were doing all the talking. When she picked up the pencil, it told me you had said something that touched a nerve. She apparently liked the idea that you would take over a piece of work she dislikes—inventory control. From that point on, the sale moved along rather smartly."

"I thought she became really receptive after I went over how I would be at the warehouse the day after the delivery to talk with the supervisor about the best ways to stack the cases."

"You're right. She really warmed up when you said that. All in all, it was a very successful sales call. I'm glad I was able to be along, even though there was no need for me to be with you."

"You had me worried for a minute, Harry. When you said you wanted to review this sale, I thought I had made a bunch of mistakes."

"No, you did fine. But I really wanted to alert you to the fact that you now have your work carved out for you."

"What do you mean?"

"Well, you made a number of commitments. You told Mrs. Silvers you were going to set up an inventory system. Heck, that takes a little doing. When you get started, let me know, and I'll try to help you with it. If you want to meet our warehousing people before you go to help their storage people, that might be a good idea. I'd also check with the credit department. Some of the information we have may be outdated, and you wouldn't want this order delayed because of a credit misunderstanding."

"Gee, that's going to cut into my selling time. Is there anybody at the home office who can take care of some of these details?"

"That's why I thought we'd better have this chat. You did a good selling job. But a sale isn't complete just because you took an order. Part of the reason Mrs. Silvers wanted to buy was because she was impressed with all the other things you told her you would do besides taking an order."

Ronald stirred his coffee aimlessly. "Yeah, I guess I said a little too much."

"No, no, no. You did the right thing. But you're just beginning to complete the sale. It's like a follow-through to a golf swing. You can do everything right up until the club makes contact with the ball, but that isn't enough. Only proper follow-through will ensure that the ball flies straight where you want it to go. It's up to you."

For a few moments Ronald sat in deep thought. Then he smiled, "Yes, I guess it's just the beginning."

AFTER THE SALE IS OVER

As the drama of the sale has progressed, we have devoted considerable time and attention to the Heart of the Sale and the Base of the Sale. The student is apt to get the impression that once the salesperson writes the order, the play is over. Not so, because the process of selling is circular, and one order leads quite naturally to the next. Between orders comes service, that almost indefinable relationship that cements one sale to the next and ultimately results in a long-term understanding between customer and salesperson.

The Base of the Sale has been defined as everything that takes place prior to actually calling upon the prospect. This includes the development of personality, preapproach study, prospecting, and even the search for product knowledge. Embodied in the Base of the Sale is all the practice and thought the salesperson should undergo before meeting the prospect.

On the other hand, the Heart of the Sale has been defined as everything that takes place from the first moment the salesperson is face to face with the prospect until the interview is concluded—either successfully or unsuccessfully. Inasmuch as the Heart of the Sale is portrayed as ending with the close, it is significant to note how the salesperson can gracefully depart. Under any circumstances, with or without an order, the salesperson must leave the prospect.

A very happy salesperson of plastic bottles showed pleasure and excitement as the purchasing agent signed an order for a full truckload of the product. "I certainly appreciate this business," said the factory representative.

"That's nice," answered the purchasing agent, who then sat back to see what would happen.

"Yes, I certainly appreciate this order," continued the salesperson.

"Good," smiled the buyer.

"I know your production people will be happy with the quality of these bottles. Did you know that the threads are reinforced to ensure tight sealing?"

"Yes," said the buyer.

"When our truck arrives, you know our drivers will load the merchandise right onto the loading platform."

"Yes."

"This is probably one of the nicest orders I have received this week."

"Let me offer you a tip," said the friendly purchasing agent. "When you have your order, why not just say, 'Thank you, I'll see you next month.' "

"Gee," stammered the salesperson. "That seems so cold. I thought it was only polite to sit around and talk for a few minutes. Like the person who comes to dinner—it isn't nice to eat and run."

"But we have concluded our business. Let's move along. Take my advice. When you get the order, clear out."

Unfortunately, no one had ever instructed this sales rep in the proper way to depart. Earlier in this text, we offered one good method: Thank the prospect for the order, attention, and courtesy, and leave. It might be just as simple as, "Thank you for the order. I'll be back in two weeks. Good-bye." Easy as that sounds, many salespeople have difficulty getting the words out.

Probably more complex is the departure when the salesperson does not get an order. Some skillful salespeople sense that no order is forthcoming and seek to make their departure before the prospect makes some sign that the interview is over. This ability to identify a no-sale situation is beneficial in not antagonizing the prospect; yet it is also a cop-out on the part of the less aggressive salesperson. It is almost impossible to tell whether or not you will make the sale, and planning what to do if you don't get an order is preparing for defeat, hardly an attribute to professional selling.

A minimum requirement of the departure is to leave the door ajar for the next sales call. If the salesperson does not get an order, a perfectly proper way to leave is to say, "Thank you for your attention, Ms. Prospect. I'll be in this territory in two weeks, and when I call again, I'll have a sample of our latest model thermocouple. Have a good day." Then pick yourself up and walk out the door.

Another way to take your leave is to ask, "When I'm in this territory again in two weeks, would you prefer if I call in the morning or in the afternoon?" This question may not deter the prospect from saying, "Don't bother to stop." But it is another way to continue the conversation. You might then add, "I know you will want to hear about our monthly specials. I'll bring along the survey report we were discussing today."

It may be repetitive, but it is important to once more caution you against thanking the prospect for his or her time. Remember, the time of the salesperson is of equal value!

Under any circumstances, when the interview is over, the salesperson must depart. The next natural sequence is for the salesperson to perform a service, or a group of services. In the event that there is no order, the service will revolve around a search for those things that will make the prospect want to buy. However, the concern of this chapter is the service that takes place after the completion of a successful sale. You may recall the expression, "The only things I have to sell are price, quality, and service. Price and quality are almost identical. But I give service."

WHAT IS SERVICE?

Any job description of the profession of selling will include a number of tasks, most of which are properly called "service." That is, beyond the process of taking an order, the salesperson is expected to perform certain chores as part of the total sale. For instance, verifying that the order, the written piece of paper, is properly processed is also part of any sale. Seeing that the order is delivered to the order department and then to the delivery department is a portion of the service attached to selling. A further step is to ascertain that the warehouse has the material on hand, and that it is in fact delivered on time. This does not mean that the salesperson has to physically go into the warehouse. It does mean that the mechanics of the company operation should allow for the salesperson to trace the order as it moves through the organization.

There are times when an order must be revised. In all good faith, a food sales rep took an order for California-pack tomatoes. When checking with the office, she discovered that this quality was sold out. She then had to call the prospect and ask if it would be all right to ship Jersey-pack tomatoes as a replacement. This is a fairly common occurrence, not only in the food industry, but in virtually every field. Following the order along to its completion is a service.

Even more complex is the necessity for a salesperson to visit the prospect after a product has been delivered to instruct the prospect in the proper use of the merchandise. Even after a customer visits the automobile showroom, discusses the relative merits of a particular model, negotiates the price, and signs the order, the sale is not complete. When the car is picked up two days later, the salesperson should be on hand to take the new owner for a ride and to explain all the little features, even though they were discussed during the original sale. One man was livid when he discovered that depressing the gas pedal to the floor gave his car an extra burst of "passing speed." The reason he was upset was that he didn't learn about this capability until six months after he owned the car. The salesperson had failed to take him for a ride and show him this feature.

These after-the-sale considerations are very important. Take the case of the couple who purchased a very expensive living-room couch. They

PROFESSIONAL SALESPEOPLE
PERFORM MANY SERVICES, NOT
THE LEAST OF WHICH IS
MAKING AN OCCASIONAL
DELIVERY.

Figure 15-1

purposely went to a reputable store because they sought the assurance of "touch-up" service, which might be needed if the wood parts were scratched during delivery. Although it was not the responsibility of the salesperson to repair the scratches, it was necessary for him to confirm that the couple was satisfied with the purchase. When they had to call the store and ask for a repairperson to call, they lost confidence in the salesperson and the store.

Service then, is everything the salesperson does other than the actual order-taking procedure. If a prospect asks a question that requires a search through the catalogs for the answer, if the prospect needs further explanation of how to get maximum use from a product, or if the prospect wants some special delivery or credit terms, these all constitute service. Sometimes service takes on a strange hue, such as the time a representative for a shoe manufacturer picked up three pairs of shoes at the factory for personal delivery to a valued customer. Acting as a special-delivery agent is also part of the service function of selling.

POSITIONING THE SALES DEPARTMENT

Every business enterprise requires a number of departments to carry out specific functions. We are primarily concerned with the sales function in this text. However, it is significant to take note of the other functions that must be performed and somehow relate them to the sales function.

Regardless of the size of any organization, someone will be in charge of purchasing, warehousing, delivery, accouting or bookkeeping, executive management, and marketing. Sales fall under the marketing department. Each of these departments must perform an important piece of work if the business is to be successful.

In smaller organizations, certain people may be assigned to perform more than one function. For example, the owner of a distribution company may also be the head buyer. The partner in the same company might be the total sales force and also one of the managers. There may even be times when these two partners stack cases in the warehouse and load trucks for delivery.

A small retail store may find the owner performing the function of buyer, bookkeeper, seller, shipper, and manager. Even in medium-size organizations, it is common to find people with multiple tasks or functions to perform. However, in larger organizations, these specific tasks are spread among a number of people, and each has a different perception of the contribution members make to the organization.

Because of the interesting nature of the sales function, because salespeople generally have huge amounts of liberty, and because salespeople frequently control a major portion of their work style, they are often viewed as a group apart. Many people are envious of the free-wheeling aspects of the sales department.

Management generally recognizes the inherent need for and talent of the sales force. As a group, salespeople are treated with more consideration, they meet more often, discuss problems with more regularity, confer with top management on a more routine basis, and, in the final analysis, make more money than employees in most other departments.

It is the contention of most salespeople that a professional sales force can lead an organization to success, that all other functions of the organization are performed to serve the sales department. This frequently leads to disagreements and misunderstandings. Members of other functioning departments view their own work as the most important aspect of the dynamic enterprise. These differing views tend to disrupt the forward progress of any organization.

Just as the salesperson would find life in the office stultifying, the office worker would find selling a frightening adventure. The format of modern organization suggests that all elements must work together to bring about customer satisfaction and company success.

Is selling the most important function of a business? The best sales force would be hard-pressed to satisfy the customer without the support of all the other members of the organization. Any business is like a hockey team, which requires that each player become part of the whole team. When one is penalized and forced to sit on the sidelines, the other players must devote all their energy to keeping the opposition from scoring, and they certainly do not have the time and strength to press onward and score.

WHY SERVICE CUSTOMERS?

An interesting transformation takes place when the salesperson gets an order. The prospect becomes a customer—and is therefore entitled to all the friendship, respect, and affection one accords to an old acquaintance. This is not to say that every prospect should not be treated courteously, but no matter how hard salespeople try to create an atmosphere of openness and cooperation, there is a change when the prospect becomes a customer. Suddenly, you, the salesperson, become part of the customer's team and are expected to perform almost as a member of the staff. In a sense, the sales representative has moved from the opposite side of the fence and is now working together with the customer toward a common goal. This is the moment that most salespeople cherish. They can now perform many services and not be overconcerned about orders. It's like becoming part of the family.

Because of this change in the total atmosphere, the salesperson is more than ever concerned that the customer receive all the benefits of the purchase. This may mean visiting the customer at home to verify that the dishwasher is properly installed or that the clothes washer really cleans the clothes. Obviously, this kind of "plus" service offers the salesperson an opportunity to prepare the way for future sales. At the same time that the professional salesperson is performing a service, the grounds for a long-term relationship are established.

Another reason for offering this kind of service is to discover new prospects. A termite-control salesperson called on a prospect and, after successfully completing the sale, arranged for the installation team to do the work two weeks later. Three days after the installers had done their job, the salesperson called, inspected the work, and verified that the prospect, who was now a customer, was satisfied. Then, quite naturally, the sales rep said, "If you know any other people who need termite control, I hope you will recommend our company." Needless to say, this extra concern brought forth a stream of names as potential prospects. By adding follow-through to the sale, this professional continued to develop a list of prospects.

Essentially, there are three reasons why customers should be serviced: to see that they have received everything for which they paid, to retain their friendship, and to discover new prospects.

WHAT HAPPENS TO THE ORDER?

Depending on the industry, the order a salesperson turns in to the office makes a circuitous journey. Let's follow that slip of paper and see what happens.

John Green smiled happily as he slipped the three copies of the order from the Wonderful Furniture Store into an envelope. He sealed the envelope and dropped it into the nearest mailbox. Ultimately, the mail carrier picked up the envelope and routed it to the central office, where it was sorted into a pile slated to travel from Boise, Idaho, to Grand Rapids, Michigan. Two days later, the envelope passed through the Grand Rapids post office and was delivered to the office of the Grand Manufacturing Company.

Because it was addressed to the order department, a clerk assigned to the job of routing orders slit open the envelope, separated the three parts of the order form, and sent one to the credit office, a second to the accounting department, and a third to the production department. These three slips of paper worked their way through the system. The credit office verified through a complex process that the Wonderful Furniture Store was an acceptable credit risk, the accounting department prepared an appropriate bill of lading and delivery slips, and the production department either prepared to manufacture the items ordered or pulled them from existing stock.

Ultimately, the credit, accounting, and production department gave an OK to deliver the merchandise to the shipping department. When the delivery department accumulated enough orders to make up a trailerload of merchandise, the order for the Wonderful Furniture Store was loaded aboard for delivery. About six weeks after the order was placed, it was delivered to the dock of the Wonderful Furniture Store.

In the meantime, John Green had called at the store for further orders before the initial order had been received. Since both the prospect and the salesperson understood that normal delivery might take six weeks, they were both prepared to continue the process of buying and selling, even though there were deliveries en route.

Assuredly, this explanation has been oversimplified. When you consider the number of hands that have touched the order, the variety of people who have added to the total process, and the inherent difficulties of bringing about what seems a simple operation, it is amazing that there are not more errors. It is incumbent upon the professional salesperson to understand this complex situation and be prepared to respond when the prospect asks, "Where is my order?"

OIL FOR THE SQUEAKY WHEEL

If you were going down the highway and one of your wheels squeaked, you would go to the nearest service station and have the attendant give that wheel a shot of grease. However, if you were a professional racing driver, you would not wait to hear a squeak before servicing your vehicle. Just as nonprofessional drivers pay attention only to squeaking wheels, nonprofessional salespeople only heed the squeaks of dissatisfied customers. The old expression, "The squeaky wheel gets the oil," ought not to apply to the profession of selling.

To whom does the professional salesperson give the most service? This requires an analysis of the current list of customers and an examination of many customer characteristics. For example, the customer who places the most business in the course of a year will naturally get and deserve a good deal of service attention. However, the customer who has great potential might also require a good deal of service. In other words, as the salesperson attempts to develop more and more business from a particular source, one way to build that volume is to give additional service, which makes the salesperson more valuable and deserving of extra business. So there is a direct link between volume and potential volume as the salesperson decides where to place the best service efforts.

There are other considerations. Some customers may reject offers of service. A large department store had just ordered a new and intricate baby stroller. The factory representative said, "If you wish, I will spend half a day with the people in the juvenile furniture department and explain the benefits of this model," to which the purchasing agent responded, "Don't bother. We'll have our own training department prepare a written description of this model." It is not clear why this customer did not want the factory person to demonstrate the new model. Whatever the reasons, an offer of service had been summarily dismissed.

This salesperson made the same offer to a chain of discount houses and met with a different response. "Yes, we'd like to have you come into our stores. In fact, you can arrange to spend a half-day in each of our six outlets in the metropolitan area." In this instance, the customer wanted more service than had been offered. The point is, the professional salesperson may not always be allowed to deliver the extra services offered—and sometimes may be called upon to give more service than has been offered. The cooperation of the customer has a lot to do with the amount of service offered and given.

Geographic location is also a determining factor in the amount of service a professional salesperson can give. In a small community, it might be unwise to do something for one customer and not for another. A drug sales specialist helped a customer set up a display of product near the entrance to the store. Within a week, the specialist received a note from the sales manager relaying a complaint from another drugstore in the same community. The only response was that the specialist had offered to set up a display for the complaining customer, but those efforts had been thwarted.

Many times, customers need a service because they lack the ability to perform certain tasks. Distributors serving small grocery stores are expected to include suggested resale prices of products. Originally this was necessary because many of the small grocers had little idea of how much to mark up their products. Not only do some companies help their customers with markups, they even keep books for them. Providing these services is the result of devoted, service-oriented sales professionals who see a need and work to satisfy that need.

The decision as to which customers get the additional services salespeople can provide revolves around the dollar volume of business, the sales potential, geographic location, need, competition, and the willingness of the customer to cooperate with the salesperson. Even though the service is cost-free, many customers just do not expect, and subsequently do not receive, the extra services that go with placing an order.

SERVICE—THE DAY AFTER THE SALE

Each level of selling has a different type of service that helps to round out the relationship between the customer and the salesperson. Since we have sought to define the sales profession along these lines, it is appropriate to relate the service functions that accompany the different levels of selling.

There are no hard and fast rules about the kinds of service different sales-people will offer. What is important is to recognize that once a sale has been made, the new relationship that evolves makes the salesperson a member of the team, which translates into doing for the customer whatever you would want done for yourself. It is correct to offer any help you think the customer might want or need.

Retail

Probably no facet of selling is more in need of repair than the quality of professionalism at the retail level. The assumption that the sale is complete when the customer walks out of the store is responsible for the demise of many small business organizations. Yet there are a number of retail estab-lishments in any community that sparkle because of the devotion of the sales staff. Here is a recent experience of a husband and wife who purchased a dishwashing machine from a large chain of stores:

Two days after the machine was installed, the husband received a phone call. "The is Tom Brown, Mr. Bloom. You remember me, I'm the person who sold you the dishwasher."

"Yes, of course, Tom. What's on your mind?"

"I just wanted to know if the machine was doing the right kind of job."

"Yes, I guess so."

"Also, I wanted to remind you that all the new models come with an energy-saver button. This means you can save about 28 percent of the energy needed during the drying cycle."

"You told us that when we were in the store."

"I know, Mr. Bloom. But it's an important feature, and you can save a few dollars by using the energy saver. I wanted to be absolutely certain you knew about it."

"Well, I appreciate your interest."

"One other thing. I'm going to put my business card in the mail to you. If there are any problems, I want you to contact me."

"Okay."

"And if there is anything else you need, I hope you'll remember me."

Sure, this was a pitch for future business. But it also showed real concern over the opportunity for the customer to save money. It is an example of service after the sale.

What else can retail salespeople do? They can alert the old customer about an upcoming sale, advise the customer about a possible price increase, and tell the customer when a particular style or model is due to arrive. A simple phone call will often set a chain of events in motion.

A retail children's clothing store started a savings club. The two partners spent three afternoons each week going from customer to customer, collecting 50 cents from each of them. When the customers had accumulated $20 worth of savings, the store allowed them to buy $22 worth of merchandise. That was a long time ago; the store now employs more than 60 people involved in selling. Today they perform other services including special after-hours sales for treasured customers who have been with them for many years.

Distribution

Few areas of selling allow for the creativity and imagination needed at the distribution or wholesale level. You will recall that distribution salespeople often visit their customers every week or every two weeks. This means that the relationship between the customer and the salesperson becomes very close. They truly form a team, and the salesperson has the opportunity to perform a boundless number of services.

Joyce Brog was a regular supplier of wrapping paper, twine, and paper bags to the Hotel Gift Shop. After she had been selling the account for several months, the owner asked her to check a bill from the file. Together they examined the bill, and then the owner said, "While you have this bill out, why not write a check for the amount, and I'll sign it." It was not an unusual request; many customers have bookkeepers or accountants who prepare checks for their signatures, and Joyce proceeded to fill out the appropriate amount. Then the customer said, "While your at it, would you mind writing these checks for the electric company and the gas company?"

At this point, Joyce realized she had become a confidante of this customer. There weren't many people who came to know the truth: that the owner of the Gift Shop couldn't write! So it was that every week, Joyce Brog spent an extra 15 minutes writing checks for this customer. It was a different service. True, this was a unique situation, but the need for strange services happens quite often.

Many distributor salespeople see service as the most important element in the entire sales package. One sales manager advised the sales force to take a night-school course in accounting so they would be better able to deal with the bookkeeping problems of their customers. Another manager had the sales force attend classes in window displays so they would be able to help their prospects properly dress windows. A third recommended that the sales force take courses in personnel management so they could serve as a resource for company clients.

Distributor salespeople are usually expected to gather credit information, particularly when the account is new. Although it is true that the company may provide credit inquiry forms, an on-site evaluation of the ability of the prospect to pay bills is often given heavy weight in making decisions about how much credit should be extended. When bills are overdue, the salesperson is often given the difficult task of collecting outstanding accounts. There are even times when the salesperson helps the customer work out a plan to pay past-due bills that is acceptable to the company as well as the customer. Thus, the distributor salesperson should have a fair idea about what makes for good credit relations.

One hallmark of the distributor salesperson is the regularity of sales calls. A frequently heard expression is, "You can set the clock by the distributor's appearance each week." This is imporant, because it enables the customer to rely on placing an order and knowing when the merchandise will be delivered. This means the customer need carry only a small inventory. Another point is that distributor salespeople often take a physical inventory for the customer and many times will write their own order, because the relationship allows that the sales representative is a member of the team and will not take advantage of the customer. Imagine the significance of this service. The customer can arrange for the salesperson to take inventory, write the order, and see that every need is covered, all of which means that the customer does not even have to be present. This automatic ordering system is in effect in many operations, and it places a heavy burden on the salesperson to be honest, forthright, and fair. No salesperson who accepts this responsibility would overstock or take advantage of an absent customer who has placed this authority with him or her.

The salesperson at the distribution level is admonished to study the business of the prospects and be prepared to offer help or service in any area. This may be in building displays, instructing the retail sales force, working in the kitchen, making deliveries, assisting with accounting problems, and even writing checks. All these things are in addition to, or complement, the actual process of selling.

Manufacturing

Sales life at the manufacturing level tends to be somewhat slower in pace. Calls are made with less frequency than at the distribution level, and although the relationships may be warm, the customers require a different type of service. Since deliveries tend to be slower because of the distance of the manufacturing plant from the customer's warehouse, there is need to track the order and ascertain that every step of the way, all conditions are "go." If the actual delivery is by railcar, the salesperson ought to be able to provide that information and include some data as to arrival date and where the car is at any given moment. This function might well be carried out by someone in the manufacturer's office, but the customer may not know anyone at that office. The singular contact is with the salesperson.

Sometimes manufacturers' representatives have to sell through a distributor, and this requires a superior form of service. Here's an example: A detergent manufacturer produces a line of machine dishwashing compounds for use by hospitals, nursing homes, and hotels. The merchandise is sold to distributors, who in turn call on these institutions. However, since the sale is complex and requires the installation of a dispensing device, the manufacturer's sales force works very closely with the distributor's sales force. As each sale is consummated, the manufacturer's sales rep installs the dispensing device and generally oversees the initial delivery of product. Regular follow-up orders are taken by the distributor sales force. However, the manufacturer's salesperson must still call on the account from time to time to ascertain that all is well. This salesperson is calling on the customer's customer.

In many instances, this kind of service is the chief reason a distributor will buy from a manufacturer. Suppose you were the purchasing agent for a distribution firm, and the difference between two salespeople was the fact that one would make sales calls for and with your own salespeople. That's a service that is hard to beat. For the manufacturer's salesperson, it means not only a ready knowledge of the company the sales rep is trying to sell, but also a complete understanding of the problems this company has with its customers. Many distributors feel that this service by the manufacturer is actually worth the cost of having an additional salesperson in the field.

Sometimes the manufacturer's salesperson has to be a sales trainer, someone qualified to teach the distributor's sales force how to sell the product. This is true particularly when new products are introduced to the market. Someone has to explain the benefits, capabilities, and uses of these products, and the task often falls on the shoulders of the manufacturer's sales force. This is a heavy responsibility and has little to do with the process of selling or taking an order. It is a service that accompanies the purchase of product.

As with the distributor, the manufacturer's salespeople may keep a running product inventory for their customers. This may or may not entail an actual physical count every month or so. But it will generally include a fairly accurate accounting of purchases from period to period. This also affords the sales representative the opportunity to alert the buyer to changing seasonal demands with reference to what took place the preceding year. When promotions come along, this salesperson is expected to assist the distributor in every way to meet quotas and goals that may afford additional trade discounts, a chance for the distributor to make some extra dollars.

Even though the life of the manufacturer's salesperson is somewhat slower in pace, the services tend to be extremely important. A sale is usually

ONCE THE PROSPECT BECOMES
A CUSTOMER, A NEW RELATIONSHIP
DEVELOPS WITH THE PROFESSIONAL
SALESPERSON.

Figure 15-2

only the beginning; the salesperson must be prepared to perform in a number of ways to ensure the continued purchase of the product. Sales training seminars and work in the field are generally accompanied by help in planning and promoting sales campaigns for the customer. Other forms of assistance run the gamut of establishing selling prices, warehousing, credit, and sometimes stock control. In the last decade, manufacturing salespeople seem to spend less time selling and more time performing services.

Industrial

Selling at the industrial level is very similar to selling at the manufacturing level. However, the kinds of service will probably extend to providing knowledge and information to production people, who will want to know more about the product. In fact, few sales at this level are made without the advice and consent of the engineering department. Even though the actual purchase is made by a professional purchasing agent, the technical aspects of what the product will do or how it will perform under test conditions will have to be approved by those who will work with the material. This information may range from the tensile strength of steel to the heat-resistant properties of plastic.

A salesperson for a farm cooperative was confronted each year with a lack of storage capability by the manufacturing plant to which he sold tomato products. During the packing season, all available storage was at a premium, and this cut into sales to the packing house. To overcome this problem, the sales rep arranged for the customer a flow chart, which allowed for the raw product to move through the packing lines while huge supplies of backup product were stored in waiting tractor trailers.

This might be viewed as problem solving, which in truth it was. It also represents a service over and above simply taking an order.

Other services supplied by industrial salespeople include assistance in arranging advertising campaigns, publicity, profit margins, training seminars, and often, calls on the manufacturer's customers. Certain distinguishing characteristics of industrial selling overlap with the kinds of services offered at the manufacturing level. Some even seem similar to the services at the distribution level. The essential differences are that sales calls are less frequent, and the amount of time and attention paid to the service factor is greater, than at the other levels of industry.

This brief discussion of the kinds of services rendered by salespeople at the different levels of selling is intended to add to the distinctions among these levels. The life-style of these salespeople was partially described in Chapter 1. There is a great similarity among them in the methods, techniques, and characteristics required in the Base of the Sale and in the Heart of the Sale. However, the kinds of service performed at these levels differ greatly.

VALUE ADDED

As companies and business organizations seek to find ways to provide more or better services, the notion of "value added" has become part of the language of selling. In this context, the term means that many things are added to the basic sale to make the purchase of product or service more desirable. Thus, although the price of a product or service may be the same as that of a competing brand, the salesperson will do other things to earn the business. The litany of services is so long and involved that each industry has identified those services that best meet the needs of its customers.

One interesting sidelight of the value-added concept is that the salesperson may now be in the position of selling all the services, concentrating on these values, as opposed to simply selling the primary product or service. In those industries whose products seem to differ very little, companies seek to add other values to set themselves apart from their competitors.

In total, this means that salespeople have to expand their sales thinking to include all the value-added services offered. Not the least of these is the concentrated attention the salesperson gives to each and every customer.

SUMMARY

Few things are so disconcerting to the prospect or the salesperson as the moments at the close of a sales interview when the salesperson doesn't know how to depart gracefully. It is difficult for some people to simply say, "Thank you for the order," and then leave. Under all conditions, whether a sale has been consummated or the interview is concluded with, "See me on your next trip," the salesperson should remain calm and collected. A degree of excitement at this time may telegraph to the prospect that sales are few and far between, which raises the question of whether purchasing the product may be a mistake. Be like the professional baseball player who strikes out. He doesn't yell and scream—he walks quietly to the dugout, promising to do better next time.

To seal a sale requires a considerable amount of service. In its broadest terms, this may be described as virtually everything the salesperson does after the order has been placed. Remember, this text has dealt with how professional salespeople prepare to meet the prospect and how they plan to present the product or service. It is when this preparation has proven successful that the salesperson has the opportunity to perform many small tasks, all of which qualify as service.

There are several reasons why service is a significant function of the sales profession. It signifies that both customer and salesperson are working toward the same goal. As they work together to solve a problem or meet a need, it is the responsibility of the salesperson to ascertain that the customer received fair treatment and performance for dollars expended. This continuing effort reaffirms the friendship and even opens the door to new prospects. A happy customer will be glad to recommend a salesperson who has offered good service.

One of the main services the salesperson performs is to see that the order is properly processed and the merchandise delivered when promised. Any problems encountered along the way have to be explained to the customer. Just because the salesperson has written an order does not absolve him or her from further responsibility. The sale really only begins with the writing of an order; it is joined to the next sales effort by the service that takes place between sales.

Some salespeople feel that they have to react only when a customer complains about late delivery or a faulty product. The true professional anticipates problems and makes the service function a regular part of the sale. Recognize that some customers will naturally require more service because they are larger or more cooperative. Other customers will demand all the possible services to which they are entitled, and a few will overlook or refuse this valuable offering.

How a salesperson carries out the service function of the job will vary from level to level of industry. Essentially, all embrace the idea that any task that will enhance the relationship between the customer and salesperson should be performed. There is a long list of potential services that the salesperson might perform for the customer. Among these are the follow-up phone call to verify that delivery and operation of a purchase are satisfactory, keeping the customer aware of upcoming specials and new product lines, training the salespeople of the customer, assisting in the planning and promotion of products, credit help, making sales calls on the customer's customers, warehousing advice, inventory control plans, ad infinitum. There is no end to the service function—it is an integral part of the selling picture.

We have suggested that the only things a salesperson has to sell are "price, quality, and service." If you dwell on these three points, you will probably come to the conclusion that the salesperson can do very little about price and quality. But in the area of service, the salesperson is really the one who makes the determinations. The salesperson gives the service and carries out the service function. There is a direct relationship between service and success. The more service, the more success.

A SUCCESS STORY

"You are looking at what used to be a salesperson," moaned the unhappy figure sprawled at the desk.

The startled sales manager looked askance at George Seltzer, who had slipped into the chair and now lay prostrate over the papers and reports of the previous week. Deciding it was wise to permit the salesman to lie quietly, the manager asked, "Do you want to tell me about it, or should I put a call in for the local shrink?"

George raised his head, intrigued with the idea of a psychiatric examination. "Hey, maybe that's the solution. I don't know who I am, and I need a doctor to help me sell tricycles."

"Ah, yes," smiled the sales manager. "I was thinking of doing postgraduate work in analysis. You salespeople drive me nuts. Now, are you going to talk to me?"

"Do you want it from the beginning, or just the highlights?"

"Spare me as much as you can, please. I have other work to do today."

George straightened up at the desk. He pulled a cigarette from a crumpled pack and felt obliged to say, "You see, they have driven me back to smoking."

"Just what I need," said the sales manager. "A lecture on the health habits of an extinct species of salesman."

"I just came from the Gold Coast, you know, where all the fancy houses are, near Bay Drive. You may wonder what I was doing there in the middle of a workday. Quite simple. I was teaching a five-year-old how to ride our new tricycle."

"That's nice," said the sales manager with a sarcastic tone to his voice. "How lovely of you to take time from your otherwise busy schedule."

"Knock it off," snarled George. "This kid is the son of the owner of the Thrifty Toy Store."

"Oh, isn't that nice? You were playing with the son of a store owner."

Shaking off the remark, George continued. "I was working with an Uppity Toy Distributor sales rep and we made a call at Thrifty. The P.A. was in conference, and while we were waiting, in walks Mr. Big himself. Well, I know him from the golf club, and we chatted a few minutes. We just casually mentioned the new tricycle line, and he says his kid needs a new bike. So the Uppity sales rep suggests that we drop one off for the youngster. Compliments of the house, of course. Well, Mr. Big says he won't accept the bike, but if his kid likes the model, he'll mention it to the P.A., who is his brother."

"George," said the sales manager. "I have to ask you this. Did you do any work today?"

"Nuts," replied George wearily. "So after the interview, the Uppity rep tells the buyer what Mr. Big said, and he suggests we go on out to the house and demonstrate the bike to the kid. So off we go, over to the Gold Coast to teach some little shrimp how to ride a bike."

"I knew from your background that teaching kids to ride bikes is probably the thing you do best."

"Anyhow, the kid is playing out front, and we bring three bikes out, assemble them, and let the kid ride up and down the street."

"You'd make a wonderful father. If anybody would marry you."

"When we finally asked the kid which bike he liked best, he said he liked them all."

"Sounds reasonable. You don't wear the same shoes every day."

"So we left all three bikes and shot back to the store. By the time we got there, Mrs. Big had called and left a message to get two bikes out of her garage. So I left the Uppity rep there to talk to the buyer and drove back to the house to get two bikes."

"Now that you mention it, you do look like a delivery driver."

"See this bump?" George said, raising one trouser leg. "That kid kicked me in the shins. Even when I tried to explain that riding three bikes at once is a difficult procedure."

"Next thing I know, you'll ask me for combat pay."

"When I got back to the store, there was the Uppity rep waiting for me out front."

"I have the feeling that the end is drawing near. Notice that night has fallen and the day is over. It's time to go home."

Reaching into his pocket, George withdrew a pink order sheet. "What do you think of this?" he asked.

The sales manager whistled softly. "Quite an order," he smiled.

"But I didn't really do any selling today," wailed George.

Slowly the sales manager fingered his moustache, deep in thought. "Here's what you ought to do, George. First thing tomorrow morning, find yourself a bunch of kids to play with. Just you keep teaching them how to ride tricycles. We'll deliver all the orders that come in."

QUESTIONS FOR CLASS DISCUSSION

1. Explain the meaning of the expression, "When the sale is over, service begins."
2. What are the benefits of service to the salesperson? Do they help to make sales?
3. What factors help the professional salesperson decide the kinds of service to offer to any particular customer?
4. If you had just purchased an electric saw, what kinds of service would you expect of the salesperson?
5. What is the responsibility of the salesperson if the shipping department fouls up the delivery of merchandise?
6. Assume you are a salesperson for a distribution firm selling candles to a card and novelty store. What kinds of service might you perform for the customer?
7. Assume you are a salesperson for a manufacturing company that sells machine-tooled parts for use in assembling electric lawn mowers. Describe the service functions you might perform.
8. Describe the relationship between the salesperson and the customer once a sale has been consummated. Is there a change in the attitude of the customer? Why?
9. Explain the meaning of the slogan, "Service after the sale."

CASE 15—THE CASE OF THE RELUCTANT DISTRIBUTOR

"I'll do my best," said Lou Wright.

"Just what does that mean?" asked Edna Broom.

"It means I want your business and I certainly have worked hard to earn your respect, but there are a lot of details to be ironed out."

"Like what?"

"Well, like you want me to call twice a week. Most of my customers want to see me only once a week. Perhaps we can work out a better schedule."

Edna's jaw dropped in surprise. "I don't think I quite understand what you mean. You have been calling on me for over a year. So far, all you have sold me were pretty small orders. This is your big chance."

Lou examined his price book, flipping the pages aimlessly. "Well, we have certainly come up with some tremendous prices, and the warehouse has agreed to ship you merchandise at least twice a week."

"Wait a minute," Edna snapped. "Anybody will do that for my business. Do you realize I purchase over $2,000 worth of merchandise every week? That's big business!"

The raised tone of her voice was a warning to Lou. He realized her patience had worn thin and he had better smoth things over. "Look, what else do you want me to do? I'm here to serve you in the best way possible."

"I'll tell you what I expect. I want you to call twice a week and take inventory of the freezer, storeroom, and icebox. If I'm here, tell me what I need. If I'm not here, we can set up buying limits, and you can write your own order. I want a complete invoice and statement every two weeks. I want a one-hour conference with you at least once a month to review new products. I want to visit your warehouse at least twice a year to inspect the sanitary conditions."

"Gee whiz, I never realized you required so much service. I won't have any time to sell."

"I don't believe what I'm hearing," exclaimed Edna. "How about if I call in the XYZ Distributors? They're plenty anxious for my business."

"Don't get me wrong," Lou apologized. "I'll do all these things, but I want you to know it's a problem. Heck, I have almost 100 customers. If they all required this much service, I'd never be able to make a living."

Edna looked at the sales representative and just shook her head in disbelief.

1. What do you think of Lou Wright's attitude?
2. How would you handle this sales problem?
3. Why did Edna Broom want to give her business to Lou?
4. Is there any way to give this much service and still be successful?

EXERCISE 15

The Atlantic Typewriter Company specializes in the distribution of equipment to professional people such as doctors, lawyers, and consultants. The title of the company is somewhat misleading, because Atlantic also

SALES PROBLEM 15—"WHAT, SHORT AGAIN?"

Jenny could see that her biggest account was about to explode like a volcano.

"Can't you ever get the order right? For the past three months, every time I tell you what I want, either I get a substitute or I get nothing at all. What is going on?"

Actually, Jenny knew there had been shortages. And she herself had made most of the substitutions. These times were just very unnerving.

Here is how three sales reps say they would handle this situation:

Sales Rep #1:   If your company doesn't have the product the customer wants, it's up to the salesperson to find something of comparable value. I would substitute the best possible product, even if I had to take a loss.

There was a time when our company decided to stop handling meat trays. I went out and found a comparable substitute. But I did tell my customer what I had done, and I also proved that I had the customer's interests at heart.

Sales Rep #2:   First off, I would be sympathetic to the customer. Then I would try to locate the source of the problem. Was there a mistake in the placement of the order? Was it transmitted in error to the office? Did the shipping department make an error? Was the computer doing the right things? Did the delivery people bring the right product?

It's only when you know the source of the problem that you can correct what has been happening.

What customers need is a whole lot of attention. They deserve it, and the best thing to do is remind them that you have been servicing them for a long time. Then review the entire process to ensure improved service in the future.

Sales Rep #3:   I think the sales rep should have been on top of this problem. To allow shortages or substitutions to continue for a month proves that the salesperson wasn't really watching out for the customer.

Probably the salesperson could set up some form of inventory control or purchasing control for the customer to ensure a continuity of supply. And it should be noted where substitutions are allowable.

It is important to get the customer involved in this problem-solving phase of your relationship. Really, there's not much use in identifying what is wrong. The important thing is to be sure it doesn't continue to happen.

handles calculators, duplicating machines, desks, chairs, filing cabinets, and office supplies.

The Alpha law firm recently merged with the Beta law firm, and they are about to renovate and expand their offices. The furnishings and equipment are to be purchased on an informal bid, which means that each distributor will have the opportunity to demonstrate quality, products, and price.

You feel that the best way to make the sale is by demonstrating the services you plan to offer with the purchase.

Prepare your presentation in the form of a group sale.

16

MANAGING YOUR SALES TIME

PERFORMANCE OBJECTIVES

After you have read this chapter and completed the Questions for Class Discussion, the Case, the Sales Problem, and the Exercise, you should be able to do the following:

1. Explain the effect of "selling time" on sales volume and income.
2. Prepare a personal time study.
3. Analyze the time study you have prepared.
4. Construct a plan to save an hour a day.

THE TIME OF YOUR LIFE

"You may find this hard to believe," Tom said, "but I really enjoy getting up at five o'clock every morning. Sometimes I'm on the road before six, and I want to tell you, there is a certain sparkle on the leaves that is hard to describe."

His two sales friends looked at him and smiled. "That may be all right for you," said Sally. "But I have been specializing in the bigger stores, and generally the people who do the buying don't start till after nine. There's no sense in getting there before they arrive."

"Not me," added Lenny. "I like to sleep late and work late. Some days I don't see my first account till ten or eleven."

Tom appeared crestfallen, as if someone had told him he was approaching his sales career from the wrong angle. It just made good sense to get out and hit the line early in the day. "If you start that late," he asked, "how can you see enough people to do business?"

"Hey, man," Lenny snorted, "I'm a late-night person. If I have to stay out till midnight to make my calls, that's the way I want to live. There are plenty of times I can be having dinner with a customer and then go back to his place and write an order."

"Maybe you two hotrods don't have any responsibilities at home," said Sally. "My husband and I share the work around the house, and at least three nights a week, I have to get dinner together."

"Wait a minute," interjected Tom. "My wife does all that during the week, and I help out on weekends. Don't get the idea that I don't want to spend time with my kids and all."

"You're both missing the point. People have to live the way they want to live," said Lenny. "My wife leaves home before I do. You know, she has this job down at the ad agency. Well, she has an arrangement with her boss, and lots of times she can take her design work home. Of course, we don't have any kids, so there's not much of a hassle."

"What I was trying to say," explained Tom, "is that the early morning is the best time of day. There's a cold snap in the air, and the world is just waking up. I find my customers are anxious to see me, and I can get my orders taken and write my reports in the late afternoon. By noon, I have most of my selling done."

"But I tried to tell you," Sally said, a little annoyed, "that my people don't get in that early. I have no objection to getting up a little earlier. I have to live with the conditions that exist in my territory. Maybe if I had early morning stops, I wouldn't like the job and I'd find one with later stops."

At that moment the sales manager walked in and exclaimed, "What's everybody doing here? All the business is out there."

"What's everybody doing here?" the three salespeople chimed in. "It's Saturday morning, and you told us to be here for a meeting."

"I know," laughed the sales manager. "I couldn't help overhearing your conversation. You know, I have a similar problem. My husband leaves home very early in the morning for his plant, and I have to see that the kids get off to school. But then he gets home before I do, and he starts dinner."

"But that doesn't answer the question of when is the best time to call on the trade."

"Well, I've been in this business for 13 years. In the beginning, when I was selling, I was single and tried the early schedule. That gave me time to get home early and go out on dates. After I got married, I found the late schedule, like Lenny's, more to my taste. Now, I'm sort of back to the middle ground."

"You mean there is no right schedule to follow?"

"I mean the proof of successful selling is the volume of business. If you start late and your volume is down, then get out an hour earlier in the morning. If you start early and you need extra business, work a little later. Heck, this is your life. Where else can you vary the routine to suit your own personal needs?"

"Sure, that's easy to say. Work harder."

"Look, selling is a way of life. It's a good life, and you have a lot of options. But I'm not about to hold your hand and tell you when to go to work. There's room in this field for every style and desire."

The three salespeople nodded in agreement. "There is one thing I would suggest," added the manager. "Don't get yourself locked into one schedule forever. There's a whole lot to be said for trying a new work style. You may find you like the other person's system better than your own. Besides, varying your time schedule may expose you to a lot of opportunities you didn't know existed."

"That sounds like a good deal of freedom," Lenny said.

"It is," said the sales manager. "I hope you can handle it."

MATURE TIME MANAGEMENT

Few professional careers allow as much freedom of choice as selling. The only real payoff is how much business you do. An almost classic story in selling is the tale of the man who complained to his partner, "Can you imagine the nerve of that Sam Jones! He told me to mind my own business. Who does he think he's working for? Who does he think I am?"

"Calm down a minute," replied the partner. "Let's take a look at his sales figures. Last year he sold almost a million dollars worth of merchandise."

"I don't care. When I tell him we have to start the day before ten o'clock, I don't want any lip from him."

"Listen, Harry," explained the partner. "I'm sorry you are upset. But we don't have any other salespeople who do as much business as Sam Jones. Why don't you forget what happened? Who cares what time he starts work?"

The story may well be apocryphal, but the message is clear. Salespeople are measured by their productivity, and that means sales. This is not to say that strange behavior will be tolerated for long. But most of us who have found a modicum of success in the sales field recognize that how we spend our time is extremely important, and we rarely trust to luck. Our chosen work and life-style impose the need for a mature approach to how we allocate our hours.

Time is a prime commodity of the salesperson; it is the yardstick by which efforts can be measured. A comparison of time spent and sales generated is the only way to determine the quality of selling. Once we establish the relationship between time and sales, we can gain some insights into the need for further work in perfecting the total sales plan.

Table 16-1 tracks the efforts of two salespeople for three weeks. Between the first week and the second week, both these salespeople revised their sales plan and improved dollar volume by producing more orders. They became more effective. During the third week, Mr. Red, anxious to

ONLY A MATURE APPROACH TO TIME WILL GUIDE THE PROFESSIONAL SALESPERSON TO SUCCESS.

Figure 16-1

earn more money, spent more time in the field (47 hours) and increased his dollar volume of business. The lessons to be learned from this example are twofold. First, improving sales methods and techniques will result in more orders. Second, volume will increase as more time is devoted to making sales calls.

Although these examples may seem oversimplified, they are symbolic of numerous case studies that reveal the same conclusions. Better-quality selling and more time spent in the field both lead to more dollars of business. However, since salespeople guide their own lives and make decisions about how their time is to be spent, they are the ones who must police themselves. The individual must make a personal commitment to a sales way of life.

Table 16-1 Time-Study Comparison

	Ms. Blue	Mr. Red
First week		
Hours worked	40	40
Sales calls	20	20
Orders	9	9
Dollar volume	$2,000	$1,500
Second week		
Hours worked	40	40
Sales calls	20	20
Orders	11	11
Dollar volume	$2,700	$2,100
Third week		
Hours worked	40	47
Sales calls	20	25
Orders	12	14
Dollar volume	$3,100	$2,900

HOW SALESPEOPLE SPEND THEIR TIME

Unlike some other commodities, time is inelastic; it has definite limits. Because of this inflexibility, many studies have been conducted to improve performance. On the production line, every movement, every gesture, every turn of a nut or bolt has been photographed, categorized, and scrutinized to find the best single way to accomplish specific tasks. It is far more difficult to determine accurately how a salesperson spends time and what motions can be improved upon. Nonetheless, many studies have attempted to spotlight the various aspects of how salespeople spend their time. Since we have separated the sales profession into four categories—retail, distribution, manufacturing, and industrial—it is only proper to deal with these with regard to time. This aspect can be handled in two parts. The first relates to the retail salesperson.

Retail Sales Time

One unique characteristic differentiating retail selling from all other forms of selling is that the prospect comes to the place of business. The salesperson must wait for the prospect. This is a major distinction, because many professionals feel that the prospect who enters a store is already half sold. Some people roam through retail stores claiming to be "only looking," but the fact that they are there is sufficient for us to assume that they are really looking for something to buy. Thus, the task of the retail salesperson starts further along in the Heart of the Sale, because lurking beneath the surface is an unmet need or desire ready to burst forth.

Although retails salespeople have little control over "sales" time, their responsibilities are significant. Most of them have inventory accountability, which means they have the duty to replenish diminished stock and to see that soiled merchandise is removed from the shelves. This takes time. In addition, retail salespeople (even if they are only clerks) must study the location of merchandise in the store and be at least familiar with the qualities and features of the product line. An engineer who enjoyed part-time selling was the "in-house expert" on power tools in a large department store. However, when customers asked for help with hand tools, he usually responded with a dull stare. He had no idea where inventories were kept and only wanted to explain how the large equipment worked.

Because the retail salesperson is easy to locate, he or she will handle a number of "service" calls. These requests seem endless, and each requires immediate attention. During a presentation, the furniture salesperson in a large furniture store was called to the phone. The caller had tried without success to reach the serviceperson who was supposed to remove the nicks from a dining-room table. Now, the customer in desperation called the salesperson who had taken the order and expected her to carry the message to the repair department. Even people stopping for directions to the bathroom infringe upon the time of the retail salesperson.

The highly professional retail salesperson will usually set aside some time each day for making telephone calls to prospects or reminding old customers about special deals or the arrival of new merchandise. This is one way for the "inside" person to stir up new and fresh business. What this all adds up to is a reduced amount of actual time spent with prospects and customers in creating or completing a sale.

One further unique quality about retail selling deserves consideration.

The freedom of movement that is so much a part of professional selling is greatly diminished at the retail level. Stores open and close with a certain regularity. There is a "time-clock" aspect to retail selling, and unless a person is accustomed to arriving and leaving at a definite time each day, this type of sales career may have little appeal. To compensate, the absolute necessity of discovering prospects does not exist at this level of selling.

Clearly, the retail salesperson is time-bound by the opening and closing of the store. The opportunity to make after-hours prospecting calls exists but is little practiced. Thus, the limitations of creativity and innovation are restricted to the hours set by the store, and this may force the salesperson to improve the quality of sales performance. Given a limit to the number of hours or minutes allotted to selling, each of these precious moments must be made to count.

Distribution, Manufacturing, and Industrial Sales Time

The life-style of "outside" salespeople is very similar, regardless of the level of selling. The difference is in degree. The industrial salesperson may call on only two or three customers or prospects a day, each separated by many miles, requiring additional travel time. The distribution salesperson may be able to schedule as many as 20 stops per day by reducing the amount of travel time. However, all salespeople at these three levels pursue their careers in about the same fashion. Built into the sales pattern is considerable freedom of how to regulate the work.

Because the outside salesperson has little close supervision, reports for the home office must be completed. This takes time. Traveling salespeople are also confronted with the necessity of waiting for customers and prospects. This simply means that whether they have an appointment or not, they may have to sit in an outer office and wait till the prospect is ready to be interviewed. It is not unusual to find that time spent waiting is an important facet of how outside salespeople spend their days. To compensate for this "wasted" time, many salespeople write their company reports while seated in the waiting rooms of prospects.

Travel time is a major portion of the daily routine of the outside salesperson. In the case of the industrial or manufacturing salesperson, this might very well mean an early-morning drive to the airport, a flight to a nearby city, a taxi ride to the client's office, and then a short wait before the face-to-face meeting with the prospect. These valuable hours are generally utilized in keeping up with company bulletins, reading trade publications, reviewing plans for the week, writing reports, and otherwise seeking to capitalize on time that cannot be used for selling.

Here is a sample day illustrating how an outside salesperson spent the time:

Travel	4 hours, 52 minutes
Waiting	1 hour, 6 minutes
Reporting writing	46 minutes
Service activities	52 minutes
Selling time	2 hours, 8 minutes
Soliciting new business	16 minutes
Total	10 hours

Even a casual study of this day indicates that the person had very little face-to-face conversation with potential and real customers. Still, this recording of time is fairly typical of outside salespeople. Perhaps the student can now recognize why salespeople should not thank prospects for their time. It is obvious that the time actually spent in dealing directly with prospects is indeed limited.

The time study above relates to a distribution salesperson, and it is interesting to note that after a regular routine of sales calls has been established, very little time remains for the solicitation of new business. Essentially, the most productive time is that brief period spent in selling. Based on a yearly income of $20,000, the value of each hour spent with customers is about $40. ($20,000 divided by 250 working days equals $80 per day income. If two hours is spent in selling, then each hour is worth $40.) Using this same approach, a $40,000 yearly income would expand the value of each sales hour to about $80!

The reasons for analyzing and pricing the value of an hour spent directly in selling is to impress upon the student and the beginning salesperson that every attempt should be made to squeeze more selling time into each day. All the other activities, each of which consumes valuable time, are needed to prepare for those moments when the salesperson is trying to sell. Any increase in time spent with prospects will ultimately yield higher income—if the quality of selling is improved. Remember what was said at the beginning of this section: More time and better quality both lead to increased earnings.

Any set of time studies must take into account the industry and the nature of the sales work. What we do know is that an eight- or ten-hour day does not consist of eight or ten hours of selling time. Obviously, the salesperson who sells heavy equipment may find it necessary to devote many days to explaining to the workers who will run the machine how it is to be used. Even duplicating equipment for office use may require a good deal of explanation and practice before the salesperson is completely satisfied that the customer can adequately handle the machine.

This service factor in some industries has led to the development of an "in-between" person who installs machinery and instructs the customer in its proper use. This service installer is neither pure salesperson nor pure serviceperson. Hence, most of the time is spent in placing and explaining equipment, and perhaps a few minutes in the act of selling. Generally, a potential sale is turned over to the regular salesperson.

How the individual outside salesperson divides a day of work is usually a personal choice. Many fields seem to require an early start in the morning; others tend to incline towards evening selling. Life insurance is historically sold at night, when the husband and wife can both be interviewed. However, many insurance people prefer to work during the day and so have carved out their own type of customers, people who can be seen during the day. The opportunity to vary the schedule is usually in the hands of the salesperson.

TARGET SALES EFFORTS

A dynamic sales manager was addressing the sales force one morning and posed the question, "What is it that each of you wants from your sales career?"

One person called out, "A lot of money!"

A woman in the rear of the group said, "Maximum results for minimum input."

Two people answered simultaneously, "Money!"

Off to one side, a man drawled, "A strong foundation for continued earning."

"This may surprise you," smiled the sales manager. "Each of you can reach his or her goal with our company." Then he went to the chalkboard and on the extreme left drew a sketch of a person and on the far right a picture of a house. "Let's assume that each of you is represented by the drawing on the left and the house on the right is your goal. Now, what are you going to do to get from the left to the right? How are you going to get home?"

The assembled group mumbled to themselves, not quite certain how to answer. Then, haltingly, one person said, "Well, I guess you just have to amble on over to the house."

"Not me," called out another. "I'd jump in a car and zip on over."

After the laughter subsided, a woman in the front row said, "First you have to figure out how far you have to travel. Then you have to decide how far you can go in one day. Simple arithmetic will tell you how long it will take to reach your final goal."

"Exactly," exclaimed the sales manager, "and the key is to have a plan of action. Once you have decided where you want to go, you have to establish a step-by-step procedure for getting there."

He paused and watched as the audience looked quizzically toward the front of the room. "Let's assume," he continued, "that tomorrow you have to sell $1,000 worth of product as a first step toward reaching your individual goal. What should we do about tomorrow?"

"That's easy," the woman in the front row said. "You schedule ten sales interviews. From my own averages, I know I will sell four of them, and that represents about $1,000 worth of product."

"She's better than I," said a man off to one side, "but the idea is the same. I can see only about seven people a day. From experience, I know I can sell about three of them, and that should add up to about $1,000 worth of business."

"I hate to say this," one man laughed, "but I would have to reduce my number of calls, because I currently write better than $1,000 a day." His colleagues laughed with him.

"You all seem to be on the right track," said the sales manager. "What's important is to target your sales effort. We have to know what we are trying to accomplish and then create a plan to reach that goal. Each of us has to get maximum use out of time, and the only way to do this is to plan our time."

Targeting sales efforts begins with an achievable goal and a timetable of how to reach that goal. Every day, the professional salesperson knows exactly what is to be done and how much time will be required to do it. In many instances, this timetable will be written out the preceding day. Also, even though the salesperson knows that not every day will be equally productive, at the end of a short period of time there is a balancing out, an averaging of efforts that validates the need for a plan.

A written plan of sales calls is important for three reasons. First, it sets a force (the salesperson) in motion for a period of time. Laying plans for a day of activity will overcome the tendency to relax after a successful interview. Many times, a big sale in the morning will be so satisfactory that a salesperson will decide to go to the movies in the afternoon. An opposite syndrome exists for the less stalwart. Defeat early in the day is reason to throw up the hands in disgust and say, "This is one of those days; I think I'll just go to the movies." But professional salespeople know that win, lose, or draw, they must make a specific number of calls each day. Some days will be more productive than others, but all require a set number of sales interviews. The sure knowledge that they have appointments for the entire working day will spur salespeople to continue to fulfill the daily schedule.

A second reason why a daily call plan is important is that special situations, such as service calls, will invariably interrupt some of the sales effort. By setting daily goals, professional salespeople ensure that delays or disturbances will not distract from the true course toward success that they themselves have determined. Consider the salesperson who, leaving home in the morning, discovers a flat tire on the car. This may upset the daily schedule of stops, but it should not prevent the professional from fulfilling a

TIME IS SO VALUABLE THAT
PROFESSIONAL SALESPEOPLE
LEARN TO MAKE THE MOST
OF EVERY WORKING MINUTE.

Figure 16-2

complete round of calls. The target of daily calls tells the professional what has to be accomplished that day.

The third reason for establishing a daily schedule is that, left to their own devices, most people will shoot for higher goals than their company would establish for them. This will undoubtedly come as a surprise, but enough surveys have been taken with regard to sales quotas to confirm that when the salespeople themselves are involved in quota setting, they expect more of themselves than their superiors expect. If you think back to Chapter 2 ("The Human Side of Buying"), you will recall the hierarchy of human needs. This striving or motivation to higher levels of needs also affects the individual salesperson. As salespeople fill the safety need, they are propelled upward toward the need for belongingness, esteem, and ultimately to self-actualization. These psychological forces are abundant in all people, and the professional salesperson demonstrates them by constantly reaching for higher goals.

Self-imposed goals and objectives are the natural result of skill and professionalism. Prodding and support by a sales manager are only temporary measures intended to set the salesperson on the right track. From that moment on, the person devoted to a sales career must make his or her decisions to improve. This is surely one of the major challenges to the profession of selling.

Targeting sales efforts requires salespeople to first make a decision about where they wish to go. Then it is necessary to actually spell out in detail how every hour of the day, week, and month are to be spent. Interruptions and service problems will then be blended into the daily routine. However, the salesperson will know exactly how many calls have to be made and how many successful interviews will result. As the drawing of the house on the blackboard illustrated, if you don't know where you want to go, you won't know how to get there.

MORE MINUTES MEAN MORE MONEY

"Too bad," said the purchasing agent. "I don't need anything. Guess that means you're only going to make a quarter from me today."

"Those are the breaks of the game," smiled the salesperson. "I see you 25 times a year. Usually I make a dollar because you order something. I guess every once in a while, I have to settle for a quarter."

The two laughed. This salesperson had earlier told the customer, "Last year I added up all my sales calls. From these I figured that every time I made a sale, regardless of the size of the order, I made a dollar, and every time I made a sales call and didn't make a sale, I earned a quarter. It keeps me making calls. There is no way I can lose."

There is considerable truth in the little device this salesperson was using. By the juggling of money, some recognition was given to the absolute necessity to make the many sales calls that do not result in orders. This person had decided that one of the goals for the following year might be to increase the value of "nonsales" interviews. That would mean an improvement in the sales-to-calls ratio. There is no such thing as batting 1.000—getting an order on every call. But there are a number of ways to improve selling averages—that is, having more successful sales interviews each and every day. Each of the following suggestions has to do with spending more productive time with prospects who can make a purchase.

Make Appointments. Some professional selling does not allow for making rigid appointments. To the extent possible, a salesperson should try to arrange a definite time to meet prospects. Actually, the task of calling for appointments is carried out during the prospecting and preapproach stages of the sale. However, as appointments are made, the salesperson notes them on the daily call schedule and fills a personal calendar. Those sales that tend to be repetitive or recurring may not require a definite date and time. For instance, the manufacturer's rep who calls every month may have only a loose arrangement to be seen during the first week of the month. Distributor salespeople who see their customers every week will be known to arrive with regularity. But an insurance person who calls once in several years must have a definite time and place for the sales interview.

Group Calls.   It just makes good logistical sense to group sales calls geographically. If you are working in one quadrant or section of a city, why plan to make a sales call on the other side of town? In the case of people who travel by plane, a trip to Chicago should incorporate several calls that can be completed in a single day or during a single trip. It is patently foolish to go to Chicago twice in one week if you have to fly into town. Salespeople who cover large areas by car often schedule stops along the way in small communities. Others prefer to arrive at a major city and work that area in particular. Any number of salespeople leave their cars at a convenient location and walk the crowded streets, stopping every few blocks to make a sales call. By eliminating travel time or grouping calls, salespeople are able to devote more time to calling on prospects and customers.

See the Right Person.   Certain aspects of professional selling bear constant repeating. One is that you should see the person who can place an order. An advertising salesperson traveled halfway across the country to make a presentation only to find that the person who could make the buying decision had not agreed to see the presentation. An assistant had arranged for the interview without clearing it with the media buyer, and the salesperson had not taken the trouble to ascertain that the person with authority would be present.

Miniaturize the Presentation.   A sales presentation should be just long enough to secure an order. If it takes 30 minutes to properly present the proposition, try to do it in 25 minutes. If that works, try to squeeze the material into 20 minutes. The professional task is to adequately explain what you have to sell in the least time. Try not to judge what is meant by "adequate"; better let the prospect be the judge. At any moment that the prospect seems willing to place an order, take it. This is not to say that the presentation should be without facts and data, but rather that different prospects require more or less explanation, and the salesperson should be prepared to take an order based on a minimum presentation. As we expressed this idea during the discussion of the close, one objective is to get the order.

Don't Talk Baseball.   It's very nice that the prospect and the salesperson support the same baseball team. But that has nothing to do with successful selling. Any conversation that is not directly related to the proposition at hand should be avoided. It is a never-ending source of dismay to professional sales managers to discover how much time their salespeople spend on conversation other than business. As this text has brought out several times, any talk other than pure business may divert the attention of the prospect from the expressed purpose of the visit. You just don't know what you might say that will turn a successful sale into a wasted effort.

Start Each Day with an Order.   There is a whole lot to be said for planning days so that the first call yields an order. Despite all the professional training in the world, we are each subject to the debilitating effects of being turned down the first thing in the morning. As the salesperson sets quotas of calls and orders for any given day, it is helpful to know that there are a few winners in the bag. Many stories tell about salespeople who didn't miss an order in 12, 20, or 50 calls. But an equally large number of stories tell about people being turned down 10, 20, or 50 times in a row. Therefore, to avoid these peaks and valleys, it is wise to build a daily schedule that starts with an order.

Sell Seven Days a Week.   The very nature of selling is to be constantly aware of prospect possibilities. At a Little League banquet one night, the speaker, a retiring baseball player, said that he planned to open a sporting-goods store in the area. Immediately, a salesperson in the audience made a mental note to chat with this speaker after the meeting was over to discuss store fixtures. On another occasion, a salesperson and her husband met a couple at a social gathering who turned out to be worthy prospects; they were looking for a new home. In the field of professional selling, you never know when or where you will meet someone who has the potential to buy your product or service.

Avoid Golf Traps.   There are times when a friendly game of golf will seal a relationship and prepare the way for big orders. Good. But golfing with a prospect who has never bought is hardly the time or place to make a major presentation. Many of the stories we hear about golf with customers have become distorted. It is very difficult to demonstrate new products while swinging a golf club. It is equally difficult to tell a prospect about the benefits of a proposition while a halfback is running for a touchdown. Enjoying extracurricular activities with a friend who is a customer is fine, but don't confuse it with professional selling.

The end result of adhering to these suggestions is to crowd more selling time into a day. By eliminating unnecessary talk, trimming the presentation, seeing the proper person, grouping sales calls, and being constantly aware of one's sales career, a person can increase the number of hours of face-to-face sales time. As we have already demonstrated, increasing selling time will effectively increase income. Every minute is important to the professional salesperson.

THE "DROP-ONE, ADD-ONE" SYSTEM

Every professional salesperson will devise his or her own method of self-created pressure that ensures proper use of sales time. One of the most popular methods is the "Drop-One, Add-One" system. Simply stated, this means making a list of regular customers in order of the dollar volume of business they place and dropping the last one on the list. Then go out and add a fresh name to the list; develop a new customer.

One distributor salesperson does this every six months. It takes that long to ascertain whether a prospect will be come a good account. Twice a year, this salesperson makes an arbitrary decision to get rid of the least productive and hence the least profitable customer. With the added time, a more profitable prospect can be solicited. This may seem like harsh treatment, but it has the effect of forcing the salesperson to reexamine time allocations at the same time that it analyzes sales volume.

Another way of examining time and volume is to average the volume of business each customer places. Those who fall below the average deserve either more attention, or less. If the potential volume is sufficiently enticing, the salesperson may decide on an all-out assault on that customer in an attempt to gain more business. If not, the decision to drop the account may be made. It is amazing to observe the effect on a professional salesperson when the decision to drop an account has been reached. It takes plenty of guts to give up a piece of business, no matter how small. But when the professional does, the result is more time and more opportunity for increased sales.

This "dropping and adding" process is applicable at the prospecting level as well. An insurance agent called a prospect and said, "This is the fifth and last time I shall call for an appointment. I realize you have had a busy schedule. But unless we can make a definite appointment now to review my proposition, I shall never call again."

It may appear that a threat was implied in this conversation. This was not the true intent. This insurance agent had a prospecting plan that allowed for five phone calls in an attempt to gain an interview. This was all the time that could be allocated to this phase of the overall sales program. Years of personal experience had proved that if the agent could not get an interview after five phone calls, it was time to go on to some other prospect and stop wasting time. The principle is identical to dropping the least valuable customer.

THE RAINY-DAY SYNDROME

Very few people like to work on a rainy day, and salespeople are no exception. However, outside salespeople face a different problem when the weather is inclement. First is the not very happy prospect of getting in and out of a car, slogging through rain and sometimes snowdrifts. Other types of work may allow for not showing up, but the professional salesperson is expected to appear under all circumstances. Therein lies an opportunity that many professionals capitalize upon. Regardless of the weather, they appear!

They simply do not acknowledge any reason for not calling on customers and prospects.

Because everyone is subject to the vagaries of poor weather conditions, some salespeople save their best clothes for the worst weather. A novice salesperson, hearing this, remarked, "That doesn't make sense. Why take the chance that a new suit will get wet or soiled?"

To which the old timer replied, "When the day is dark, I always try to wear something light. It is when all the world seems to be coming apart at the seams that the professional salesperson needs inner encouragement and the prospect has to feel that here is a bright spot in the day."

"Not me," said the sales beginner. "I am trying to be truly professional, and I don't need any kind of extra help."

"That's okay with me," said the old pro. "But just think how you feel about yourself when you put on an old and worn suit. I need the boost, and my customers look forward to my appearance. When the weather is down, I try my best to be up."

An early-morning discovery that it is raining is no reason to slip back into bed. Like the Postal Service, professional salespeople are on the go; "Neither snow, nor rain, nor heat, nor gloom of night stays these couriers from the swift completion of their appointed rounds."

PERSONAL TIME STUDIES

Tracking time is not a totally new idea. For the beginning salesperson it may come as a shock, as if the boss is watching over your shoulder. Many companies meet opposition when they institute periodic time studies; the salespeople exhibit resentment. In the final analysis, a recounting of time is more important to the salesperson than to anyone else. More than ever, the thought that "time is money" applies to the activities of the professional salesperson.

Unlike the case with other types of work, there is a direct link between the productivity and income of the professional salesperson. Although sales may increase in several ways, a better use of available time is one of the easiest ways to upgrade productivity. If three hours a day of face-to-face selling can be increased to four hours a day, it is a pretty fair assumption that sales will go up by one-third. Built into any time study are immediate and direct benefits to the salesperson.

The time study in Table 16-2 can prove instructive. The salesperson spent less than three hours that day with customers and prospects. During that time, a dispenser was repaired, banquet tickets were discussed and purchased, it was necessary to call the office for some information, an inventory system was established, a bill was collected, and inventory was actually counted. How many minutes were actually devoted to "selling"?

Table 16-2 Time Study

SALESPERSON Joan Jones	DATE 12-2-85				LEFT HOME 8:40 A.M. RETURNED HOME 4:30 P.M.
Customer	Arrival Time	Travel (Minutes)	Departure Time	Activities	Sales Time
ABC Company	9:10	30	9:25	Order	15
DEF Company	9:40	15	10:15	Repair dispenser Order banquet tickets	35
GHI Company	10:45	30	10:50	Buyer out	0
JKL Company	11:15	25	11:25	Order	10
MNO Company	11:45	20	12:05	Order Called office	20
			LUNCH		
PQR Company	1:20	20	1:40	Order Set up inventory	20
STU Company	2:05	25	2:30	Order Collected bill	25
VWX Company	2:45	15	2:55	No order	10
EPA Company	3:15	20	3:30	Order and inventory	15
FED Company	3:45	15	4:00	New prospect	15
Total		215 minutes			165 minutes

Because this study is simplified, there is no way to accurately answer that question, but certain conclusions can be drawn. The most important: There simply wasn't a great deal of time for pure selling.

A single time study has little value. By repeating this exercise at some later point, Joan Jones can check to see if her use of time has improved. Moreover, based on two, three, or four time studies of the same weekday, she can make decisions about how to get more selling and less traveling into her daily schedule. This might require rerouting accounts, starting a little earlier in the day, working a little later, or having lunch with a prospective account. Whatever decisions are made, it is clear that salespeople must control, police, and direct their own efforts.

Because people are individuals, each with his or her own desires, needs, and goals, the salesperson has the opportunity to design a time study that applies to himself or herself specifically. Over and over, the freedom of movement afforded professional salespeople is emphasized. Needless to say, the salesperson must accommodate a schedule to satisfy the needs, desires, and wants of the customers. It would be foolhardy to expect to call on the purchasing agent of a steel company in the middle of the night.

Inasmuch as time is such an important commodity, many companies have undertaken time studies in sales departments. However, the professional will probably want to have a better understanding of where the time goes and therefore institute a personal time study. These will increase in value as they are carried out every three or four months. As a minimum, the professional salesperson should study time allocation at least twice a year. As one sales pro put it, "Good time study results in more talk and less walk."

An interesting variation of the traditional time log is presented in Table 16-3. In this form, the salesperson can account for every minute of every day by category of activity, and equally important, minutes spent with each customer. This concentration of time and effort can then easily be measured against sales results. Ultimately the salesperson can make positive decisions about the best place to give professional attention.

WHEN TO GIVE UP

A perennial question asked by new salespeople is, "How often should I call on a prospect before giving up?"

It is appropriate to deal with this problem in the midst of a time study. From the earlier chart, it is fairly obvious that the time allotted for soliciting new business is brief indeed. Moreover, the type of selling will dictate the number of times a prospect ought to be solicited. For instance, insurance salespeople require a constant stream of new prospects, because their product represents an occasional purchase. On the other hand, the manufac-

Table 16-3 Time Log

	1	2	3	4	5	6	7	8	9	10	11	12	13	14	15	16	17	Total (minutes)
Travel time																		
Taking order																		
Showing new product																		
Collecting money																		
Inventory																		
Waiting																		
Office calls																		
Paperwork																		
Conversation																		
New business calls																		
Total (minutes)																		

Date _____

353

turer's representative must call on the same people over and over, anticipating orders every month or every season. A distributor salesperson might call on the same customers every week, and possibly get an order every week. All must prospect for new customers!

Many studies reveal that most first-time sales are made after the fifth sales call. That means that the salesperson will make a presentation five or more times before the prospect will agree to buy. In fact, sales increase rapidly as the number of calls increases. In certain industries, a prospect is not dropped from the list of potentials until after the tenth call.

Meeting the rebuffs of a prospect is one of the most difficult jobs of the salesperson. Here is the experience of a distributor salesperson:

"I called on Smith every week for eight weeks. He had a reputation as a tough apple, and I really wanted to get some of his business. Before each call, I prepared a demonstration on a different line of our products. He was always cordial but never receptive. Now, I'd like to tell you I finally sold him. I didn't. Finally, I ran out of time and told him I wouldn't call again for maybe a year. He smiled and said, 'Okay.' That's all there was to it. But I just couldn't continue to call without getting business, so I gave him up."

Every salesperson will establish what he or she feels is an adequate number of prospecting calls before deciding to stop trying to sell a particular account. The barrier each salesperson must overcome is willingness to concede defeat too soon in the game. No prospect worth selling should be abandoned without a great deal of effort. Some salespeople actually refuse to give up until they have called at least ten times. Every industry may have its own guidelines; however, as a general rule, the salesperson should show determination and be prepared to make up to ten sales calls before relegating the prospect to the inactive files.

One point worth remembering is summed up in the comment of a veteran of 25 years in selling: "The harder it is to get a prospect to buy, the harder it is to lose that customer."

SUMMARY

Professional salespeople may improve their sales and income by perfecting sales techniques and methods. Another excellent way to increase sales is to jealously scrutinize and guard sales time. Only when you have studied where the hours are spent each day will it be possible to reach conclusions about how to increase the actual number of minutes spent in pure selling activities.

Retail salespeople usually wait for prospects to enter the store. Even at this level of industry, it is possible to generate interest by calling old customers to keep them informed of changing styles and special sales. At the other levels of industry—distribution, manufacturing, and industrial—the salesperson finds a good deal of time devoted to such nonproductive activities as travel, waiting, report writing, and even service. Any increase in the time spent in selling should result in increased volume and therefore increased income for the salesperson.

To assist in analyzing time, the salesperson should target sales efforts by first deciding what is to be accomplished. The salesperson who participates in determining sales quotas and goals can determine a better use of time. Written schedules are significant because they tend to force the salesperson to complete a given number of sales calls, make allowances for disruptions such as service activities, and invariably set higher goals.

To conserve time, the professional salesperson will try to make definite appointments, group sales calls geographically, try to always see the correct person, trim the sales presentation to workable dimensions, avoid extraneous conversation, try to start off each day with a sale, recognize that selling is a seven-days-a-week activity, and realize that social activities with a client are not the same as selling. By applying these rules, the salesperson can squeeze more selling time into the normal day.

As a further effort to conserve time, the professional salesperson will analyze the volume of business from all customers and accept the fact that from time to time, some old accounts should be dropped from the books. It is always difficult for a salesperson to give up established business. Yet this singular effort may spell the difference between roaring success and acceptable performance. The professional salesperson will never let bad weather or a flat tire impinge upon maximum performance.

As a prod to improve time usage, the professional salesperson will create a personal time study. This means an in-depth time-keeping chart made at least twice a year. As these studies accumulate, the salesperson can reexamine past efforts to evaluate where improvement has been made and where further improvements can be effected. What each person does relies on the industry and the personal desires of that person.

There are times when prospects have to be drawn back into the "maybe" pile. After the professional salesperson has called ten times on a prospect, it may be time to concede that there is nothing to be gained from further calls. The mature salesperson will recognize the necessity of making those ten calls and will also recognize when to stop wasting valuable time.

The profession of selling is a mature activity, and it remains essentially in the hands of the salesperson to make those decisions that affect personal life-style. How the salesperson spends time is almost always up to that person.

A SUCCESS STORY

Ted Maul studied the sales report very closely. A splatter of figures covered the pages, and he sat quietly trying to wade through the complex set of data. "Too much information can be as much trouble as too little," he thought.

The major question on his mind was how to increase sales without devoting more time to his business. Some facts seemed to leap from the page. His average order was running close to $100. Every week he was turning in 50 orders, which meant about ten a day. Based on his territory and the need to spend time taking inventory for each customer, he couldn't see any way to raise the volume per call or the number of calls per day. Unless, that is, he decided to work more hours each day.

When Ted compared his own figures with those of the other sales-people, he discovered that one person had average orders of almost $200. This person was doing almost twice as much business, and yet the respective territories appeared comparable. Before seeking an answer from this salesperson, Ted ran a time study of his own efforts. After three weeks of recordkeeping, he could not discern any way to save time, and this meant that if he wanted to increase his sales, he would have to work more hours—not a very happy prospect.

After more study, Ted decided to confront the salesperson writing $200 orders to see what he might learn. "Arlene," he said, "how are you able to do so much business with your accounts when we seem to have similar territories?"

"I don't know how to answer that question," she responded. "You're welcome to examine my routing and my own time study. I imagine the figures are similar to yours."

Together the two pored over the hours spent selling and the volume of business. "Wait a minute," Ted exclaimed. "You seem to have almost twice as many customers. How is that possible?"

"That makes sense," she answered. "I do about twice as much business as you, so I need about twice as many accounts."

"But if you don't work any more hours than I do, how can you see them all?"

Once again the two salespeople studied the figures. Only in the last moments of desperation did Ted ask, "How often do you see each account?"

"Every two weeks," Arlene replied.

"My goodness. No wonder you can do more business. I see my people every week. How did you manage to switch them to a two-week schedule?"

Now that the answer had been found, Arlene had no difficulty in recalling her own decision to test her accounts by calling every other week instead of every week. "Remember when the price of gas went up so drastically? Well, I asked my customers if they would mind my calling on alternate weeks so that I could save gas. They were all willing to cooperate, and it's been that way ever since."

Banging his fist on the table, Ted declared, "That's a fantastic idea! One change in scheduling and you were able to double your sales. Oh, my. Why didn't I think of that?"

"You did," she smiled. "At least you did just now."

QUESTIONS FOR CLASS DISCUSSION

1. Compare sales success to a baseball batting average. What are the two ways to improve sales success?
2. Explain at least five ways outside salespeople can improve the use of their time.
3. Generally speaking, salespeople control their own working hours. What are the advantages and disadvantages of this responsibility?
4. Prepare an imaginary day in the life of a salesperson in the food-distribution industry. Prepare a comparable day in the life of an insurance agent.
5. Prepare a personal time study, with specific attention to the amount of time you spend in school or learning activities. Is there any relationship between the "business" of going to school and the "business" of selling?
6. What changes can you make in your personal life-style to afford an extra hour of time each day? Explain.
7. What are the prime differences in the way retail salespeople spend their time as opposed to time spent by outside salespeople?
8. What is meant by the expression, "Time is inelastic"? Is there any way to make time more elastic?
9. If a salesperson earns $25,000 a year, what is each hour of "selling" time worth?
10. Explain the meaning of "targeting sales efforts."

CASE 16—THE CASE OF THE UNHAPPY BUYER

Gusts of wind whipped across Market Street and gathered the few shoppers into weary knots, each seeking to hide from the driving rain. Head bowed against the whirl, Marian Sack forged her way across the street toward Harold's Epicurean Shop, where she had an appointment with Mervyn Harold. Eight previous sales calls had finally resulted in a small order, and today was to be a true test: Did the new line of fancy kitchen cookware sell?

She stopped for a moment to admire the display of cooking utensils in the window. Harold had certainly given her products a fair amount of exposure. "Placing those copper pots in the window is a great break," she thought. "Now, if he did some business, I'm in good shape."

Briskly she pushed her way through the glass door and headed for the purchasing office on the second floor. Midway up the stairs, she heard Harold's voice. "Ms. Sack. Wait a moment."

Turning, she saw Harold beckoning her to return to the first floor. She smiled and retreated to the waiting purchasing agent. "Good afternoon," she said.

"Precisely," he snapped.

"Sorry I'm late. Bad weather and all."

"What does the bad weather have to do with arriving three hours late for our appointment?"

Now the joy and happiness of seeing her products in the window drained from her face. Harold's attitude was hardly encouraging. "The motor of my car got wet, and I had to wait while the service station dried out the wires," she explained. "But I didn't realize we had a definite appointment. I was under the impression you were available all day. That's why I wasn't too concerned about the time. But surely you knew I would be here?"

"Why surely?" he asked. "We have only just begun to do business."

"I'm sorry. I guess I should have called. But I value your business so highly that I feared a phone call would be too impersonal."

"Ms. Sack," he said, "when you didn't arrive at eleven o'clock as you have in the past, I called your office and placed a second order. Next time, please arrive on schedule." With that, he turned and stalked off into the back storeroom.

Sack stood dumbfounded, uncertain over whether to be happy for a second order or sad because she had upset a big buyer.

1. How many sales mistakes did Marian Sack make?
2. If you were Sack's sales manager, what advice would you offer?
3. How would you relate this story to an improved use of time?
4. Was Mervyn Harold justified in his arrogant treatment of the salesperson?

EXERCISE 16

Few learning activities are as effective as observing reality, which is why this exercise calls for the student to work a full day with a salesperson, making sales calls.

During the course of this day, you are to track time in the following categories:

1. Travel
2. Waiting
3. Order taking
4. Presentation of new products

SALES PROBLEM 16—ONE IDEA FOR TWO CUSTOMERS

When both companies came out with the same promotion at the same time, Bill knew he had real problems.

He had thought they were far enough apart geographically to use the same kind of promotions. Was he wrong! Now, both firms had invested in inventory, promotions, and printed materials to sell his products. Not only that, one company was selling the merchandise for less than the other. Both were angry.

Here is how three sales reps confronted a very sticky problem:

Sales Rep #1:   When you sell to a variety of customers, you have to give them all the same opportunities. If a good deal is coming down the pike, it is the responsibility of the sales rep to make the most professional presentation possible.

In this instance, two companies decided to jump. The sales rep doesn't set the prices for the companies. Therefore, it simply makes good sense to explain that everybody started from the same point. Your job as a sales rep is to keep everybody in your territory very well informed.

Sales Rep #2:   No sales rep should get involved in telling a customer what to charge for merchandise, other than industry standards or norms. Second, I would never sell anything on the basis of exclusivity. I want to sell each of my accounts as much as I can. I also want them all to be successful.

However, I must be certain that each account knows that the deal offered to one was the same as to the other. The fact that one person saw a larger opportunity and chose to cut the selling price is just part of being in business.

Sales Rep #3:   Probably there was a deal on the merchandise, and that is why both these customers made the purchase. The fact that one passed the savings along to the ultimate consumer is just the way some people prefer to do business.

There is also a possibility that one account purchased a larger quantity and benefitted from a larger discount, or saved money on freight. One thing is certain, the sales rep did not set the selling price.

The key here is to continue to bring specials and ideas to all your customers. Ultimately, they will understand that that is part of the selling job. Maybe they will learn to jump in on more deals in the future.

5. Prospect calls
6. Paperwork and phone calls
7. Selling

Prepare some brief comments on the time of this salesperson.

In the event that you cannot find a salesperson with whom to travel, here is a substitute exercise: Maintain a study of your own time for two consecutive days, tracking your time in 15-minute increments.

Include a brief report on what changes you intend to make and the resulting allocation of your time.

17

CAREER OPPORTUNITIES IN SELLING

PERFORMANCE OBJECTIVES

After you have read this chapter and completed the Questions for Class Discussion, the Case, the Sales Problem, and the Exercise, you should be able to do the following:

1. List and describe the six advantages of a sales career.
2. List and describe the six elements of a sales compensation package.
3. Differentiate between "inside" and "outside" selling.
4. Prepare a sales plan to convince (sell) the instructor of this course to give you an A.

A REVEALING INTERVIEW

"Your credentials certainly seem to be in order, Mr. Stellman," said the personnel manager. "Tell me a little more about your experience as a newspaper carrier."

"Gess, there's not much to tell. I needed a job when I was in grade school. It was a wonderful way for a youngster to earn a lot of money."

"Did you enjoy the work? What I mean is this business of getting up at the crack of dawn. Did that bother you?"

"Sure did. But I knew that the rewards were worth it. From the time I was 12 years old, I never asked my parents for any money. It was a great feeling to know that I could support myself."

Impressed with this response, the personnel manager probed further. "Did you ever lose a customer?"

"Oh, sure. A lot of my people were elderly, and every once in a while one would die. Also, when the Naval Air Base moved, I lost a lot of customers."

"Didn't that bother you?"

"I guess it did at the time, but I knew how to deal with that kind of problem."

"What do you mean?"

"We were trained to keep looking for new customers. When you just plug along, you realize that some you lose and others you gain."

"Do you understand the nature of this field marketing position?"

"Well, I spoke with some of the other people, and they tell me it's more selling than anything else. Quite frankly, that's pretty much what I'm looking for."

"Actually, there's much more to it than selling. There's a great deal of service, being able to show the customers how to best display these products. There are also times when you may even be asked to demonstrate profit margins and how to promote new lines as they come on-stream."

"I recognize the need to learn a good deal about how your products are manufactured, but the thought of hitting the street and producing sales is really my meat."

"Yes. Well, there are other responsibilities. There are monthly reports and sales meetings, and at least twice a year, we have to attend conventions. How do you feel about that?"

"Great. Even though I really enjoy selling, I know that once in a while, the chance to see and learn new things is important."

The personnel manager appeared somewhat disturbed. "This is much more than merely selling," he said. "You will have lots of responsibilities. You see, the general manager came up through the sales ranks, and she takes a particular interest in how the sales department is doing."

"You have me a little out of kilter," said Stellman. "I was under the impression that this job was selling. That's what I do best."

"If selling were the only thing involved, we wouldn't give this position the title of Field Marketing Representative. Oh, no. There are many other things you will be expected to do, including the possibility of going to school at night."

"But I already have a two-year degree."

"Of course. That shows in your application. However, this is a growth company, and we find that most of our junior and even some senior executives come from the sales ranks."

"But all I want to do is sell."

"In this company, you will be expected to do much more than simply selling."

"Heck, I spent four years with another company, and they really added to my college training in sales. I like the freedom and the chance to run my own life. Are you telling me I have to become an executive and sit behind a desk?"

"Anything wrong with sitting behind a desk?" asked the personnel manager, a little annoyed.

"Nothing in the world, if that's what you want to do. Me, I like to be out on the street, meeting people, seeing new things, breathing fresh air."

"How about being away from your family overnight?"

"Once in a while it's okay. My family knows I love my work. No, I don't like being away, but if that's what the job entails, I want to do it. In my last position, I spent most of the time away from home doing all the reports and making appointments for the next day's work."

"You don't mind all these other responsibilities that go with the job?"

"Of course not. But do you mind if I just call myself a salesperson?"

"Why do you want that kind of title?"

"That's easy. Selling is my profession."

Like a diamond, selling has many facets. There are responsibilities and tasks, functions to be performed, and needs to be filled. Whatever title you assign to the profession, it is still a matter of meeting people and conveying a message, hopeful that they will buy. In the simplest terms, "selling is the transfer of product or service from one person to another." But that big, wide, wonderful world calls us by many names. Reduced to basic terms, the job is still selling.

THE PERVASIVE NATURE OF SELLING

According to the ethical standards accepted by the medical profession, doctors may not advertise their services in the conventional fashion. A newspaper notice announcing the opening of an office, the removal of an office, or the joining together of two doctors as a team is the extent of advertising allowed. But there is currently in medical schools a course that can best be described as "Bedside Manners." That's right, people entering the medical profession are being trained in the best ways to treat their patients as human beings. This training might well be called "selling."

Until recently, lawyers were not allowed to advertise in the conventional sense either. Still, they found new clients by joining business associations, becoming active in politics, belonging to social clubs, and engaging in a multitude of activities that tended to bring them in contact with the public from whom they draw their clients. This mingling with people is the kind of exposure that permits them to become known and have their services sought out. In a very prosaic sense, they are "selling themselves."

Time studies prepared by the presidents of large corporations are filled with notations of the amount of time spent with customers and prospects. Some of these high-placed officials regard their jobs as nothing more than developing sales at the upper levels of industry. Few would refer to themselves as salespeople, despite the fact that their every waking hour is devoted to increasing the dollar volume of business done by their companies.

This notion, this concept, this ability to persuade others to our way of thinking, this profession known as selling is all-pervasive. The major distinction between a 21-year-old "green" salesperson and a company president is one of degree. Both are salespeople. Some of us have studied our profession and brought our understanding to a fine degree of performance. We recognize that the business of selling requires easily as much effort and study as do many other professions.

To those of you who opt for a career in selling: Make your choice a positive one.

ADVANTAGES OF A SALES CAREER

Every career or life-style contains advantages and disadvantages. In the world of professional selling, all the disadvantages can be advantages in disguise, because every aspect of professional selling requires people to make decisions about the type of work and the kind of life-style they prefer. Unlike many other careers, selling is replete with opportunities for a person to set a pace that satisfies, to relocate, to advance, or to move into another field. This need to make choices may overpower some, but for others it is the best possible way to grow and develop.

"Excelsior"

The "Excelsior" syndrome is similar to climbing a mountain—passing through rings of clouds, hoping that beyond the next white covering will be the top. Yet deep down, the professional salesperson knows there is no limit. There is no top to the mountain, because there is always a better way, a higher goal, something more to achieve. What can be said about selling is little different than what can be said about life itself.

This challenge to continue forward is a major part of the profession of selling. Each day provides new hurdles to overcome and new problems to solve. The process feeds upon itself; new products beget new products, and new services beget new services. Just when the salesperson feels a sense of competence, there is another barrier to vault. The cry, "Ever onward," which is what the word *excelsior* means, is the byword of selling. Selling is a heady activity that constantly rejuvenates the willing and further enfeebles the weak.

Thus, a sales career has both an advantage and a disadvantage. The profession of selling is for mature and dedicated people who welcome the ever-present challenge. If this quest for new and better ways diminishes, the professional salesperson knows something is missing. It might almost be said that a career in professional sales is never dull.

Transferability

One of the qualities of professional selling is the fact that learned methods and techniques are transferable, which means they may be used in other activities. The ability to persuade and convince has long been the strength of many politicians. In fact, if you listen closely to a political speech, you may detect many of the methods this book propounds—appeals to the emotional or psychological needs of the audience. However, the ability to sell may easily serve in a number of other ways.

A long-time professional salesman was forced to give up his profession because of an automobile accident. He chose teaching as his new career and found great success when he approached each class session as a sales opportunity.

A professional saleswoman, who took time out to have two children before returning to her work, marveled at the amount of "selling" she did on her children. "I found it much easier to present them with ideas rather than force my thinking on them," she said.

Another professional saleswoman, promoted to a management position with her company, remarked, "It's amazing how much selling I still do—to both my subordinates and superiors."

The knowledge of selling will stand the student in good stead in a multitude of other careers. As we shall soon see, the ability to "sell" is a valuable asset when applying for a job. Asking the boss for a raise is often best done by first developing a sales plan.

Maneuverability

Wherever there are people, there are salespeople. No section of the country, or the world for that matter, is lacking in demand for skilled and competent salespeople. This quality of maneuverability is significant to many people who decide to move to another part of the country. Somewhere their professional talents are needed.

When Ray Lowry and his family decided they wanted to move to the West Coast, it meant a number of changes. However, Ray knew that his experience in selling shoes at the retail level was a talent in demand all over the country. He had little trouble finding a new position in the San Francisco area, where his professional sales skills were needed.

In another instance, a woman who worked her way through college selling for a book company easily found employment with a competitive firm where she wanted to live, over 1,000 miles away.

Often salespeople will be moved by their companies as openings in different parts of the country appear. One man, who worked in New Jersey for ten years, jumped at the chance to move back to Wisconsin. The woman who replaced him in New Jersey had been brought into the company from another field of selling because she had exhibited the kinds of drive the original company desired in its sales force.

Once you have learned the profession, the opportunity to select where to live is pretty much up to you.

Advancement

The ranks of management are filled with people who have risen through sales departments. If a position in management is the ultimate goal, there is probably no more direct route than through the sales field. Each year, a survey of the number of presidents of top corporations reveals that a large percentage gained access to the executive suite through a progression of sales positions.

There are other ways to executive jobs. Specific knowledge in engineering, finance, production, or even the profession of management can often lead to these high-powered offices. However, there is little doubt that a basic career in selling prepares many people for executive jobs.

The positions immediately above sales, such as sales supervision, sales management, sales training, and marketing, all require a deep understanding of professional selling. Often a person will refuse promotion, because it is not unnatural for a salesperson to earn more dollars than a sales supervisor. Needless to say, anyone interested in starting his or her own business would be well advised to study basic selling as an absolute necessity for business success. Every business requires a fair amount of selling.

Atmosphere

Along with success in professional selling comes the right of salespeople to create an atmosphere in which they wish to work. In many instances, this may mean not selling to prospects who the salesperson finds are miserable or uncooperative. It is important that the salesperson not take refuge in this attitude as a reason for not calling on difficult prospects. However, if any one or two or three prospects are mean and nasty, the professional salesperson can survive without them.

Even the relationship between the salesperson and the sales manager or owner can be controlled. Physical contact is usually limited to a few hours each week. Beyond that, salespeople are pretty much on their own. The process of report writing tends to limit contact and allows the professional salesperson to establish an environment conducive to happy living.

It is an interesting sidelight that salespeople, in particular outside salespeople, live in a world that is largely of their own making. They have the choice of working early or late, visiting distant places, and stopping along the road. Frequently, this will take the form of picking up fresh fruit from a roadside market, collecting antiques from stores in the territory, or meeting people in cities and communities around the state. The atmosphere salespeople create is known as freedom of movement. No one breathes down their necks, and they work the way they want. To compensate for hours diverted to other activities, they may choose to start the day before dawn, or work until midnight. The point is that they can do pretty much as they wish, as long as they achieve the sales goals they have carved out for themselves.

Money

Income is no small advantage to the sales profession. High-risk selling in which orders are infrequent, such as insurance, can offer a tremendous opportunity for high incomes. Steady, repeat-order selling, such as the distribution field, offers a good income with only a slight chance to make "big" money. There is a tradeoff: The more difficult the sale, the higher the income potential.

By any measure, the income possibilities in the sales field are without limit. This is in itself one of the most attractive qualities of a sales career. Just as the professional creates the work climate and the schedule of activities, the amount of income desired can be an attainable goal.

THE SALES COMPENSATION PACKAGE

At an earlier time, the compensation package of professional sales-people was fairly simple. They earned either a straight commission or a combination of salary and commission. To better understand the complexity of today's sales profession, it is first necessary to have some grasp of the tasks for which salespeople are paid.

Do you pay a salesperson a commission for orders taken, or for orders that have been delivered and paid for? What do you do about paying a person who services an account when no order or possible commission can result? Do you pay for sales to major national accounts that are sold by someone at the company's headquarters? How do you compensate a salesperson for introducing new products? Is it right to pay a salesperson for gathering market information?

These and other questions bedevil sales managers and are scrutinized by those charged with the responsibility of arriving at a fair method to compensate salespeople. In other words, salespeople perform many tasks and should be paid for whatever it is they do. That is why the total compensation package is so complex—because management is trying to fairly equate some form of remuneration with all the work salespeople do besides taking orders.

Salespeople should be paid for taking care of "house" accounts. Here is a clear example. A national drive-in restaurant chain may agree to use a specific brand of catsup. It contracts with a national manufacturer to use that brand. The manufacturer then arranges to ship the product through its distributors all over the country. These individual and frequently independent distributors ask the route salespeople to stop and take orders from the stores on a weekly or biweekly basis. Price concessions may have been part of the original contract, and there may not be a sufficient margin of profit to pay the salesperson a full commission on the individual sale. Besides, the salesperson did not make the sale. Nonetheless, the salespeople have to receive some form of compensation or they won't bother to take the orders.

Drug detail people who call on doctors to explain new pharmaceuticals rarely take an order. Their goal is to interest doctors in a new product so that they will prescribe it. Ultimately, the distributor of drugs to drugstores will benefit from this effort. How do you compensate detail people?

These various elements disturb the thinking of salary and wage administrators who must develop formulas for paying salespeople. The end result is a package consisting of a number of ways not only to satisfy the salesperson but also to motivate the sales force. Here are some of the best ways salespeople are paid:

Base Salary.   To ensure that the salesperson earns a living wage, many firms start with a salary that may appear modest. This salary is intended to compensate the salesperson for calling on old established accounts, servicing "house" accounts, collecting bills, and gathering market information. There may also be provision for the introduction of new products about which the company is uncertain. Each of these activities detracts from "real" selling time, and the salesperson has to be paid for efforts expended.

Commission.   Variable commissions may be paid based on sales. There may be a minimum sales goal, after which the salesperson receives a percentage commission. The commission scale may be sliding—that is, higher for more sales, or sometimes lower as the volume goes up. The varieties are infinite. This aspect of compensation is intended to serve as a motivator. Although money may not be the most important facet of motivation, there is no denying that salespeople in particular are motivated to higher productivity because the money goal is important. A number of surveys have confirmed that most employees classify money as less important as a motivational factor than general working conditions and happiness with their work. In the selling field, money is still conceived of as a great motivator, which is why commissions become so important in the compensation package.

Bonuses.   In addition to commissions, salespeople often participate in a bonus arrangement for meeting or exceeding sales quotas. Again, this part of the compensation package may be tied to profits, volume, or even how the entire sales force has met its goals. There are no specific rules for how any company will set up its bonus plan. It too is intended to spur greater activity and participation on the part of salespeople.

Car Allowances and Travel.   Inasmuch as travel is such an integral part of the sales picture, most companies have devised a plan to meet all or part of this expense. In some instances, the company will provide a car with no other allowance. In other instances, it will provide allowances but no car. In still a third system, it may provide both a car and an allowance.

If travel by plane is required, the cost of the fare, cabs, food, lodging, and an occasional cocktail are generally paid by the company. If it is necessary to rent a car, the company pays. When salespeople are away from home, the company usually treats them in splendid fashion.

Expenses.   Theater tickets, magazine subscriptions, and dinner invitations to big buyers are often part of the expense portion of a compensation package. Every company has its own rules with regard to these items. However, a handsome expense account is often held out to a salesperson as an added inducement to work for a firm.

Peripheral Benefits.   Part of salespeople's compensation consists of peripheral benefits such as Blue Cross, retirement plans, health insurance, life insurance, major medical payments, college scholarship programs, and even two new items, Blue Tooth and Blue Eye. Some organizations pay for employees to go back to school; others provide for a leave of absence every seven years as a sabbatical. There is no limit to the variety of things some companies provide to further compensate salespeople.

Given all these methods for compensating salespeople, it is important to recognize that no matter how the pie is sliced, salespeople receive a percentage of the sale; that is to say, a certain portion of the total dollars of revenue is devoted to compensating salespeople for their efforts. How this sum is arranged—partially in commissions and partially in bonus and salary, or all in commissions, or all in salary and expenses—is of only relative importance. Some sales positions are strictly on commission. The salespeople pay their own expenses, insurance, travel, and so on. There is no right way!

The end result of all this figuring and planning brings to the salesperson more dollars than do many other types of work. Most important is the idea that since income is directly related to sales volume, there is no upward limit. You earn what you earn. That's quite a challenge, and one to which most professional salespeople respond best.

OTHER VIEWS OF THE SALES PARADE

The profession of selling is open to several interpretations. This text has divided the differences in types of selling into four main categories—retail, distribution, manufacturing, and industrial—but other views are worth mentioning. Some experts feel that the only distinctions in selling arise because of the nature of the product or service. They generally suggest that selling is broken down between tangibles and intangibles.

Tangibles easily fall into the category of products; that is, they are things that can be seen, touched, smelled, tasted, or heard. Therefore, it is easy to understand that cars, golf clubs, typewriters, furniture, clothes, and anything that qualifies as a product requires a somewhat different kind of sales plan. When the salesperson can hold up a product for the prospect to examine or touch, the presentation has certain advantages.

On the other hand, *intangibles* are those things that cannot be identified by the five senses—things such as insurance, advertising, consulting services, travel, or even stocks and bonds. How these services are presented to the prospect makes for a distinctive kind of sales problem. Thus, the point of view that differentiates between product and service is valid. However, even though selling tangibles and selling intangibles differ, this text has sought to provide the framework for all kinds of selling, because regardless of the product or service, a sales plan is a prerequisite to sales success.

Sales Specialists

Still other experts feel that the various specialized activities of selling spell a difference. Here are some descriptions of certain of these specialized areas:

Merchandiser. Many industries require the services of a "salesperson" whose time is devoted to overseeing displays and point-of-purchase materials for retail stores. For instance, the person who regularly restocks the pantyhose section in the supermarket is referred to as a salesperson. Initially, this person may have actually created the need and demand for the product, but the follow-up is one of seeing that the display is adequately stocked. Another example is the representative for a food packer who checks the display area in grocery stores and attempts to gain more shelf space for his or her company.

Telephone Sales.   The amount of selling that takes place over the telephone is astounding. There was a time when this kind of selling was restricted to magazine subscriptions and newspapers. In recent years, however, some large organizations have recognized that the time and effort of a salesperson on the road are very expensive, so they have tried to replace these people with telephone sellers. Moreover, many professional salespeople are willing to turn over their new-found customers to the telephone squad in return for a reduced commission based on the fact that they no longer have to make regular calls on those customers. Some may regard telephone sales as little more than order taking. However, if the telephone sellers are to do a good job, they must acquire a sales skill unique to the task.

Detail Person.   As mentioned earlier, drug salespeople who spend time calling on doctors are referred to as detail people. On the surface, their task is to acquaint the marketplace with the products of their company. There appears no direct link between sales volume and their efforts. It is true that they may not take orders, but the volume of products sold in their territory is a direct reflection of their efforts. Every time manufacturers decide to do away with this type of salesperson, they have second thoughts, because definite results are attributable to this activity.

Promotional Person.   To give sales a "shot in the arm," many companies have a small staff of action-oriented salespeople who can generate immediate sales. These people may be experts in a particular line or group of products who are called on for a "one-day blitz" of the territory. In the parlance of the trade, they are known as "high-pressure salespeople." However, since this text does not differentiate between "high" and "low" pressure, we suggest that because these people thrive on calling once and only once on prospects, they give the impression of being what is commonly called high-pressure. (Note: The distinction between "high"- and "low"-pressure selling is a matter of appearances and activity. There is no middle ground—you either want to make a sale or you don't want to make a sale. It is difficult to conceive of not being certain. However, we concede that how the salesperson goes about achieving that result may give the impression of unconcern, which is sometimes misidentified as "low" pressure.) The promotional person simply prefers a life-style filled with new faces each day. This person will flourish on the challenges inherent in constantly breaking new ground. Not every person will find happiness in this daily routine.

Broker.   Many industries have brokers, who are really sellers representing manufacturers but who work on a straight commission. Brokers may handle several lines of interrelated but noncompetitive products. For example, a broker selling vegetables for a cannery on the West Coast might also represent a fruit packer from the Midwest. Since many canners are relatively small and cannot field their own sales force, they engage brokers to carry out the sales function for them.

Each of the foregoing descriptions presents a somewhat divergent view of selling. They all exist, and they all require a similar approach to the business of selling. The fact that they represent different opportunities is absolutely true. However, the overwhelming majority of sales positions fall into the broad categories described in this text. For that reason, we shall seek to further define sales life within our four categories.

THE FOUR LEVELS OF SELLING

Any description of selling is at best an arbitrary decision to divide the types of selling into specific categories. For the aspiring student in search of a career opportunity, it is convenient and appropriate to think of selling along the four lines we have suggested. To add further to your understanding of the distinguishing qualities and characteristics of these four levels, we shall make some additional observations about the life-style at these levels. However, within each category are exceptions, and we hasten to caution the student that merchandisers, promotional salespeople, and detail people may exist at all levels. By the same token, there is an overlap in life-style and work activities. Finally, income potential at all levels covers such a wide range as to be almost beyond description. A retail salesperson may earn more than a manufacturing salesperson, and a person in distribution may earn more than a person selling at the industrial level. No specific income line is drawn between levels.

Retail

The range of retail sales activities extends all the way from the clerk in a five-and-dime to the design consultant in a furniture store. There is also a range in income, from the bare minimum required by law to the upper reaches of $20,000 or $30,000 a year, sometimes higher.

The work style, regardless of the income level, usually consists of approaching the prospect who has entered the store, discussing merchandise, and writing an order. Depending on the type of product, the salesperson may actually wrap the package and hand it to the waiting customer. Knowledge of how to work a cash register might be part of the responsibilities. Other tasks include keeping the stock clean and updated, running a simple credit check, making change, and on some occasions, handling complaints.

To prepare for a retail sales career, a person may receive on-the-job training. This will usually be minimal, since many retail stores have little feel for either sales training or product knowledge. They expect salespeople to "pick it up as they go along." Nevertheless, in more sophisticated stores, sales personnel may spend some time visiting manufacturing facilities to gain more insight into the lines of merchandise. Factory representatives may sometimes conduct training sessions for retail salespeople. In the main, the salesperson will learn while doing.

Compensation at this level of selling is generally low. Many stores offer salespeople a small commission override on a nominal salary. Few retail positions are straight commission jobs. For some people, this represents security of a kind. Bear in mind that even at this level, the opportunity for innovative and creative thinking exists—but it usually remains for the salesperson to institute this type of thinking.

Little prospecting is done by retail salespeople, not because they do not have the opportunity, but because they are not encouraged to develop business in this way. Advertising is expected to bring prospects to the store for the retail person to sell. In brief, the notion that a person can become a proficient salesperson rarely enters the minds of store managers. Selling is assumed to be a career that requires only living experience. Needless to say, that thought is anathema to this text.

Distribution, Manufacturing, and Industrial

If there is any distinction among these three levels of selling, it is only a matter of degree. Distribution salespeople may have as many as 5,000 items in their price books. Obviously, they cannot be completely knowledgeable about each of these products. Nonetheless, distributors make a considerable effort to transmit product knowledge to their salespeople. Many also recognize the need for further instruction in the basics of selling. As scientists do research in human behavior, new understandings of how people act and react are woven into the sales fabric.

Recently, the idea of transactional analysis has reached popularity as a method to deal with children and adults. Wide-awake sales managers have converted these techniques into sales training programs. Audiovisual aids have been adapted for home study as a way to impart sales knowledge and techniques to professional salespeople. The learning process is never-ending.

Mingled with product knowledge and sales training are additional inputs of business knowledge, ranging from economic theory to management techniques. Salespeople at each of these levels are constantly being prepared for some form of promotion or further readied to continue successful sales careers. We cannot overemphasize the continuing education of the professional salesperson at each of these three levels. It should be noted that in organizations that are small or relatively unconcerned, this drive for further learning is generally left up to the individual. Once again, the thrust into the future is left in the hands of the salespeople themselves.

Each of these levels speaks of people on the "outside." They are not boxed in by opening or closing hours. Freedom of movement is a chief attraction for anyone who wants to work on the outside. Braving the vagaries of weather is only one example of the difficulties to be overcome. Probably no consideration is of more importance than the ability to be a "self-starter." Still, this characteristic is a learned trait; few are born with the desire to initiate their own work style. Salespeople are not born, they are made!

Travel and love of the open road attract people to outside selling. The romance of spending one night in Des Moines and the next in St. Louis appeals to many people. In reality, a considerable amount of spare time is spent in strange places where little is happening. Stories about the free-living style of traveling salespeople are highly exaggerated. More often than not, the evenings away from home are devoted to report writing, reading trade journals, and occasionally taking a client or prospect to a ball game or to dinner. What attracts people to this work? There is no easy answer. Many people flourish and revel in the chance to see new faces and new places daily. A flight to the Coast will frequently find the sales rep seated next to someone with a story. If you show even a moderate amount of interest, by the time you have reached your destination, you will be privy to the innermost secrets of someone's life. The natural curiosity of outside salespeople sustains them through many a long night.

Even though they are under the guidance and supervision of a sales manager, outside salespeople must still confront the reality of establishing new prospects and creating new demands for their product or service. Rolling out of bed in the morning determined to beat the world and equally prepared to know defeat, these people do make things happen. One man used to look at himself each morning in the mirror and say, "Murphy, be enthusiastic!" It was his way of getting ready to sell the world, because he knew that each call was a fresh challenge and a fresh opportunity. Over a period of many years, the challenge of each sale seldom dimmed his energy or failed to inspire him to new heights.

Among industrial and manufacturing salespeople, there is probably more overnight travel than is found among distribution salespeople. Naturally, larger expense accounts go with their widespread territories. Also, as a general rule, these salespeople will earn more dollars than distributor salespeople. Starting salaries probably begin in the $17,000 to $20,000 bracket. There is literally no upside limit. At the distribution level, starting salaries are in the $14,000 to $18,000 range, travel expenses are far less, and although there is no outside limit, the sheer weight of calling on regular customers over and over often deters the salesperson from fulfilling the mission. Only by adopting a "Drop-One, Add-One" system can the distributor sales-person skyrocket sales.

In the final analysis, outside salespeople find and make their own way in the world. They receive ample support from the home office in terms of training, information, and backup service. However, when salespeople leave home on Monday morning for a swing through the territory, they are singular agents doing what they do best. They move through the landscape adding value to their product by bringing a proposition to the very doorstep of the prospect. Professional selling is a very sophisticated frontier where the unexpected lurks beyond every hill.

HOW BIG IS THE SALES MARKET?

Huge! That is the only way to describe the number of opportunities in the sales field. Despite numerous efforts to be specific, it is almost impossi-ble to clearly define this amorphous segment of the labor pool. A fair approximation of the number of people involved in sales work probably approaches 10 percent of the work force, or about 10 million people.

However, as has been stated over and over, all too few of these are what we have referred to as "professional." Moreover, the titles assigned to certain kinds of work may sound a long way from selling. Field representa-tive, market area manager, district coordinator, field service representative, and factory representative are but a few of the names that describe what is primarily a sales function. In addition, some positions require only part-time sales efforts. The manager of a retail store might well take a turn covering the floor, and the sales supervisor for a distribution firm will quite possibly spend 20 weeks a year in sales work, covering for vacationing salespeople.

Clerks in retail stores are rarely described as salespeople. The chief executive officer of a large corporation may not think of herself as a sales-person when in fact one of her main functions may be to retain relationships with superzize clients. Thus, any statistics on the total number of people who sell for a living are suspect. It is sufficient to say that there are ample opportunities.

Probably of more importance is the idea that the requirements for salespeople will increase as the economy grows. No new product has yet been devised that can in any way replace the salesperson or reduce the need for people to go into the marketplace and present new ideas. The demand for competent salespeople in a free and democratic society is absolute. Under other forms of government and other social doctrines, there may be no need for people to "sell," but in this country, the need for this talent is insatiable.

As further evidence that sales careers are on the increase, it is interest-ing to note how the new industries that have appeared over the past few decades have called for more and better salespeople. The boom in TV has created needs for a divergent range of products, all of which have to be bought and sold. Cameras, electronic devices, and services that were unknown 25 years ago are needed to fill a gap, a need of those particular industries. All these have inexorably been provided by salespeople leading the parade of new products and services. Electric typewriters did not do away with the need for salespeople to sell manual typewriters; they expanded the market and increased the number of salespeople. Those distribution salespeople who called on small grocery stores did not disappear with the advent of the supermarket—they became detail people and broker representatives.

The ability in and knowledge of professional selling is at all times a marketable talent. During times of economic strain, corporations and companies may reduce the ad budget, decide against building a new warehouse, eliminate research and development, and cut back on the replacement of equipment. Only at the last, most desperate moments do they trim the sales force. The salespeople are, after all, an immediately productive element of any business operation.

THE PROJECTED NEED FOR SALESPEOPLE WILL GROW WITH THE ECONOMY.

Figure 17-1

Inherent in the professional ability to sell is the security a person feels with the knowledge that this ability can be applied in a variety of fields regardless of geographic location. Many professionals—engineers, computer programmers, and even airline pilots—may rise and fall with the times. For salespeople, there is always an opportunity. Once the basic techniques and methods are mastered, the salesperson may opt for a career at the retail level or move into outside sales. The point is that wherever there are people, products and services are being sold.

THE ROAD TO SALES MANAGEMENT

A successful sales career more often than not leads to opportunities in sales management. There is a natural progression as organizations develop and grow that requires more and more people at supervisory levels. Along with this is a basic assumption that sales experience prepares a person for sales management.

It is absolutely true that a sales background is an advantage; it gives a person exposure to all the trials, tribulations, and excitement of the sales profession. It also trains a person in the best ways to get along with people, a very necessary attribute of management. However, the skills and knowledge required of managers are somewhat different from the requirements of professional selling.

Here are some of the levels of sales management to which competent and successful salespeople aspire:

Field sales management is the next level upward. These managers work in the field with the sales force, assisting, counseling, and training salespeople. Probably the field sales manager will be responsible for five to ten salespeople, devoting virtually full time to working with them.

Five to ten field sales managers might report to a *division or district sales manager,* who probably doesn't get into the field too often but who is responsible for arranging sales meetings and convention dates, and may even call on a few big accounts. The divisional manager usually has to oversee an office, interview sales applicants, draw up annual budgets, implement pricing schedules, and sometimes become involved in problems with the shipping and production departments. In some organizations, the district or division is a profit center with broad corporate responsibilities.

National sales managers may have five to ten districts reporting to them. These are administrative positions of the highest level, which require still other kinds of skills and background. Often managers at this level confer regularly with corporate officials, deciding on new product lines, pricing philosophy, corporate goals and objectives, and sales budgets. Needless to say, these managers might also have limited sales responsibilities with regard to the large national accounts that demand attention at this level.

The professional salesperson who wishes to move into a management position has a good head start. Virtually all the skills and techniques of professional selling can be employed in other positions. However, upward mobility is also a matter of preparing for the next level of work. The professional salesperson is already equipped to investigate, analyze, and proceed to fulfill an objective in terms of selling. The application of this same method is appropriate when the salesperson aspires to a sales management position.

However, a great many professional salespeople are completely happy in their chosen careers. They find the life-style, the chance to make money, and the nature of professional selling absolutely satisfying.

HOW TO GET A SALES POSITION

When job applicants are asked why they want to get into sales, the most frequently heard reply is, "I like to be with people." If this answer is accurate, then the job applicant ought to walk down the streets of any major city and rub shoulders with people. Selling is far more than just "being with people." As a matter of fact, we have seen that the actual process of selling ("being with people") may occupy only a small percentage of time. Selling is an exciting career, and the decision to enter the field should be both positive and forceful.

A good deal of conventional advice has been given about how to apply for a position. Applicants are taught to prepare a resumé, how to sit, how to stand, when to smoke, what answers to give, how to dress, and how to fill out an application. All these notions we leave to others. Instead, we suggest that the applicant view himself or herself as the product to be sold and the company as the prospective buyer. That's correct, seeking a job is almost identical with selling a product or service.

The starting point is to study the product. Be able to describe the physical attributes—the strengths, and be mindful also of possible weaknesses. Think through where that product will fit into the potential employer's scheme of things. (If thinking about yourself as a product is disturbing, pretend you are trying to explain the virtues of someone else who has your characteristics, desires, and attributes.) What does this human being have to offer that will make that company a better place than it is currently?

Also, consider what the benefits are of employing this person (you). Think back to the consumer benefit approach. You will recall that this was a statement telling what the use of the product would do for the prospect. Not a description of the product, but what would accrue to the prospect from having bought the product—how would the prospect benefit? This same line of reasoning is true when you are applying for a position. "What can you do for the company that is not now being done?" Answer that question and you will have your job.

The next step is to study the market, do some prospecting. What kind of sales job do you want? Will being away from home overnight disturb your home life? Do you mind flying? How much money do you need? How much money do you see as a long-range goal? Find the company that meets as many of your desires as possible. Then do further research into these companies in the geographic area you find most desirable. Are they looking for salespeople? If you think Company A is the place you want to work, and it is not currently in need of a salesperson, do not be deterred. You should apply as if you want that job today! Many competent and professional salespeople have made their own place in a company. They have sold themselves into a job.

After you have studied the product (you) and completed prospecting and preapproach work, it is time to write a sales plan. Oh, yes. You can sit down and prepare approaches, presentations, demonstrations, the meeting of objections, and closes for gaining that position. If you think this is an unconventional idea, you are absolutely correct. However, if you were a sales manager interviewing an applicant, what would impress you the most: a conventional interview, or a dynamic presentation of this unknown product—YOU?

Once you accept the idea that applying for a job or sales position is similar to a sale, then fitting all the pieces together is merely creating a dynamic sale. That's what this entire book is about. The fact that you may be selling yourself should not stop you from using all the methods and techniques at your disposal. None are better than the exercises and activities that have been explored in this book. To those who claim that "selling is really selling yourself," we respond, "Instead of saying it—do it!" Prepare and carry out that dynamic sale of yourself.

SUMMARY

Selling—the process of persuading or convincing others to your way of thinking—is all around us. Everyone, regardless of position or profession, sells to some extent. However, a career in professional selling has distinct advantages. There is a constant challenge in sales work, the opportunity to transfer learned abilities to other fields of endeavor, a decided maneuverability—which means controlling your style of work and living where you wish—a chance for advancement into management if you consider that desirable, an atmosphere of your own making, and income levels without limit.

Perhaps the income area is most important to some people. Sales compensation is complex and allows for a variety of ways not only to cover travel expenses but to reward people for efforts expended. To professional salespeople, this is an important incentive to produce more business.

Through a series of salary, commissions, bonuses, expenses, and peripheral benefits, professional salespeople can more than provide for themselves and their families.

Selling can be divided into a variety of categories. One view is that sales are either products (tangibles) or services (intangibles). A second view is that the proper division is in terms of the type of work—for instance, merchandising, telephone, detail, or promotional. Both views are correct. However, this text has separated selling into levels that appear to correspond to the structure of business in general. Our view suggests that retail selling is somewhat different from the other levels—distribution, manufacturing, and industrial. Despite this, there is considerable overlap, and to draw any definite line of demarcation would be unrealistic.

An overview of the total sales field reveals that there are, and will be, plenty of selling jobs and positions. New products and services meld to create the need for an increasing number of sales professionals. Our system of government, our economic structure, our very way of life require vibrant selling and dynamic salespeople.

How to gain a foothold in this absorbing work life is a great consideration. Along with the conventional methods recommended by many, this text suggests that the application process should be viewed as a "sale." As the applicant conducts a self-analysis, benefits will come to mind, and relating all these aspects to a sales plan will provide for a vibrant presentation of the applicant as a potential professional salesperson.

The challenge and opportunity for an exciting sales career are there. It is up to you to get out and make the sale.

A SUCCESS STORY

"George," said the woman, "let me give you some advice as one who has been through the mill. Find yourself some kind of work in which you'll be happy."

"I appreciate what you are saying," replied the young man. "But you seem to have done all right."

"True, true," she murmured. "The only thing I regret is that I didn't spend more time with my family."

"That's not altogether right. Sure, you were away from home overnight once in a while, but we understood the nature of the work kept you from us. There was never any bad feeling about your absence."

"Let me tell you, it was fun. Did I ever tell you about the time in Atlanta when I went to see Hank Aaron play ball? Or that trip to the West Coast when the Dodgers moved to Los Angeles? Did you know I was in Chicago the year they reopened McCormick Place? Those were exciting times."

"Hey, you still do some pretty exciting things."

"There is no substitute for being on the road. There's a sense of freedom, a rush of feeling when you fly into a new city or drive along a country road. Always something new to see and experience."

"Sounds like you want to write a book of memories."

"You know, there hasn't been a really great book extolling the virtues of selling. Oh, there are a few around that tell the seamy side. But I don't know of any that really tell the story about those of us who traveled and criss-crossed the country."

"Well, I have to go now. My flight leaves in an hour. Can I bring you back anything?"

"This is your first big trip. I just want to wish you well. I hope you'll like it, and I hope you'll stick with it. You just have to know that I'm happy and proud that you decided on a sales career."

"Thanks, Mom!"

QUESTIONS FOR CLASS DISCUSSION

1. How does an ability to sell help the manager of a trucking company? the administrator of a hospital? a superintendent of schools?
2. People involved in selling make up about 10 percent of the work force. What might happen to our economy if that number were reduced appreciably? Are they needed?
3. A mature approach to life is an absolute necessity for a successful sales career. What are the advantages of a sales career? Can you describe them?
4. What forms of compensation constitute the total package for paying sales-people? Would you prefer more salary, or more commissions? Why?
5. Explain what is meant by the statement, "Any salesperson worth his salt will want to work on a straight commission basis."
6. Write at least six different approach statements you might use if you were applying for a sales position with a distribution company.
7. Using yourself as the "product," write four consumer benefit statements you might use in making an approach to an industrial firm when applying for a job.
8. Money is a strong motivator of salespeople. Can you think of any other motivational factors?
9. Would you like to be a salesperson? Why?

CASE 17—THE HAPPY JOB HUNTER

Jack Pierce sat at his desk, shuffling papers and preparing lists. On one page he had ranked the names of some of the largest corporations in the city. On another he had listed the names of distributors, and on a third he had ranked the retail outlets in his community. "Every one of these organiza-

SALES PROBLEM 17—HOW TO GET THE CUSTOMER
OFF THE DIME

The store looked the same as it had for the last ten years. This disturbed Martha Young, who sells all the dolls, plates, figurines, and novelty items typically carried by card shops. As she reviewed her business with Harry's Card Corner, she realized that sales were flat, orders were flat, and the flavor of the store was flat.

As a professional sales representative, she had many ways to freshen the store and give it a more exciting appeal. The problem was that neither Harry nor his two assistants wanted to do anything to change what they felt was the strength of the store. "I can't get them off the dime," Martha complained to her sales manager. "They just won't do anything to make the store more attractive. And it's hurting my sales with them."

Here is how three salespeople confronted this problem:

Sales Rep #1:   First I would try to get Harry to get rid of some of the old inventory, those things that have been hanging around for a long time. If you have to lose money on a few items, it's better to make room for merchandise. Then I would recommend that he post a few signs around noting special new products that might interest shoppers.

Getting people to take a fresh approach to their business is really very hard, because they tend to be successful, and your suggestions may be taken as an insult.

Sales Rep #2:   If Martha has been selling Harry's for a long time, she should have close rapport with the owner and the others in the store. This means that she should be able to make lots of suggestions to improve sales.

The idea of running specials is always good. First they should push new items. If there are old products hanging around, it might be best to return them for credit, or even to give them to a charity. The tax writeoffs might be better than selling the merchandise.

I travel all over and pick up lots of things that other stores are doing. If Harry realizes how much information I possess, he would surely tap my brain.

Sales Rep #3:   It's awfully hard for a sales rep to try to tell a customer how to run the business. Many times, customers will resent that you are showing how much you know when they are the ones actually taking the chances.

Every customer is different, and I would be very hesitant about telling anybody how to run a business. If the sales are slow, that's just part of the selling business.

tions needs salespeople," he thought. "It's up to me to decide where I think I will be happy."

From a drawer he took a yellow lined pad on which he had written approaches to the personnel managers of these business houses. He mused over a consumer benefit approach. "When you assign me to a territory, you will be able to relax, because you will know I am calling on every prospect in the area." This, he felt, coupled with the new tie and muted gray shirt, was the kind of thing that would convey his ability to the interviewers. "Sure, I can tell them about my good grades in college," he thought. "But that kind of information they can read in my application; what else can I do to make a favorable impression?"

As he sat there considering, "Jack Pierce—job hunter," he found other important facets of this human being.

"What do you think of this, Ms. Interviewer? I missed only six days of school in two years."

"Here is a recommendation from my college instructor in professional selling."

"I want to be a salesperson."

In his mind he turned over the objections that would be raised. "You don't have any experience." "We want an older person." "We're not looking for anyone right now."

He reviewed the six ways to meet these objections, and then he considered what might be appropriate closes. "When do you think you will be ready to hire a devoted salesperson?" "Would you prefer to have me start in October or November?" "You're right, Ms. Interviewer, I don't know anything about welded jaddydiffles. I will spend two weeks in your laboratory learning. Will that be enough time?"

Encouraged by his own inventiveness, Jack reached for the telephone and started to dial, ready to make his first job-interview appointment. His confidence soared, because he knew the product and he was certain his sales plan was well organized. "Getting a job, after all, is merely selling yourself."

1. How might Jack Pierce have enlarged his plan?
2. Do you think this is the proper approach to job hunting?
3. How would you prepare for an interview?

EXERCISE 17

Prepare a sales plan to convince (sell) the instructor of this course to give you an A.

appendix

Professional Sales Representative's Job Description

Sales representatives are responsible for personal contact with prospects and customers. All efforts and activities shall be directed toward fulfilling the goals and objectives of the company.

During the annual (semiannual or monthly) performance evaluations, the sales representative and the sales manager (or the field sales manager) should review this job description. They should agree to objectives that are consistent with organizational goals and objectives, and to the performance required by the sales representative to meet those objectives.

This job description is prepared in five sections. Section I designates the particular functions of the sales representative. Sections II and III identify the areas of information exchange and interpersonal relationships. Section IV indicates self-improvement and development methods. Section V specifies measurable performance standards.

I. FUNCTIONS

1. Take orders from customers.
2. Make prospect and customer calls regularly and systematically.
3. Maintain a list of prospects.
4. Analyze prospect potential within the territory.
5. Demonstrate products to prospects and customers.
6. Inform prospects and customers of sales promotions.

7. Maintain records of customer purchases.
8. Take customer inventory when indicated.
9. Maintain records of information relating to prospect calls.
10. Make emergency deliveries to customers when necessary.
11. Make minor repairs and adjustments to equipment.
12. Collect accounts receivable (current and delinquent).
13. Gather credit information.
14. Prepare sales forecasts.
15. Assist in taking inventory.

II. INFORMATION EXCHANGE

1. Submit all reporting forms (call sheets, prospect calls, daily routes, etc.) to the sales manager or the field sales manager.
2. Report on competitor activity to the sales manager or the field sales manager.
3. Report high potential sales opportunities to the sales manager or the field sales manager.
4. Report collection problems to the credit manager.
5. Read and understand company policy.
6. Maintain product manuals, sales manuals, price books, order-taking systems, etc.
7. Attend sales meetings.
8. Conduct portions of sales meetings.
9. Demonstrate a working knowledge of all product categories.
10. Be conversant with industry's trade publications.
11. Provide information to customers on product uses and applications.
12. Understand and utilize professional sales skills.

III. INTERPERSONAL RELATIONSHIPS

1. Assist in training new personnel (sales, warehouse, delivery, office, administrative).
2. Report directly to the sales manager (or field sales manager).
3. Cooperate with other members of the sales team.
4. Cooperate with customer service personnel.
5. Cooperate with the office manager.
6. Maintain a businesslike relationship with customers and prospects.
7. Participate in trade shows, conventions, or distribution-center tours.
8. Represent company at industrywide functions or affairs.
9. Work with manufacturer (broker) representatives.
10. Work with company specialists.
11. Adjust customer complaints and problems.
12. Participate in the selection of new products.

IV. SELF-IMPROVEMENT AND DEVELOPMENT

1. Conduct a personal time study twice a year.
2. Attend training seminars.
3. Read sales books and business periodicals.
4. Take sales courses.

V. PERFORMANCE STANDARDS

(All or some of these performance standards may be applicable, depending on the objectives of the organization.)

	Budgeted	Actual	Over/Under
1. Sales volume			
2. Percent gross profit			
3. Dollar gross profit			
4. Average number of accounts			
5. Sales volume per account			
6. Number of orders:			
weekly			
monthly			
7. Frequncy of orders (ratio)			
8. Average order			
9. Accounts receivable (ratio)			
10. Bad debts			
11. Dollar gross profit:			
Product group 1			
Product group 2			
Product group 3			
Product group 4			
Product group 5			
12. Percent gross profit:			
Product group 1			
Product group 2			
Product group 3			
Product group 4			
Product group 5			
13. Sales by market segment:			
Group 1			
Group 2			
Group 3			
Group 4			

14. Other sales performance standards, as may derive from company goals and objectives from time to time.
15. A written self-evaluation of personal performance.

GLOSSARY

ABCs of Selling.   Always Be Closing.

Approach.   The first 60 seconds of the sales interview.

Aptitude tests.   Tests measuring those areas in which a person is proficient.

Barter.   The exchange (or trade) of product or service between two people without the use of money.

Base of the Sale.   See *Sales plan.*

Broker.   Salesperson who represents several manufacturers on a straight commission basis.

Canned sales talk.   A pre-prepared and memorized sales presentation.

Close.   The last phase or segment of the sales interview, in which the salesperson seeks to get the order.

Cold canvass (cold turkey).   Making sales calls on people you do not know or whom you have never seen.

Customer.   A person who has bought the product or service; one who has accepted the proposition.

Demonstration.   The third phase or segment of the sales interview, in which every aspect of the proposition is reviewed.

Detail people.   Salespeople who call on doctors to interest them in prescribing their company's products.

Drop one, Add one.   A system of examining customers by volume and deciding to drop the least valuable while adding a fresh prospect.

Emotional motivation.   Actions (motivations) based on subjective feelings.

End-user.   The customer of the prospect; sometimes called "the customer's customer."

Excelsior.   The challenge to continue to grow.

GPO.   Government Printing Office, Washington, DC 20402.

Group selling.   Selling to more than two people in the same organization at the same time.

Heart of the Sale.   See *Sales plan.*

Hierarchy of Human Needs.   A theory of psychological needs that motivate people; propounded by Abraham Maslow.

Ideal other.   How a person thinks other people would like him or her to be if he or she were "perfect."

Intangibles.   Those products or services that cannot be identified by the five senses.

Intelligence (IQ) test.   A measurement of a person with relation to other people in the ability to absorb and learn at that particular moment.

Interest test.   A way to relate the interests of a person to similar interests of people in various work or professions.

Meeting objections.   Answering a prospect's questions that stand in the way of completing the sale.

Merchandiser.   Salesperson responsible for overseeing the displays in a retail store.

Motivate.   To provide with a motive or motives.

Motivation.   The act or an instance of motivating; the state or condition of being motivated; that which motivates.

Motive.   Something that prompts a person to act in a certain way.

Nonverbal communication.   The use of body language, motions, or gestures to convey or transmit a message.

Other self.   How a person would like to be if he or she were "perfect."

Personality test.   A measurement of how traits or characteristics will help or hinder a person in dealing with other human beings.

Preapproach.   Gathering information about the prospect before making the sales call.

Presentation.   The second phase or segment of the sales interview, in which the salesperson seeks to establish confidence in the company.

Product benefits.   What the product will do for the prospect.

Product features.   The characteristics or properties of the product or service to be sold.

Profile cards.   A collection of information, both personal and business, about the prospect, recorded on file cards for easy reference.

Promotional person.   Action-oriented sales specialist who calls on prospects only once in an attempt to generate immediate sales.

Proposition.   The complete explanation of the product or service, what it will mean to the prospect, how much it will cost, credit terms; everything the prospect may want to know before making a purchase.

Prospect.   A person who probably has need for the proposition, and who more than likely has the ability to pay for it.

Pulse taking.   Open-ended questions that help determine if the prospect understands the proposition. Sometimes known as a "trial balloon" or a "trial close."

Rational motivation.   Actions based on objective reasons.

Real other.   How a person thinks other people really think of him or her.

Real self.   How a person thinks of himself or herself.

Sales personality.   Those personal characteristics that portray professional selling.

Sales plan.   The overall concept of the sale, which consists of two elements—the Base of the Sales, which is made up of knowledge, traits, characteristics, time management and other background material; and the Heart of the Sale, which is made up of the phases in the inclined plane of the sales interview.

Self-actualization.   The need for a person to be everything he or she is capable of being.

Selling.   The activity that effects the transfer of products or services from one person to another for money.

Service.   Everything the salesperson does for the customer beyond taking the order or concluding the sale.

Sphere of influence.   Those people who tend to have an undue influence on a variety of other people.

Sponsor.   The person who brings the salesperson to a group-selling opportunity.

SS = 2E − M.   Sales success equals two ears minus one mouth.

Suspect.   A person who might be able to use your product or service; one who might find your proposition acceptable.

Tangibles.   Those products that can be identified by the five senses.

Value added.   All those things added to the basic product or service that make your proposition more appealing to the prospect.

Verbal communication.   The use of the spoken word to transmit messages.

WOLIPPP.   A mnemonic device to ensure that you have covered all the steps in a group sale; stands for Who and what, Objective, Leader, Identifying the dissident, Plenty of literature, Poll taker, and Pounce.

BIBLIOGRAPHY

ANDERSON, B. ROBERT, "The Benefits of Selling," *The American Salesman* (October 1972), pp. 51–54.

———, *The Professional Salesman, His Methods and Techniques.* Falls Church, Va.: International Foodservice Distributors Association, 1984.

———, "What Business Are You In?" *The American Salesman* (November 1973), pp. 51–53.

———, "Who Does the Buying?" *The American Salesman* (January 1971), pp. 4–7.

BROWN, RONALD, *From Selling to Managing.* New York: American Management Associations, 1968.

GOODMAN, GERSON, *Cold Call Selling.* New York: Sales and Marketing Management, 1985.

GORMAN, WALTER, *Selling.* New York: Random House, Inc., 1979.

HAAS, KENNETH B., *Professional Salesmanship.* New York: Holt, Rinehart and Winston, 1966.

HASS, KENNETH B., and JOHN W. ERNEST, *Creative Salesmanship* (2nd ed.). Beverly Hills, Calif.: Glencoe Press, 1974.

HAAS, KENNETH B., and ENOS C. PERRY, *Sales Horizons* (3rd ed.). Englewood Cliffs, N.J.: Prentice-Hall, Inc., 1968.

HANAN, MARK, *Organizing for Profitable Selling.* New York: Sales and Marketing Management, 1985.

IVEY, PAUL W., and WALTER HORVATH, *Successful Salesmanship* (4th ed.). Englewood Cliffs, N.J.: Prentice-Hall, Inc., 1968.

JONES, MARK, and JAMES HEALEY, eds., *Miracle Sales Guide* (3rd ed.). Englewood Cliffs, N.J.: Prentice-Hall, Inc., 1974.

KUESEL, HARRY N., *Kuesel on "Closing Sales."* Englewood Cliffs, N.J.: Prentice-Hall, Inc., 1965.

LAPP, CHARLES L., *Training and Supervising Salesmen.* Englewood Cliffs, N.J.: Prentice-Hall, Inc., 1960.

LUND, PHILIP R., *Compelling Selling.* New York: American Management Associations, 1974.

MARSH, U. GRANT, *Salesmanship: Modern Principles and Practices.* Englewood Cliffs, N.J.: Prentice-Hall, Inc., 1972.

MILLER, ROBERT B., and STEPHEN E. HEIMAN with TAD TULEGA, *Strategic Selling.* New York: William Morrow & Company, Inc., 1985.

RATHMELL, JOHN M., ed., *Salesmanship,* for American Management Association. Homewood, Ill.: Richard D. Irwin, Inc., 1969.

ROBESON, JAMES F., H. LEE MATHEWS, and CARL G. STEVENS, *Selling.* Homewood, Ill.: Richard D. Irwin, Inc., 1978.

ROBINSON, O. PRESTON, WILLIAM R. BLACKER, and WILLIAM B. LOGAN, *Store Salesmanship* (6th ed.). Englewood Cliffs, N.J.: Prentice-Hall, Inc., 1966.

ROTH, CHARLES B., *Secrets of Closing Sales* (4th ed.). Englewood Cliffs, N.J.: Prentice-Hall, Inc., 1970.

SENG, ROGER W., *The Skills of Selling.* New York: American Management Associations, 1977.

SHOOK, ROBERT L., *Ten Greatest Salespersons.* New York: Harper & Row, Inc., 1978.

SLOAN, DAVID F., "Averages Favor the Salesman," *The American Salesman* (June 1971), pp. 5–8.

THOMPSON, JOSEPH W., *Selling, A Behavioral Science Approach.* New York: McGraw-Hill Book Company, 1966.

THOMPSON, WILLARD M., *The Basics of Successful Salesmanship.* New York: McGraw-Hill Book Company, 1968.

WARD, EMORY, "Offer More of What Others Are Offering Less and Less-Service!" *The American Salesman* (June 1975), pp. 54–57.

INDEX